P9-DMX-511

Law and Regulation of Common Carriers in the Communications Industry

LAW AND REGULATION OF COMMON CARRIERS IN THE COMMUNICATIONS INDUSTRY

Daniel L. Brenner

WESTVIEW PRESS

Boulder • San Francisco • Oxford

Tennessee Tech Library
Cookeville, TN
WITHDRAWN

All rights reserved. No part of this publication may be reproduced or transmitted in any form or by any means, electronic or mechanical, including photocopy, recording, or any information storage and retrieval system, without permission in writing from the publisher.

Copyright © 1992 by Westview Press, Inc.

Published in 1992 in the United States of America by Westview Press, Inc., 5500 Central Avenue, Boulder, Colorado 80301-2847, and in the United Kingdom by Westview Press, 36 Lonsdale Road, Summertown, Oxford OX2 7EW

Library of Congress Cataloging-in-Publication Data
Brenner, Daniel L., 1951–
  Law and regulation of common carriers in the communications
industry / Daniel L. Brenner.
    p.   cm.
  Includes index.
  ISBN 0-8133-8262-9
  1. Telecommunication—Law and legislation—United States—Cases.
2. United States. Federal Communications Commission.   I. Title.
KF2764.B73   1992
343.7309'94—dc20
[347.303994]   92-9088
                                                                                  CIP

Printed and bound in the United States of America

The paper used in this publication meets the requirements
of the American National Standard for Permanence of Paper
for Printed Library Materials Z39.48-1984.

10   9   8   7   6   5   4   3   2

CONTENTS

PREFACE

This book of cases and materials offers an overview of common carrier regulation and a review of leading policy initiatives. The focus is on federal regulation, principally the Federal Communications Commission (FCC), although state and international developments are also considered.

The dynamic pace of the communications industry in the last twenty-five years has required continuous updating of regulations. As technology changes, so must the government change the way it approaches regulation. The issues dealt with here are, in the author's view, the most significant ones in this rapidly changing field. Their study will provide the reader with a reasonable sample of the key policy issues confronting the FCC and those whose practice takes them before it. It is impossible to cover the entirety of the laws in this area. But the hope is that these materials will provide a structural overview to the field.

I wish to acknowledge Charles Firestone and Tracy Westin, who as previous directors of the UCLA Law School Communications Program helped to develop earlier versions of these materials. Thanks are due also to Howard Symons for his helpful suggestions in reviewing the manuscript; to Dayna Babikian and Christian Castle, who served as research assistants during the preparation of this manuscript; and to the many students and colleagues who have influenced my thinking. In particular, my own understanding of this field owes a great debt to the writings of Alfred Kahn of Cornell University.

I especially want to thank the Annenberg Washington Program on Communication Policy Studies for its generous financial assistance in preparing the manuscript.

I dedicate this book to Dorothy and John Brenner.

Daniel L. Brenner
Washington, D.C.

1

PUBLIC UTILITY THEORY

INTRODUCTION TO
COMMON CARRIER REGULATION

Introduction: The Telephone

"If I can get a mechanism which will make a current of electricity vary in its intensity, as the air varies in density when a sound is passing through it, I can telegraph any sound, even the sound of speech."

So declared Alexander Graham Bell in 1875 while experimenting with his "harmonic telegraph." On June 2 of that same year, by fashioning a makeshift diaphragm, this teacher of deaf persons discovered he could hear over a wire the sound of a twanging clock spring. Bell then knew it was possible to do what he had hoped—send vocal vibrations over a telegraph wire so they could be transformed into sound for a listener at the other end. Nine months later, on March 10, 1876, Bell transmitted the first complete sentence heard over a wire: "Mr. Watson, come here, I want you." His message was received by his associate, Thomas A. Watson, in an adjoining room of their tiny Boston laboratory.

U.S. Patent No. 174,465, issued to Bell in 1876, became known as the "most valuable patent." Yet, as had been the case with the telegraph, early efforts to popularize the telephone met with disappointment. Though people paid to hear Bell lecture on "the miracle discovery of the age," for a brief time they seemed unaware of its possibilities. However, 1877 witnessed the erection of the first regular telephone line—from Boston to Somerville, Massachusetts. By the close of 1880, there were 47,900 telephones in the United States. The following year brought telephone service between Boston and Providence. Boston and New York were connected in 1884, and service between New York and Chicago started in 1892. Transcontinental service was not inaugurated until 1915.

The telephone is an electrical device that picks up a spoken word and speeds it invisibly and inaudibly by wire, cable, or radio to another point. In this process the telephone instrument performs two functions—it converts the sound waves of the human voice into electrical waves for transmission, and, at the receiving end, it transforms this electrical energy back into sound waves that can be recognized by the human ear. The telephone system provides the highways that carry this electrical speech. Strands of copper wire link rural subscribers; more populous places use cable; fiber-optic cables, transmitting sound by light waves, are used in some areas. In big cities cables are placed in underground conduits or buried directly in the ground. City-to-city traffic is transmitted over cables, microwave radio, or satellites.

Telephones were first leased in pairs. Each subscriber had to put up his or her own line to connect with another listener. Development of the switchboard permitted interconnections to be made with fewer lines. For example, joining six subscribers with one another by private lines would require fifteen separate circuits. One switchboard can handle many times that number of lines; a switchboard serving 10,500 telephones is a substitute for 55,119,750 separate wire connections.

The first switchboard was set up in Boston in 1877. New Haven saw the first regular telephone exchange in 1878. The dial telephone was invented in about 1889, and the first dial exchange was installed at La Porte, Indiana, in 1892. By 1921 dial telephones had come into general use.

Toward the close of the nineteenth century, the myriad of overhead telephone wires in large cities became such an obstacle to effective fire fighting and were so subject to storm damage that it was necessary to develop sturdier cables composed of numerous wires. Success in enclosing many wires in a single cable eliminated the need for multiple cross-arms on telephone poles. In 1888 it was possible to squeeze 100 wires into a large cable; today more than 5,000 strands can be encompassed in a cable about the size of a man's wrist. Some cables are maintained under inert gas pressure to keep out moisture that could cause short circuits. The gas also helps detect leaks in the cable sheath. Fiber-optic lines can transmit many times the capacity of wires.

Experiments with underground telephone cable date back to 1882, but it was not until 1902 that the first long-distance buried cable went into operation—between New York City and Newark, New Jersey. In 1913 Washington, D.C., and Boston were so linked. The original transcontinental telephone line was of open wire; the first cross-continent cable line opened in 1942.

Carrier technology permits large numbers of telephone conversations to be transmitted without interfering with each other over a single pair of conductors, a coaxial cable, or a radio system. At the sending end, speech currents are translated onto different frequency bands. At the receiving end, signals are translated back to their original audio frequencies.

In the last twenty years, great strides have been made in switching technology (i.e., technology that directs calls) from the old electromechanical "clacking" switches to a system where calls are switched by computer. This use of computer switching was augmented by improvements in "out of band" signaling systems, which transmit billing and other information about a particular call. In addition, "packet" switching technology allows voices or other data to be broken into bits of impulses, combined for maximum efficiency during transmission, and reassembled (see Figure 1.1).

Until recently the United States was virtually alone in providing telephone service wholly by the private sector. Telecommunications companies are, under law, subject to government oversight to ensure a high quality of service and reasonable charges to subscribers. This regulation is exercised at the federal level by the Federal Communications Commission (FCC) and at the state level by public utility commissions (PUC) or public service commissions (PSC). Based on the U.S. experience, there is an increasing trend toward privatization of markets in the United Kingdom, Germany, and Japan.

Regulation

Though several earlier acts of Congress related to specific telegraph matters, federal regulation of interstate electrical communication as a whole dates from passage of the Post Roads Act in 1866. This legislation was intended to foster the construction of telegraph lines by granting, among other things, rights-of-way over public lands. Federal regulation of the rates and practices of interstate communication carriers was initiated by the Mann-Elkins Act of 1910. This extended certain provisions of the Interstate Commerce Act (a nineteenth-century law) to cover common carrier services, both wire and radio.

In brief, a communications common carrier is defined under law as one whose services are open to public hire for handling interstate or international communications by electrical means. Broadcast stations are not considered common carriers. The Communications Act of 1934 coordinated in the FCC regulatory powers formerly exercised by various federal agencies and broadened considerably the scope of such regulation. The act, reproduced in Appendix B, is designed "to make available, so far as possible, to all the people of the United States a rapid, efficient, nation-wide, and world-wide wire and radio communication service with adequate facilities at reasonable charges. . . ."

The FCC regulates interstate and international communication such as telephone, telegraph, facsimile, telephoto, and broadcast program transmission, whether by wire or radio, including cable and satellites. Common carrier communication that is purely *intrastate* in character is not, in general, subject to FCC jurisdiction but does come under the authority of state PUCs.

There is an inherent difficulty in separating intrastate and interstate components of communications services and facilities. Some equipment and services can be identified as serving only one sector. Most resources are a combination, however, and the issue of overlapping jurisdiction has significant policy effects. The federal approach has tended to favor competition in the provision of equipment and services, whereas many states have retained

FIGURE 1.1 Local Distribution Network

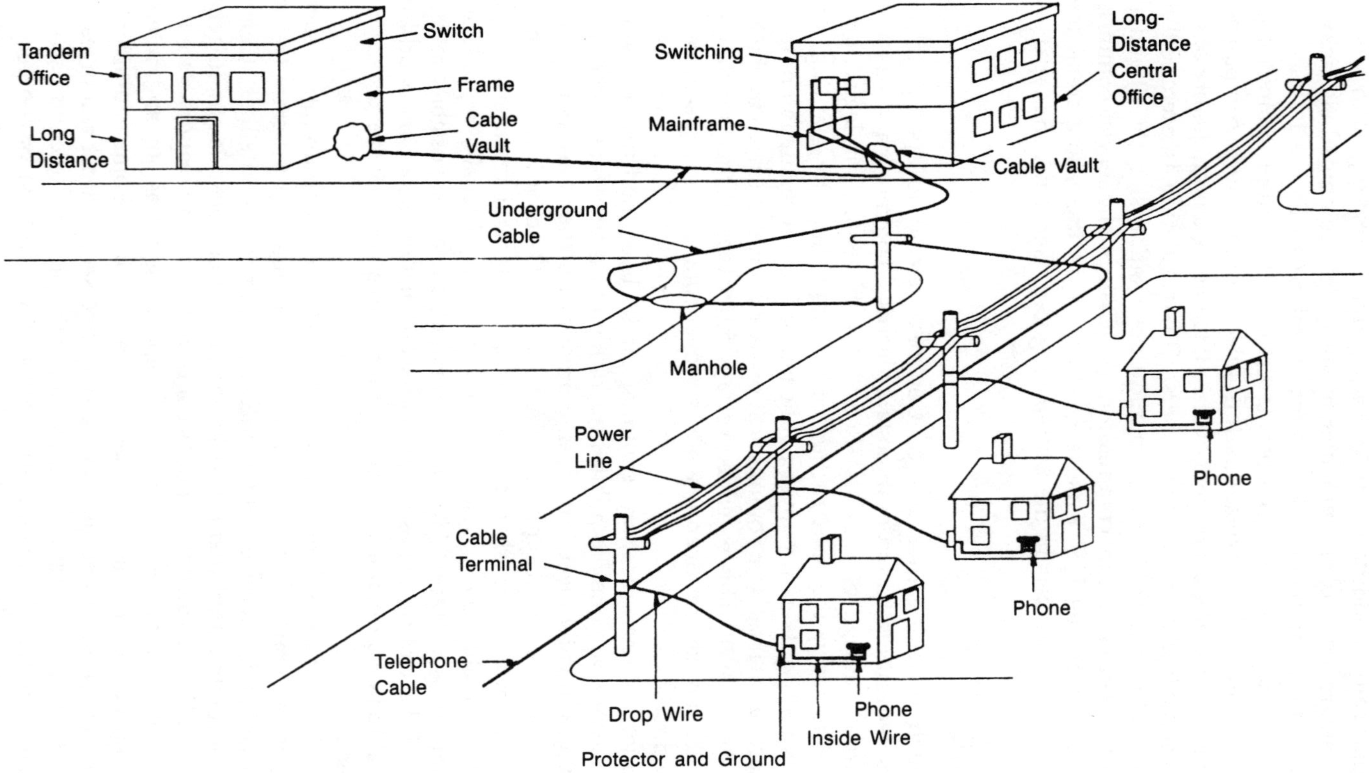

more regulation of providers, meaning less free entry for competitors. Thus, where jurisdiction overlaps there may be a conflict as to whether to permit competitive entry.

Operating under licenses granted by the FCC, common carriers use radio facilities for a substantial portion of their long-distance communication pathways. These as well as other radio facilities are regulated to curb interference and avoid inefficient use of the limited frequency spectrum. Only citizens of the United States may hold a radio license. Licenses are denied to corporations in which any officer or director is an alien or of which more than one-fifth of the capital stock is owned by aliens or foreign interests.

The FCC reviews applications by carriers to construct wire or cable transmission facilities to assure that the proposed facilities are adequate but not excessive and that their costs are reasonable and prudent. The Commission is charged with domestic administration of wire, cable, and radio communication provisions of treaties and other international agreements to which the United States is a party. The Communications Satellite Corporation (COMSAT), the U.S. signatory to the INTELSAT agreement (which governs international satellite transmissions), is subject to the same FCC regulatory controls as are other communications common carriers, as well as to certain additional regulatory requirements.

Government regulation of telecommunications companies serves as a substitute for competition in the marketplace, which normally regulates private enterprise. Traditionally, regulators have required each company to file a tariff that proposes the schedules of charges for service to the public as well as the various rules and regulations that govern the application of the charges and the use of service by the subscriber. The FCC reviews the tariff. If the charges and regulations are ascertained to be just and reasonable, the tariff becomes operative. Should the Commission decide that the proposed tariff is not just and reasonable with regard to any charge, practice, classification, or regulation, the tariff may be rejected and the company required to remedy the defect. Another course of action is to prescribe the rate structure the company will employ. This latter option is taken infrequently, however, so the initiation of telephone rate structure is primarily in the hands of the telephone companies.

The private enterprise approach requires in the design of rate structures a balancing of the public interest with the interests of the investors in the venture. In other words, there is the need to provide high quality, universally available service at reasonable charges to subscribers while generating enough revenue to cover the cost of service. Those revenues must also yield sufficient return on the capital invested to encourage continued private financial support. In one form of review, called rate-of-return regulation, the FCC sets the carrier's allowed rate of return on investment. Price regulation, or price caps, where the regulator focuses on rates charged, rather than the profits of the carrier, is another approach that has gained acceptance.

Universal telephone service has been an expressed governmental, corporate, and social goal since the turn of the century. Looking toward this goal, the old Bell System (i.e., the predivestiture American Telephone and Telegraph Company, or AT&T) tried to structure rates so that revenues from business and optional services helped support basic residential service. The former were priced at levels above their directly attributable costs to provide a contribution to the common costs of the enterprise. This type of rate structure kept basic residential rates low while still generating enough revenue to cover the overall costs of the enterprise.

In a free market environment, rate structures have to be more closely related to the directly attributable costs of each telecommunications service. Otherwise, competitors will undercut a firm that is charging exceedingly high prices for one class of service in order to subsidize another. Subsidies are harder to sustain if competitors can enter the market without having to inflate prices to underwrite unprofitable services. Thus, the idea of one class of service contributing to the benefit of another has become less feasible. In addition, as the diversity of the phone network has increased, "universal service" has become more subject to interpretation. Does universal service require all users to have touchtone capability? What about call waiting?

Under the Communications Act of 1934, the FCC has primary jurisdiction over all interstate and international communications. State regulators oversee local (exchange) services, terminal equipment, and intercity services provided wholly within the borders of their respective states. However, federal law grants to the FCC authority over three matters that have a direct effect upon the cost of providing service and, therefore, the intrastate rate structure:

1. The FCC prescribes a uniform system of accounting to be followed by all communications companies.
2. The FCC prescribes the depreciation practices to be followed by the companies.
3. The FCC has the authority to set the value of the communications property used in furnishing the service.

A unique accounting aspect of this third function is the allocation of property between federal and state jurisdiction. The allocation, known as "jurisdictional separations," is necessary because of the two levels of regulation practices in the United States. There is, therefore, federal-state cooperation in establishing basic costing procedures that underlie the determination of rate structures.

The former Bell System companies are the dominant suppliers of telephone service in the United States, but there are also some 1,500 non-Bell companies providing telephone service in their respective franchised territories. Despite the number of firms providing telephone service throughout the United States, the basic rate structures are similar from firm to firm.

Exchange and Interexchange Service

Local exchange rates generally are established on a statewide basis. Phone companies determine their revenue requirement (total cost of providing service) for the state as a whole and then work out a schedule of rates that meets the revenue requirement. If more than one company operates within a state, each company determines its own revenue requirement.

This approach has the effect of averaging the costs of phone service throughout the state. Therefore, rates may depart from the actual cost of furnishing service within any particular community. For example, in sparsely populated areas—where low customer density per mile of line makes it expensive to provide service—rates are lower than warranted by the phone company's costs. However, the charges to subscribers still reflect the "value of service," because they correspond directly to the number of telephones within a designated local calling area. Rural residents may pay less relative to cost than urban residents, but they also can reach fewer numbers at the "local" price. *Value*-of-service pricing, rather than *cost*-of-service pricing, has been employed traditionally in constructing exchange service tariffs within the United States as a means of equalizing subscriber charges and thereby encouraging telephone development in high-cost areas.

Another factor affecting revenues is the way customers are charged. If the subscriber has *measured service,* the basic monthly charge covers a certain number of message units, i.e., local calls, that may be used before any additional local service charges accrue. A *flat-rate* subscriber, conversely, may make unlimited local calls in a designated area without additional charge. Over the years, telephone companies generally have encouraged flat-rate local service outside of major metropolitan areas. However, in an era of rising costs, usage-sensitive rate structures may become more appropriate as part of the movement to cost-based pricing.

The long-distance, or "interexchange," rate structure, unlike the local service rate structure, is completely usage sensitive throughout the United States. Long-distance message telecommunications (toll) services are furnished by AT&T, MCI (Microwave Communications, Inc.), and others at uniform statewide rates for *interstate* calls. (Pay phone and hotel rates may differ, however.) The rate structure does not explicitly recognize that costs for calls on heavily used routes between urban centers may vary from costs on lightly used routes in sparsely populated areas. In the *intrastate* service, a fifty-mile call will cost the same irrespective of the points served within the particular state. However, a fifty-mile call in one state may cost a subscriber more or less than a fifty-mile call would cost in another state—or, for that matter, a fifty-mile *inter*state call. This situation is the result of the separate jurisdictional responsibilities of intrastate and interstate operations divided between the FCC and the PUCs.

Competition and the AT&T Breakup

Until the 1970s there was essentially no competition for local or long-distance telephone carriers. Local companies enjoyed public utility monopoly franchises granted by state governments; AT&T was a de facto monopolist of long-distance services, protected by the FCC from competition. In the 1950s, however, a new technology—microwave communications—transformed the prospects for competition in long-distance services. Entrepreneurs such as MCI began offering service that competed with AT&T's long-distance service. In 1969 the FCC allowed MCI to enter the market, opening the door to competition, if only by a crack.

MCI used microwave links to provide unswitched service between pairs of points predetermined by the customer. The service initially did not allow MCI customers to call anyone, anywhere; for that switched service, AT&T controlled the market. Over the next decade, the door swung open much wider for AT&T's rivals. MCI began expanding the pairs of points it offered and negotiated the rights to hand off traffic from its facilities to local exchanges in order to complete customer calls. Others, including Southern Pacific Railway (U.S. Sprint), which already owned rights-of-way to install transmission facilities, joined the field. To serve areas where they had no facilities in place, MCI and Sprint purchased AT&T links in bulk and resold them. Other new entrants were pure resellers who only resold AT&T service, which they purchased in bulk. Drawing on digital technologies, competitors offered customers data transmission service, more sophisticated terminal equipment, and a variety of services—such as fiber-optic transmission—that AT&T was either unable or unwilling to offer.

In the mid-1970s AT&T had a large, prestigious research organization, Bell Laboratories. But "Ma Bell" also had an enormous amount of obsolete customer equipment on its books and aging analog technology that was being threatened by competitors offering the new digital technology so crucial for the transmission of data. AT&T was forced to defend its monopoly by arguing that letting aggressive new competitors enter the field would force AT&T to raise local rates as it lost business.

Once the FCC let competitors into the long-distance and terminal-equipment markets, AT&T fought back in the marketplace. This aggressive defense attracted the concern of the U.S. Department of Justice, which brought a major antitrust suit against AT&T in 1974. After more than seven years, the suit was settled by a consent decree. AT&T was required to divest itself of its operating companies; in return, AT&T was freed from the restrictions of a 1956 court ruling that had kept it from entering any business other than regulated communications. Thus, AT&T was allowed to enter the computer business.

In 1984 AT&T completed the divestiture of its operating companies. The divested Bell Operating Companies (BOCs) are now managed through seven regional holding companies (RHCs), sometimes called regional Bell Operating Companies (RBOCs). These include NYNEX Corporation (New York and New England), Bell Atlantic Corporation (mid-Atlantic), BellSouth Corporation (South), American Information Technologies (Ameritech) Corporation (Midwest), Southwestern Bell Corporation (Texas and Southwest), US West, Inc. (Rocky Mountains), and Pacific Telesis Group (California and Nevada).

The Modified Final Judgment (MFJ), which governed the broken-up AT&T, reconfigured the Bell System, redefining basic exchange areas and making them much larger. Before divestiture, an *exchange* was an area with a single uniform set of charges for telephone service. Calls between points in an exchange area were *local* calls. The MFJ redefined an exchange to be more or less equivalent to a U.S. government statistical unit called the Standard Metropolitan Statistical Area (SMSA). The Bell System territory was divided into about 160 of these new exchanges, called *local access and transport areas* (LATAs), ranging from large metropolitan areas to entire states. LATA boundaries, not states or area codes, determine which entity—a local or long-distance company—is assigned to handle a call.

Under the MFJ, the BOCs provide regulated telecommunications services *within* LATAs (intraLATA), and AT&T and other interexchange carriers provide services *between* LATAs (interLATA). InterLATA calls may be within a single state and are handled by AT&T or another long-distance company. An intraLATA call may involve more than one area code.

AT&T competes in the computer and other high-technology electronics markets through its two main subsidiaries: AT&T Communications, which offers long-distance voice, data, and video transmission in the United States and abroad, and AT&T Technologies, Western Electric's successor. Now free of their relationship with AT&T, the BOCs may purchase their capital equipment from any competitive source. As a result, other communications equipment manufacturers (such as ITT or Northern Telecom) may supply the BOCs, whose customers represent more than 80 percent of American households. (In previous decades BOCs bought most of their equipment from AT&T's own Western Electric subsidiary.) In addition, the high-tech manufacturers may sell their equipment to new competitive long-distance carriers or even offer long-distance service themselves. Thus, a slight crack in the monopoly facade of AT&T caused by technological advances has now evolved into full-scale competition for communications equipment and long-distance services. Only local service remains a protected, franchised monopoly in most states.

Summary

How did the nation's phone system transform from a monopoly to a largely competitive industry? The simple answer is: technology. Improved technology reduced the cost of providing some aspects of phone system services. Competitors sometimes could provide service more cheaply than AT&T, which had a massive preexisting investment in older technology. Technology also enabled the introduction of desirable telecommunications services that AT&T could not or would not rapidly make available.

Technology-driven changes in telecommunications had three regulatory ramifications. First, the rules of entry into the market had to change. Competitors who were providing innovative offerings were accommodated. Second, since these competitors were not saddled with the cross-subsidies inhering AT&T's rate structure, they could offer lower prices, gaining a competitive advantage. AT&T and regulators had to rethink whether the system of pricing adopted under a monopoly environment made sense as competition emerged.

This rethinking led "prices" of services to move closer to their actual "costs." It also led to new approaches to pricing regulation, such as emphasizing stability through caps on prices.

COMPETITIVE CARRIER, FURTHER NOTICE OF PROPOSED RULEMAKING

84 F.C.C.2d 445 (1981)

*   *   *

The market mechanism is the major social institution for the allocation of scarce resources in the United States. Many markets, however, function with some degree of government participation that supplements or conditions the process of voluntary exchange. A particular variant of market intervention is the economic regulation of monopoly firms that have come to be considered "public utilities," such as those that produce gas, electricity, water and communications.[3] In general, the economic regulation of public utilities has traditionally included control over entry into the market, some degree of price control, the specification of both quality standards and conditions of service, and, usually, an obligation to serve all customers requesting service under reasonable, non-discriminatory terms. The historical arguments justifying the imposition of such social controls on public utility firms are diverse, varying widely from market to market and from one legal jurisdiction to another. Kahn identifies such diverse justifications as: "natural monopoly;" the need for franchises to obtain the power of eminent

---

3. Economic regulation of a market can be contrasted with government ownership and control of a firm or industry. In general, economic regulation only constrains the behavior of privately-owned enterprises while preserving private ownership and management of the firm. For a brief discussion of both the legal and economic rationale of regulation and its historical evolution, see Kahn, *The Economics of Regulation*, Vol. I, Ch. 1 (1971). A useful discussion of the "public utility concept" is provided by Bonbright, *Principles of Public Utility Rates*, Ch. 1 (1961). In many foreign countries, firms regulated as public utilities in the United States are nationalized or socialistic enterprises.

domain; the desire to promote risky enterprises; the desire to protect consumers who cannot readily evaluate the quality of goods or services purchased; the desire to prevent the emergence of "destructive competition;" the need to prevent deterioration in the quality of service; the need to control "monopoly power;" the need to prevent "cream-skimming;" and other social-political rationalizations.

* * *

Market power is the ability of a firm to raise and maintain its prices above costs, including an allowance of a fair profit. As a result, consumers pay more than the costs of production. Thus, resources that could have gone into the production of more goods are wasted.

Another potential problem raised by market power is the ability of the dominant firm to maintain prices below costs in order to forestall entry by potential competitors or to eliminate existing competitors by a predatory pricing strategy. The potential problems created by the existence of market power were perceived to be so great in certain cases that state legislatures and Congress responded by imposing direct controls over the prices and profits of the firms possessing such power.[7] Control over prices and profits of such dominant firms typically has been implemented through the institution of rate of return regulation.

Rate of return regulation has several constituent elements. Fundamental is the prescription of an allowed rate of return that provides the firm a just and reasonable profit on its invested capital. The regulator here must first determine the "proper" percentage return, the expenditures that belong in the rate base on which the return can be earned, the expenditures that are to be allowed as a current expense, and the expenditures that are to be disallowed altogether. To carry out these requirements effectively, the regulator must be able to obtain detailed cost information. Additionally, the power to disallow expenses and to order refunds is necessary to remedy such potential problems as imprudent expenditures or excessive rates of return.

All of the elements of the rate of return regulation paradigm discussed above are embodied in Title II of the Communications Act of 1934. Section 201(a) provides for furnishing service on reasonable request. Section 201(a) provides for public control of rates by requiring just and reasonable charges. Section 202(a) makes unreasonable price or service discrimination unlawful. Section 205 provides the FCC with the authority to prescribe carrier rates and practices. Section 214 provides the Commission with authority to approve investments. Other portions of Title II provide for reports and accounting systems that can be used to implement rate of return regulation. Our power to order refunds is derived from Section 204(a).

---

7. Traditional wisdom held that the market power of the dominant firm often was based on substantial economies of scale, *i.e.*, a situation in which large scale production by a single firm is essential to achieve least cost production of telecommunications services. Such a firm is said to have a "natural monopoly." This view has, of course, not prevailed in interstate telecommunications. *See Customer Interconnection*, 75 F.C.C. 2d 506 (1980).

Rate base regulation applied to a monopoly firm is conceptually straightforward. The basic idea is to control what the regulated firm charges its customers by allowing it to collect just enough revenue from its customers to recover its cost of operation.[13] In principle, the imposition of rate base regulation prevents the monopoly firm from exercising its monopoly power by pricing its services well above cost and earning monopoly (supranormal) profits. Arguably, rate base regulation provides consumers with two major benefits: (1) the cost advantages of large scale production that fully exploits the assumed natural monopoly conditions and (2) the assurance that rates charged by the regulated firm are not excessive but instead are "just and reasonable," reflecting the average unit cost of production at high levels of output. Additionally, regulation also requires the monopoly firm to serve all customers reasonably requesting service and to do so on non-discriminatory terms. In brief, the social contract between society and the regulated firms appears to protect the consumer from monopoly abuse, provide consumers with public utility service at rates reflecting the economies of large scale production; and provide owners of the regulated firm "just and reasonable" compensation for use of their property.

Rate base regulation as just described suggests only its fundamental logic in general terms and does not address the complexities of real-world application.[14] Implementing regulation requires that the agency, among other things (1) determine the property to be included in the rate base; (2) prescribe the rate of depreciation the regulated firm may use in computing depreciation expenses; (3)

---

13. This relationship is presented in textbook discussions in terms of the familiar regulatory relationship "Revenue Requirement (RR) = Cost of Service (COS)" where COS = E + T + d + r(V − D). The definitions of E, d, T, r, V and D are, respectively, operating expenses, depreciation expense, taxes, the allowed rate of return, gross valuation of public utility property used in producing public utility services, and accrued depreciation. The expression (V-D) represents the regulated firm's "rate base" net of depreciation and r(V-D) measures its "allowed earnings" on its rate base. For further discussion see Paul J. Garfield and Wallace F. Lovejoy, *Public Utility Economics* (Englewood Cliffs, N.J., Prentice-Hall 1964), Chapter 5.

14. Rate of return regulation is sometimes characterized as a substitute for competition. Unfortunately, the implementation of rate of return regulation does not cause the monopolist to behave exactly like a competitive firm. While rate of return regulation imposes some control over the monopolist's market power, such regulation introduces systemic distortions in resource allocation and may hinder the achievement of good market performance in the industry. In recent years economic theorists have examined the implications of rate of return regulation on economic efficiency. For example, Averch and Johnson in their pioneering article show that rate of return regulation creates incentives that may distort the input choices of a regulated firm away from production at minimum cost. See Averch and Johnson, "Behavior of the Firm Under Regulatory Constraint," 52 *American Economic Review*, 1053–69 (Dec. 1962). Charles Needy emphasizes that rate of return regulation may encourage the regulated firm to produce at non-optimal levels of output. See Needy, *Regulation-Induced Distortions* (1978). V. Kerry Smith shows that rate of return regulation may distort the direction of technological change. See Smith, "The Implication of regulation of Induced Technical Change," 5 *The Bell Journal of Economics and Management Science* 623–32 (Autumn, 1974). Roger Sherman and Michael Visscher show that rate of return regulation may encourage price structures that do not maximize consumer welfare. See Sherman and Visscher, "Rate-of-Return Regulation and Price Structure" in Michael A. Crew, ed., *Problems in Public Utility Economics and Regulation*, 119–132 (1979).

determine the allowed rate of return that presumably reflects the firm's financial "cost of capital," (4) establish the criteria for "allowable" operating expenses; (5) develop a regulatory accounting or information system that tracks the firm's revenues and expenses; (6) specify the criteria for reviewing tariffs submitted by the regulated firm to the regulatory agency; and (7) establish rules and procedures for exercising regulatory control. The actual administration of regulation requires expert staffs of lawyers, accountants, engineers, and economists and is implemented through a process that is often slow, subject to protracted procedural delay, and costly, to both the regulatory agency (and therefore taxpayers) and the regulated firm (and therefore consumers).

The regulatory process is also highly dependent on a constant flow of information. Detailed data on revenues, depreciation schedules, expenses, rate base investment, cost of finance, tariffs, construction plans, and numerous other aspects of the regulated firm's activities are necessary for the regulatory process. The source of this information is, of necessity, the regulated firm itself. Thus, there are additional costs to regulated firms and consumers that must be acknowledged.

This Commission over the past twenty years has attempted to respond to the shortcomings of the regulatory process by introducing competition as an additional constraint on the behavior of dominant firms. To a large extent, however, these entrants have been subjected to the same regulations as the dominant firms. Therefore, they are required to provide the same detailed kinds of data on revenues, costs, investment schedules, etc., as dominant firms. Collection of such data are expensive for firms. However one perceives the ultimate cost benefit tradeoff in the context of regulating dominant firms, it seems clear that the application of these same regulations to firms that possess insignificant market power imposes costs without any corresponding benefits.

Most importantly, the requirements of the regulatory process itself, particularly the requirements for prior review of prices and investments, take away firms' ability to make rapid, efficient responses to changes in demand and cost . . . Thus there is a danger that risky investments will not be undertaken. Many entrepreneurs may simply choose to invest their funds in other areas of the economy rather than subject themselves to the risks and costs of being regulated. This barrier to entry reduces both competition and innovation.

Additionally, the requirement that firms post their prices makes it difficult for those same firms to bargain with their customers over rates or to adjust them quickly to market conditions. This in turn means that the kind of price discounting that often occurs in a workably competitive market cannot take place. Particularly affected are the kinds of discounts that occur when a fairly large potential customer seeks service during a time of otherwise slack demand for the supplier. In competitive markets, suppliers are often willing to lower prices in order to attract such customers. Because such periods cannot always be predicted, it is often not possible to file tariffs which can take effect in time to cover this situation.

The requirement that firms file tariffs, in practice, immediately subjects them to petitions from competitors for rejection or suspension and investigation of the tariffs. Should a competitor be successful in persuading the regulatory agency to order a hearing, the firm can face substantial legal costs in defending its proposed prices. As a result, it may find it less expensive to withdraw the new rate. Conversely, the tariff filing requirement may also lead firms to file tariffs for services they are not yet ready to provide. Since such petitions are filed more often over proposed rate decreases than proposed rate increases, the consumers are the losers in such battles.

Tariff posting also provides an excellent mechanism for inducing noncompetitive pricing. Since all price reductions are public, they can be quickly matched by competitors. This reduces the incentive to engage in price cutting. In these circumstances firms may be able to charge prices higher than could be sustained in an unregulated market. Thus, regulated competition all too often becomes cartel management.

The requirement for prior approval of facilities construction, with the requirement that the regulatory agency obtain public comment on such requests, similarly imposes costs beyond those of preparing the applications. If the application calls for new technology or a new service, the proposing firm not only is required to give its competitors an early blueprint of such technological innovations but also its exact plan for deployment. Because such early warning does not take place in markets not subject to price and entry controls, technological innovation by existing competitors or new entrants is discouraged in regulated markets compared with unregulated ones. However, to the extent that firms prefer to avoid regulation, these same regulatory requirements result in wasteful use of resources. Firms with private microwave facilities, for example, are unable to sell their excess capacity without becoming common carriers.

Finally, there are additional costs in regulating competitive carriers that are borne by the agency and thus the public interest that it is designed to protect. The resources devoted to regulating and to complying with regulations are wasted, since the firm would be unable to earn excess profits in any case. That is, lacking market power, nondominant firms are unable to do what the rules are designed to prevent them from doing anyway. The costs of resources wasted on competitive carriers could be used to attempt to do a better job regulating the dominant carriers. The resources used by the regulatees are inevitably passed on to the public in the form of higher prices.

The implication of this review of the consequences of rate of return regulation is that similar regulatory restraints applied to firms with diverse characteristics (particularly varying degrees of market power) can have disparate results, often in conflict with the statutory goals of regulation itself. The extent to which a firm is regulated should depend upon the economic consequences of the regulation and other public interest considerations. In our opinion, regulation should be applied only where the benefits of that regulation for consumers exceed the costs.

In summary, the central issue we face is to reconcile the use of traditional regulatory tools (control of entry and exit, expansion of facilities, rate and revenue requirement regulation) with the characteristics of the firms operating in the communications arena. Regulation of those carriers with little or no market power can have negative effects on market behavior and on costs to consumers. These firms typically face a series of rival firms offering similar service to the same locations. Their ability to price and diversify their services as the market dictates may be impeded by regulation, while they have no power to engage in practices detrimental to the public. There is no anticipation of overcapitalization nor excessive rates because the market constrains their behavior. Further, the fact that immediately-available, close substitutes exist means that exit regulation need not be of critical concern. Retention of significant Commission control over entry would only serve to delay the availability of new sources of supply and new services. Current entry regulation causes firms to declare their strategies before entry, thus reducing any time-related advantages that a new firm would have over existing firms by giving the latter more opportunity to react to the entrant. The import of these matters certainly varies from firm to firm. Therefore, our regulations must be flexible to account for these differences among carriers and they must reflect actual market place conditions so that they are applied only in a firm that confers greater benefits upon consumers than costs.

In performing our cost/benefit analysis, we must take into account that, while initially regulation was applied under a concept of single-output monopoly firms, today the firms supplying basic communications service participate in several markets. Recognizing the existence of multiple markets requires the regulatory authority to examine the rationale for regulation in each market. Consequently attention must be paid to the demand side, since consumers are no longer purchasing a single, indifferentiated product. If this were the case, then regulatory policy could be interchangeably and equivalently focused on either the monopoly firm *per se* or on the market it serves. The presence of the same firm in several markets, often with different characteristics, blurs this interchangeability. Continuing to formulate regulatory policies directed toward the firm itself rather than the firm's performance in the various markets it serves obscures the original purpose of regulation, i.e., the protection of consumers from the potential abuse of a monopolist's market power. Directing policies toward the regulated firm and not toward its observed or potential behavior in the individual markets it serves may lead to policies that protect competitors rather than consumers.

Finally, we have attempted here to move away from static analysis involving heavy reliance on historical data. While analysis of such data may be easier than analysing dynamic markets, the rapidly changing telecommunications industry requires forward-looking decision making.

*   *   *

III. The Communications Act

A. Introduction

The guiding principle implicit in our discussion of the economic consequences of Title II regulation is that competition will serve the public interest and achieve the Act's underlying purpose "to make available, so far as possible, to all the people of the United States a rapid, efficient, nation-wide, and world-wide wire and radio communication service with adequate facilities at reasonable charges. . . ." Section 1, 47 U.S.C. §151. This principle also has led the Commission to adopt and implement since 1959 a consistent policy of encouraging competitive entry into previously monopolized markets.

As this policy has developed and its merits have been sustained and often endorsed by the courts, *see e.g., United States v. FCC* (SBS), No. 77–1249 (D.C. Cir. March 7, 1980), and as the results of this policy have been further spurred on by rapid technological change and innovation, a dynamic, competitive tele-communications market has begun to emerge. However, the continued rigid uniform application of Title II requirements to all market participants threatens to undermine this dynamism and in turn betray the overriding goals of the Act. We do not believe that Congress intended such a result. Indeed, as the following examination of the statutory framework and the legislative history clearly shows, Congress imposed Title II regulation primarily to constrain the market power of communications suppliers and hence those carriers without such power need not be subjected to the full panoply of Title II requirements, if they are regulable under Title II at all.

B. Statutory Framework

The essential elements of Title II regulations entail control on price, publication of terms and conditions of service, prohibitions on discrimination, control on investments and an obligation to serve all. In assessing the import of this statutory scheme, we begin with the observation that Title II represents the traditional approach to public utility regulation. The carrier is required to provide service upon reasonable request, all charges and practices thereafter are to be just, reasonable and not unduly discriminatory, and facilities investments must be authorized.

We believe that this regulatory scheme was developed in recognition of the monopoly position held by the providers of what Congress deemed to be an essential public service. This belief stems from a recognition that the regulatory measures of the sort contained in Title II make sense only in the context of an industry lacking beneficial competitive restraints. A brief review of the major statutory obligations imposed by Congress on Title II firms reveals this purpose.

Section 201(a) requires Title II firms to "provide service upon reasonable request." The presence of an affirmative duty to serve suggests that Congress intended to regulate communications entities whose refusals to deal would leave consumers without an essential service.[17] By definition, in a competitive market-place alternative sources would be readily available and there would be no need to assure service to all through a regulatory device. Indeed, under both the common law and our nation's basic economic policies founded in the antitrust laws, no duty to deal exists in the absence of monopoly power. See *United States v. Colgate*, 250 U.S. 300 (1919).

The obligations imposed by Congress upon Title II firms with regard to the prices they may seek to charge are found in Sections 201(b) and 202(a). As discussed in the *Notice* and our *First Report and Order*, the legal obligation to charge just and reasonable rates need not be imposed in the absence of market power. Accepted economic theory, both in 1934 and today, informs us that competition will assure the "reasonableness" of price. The presence of market power, in contrast, is the ability to charge and maintain price above the cost

---

17. This purpose is generally set forth in Section 1 of the Act, wherein one stated purpose is "to make available, so far as possible, to all the people of the United States" efficient and reasonably priced communications service.

(including a reasonable profit) of providing service. Indeed, it has often been noted that rate regulation has been created to substitute for, and compensate for the lack of, competition.

The tariff and rate supervision responsibilities with which the Commission is charged strongly suggest a congressional concern for curbing monopoly abuse. Section 203 requires the public filing of all rates and conditions proposed, prohibits carrier activity at variance with the filing, and empowers the agency to impose fines when such discriminations occur. Section 204 invests the agency with authority to suspend new filings and hold hearings on the lawfulness thereof. Refunds may be ordered for unreasonable rates that have been collected. Section 205 provides the extreme remedy of removing the carrier's right to initiate charges and substituting governmentally prescribed rates. It is readily apparent that each of these sections seeks to monitor and prevent the exercise of control over prices otherwise resulting in wealth transfers from consumers to monopoly carriers.

Section 214 requires agency authorization of new facilities investments by carriers. At least one of the concerns behind passage of this section was the fear that consumers would ultimately suffer the burden of imprudent or wasteful investments by carriers.

As noted elsewhere, only firms with monopoly power are capable—in the absence of governmental intervention—of passing these costs along to their captive ratepayers; the inefficiency of competitive firms must be shouldered by their investors. Other sections supplement this purpose. Section 213, for example, invests the Commission with the power to investigate the carrier's rate base to assure that the rates charged reflect accurately the cost of the property used to provide the service. Other information with regard to corporate structure, earnings, expenses and management are accessible to the agency. The power to prescribe depreciation rates—a highly significant aspect of a carrier's revenue requirements—is also specifically provided. Section 220.

We have discussed the generally accepted proposition that competitive firms, in contrast, cannot profitably engage in activities of the kind Congress sought to prevent in Sections 201–205 and 214. None of this type of regulation is of any public benefit where firms lacking market power are involved, for they have no ability or incentive to charge unlawful rates. Regardless of the level of investment, their prices will be determined by the market, typically in the present context by the prices set by firms with market power. They have no ability to discriminate unreasonably and, in any case, their customers can always obtain service from a competitor in the event their rates exceed the prevailing market price. Such firms would thus be also unable to pass on to their customers the cost of inefficient facility investments.

Congress fashioned the rate base regulatory scheme of Title II to address the ills it perceived in a communications marketplace dominated by a few firms. Moreover, the language of the Act suggests that Congress did not foresee the prospects of new entry or significant competition in an industry which for years had been tending toward or under monopoly control. Although Section 214 of the Act has subsequently been applied by this Commission to new entrants, which due to technological innovation or other conditions have sought to participate in the industry, the language of that section seems primarily, if not exclusively, concerned with controlling an industry in which new entry could not feasibly occur. Thus, Section 214 addresses the public convenience and necessity for "additional or extended line[s]," but is silent on the matter of new carriers undertaking the operation of new facilities networks.

In sum, Title II can readily be viewed as a logical and consistent regulatory scheme directed at the problems associated with monopoly control or market power. While this construction is not totally free from doubt, our ensuing analysis of the legislative history and the historical context of the Act bolsters our conclusion that Congress intended to create a regulatory system to constrain the abuses market power portends. . . .

Questions

1. The purposes underlying the Communications Act of 1934 are outlined in §151. Review §151, which can be found in Appendix B. The act requires the FCC to act in the "public interest." Is this standard too broad to be meaningful? What factors might the Commission consider in determining the public interest? Are there other interests the FCC might have to consider?

2. The rate-of-return regulation paradigm is embodied in Title II of the act. Review carefully §§201–205 and see if you can construct a flow diagram of how the Title II paradigm is supposed to work. What are the basic instruction to the Commission proposed by each section? What are the time limits for Commission action?

3. Why is the communications field regulated? What is a natural monopoly? What is market power?

4. Several authors have described a type of "regulatory compact" between Bell and its regulators in the early years. For example, Gerald Faulhaber states:

> [AT&T President] Vail's regulatory strategy seem[ed] especially astute. Vail's policy of immediate accommodation ensured that Bell was the only "interested party" close to, indeed in partnership with, the regulator. By announcing a common goal, universal service, Bell gave the regulator the political justification to brush aside potential competitors, barring their entry into the regulatory game.

(Faulhaber, *Telecommunications in Turmoil*, 45–46 [1987]. See also Henck and Strassburg, *A Slippery Slope: The Long Road to the Breakup of AT&T*, xi [1988]). What did the regulators gain from this compact? What did Bell gain from this compact?

5. What circumstances brought about the recent shift in focus from regulation to competition? Was it wrong for the original decisionmakers to regulate so closely?

6. What are the explicit goals of rate-of-return regulation? What are the implicit assumptions? What are the costs?

7. The regulatory process is highly dependent on a constant flow of quite detailed information. Who are the sources of this information? What problems may arise as a result?

NORTH AMERICAN NUMBERING PLAN

Is there any method behind the ten-digit phone numbers assigned by the phone company? The U.S. system, called the North American Numbering Plan, is administered under the 1984 consent decree, which broke up the old Bell System. The plan applies a "destination code" principle, telling the system what "address," or destination, a caller is trying to reach. Each main telephone is assigned a ten-digit number comprised of 1) a three-digit Numbering Plan Area Code (NPA, better known as the area code); 2) a three-digit Central Office (CO) Code that signifies the serving or end office providing the dial tone; and 3) a four-digit station number.

The plan follows certain numbering protocols to facilitate efficient call routing. For example, the system tells whether a local or long-distance call is being placed by the second number dialed. This is because all area codes contain a 0 or 1 as a second digit, whereas until recently no CO codes may have these numbers in their second positions. In addition, codes in the form of "–11" are reserved for special functions such as directory assistance (411) and emergency calls (911). The codes 700, 800, 900, and 610 are called Service Access Codes (SACs) and are reserved for special network uses. One drawback of this special numbering format, however, is the limited number of codes available for assignment. As the number of available codes shrinks, interchangeable NPA and CO codes will have to be assigned, and a universal requirement of "1+" dialing for all ten-digit calls will have to be implemented.

A similar problem with code availability created the need to change to the present plan. An earlier plan used a two-letter, five-number scheme. The letters were the first two letters of the serving office name; the five numbers were made up of the third digit of the CO code and the four-digit station number. A familiar example is Pennsylvania 6–5000, or PE6–5000. (Because of the confusion between the letter O and the number 0, and other similar digit-letter combinations, certain codes remained unassigned.) But the plan, which was supposed to have enough capacity to last through this century, ran out of codes. In 1959 the transition to the present All-Number Calling (ANC) Plan commenced and was completed in 1980. Implementation of interchangeable codes and 1+ten-digit dialing is anticipated in 1995.

Questions

1. Who owns a telephone number? Is there a property right in a telephone number? If a subscriber moves and wants to keep his or her number, can the telephone company charge him or her? (Find out what the local billing practice is in your calling area.) Can you be charged for an unlisted number?

2. It has been suggested that each person should be assigned a telephone number for life (as with a Social Security Number). The FCC is considering this proposal in connection with introducing Personal Communications Service (PCS). The notion is that a person could always be contacted at his or her assigned number by either telephone or computer code. What privacy issues does this raise?

3. Calling Number Identification, or Caller ID, also raises privacy concerns. Caller ID displays a calling party's telephone number on a special display device at the receiving party's location. A Pennsylvania trial court found that Caller ID violates the caller's common law right of privacy. The South Carolina Supreme Court, ruling on the same issue, found no privacy-right violation for either party. What privacy rights of the parties are involved? Are there privacy rights on both sides of the call?

By 1991 sixteen states offered calling-number identification services. Only nine states, however, allowed callers to block their phone numbers from being displayed. California allows callers to block numbers on a per call basis. Why not authorize callers to block the display on all calls from their line?

RATE REGULATION

Although this is not a book about finance or accounting, it is important to understand the basic concepts behind the rate-regulation equation printed in *Competitive Carrier* at footnote 13. Only by doing so can one really understand the conflicting interests of rate-regulated firms and a rate-setting utility commission. The equation is as follows:

Revenue Requirements (RR) =

Cost of Service (COS) =   operating expenses (E) + depreciation (d) + taxes (T) + allowed earnings (r(V−D))

where r is the percentage return on capital, V is the value of the capital equipment, and D is the accumulated depreciation on the equipment for the year in question.

This equation tries to mirror economic reality in a competitive environment. It allows revenues to include only a firm's expenses plus a reasonable profit (a return on investment). However, fluctuations in any one variable can upset the goal of rate regulation by allowing too much revenue. Take depreciation, which measures the natural tendency for an asset (such as machinery) to wear out or become obsolete. Once it is decided how much an asset depreciates each year, a firm can deduct from its gross income an equivalent amount as an expense of doing business. In the above equation, depreciation is accounted for by adding the amount into COS so that the firm's revenue requirements (RR) correspond to economic reality. A problem can arise, though, where rates of depreciation do not mirror reality. Many times, firms are allowed to depreciate assets at a much quicker rate than the assets actually deteriorate. The result of accelerating the rate of depreciation is to raise RR, which in turn increases incentives for capital investment.

For instance, assume that a rate-regulated firm could depreciate a piece of machinery 100 percent in the machine's first year of operation, thereby taking the full cost of the machine as a present expense. In such a situation, the COS as computed above would be inflated; the rate-regulated firm would be allowed a 100 percent depreciation expense for a machine that actually has plenty of useful life left. This phenomenon creates an incentive for firms to buy "gold-plated" machinery (i.e., purchase unneeded assets simply to increase their depreciation expenses).

Accelerated depreciation generates increased revenues, which are then used to underwrite the costs of new equipment—even though existing equipment may still be adequate to do a particular job. This result occurs because the existing equipment has a book value of zero.

The above example illustrates the importance of deciding the parameters of the depreciation variable in the rate-regulation equation. Obviously, FCC decisions on what will be included in the valuation of public utility property (V) or what is a reasonable rate of return on investment (r) are no less significant. Some critics claim rate-regulated firms purposely overcapitalize in order to increase V, thereby increasing their rate base and allowed earnings. In any event, these Commission decisions are the genesis of many disputes, not to mention the source of high administrative costs. It is not surprising, then, that many students of public utility regulation feel rate regulation is an exercise in regulatory futility.

THE ROAD TO MORE INTELLIGENT TELEPHONE PRICING

Alfred E. Kahn
1 Yale Journal on Regulation 139 (1984)

The transformation of interexchange telecommunications from a regulated, franchised monopoly to an unregulated, competitive industry has been under

Copyright © 1984 by the *Yale Journal on Regulation*, Box 401A Yale Station, New Haven, CT 06520. Reprinted from Volume 1 by permission. All rights reserved.

way for a quarter century. AT&T now faces competition in almost all of its intercity markets, including residential toll calling, and the local operating companies face the prospect of partial displacement by a number of emerging alternatives to the wired exchange network.

It is probably a sign of good mental health that we seem to be spending little time looking back and asking ourselves whether the course on which we have embarked in telecommunications is the right one. The question is not only impossible to answer with any assurance, it is also irrelevant. Further movement toward freer competition is inevitable, at least for the foreseeable future.[2] While I "estimate" a small but positive probability that ten or twenty years from now we will look back and conclude that the entire venture was a ghastly mistake, I am convinced that this probability can be reduced substantially by the adoption of intelligent pricing policies by telecommunications companies and their regulators.

*   *   *

I. The Inefficiency of Present Pricing Policies

A. Features of an Efficient Pricing System

Economic efficiency requires that services be priced at their marginal costs. A telecommunications system incurs two types of costs. The first are the costs associated with merely connecting a customer to the network; because they are not affected by how much he then uses the system, they are characterized as non-traffic-sensitive. Traffic-sensitive costs, in contrast, are generated by the customer's usage of the system and vary with, among other factors, the time and

---

2. Historically, rapid and dramatic technological advances, both in communications and the use of communications, have made movement toward greater competitiveness inevitable. Once we had microwave technology, which opened the door to private microwave systems, then the decision in Allocation of Frequencies in the Bands Above 890 Mc. (Above 890) 27 F.C.C. 359 (1959), *modified,* 29 F.C.C. 825 (1960) (allowing customers to construct and operate their own facilities for private, point-to-point telecommunications, bypassing the telephone company network altogether), was probably inevitable. Once we had private carriage, then "specialized" competitive common carriers followed. The activities of these carriers were sanctioned in Microwave Communications, Inc., 18 F.C.C.2d 953 (1969), *reconsid. denied,* 21 F.C.C.2d 190 (1970) (permitting MCI to sell private line service in direct competition with the telephone company), and Specialized Common Carrier Servs., 29 F.C.C.2d 870 (1971), *aff'd sub nom.* Washington Util. & Transp. Comm'n v. FCC, 513 F.2d 1142 (9th Cir.), *cert. denied,* 423 U.S. 836 (1975) (competition in the private line market has no adverse technical or economic effects on the telephone network and will only benefit consumers). And once those decisions were in place, the competitive offering of general toll service became inevitable. This service received judicial approval in MCI Telecom. Corp. v. FCC (Execunet I), 561 F.2d 365 (D.C. Cir. 1977), *cert. denied,* 434 U.S. 1040 (1978), and MCI Telecom. Corp. v. FCC (Execunet II), 580 F.2d 590 (D.C. Cir.), *cert. denied,* 439 U.S. 980 (1978) (MCI can offer "Execunet" service, billing subscribers on a per call basis, with minutes of use and distance called determining the charge, in addition to flat-rate private-line service).

duration of usage, the distance traversed by the call, and whether the call is intra- or interexchange.[6]

Assuming metering costs are not prohibitive, an efficient telecommunications pricing system would therefore charge each user a two-part tariff. One part would be a fixed access charge (levied either as a lump-sum or on a periodic basis), which would cover only the marginal non-traffic-sensitive costs of connecting the customer with the existing system. Such a charge would vary substantially among customers depending on their locations and on other factors that may cause those costs to differ. The second part of the tariff, related to traffic-sensitive costs, would vary with the customer's usage of the network and would reflect the mix and duration of intra- and interexchange calls and the times the calls were made.[7]

B. Present Deviations from Efficiency

A comparison of present telecommunications pricing policies with the foregoing principles uncovers three major sources of inefficiency.

First, both access and usage rates are in large measure averaged over a number of subscribers. They therefore do not reflect individual geographic, temporal, or other factors that cause true access costs to vary among customers. (Consider, for example, the difference between the marginal costs of plugging in a phone for a new resident in an existing urban apartment and of extending telephone lines and inside wiring to a newly built, isolated rural home.) Nor do local or long-distance rates reflect the very large differences in the usage-sensitive costs of calls between persons in different locations.

Second, a large portion of the costs of providing access to the telephone network is recovered in charges for *using* the system, even though those costs are largely independent of usage. Customers impose access costs on the system when they are connected to it, regardless of whether they then proceed to place or to receive calls. Because it ignores this fact, the present pricing practice has two adverse consequences, each the counterpart of the other. On the one hand, the basic monthly service charge is far too low. People are thus encouraged to become customers and, even more flagrantly undesirable, to order additional lines, when the value to them of that access is less than the cost to society of providing it. On the other hand, the charges for using the long-distance network are artificially inflated (on the order of sixty percent) because customers are required, by the "separations and settlements" process currently followed by the

---

6. "Interexchange telecommunication" means telecommunication between a point located in one exchange area and a point or points located in a different exchange area. "Intraexchange telecommunication" means telecommunications between two points located within the same exchange area. *See* United States v. AT&T Co., 552 F. Supp. 131, 229 (D.D.C. 1982), *appeal dismissed,* United States v. Western Elec. Co., 714 F.2d 178 (D.C. Cir. 1983).

7. The argument for time of day charging is that usage during peak hours requires marginal additions to network capacity, whereas usage at other times does not.

FCC and local regulators,[10] to contribute to the payment of costs that would not be avoided even if their long-distance calling were curtailed. The result is very inefficient—the artificial sixty percent tax discourages people from making long-distance calls by grossly exaggerating the costs they impose on society when they do so. This source of inefficiency is especially serious since the demand for interexchange calling is more sensitive to price than the demands for other services. The efficiency is almost certainly understated by the sixty percent figure as well, since that figure represents the markup above average costs, or average revenue requirements as set by traditional regulatory procedures. Marginal costs, to which economically efficient prices would have to be equated, appear to be far below average.

Some state regulators are being presented with testimony purporting to demonstrate that revenues from local service cover its fully distributed costs and that the asserted subsidy of local charges is therefore a fraud.[13] In economic terms (and I cannot think what other terms are relevant) those demonstrations are nonsense. They rely on the economically false proposition, legally approved by *Smith v. Illinois Bell*,[14] that interstate usage should bear some part of the non-traffic-sensitive costs of providing subscribers access to the local exchange. Only by allocating some portion of those costs to interstate usage do these studies "demonstrate" that the basic charge for local service fully covers the "cost" of providing this service. Once one accepts, instead, the economically incontestable propositions that costs that do not vary with usage should not be recovered in charges for usage and that there is no such separate service or phenomenon as access to the interexchange (as distinguished from the local) network, one recognizes inescapably—again, as a matter of economics—that imposition of any of those costs on usage constitutes an improper subsidy.

The third source of inefficiency is that typical local rates do not take into account the amount of local usage or, more importantly, the amount of usage at busy hours.[19] Since additional local calling, at least at busy hours, requires extra

---

10. "Separations and settlements" is the process by which investments and expenses of telephone companies are allocated between the interstate and intrastate jurisdictions and, similarly, between intrastate toll calling and local exchange rates. Such allocations provide a mechanism by which revenue requirements for interstate and intrastate operations are developed. The present system of "separations and settlements" employed by the FCC is the so-called "Ozark" plan adopted in 1970, Separations Procedures, 26 F.C.C.2d 247 (Report and Order), which has periodically been reviewed and amended. See Separations Procedures, 80 F.C.C.2d 230 (1980).

13. *See, e.g.,* Testimony of Dr. John W. Wilson, *In re* Mountain States Tel. & Tel. Co., Mont. Pub. Serv. Comm'n, Docket 82.2.8 (1982).

14. Smith v. Illinois Bell Tel. Co., 282 U.S. 133 (1930) (suit by public utility to enjoin as confiscatory a state commerce commission order lowering rates for intrastate telephone service, holding that, in determining apportionment of costs between intra- and interstate service, it is improper to ignore the fact that part of the use of a local telephone company's property is in the transmission and reception of interstate messages).

19. Some local telephone companies do use metered service in some markets. New York Telephone uses time-of-day charges while Southern New England Telephone offers an economy telephone service, "Select-a-Call," under which the customer is charged a low monthly rate for

capacity, the general practice of providing service on a flat rate basis—with no charge per call or per minute—results in excessive local calling. That is, it leads people to place calls the value of which to them is less than the costs those calls impose on society.

C. Inefficient Pricing as the Instrument of Cross-Subsidization

These inefficient pricing practices are the consequence and instrument of a complex network of cross-subsidies between different customer groups. First, long-distance service under the present system grossly subsidizes local service. A customer placing a long-distance call incurs a charge per call and per minute far greater than the additional cost to society of each call or minute, while a customer placing a local call in most areas pays nothing per call or minute, which of course is less than the additional cost to society. Moreover, the subsidy is very large—about $7 billion in 1981 from interstate toll calls (with a few billion more from intrastate toll calls), which amounts to an average of $7 per month for every telephone line in the country and, at the extreme, $27 per month in Nevada.

Second, because businesses do a disproportionately large amount of long-distance calling, business subscribers in the first instance subsidize residential subscribers. Since businesses generally survive by passing their costs on in their prices, however, this means in the final instance that residential telephone service is subsidized by a kind of sales tax on all the purchasers of goods and services produced by businesses that are overcharged for their telephone service.

Third, geographically accessible customers subsidize inaccessible customers. This is generally a subsidy from urban to rural customers and encourages an uneconomically high proportion of the public to connect to the network or to demand single-party rather than multi-party service.

Fourth, customers with a preference for making local calls during off-peak hours subsidize those with a preference for peak hours.

A pricing system based on marginal costs would correct these inefficiencies. Other considerations, however, seem to argue for a departure from marginal cost pricing. These are the subject of the next section.

II. Some Qualifications and Counter-Considerations, Rational and Demagogic

There are two valid qualifications to the proposition of the previous section that all marginal access costs should be recovered in the basic monthly charge. First, subscribers benefit from being able to reach other subscribers; if some drop off the system in response to cost-based access charges, this will reduce the value of the service to those who retain it. Second, various other social or political considerations might call for subsidization of access for certain groups, such as the poor.

---

simple access and low per call charges, discounted nights and weekends, for all outgoing calls. But these offerings are typically optional to residential customers, the overwhelming majority of whom take flat rate services, at a heavily subsidized flat monthly charge.

A. External Benefits

The first of these qualifications—the external benefits that one subscriber confers on others—could in principle justify making heavy users, who presumably get the most benefit from the system, subsidize the basic access charge so that they can continue to reach those who would otherwise drop off the network.

Since this consideration is a familiar one, I confine myself to two observations about it. First, the argument can easily be overdone. It is difficult to measure the size of the externality, and it is not at all clear to what extent heavy users are interested in reaching all who would decide not to have service if it were priced at its full cost. Second, providing a universally subsidized basic access charge is an excessively imprecise and inefficient way of preserving the external benefit. The particular heavy users who are especially interested in being able to reach and be reached by particular customers who would otherwise drop service—impecunious relatives, for example—could be expected to help pay those bills directly, without forcing the burden on others who would reap little or none of the benefit.

B. Preserving Service for the Poor

The second qualification is that there may be a broad social consensus that we ought to do something about people who would be excluded by purely cost-based prices from enjoying what we have come to regard as a necessary component of the minimum acceptable standard of living, and that we ought to do so without resorting to the economically superior method of direct government subsidy. This consideration is on the one hand so familiar and on the other so frequently abused that I consider it more important to refute the demagogic contentions with which it is all too frequently associated than to discuss the qualification itself—other than to observe that there are far less costly and inefficient ways of achieving this goal than simply rejecting economically efficient pricing.

The vulgar arguments to which I refer are such contentions as that the dictates of economic efficiency are in flat conflict with principles of equity, or that shifting more costs to the monthly charge is bad for "consumers" and must therefore be opposed by all who profess to speak for them.

Clearly there are possible areas of public policy in which conceptions of fairness may conflict with economic efficiency. But the major departures from economic efficiency in today's public policies are also demonstrably unfair,[24] and movement in the direction of economic efficiency is compatible with increased fairness. It is *fair*, as a general proposition, to impose costs on people when and to the extent they impose costs on society.

The "consumer," moreover, is not a single entity but a collection of diverse individuals, with varying patterns of behavior and needs. The proper pricing of

---

24. The following examples come to mind: farm parity price supports, the benefits of which go primarily to wealthy farmers, unlimited deduction of mortgage interest and property taxes, the benefits of which go primarily to the wealthy; and quota restrictions on imports of Japanese cars and steel, which protect the salaries of highly paid auto and steel workers.

communications services requires that we determine how best to distribute a given burden of costs so as to maximize the flow of benefits net of costs for all consumers. For example, there are consumers who make local calls infrequently, or, when they make them, make them off peak or briefly; and there are others who make local calls all the time, often on peak, and talk without limit. Therefore, to oppose local metered service—as some consumer advocates do—on the ground of equity or of "protecting the consumer" is simple demagoguery. There are consumers who want to make a lot of calls in an extended area at no extra charge, and there are others who happen to live in the country, or on the borders of local calling areas, whose equally short-distance calls are subject to inflated toll rates. It is ridiculous to imply that the interests of both of these would be similarly, and adversely, affected by a more efficient pricing system.

Similarly, there is a difference between the consumer who uses directory assistance all the time and the one who takes the trouble to look up numbers in the phone book. To oppose charging for directory assistance on the ground of "protecting the consumer," as many have, is to make an argument unworthy of respect. It is not unfair to consumers, who have to bear all the costs in any case, to distinguish among them on the basis of the costs they impose on society.

And it is a reflection at best of ignorance—and at worst of demagoguery—to advocate holding down direct charges to individual purchasers by shifting costs to businesses, in the supposed interest of "the consumer." The business of businesses consists largely in shifting their costs to *their* customers, and it is the simplest and least contestable of economic propositions that consumers in the aggregate are better off paying prices that reflect directly the marginal costs of the various goods and services among which they choose.

Returning to the second qualification, how can economic efficiency accommodate our desire to keep telephone service affordable to poor people? The task of social policy is to identify the people that we agree we would like to help, and then to find a method of helping them in a way that imposes the minimum cost on all of us—which *includes* them. Our tendency to try to help "consumers" by holding all prices down ends up injuring almost everybody. If we are to retain a subsidy for basic service, it has to be less negligently and haphazardly distributed and more tightly targeted at those who really need it. . . .[25]

The one thing that is certain is that the new regime of competition, on the one hand, and perpetuation of the old regime of inefficient pricing, on the other, are fundamentally incompatible; one or the other is going to have to give. . . .

The more visible horn of the dilemma is the painfulness of the inescapable increase in the basic monthly charge. The most obvious palliative is to spread the increase out over time. Another measure, even more important in the longer run, is to offer subscribers a wider range of price and service options than is currently available.

*　　*　　*

---

25. We might, for example, issue "telephone stamps," analogous to food stamps, to those determined to be in genuine financial need. *See also* H.R. 5158, 97th Cong., 2d Sess. § 234 (1982) (proposal for National Telecommunications Fund).

Allowing for a gradual, but not too gradual, transition to efficient pricing can serve a valuable economic as well as political purpose in two ways, provided the end result is clearly announced. First, it may serve as a justification for avoiding uneconomic upgrading of service. I recently heard a regulatory commissioner from a sparsely populated western state complain of the public pressures his local phone company was under from rural customers to go from four-party to one-party service, knowing full well that he could not hope to permit the company to charge the estimated cost of $30 a month. An announcement that the costs of that superior access must eventually be added to the basic charge might help relieve those pressures.

Second a gradual transition would give alternative technologies better adapted to serving high-cost customers an opportunity to be introduced or developed, whether by the phone companies themselves or others.[43] The rationalization of rates offers hope for technical solutions to the problem of providing quality service to high-cost areas, the development of which is discouraged by the present cross-subsidized rates. Could it be, for example, that announcement of scheduled increases of local rates in rural areas would make radio telephony over those long, sparse routes economic?

*   *   *

The other horn of the dilemma, of course, is that any transitional arrangement that leaves a portion of the non-traffic-sensitive costs to be recovered out of long-distance charges will encourage bypass of local networks, a danger already magnified by the recent intensification of competition and the progress of technology. Such bypass would be uneconomic because it would result from the excess of current rates over marginal cost. The telephone companies will have to propose, and regulators consider, a variety of ways of minimizing this danger. Since the possibility of bypass grows with the individual subscriber's use of the network, an important component of the interim rate structures will probably have to be some sort of "taper," a declining rate for incremental usage that will provide a progressive quantity discount. Such a rate structure could be patterned on the familiar declining block rates for electricity, which had the same historical justification.

The economic case for the taper, in these circumstances, is unexceptionable. Marginal costs are now below average revenue requirements, and rates set at the latter level are resulting in an economically unjustified loss of customers. The rates for successive blocks of usage must not, of course, decline below marginal cost. True, such a discount will help the big users disproportionately; but if big users have an escape from economically excessive charges, a BOC will have no choice but to reduce rates to them if they are to make any contribution to the access costs which the small users would otherwise have to pay by themselves. The taper is clearly needed in these circumstances, then, in the interest of both economic efficiency and minimizing the danger that small users or impecunious subscribers will drop off the system.

---

43. Such alternative technologies might include, among others, high-speed, wide-band multipoint distribution facilities, direct broadcast satellite services or mobile radio.

*   *   *

Progress toward more efficient pricing policies has already met with formidable political resistance. However much they may be required for economic
efficiency, justified by the non-traffic-sensitivity of access costs and compelled
by the pressures of competition, increases in the basic monthly rate are political
poison. They will be even more difficult to bear because they will be magnified
in the short run by other consequences of intensified competition and technological change, notably the required increase in depreciation rates. A further imped-
iment to any rational solution is the widespread popular belief that if something
is regulated it can defy the principles of economics. The same people who are
willing to pay $15–$25 per month for cable TV, Home Box Office, and the like
seem to regard a $6–$10 rate for unlimited local calling as a God-given right.
And people buying a newly built $70,000 house regard it as heinous if they are
required to pay the $150 or more that it costs to put a telephone in it.

[W]e must patiently explain to the courts and the public at large the fallacious-
ness of the widely held opinion that if you use some facility and get some benefit
from it, it is only fair that you pay some share of its cost, even though your *using*
it imposes no sacrifice on anyone. Anyone who has argued in a public forum the
merits of peak responsibility pricing will recognize how profoundly held that
view is. I fear it is the underlying rationale of *Smith v. Illinois Bell.*

For its attempts to reconcile popular opinion and *Smith v. Illinois Bell* on the
one side, with economic reality on the other, by imposing a lump sum charge
for "interstate access," the FCC surely deserves an *A* for effort and ingenuity.
Unfortunately its proposed solution invites the response: "I don't want *interstate*
access. I don't make any long-distance calls, so why should I have to pay for it?"
And to the counter-argument that there is no way of choosing to have or not to
have interstate access apart from local access, the rejoinder: "If there is no such
thing as interstate access, how come you're proposing to charge for it?" In short,
I fear that this attempt to satisfy *Smith v. Illinois Bell* while nevertheless removing
the tax on usage may be unsuccessful.

I suspect, therefore, that it will eventually be necessary to expose as false the
notion that "interstate" is some identifiable entity onto which "local" consumers
can shift some of the costs of the system. What we must clearly explain is that
only real people, "local" people, pay the costs of telephone service, and that how
these costs are distributed among them should depend upon their respective
responsibilities for the system's incurring these costs.

Access costs are incurred when the subscriber subscribes, not to interstate
service, not to intrastate service, not to local service, but to the *availability* of any
and all of these. Therefore, to interpret *Smith v. Illinois Bell* as holding that
because the subscriber uses the facility for both interstate and intrastate calling,
much or little, the cost must be levied on that use rather than on the act of
connection that causes the costs to be incurred, would be to elevate legal fiction
above economic reality. Or perhaps the following version of the same reality
might be easier for the courts to accept, because it avoids direct confrontation
with *Smith v. Illinois Bell's* assumption that fairness requires *users* to share the
common costs of the facilities that make that use possible: Subscribers *use*
telephone facilities in a number of ways; they use certain facilities when they

Economics of Local Rates

California		
Average cost per residence line		$31.25
Price to customer		
Basic rate	$8.25	
End user (FCC)	2.00	
Subsidy		21.00
Source of subsidy		
Interstate long distance		7.00
Intrastate long distance		
InterLATA		6.00
IntraLATA		7.00
Other		1.00
Total		21.00

Source: AT&T (1986).

ask merely to be hooked up; they use others when they pick up the phone and dial a local call; they use others when they make interexchange calls; they use others when they receive calls. I have difficulty believing that *Illinois Bell* would have to be interpreted, in 1984, as inconsistent with a system of charges that differentiates these various *usages* and charges each with the costs that it imposes on society—and only with those costs.

The answer, in short, is to teach the courts elementary marginalism, but—a mild tactical suggestion—without using that word.

. . . [I]n driving home this lesson, in and out of the courts, it is important to point out that we are talking not about additional revenue requirements but only about rate structure reform—not charging consumers more but redistributing the burden among them.

. . . [T]elephone companies and their regulators must resist pressures to upgrade service without charging the affected customers the full costs. It should surely be possible to show rural subscribers the cost of going from four- to one-party service, or to show metropolitan area subscribers the cost of giving them extended area service, and enlist public support for not doing so unless they are willing to pay those costs. An informed public, one would hope, is unlikely to regard a mere improvement in the quality of service as a necessity, much less a necessity which people are entitled to receive at non-compensatory rates.

. . . [U]nbundle, unbundle, unbundle. Unbundling promises a large number of benefits which, if sufficiently publicized, should make it politically popular. In the present context, its most important benefit is that it helps pinpoint subsidized service as well as the recipients of the subsidies. Telephone companies should offer access alone, or low-priced four- or eight-party service, then make sure its availability is widely publicized. In that way companies and commissions can honestly claim to be meeting any reasonable conception of their social responsibility, namely, to ensure that there is an inexpensive service available for people who are really poor.

Unbundling probably should be undertaken even if the direct immediate benefits are less than the costs. For example, unbundling requires measured local service, which, to be truly efficient, must also incorporate time-of-use differentials. There is a serious question whether the direct cost savings generated by such measurement will in all situations outweigh the costs of measurement. Observers like Bridger Mitchell have found that, where electronic switching is readily available, costs and benefits are likely to be comparable. But even where measurement costs exceed the direct benefits, we probably should start measuring. For if measurement is necessary to move us away from the gross inefficiencies of the present system, its initial costs are a small price to pay. Besides, measured service is also fair. Heavier users, who impose heavier costs on the system, *should* pay more than light users.

* * *

The inefficiencies of present telephone pricing policies—cost averaging, usage-based access cost recovery, and flat charges for unlimited local calling—maintain an unrealistic, inequitable and inefficient regime in which certain groups of consumers subsidize others in ways unrelated to rational social goals. To correct these inefficiencies we must move to cost-based, unbundled pricing. The arguments against that kind of pricing, particularly concerns about telephone service for the poor and the desire to maintain universal service, fail to acknowledge that, in the long run, marginal cost pricing is both equitable, since it charges people the costs they impose on society, and efficient, since it decreases total costs and makes it easier to direct subsidies to those who need them most. While both fairness and political prudence clearly justify a gradual transition to more efficient pricing, failure to begin moving promptly and substantially in that direction will be self-defeating because it will encourage large users to bypass the local exchange, thus imposing a larger share of fixed costs on the smaller number of users who remain tied to it.

CHARGING FOR LOCAL TELEPHONE CALLS: HOW HOUSEHOLD CHARACTERISTICS AFFECT THE DISTRIBUTION OF CALLS IN THE GTE ILLINOIS EXPERIMENT

R.E. Park et al.
The Rand Corp. (1981)

Introduction

Most residential telephone service in the United States is provided for a flat monthly fee, with no extra charge for calls to telephones within the local area. An alternative, common in the rest of the world and increasingly discussed in the United States, is to levy a charge for each local call or each minute of local calling. This alternative—referred to as "usage sensitive pricing" or "local measured service"—holds out the possibility of being both more efficient and more equitable than flat rate charges. However, not much is known about the effects of switching from flat rate to local measured service. Will the efficiency gains offset the additional costs of measurement and billing? Who gains and who loses from conversion to measured service?

. . . The questions we attempt to answer here are: What effect does a change from flat rate to measured service have on the level and distribution of residential telephone usage? How is usage, and the change in usage, related to household characteristics?

We use data collected in a particular experimental setting—the GTE local measured service experiment in Illinois. Section II is a brief overview of the experiment and the data. Section III specifies the model that we fitted to the data. The estimation results are in Sec. IV. In Sec. V the results are applied with several purposes in mind, including a demonstration that the fitted distributions describe the data reasonably well and an illustration of the effects of household demographic characteristics on flat rate and measured rate call distributions.

Summary

We fit a model that describes the number of telephone calls a household makes each month in terms of that household's demographic characteristics, whether it pays a usage sensitive charge for telephone calls, and random errors including household-specific components. For 641 interviewed households participating in GTE's local measured service experiment in Illinois, the data include the number of calls made during each of three flat rate months and during the same three months a year later under measured rates.

Under a flat rate the number of calls tends to be larger in households that include more people, are headed by an older person, include teenagers, or have many local acquaintances. These and other less significant demographic characteristics account for 32 percent of the variance in the number of calls.[1] Persistent differences among households not associated with any of the measured demographic characteristics account for an additional 55 percent of the variance.

When measured rates are imposed, most households tend to reduce the number of calls they make. The reductions tend to be proportionately larger in households that include more people, have lower incomes, are headed by an older person, and include no small children. However, these and other measured characteristics account for only 11 percent of the total variance in households' response to measured rates. Households that consistently make an unusually large number of calls under flat rates (that is, more than one would predict based on their measured characteristics) tend to reduce their calling proportionately more under measured rates, and this accounts for an additional 10 percent of the response variance.

Mandatory measured rates for residential customers will tend to benefit households that do not use their telephones very much and harm those that use them a lot. There is a wide range of telephone use within any demographic

---

1. As transformed to induce normality.

group, so the benefits and harms of measured service will tend to be diffused across groups.

Questions

1. How is the revenue requirement computed? What factors may the FCC set in the formula? What factors are more controlled by the regulated firms? How does the FCC determine the rate of return?

2. Consider this oversimplified illustration of the rate-of-return formula: A telephone company builds a building with a ten-year life valued at $10,000,000; annual operating expenses are $1,000,000; taxes are $100,000; and the rate of return is 10 percent. 1) What is the revenue requirement in Year 1? 2) Assume operating expenses and taxes remain constant. What is the revenue requirement in Year 5? 3) Suppose the building has a five-year life. What is the revenue requirement in Year 1? 4) What can you conclude from your findings?

3. What opportunities for abuse are built into the rate formula? Can the FCC police these problems?

4. What economic inefficiencies does Kahn identify? How do subsidies harm the system? What are Kahn's solutions? Do you agree?

5. In what way is the *Smith v. Illinois* decision economically flawed? As a result of *Smith*, 5 percent of the costs of the local loop initially were assigned to interstate jurisdiction, thereby reducing intrastate calling costs. Meanwhile, microwave technology lowered the costs of interstate calling. But because of *Smith*, more and more local loop costs were assigned to the interstate ledger. By 1984, while local loops were used for interstate calling only 8 percent of the time, 25 percent of their costs were assigned to the interstate jurisdiction.

6. Some commentators contend that the rural areas are threatened with being left out of the information age because the competitive market renders communications providers unwilling to extend the expensive, advanced communications infrastructure necessary to provide such services into sparsely populated areas. Does our policy in favor of universal service include advanced information services? How might the infrastructure be established? Who should pay for it? Why?

In adopting a policy to upgrade the publicly available telecommunications infrastructure, FCC Commissioner Andrew Barrett wrote: "The competitive framework currently in place that relies on general market forces is appropriate, but we must concentrate on removing barriers and providing incentives to let it work, rather than on trying to preserve or create monopolies" (Barrett, "Public Policy and the Advanced Intelligent Network," 42 *Federal Communications Law Journal*, 413, 429 [1990]). Warren Lavey argues: "Universal information services can be achieved most effectively by combining a regulated advanced telecommunications infrastructure with nonregulated competition for the information services themselves" (Lavey, "Universal Telecommunications Infrastructure for Information Services," 42 *Federal Communications Law Journal* 151, 153 [1990]). Senator Larry Pressler and Kevin Schieffer support "subordinating the drive for deregulation and, where necessary, even competition, to the extent that it jeopardizes the realization of universal telecommunications service" (Pressler and Schieffer, "A Proposal for Universal Telecommunications Service," 40 *Federal Communications Law Journal*, 351, 354 n.7 [1988]).

2

TITLE II REGULATION

DEFINITION OF COMMON CARRIER

If the FCC determines that a firm is a common carrier, it has the authority to require that firm to submit to entry and exit regulations. That is, it can determine when a common carrier may enter and withdraw from a market and has control over what prices it may charge. Such regulations can decrease profitability, because public-utility–type rate-based regulation assumes that the utility is a monopoly and will charge prices yielding supranormal profits unless restrained by government. Rate-based regulation also adds a cost to the firm of producing data for regulatory monitoring and slows down business activity. The FCC has questioned the traditional assumption that common carriers are always capable of charging consumers a monopoly price.

The Commission's method of defining common carriers has undergone substantial revision over the last decade, evolving as technology has advanced, as competition has increased among telecommunications firms, and as the Commission has come to redefine the purposes of the Communications Act. The FCC began the 1970s with a common carrier analysis based on a firm's functions but gradually turned to an economic analysis of an individual firm's ability to exert market power—that is, to effectively charge consumers a monopoly price.

The Communications Act defines a common carrier as "any person (1) engaged as a (2) common (3) carrier (4) for hire, in interstate or foreign communications by wire or radio or interstate or foreign radio transmission of energy, . . . but a person (5) engaged in radio broadcasting shall not, insofar as such person is so engaged, be deemed a common carrier." This definition has been criticized as "circular" and as "not meaningful." The circularity in the statute allowed or even required the FCC to rely upon the common law of common carriage before it adopted economic analysis. Consider each element of the statutory definition.

1. Engaged in communication: All messages transmitted by wire or radio, even if of rudimentary informational content, come within the common carrier definition. Indeed, Section 203(d) of the act merely requires the "transmission of energy by radio," all else equal, for a firm to be considered a common carrier.

2. Common: A common carrier under the act must hold itself out to the public indiscriminately. It undertakes to serve the public at large, holding out its services to all who may choose to use them. Size of operation is not determinative, nor usually is any specialized nature of services provided. Private carrier status has been permitted, however, where communications services are shared on a nonprofit basis. Once a firm is found to be a private carrier, reconsideration of its status is still possible, and a change of status might be allowed.

3. Carrier: In order to be considered a carrier, a firm must control transmission. At common law, the mere furnishing of the means of transportation was not considered common carriage because, with the customer operating the vehicle, the furnishing firm performed no act of carriage. This principle—that a person must transmit radio or wire signals to be considered a carrier—may be found in the act by reading Sections 3(a), (b), (d), and (h) together.

4. For hire: In the "holding out" context, the FCC has taken the position that operating on a nonprofit basis is sufficient evidence of an intent not to offer one's services to all potential users, in which case the firm is considered a private carrier.

5. Not broadcasting: Broadcasters traditionally are not regulated as common carriers. One policy rationale favoring private carrier status for broadcasters is that the common carrier's duty to serve the public indiscriminately might chill editorial discretion and journalistic freedom.

Faced with evolving telecommunications technology, the FCC has reinterpreted and narrowed the statutory and common law definition of common carrier, allowing many firms to compete as private carriers.

In *Land Mobile Service*, 46 F.C.C.2d 752 (1974), *reconsid'n*, 51 F.C.C.2d 945, 957 (1975), the Commission allocated a portion of the 800MHz band to private mobile land radio, creating a new class of entrepreneurs termed Specialized Mobile Radio Systems, who would be considered private carriers. This carving-out process was upheld by the *National Association of Regulatory Utility Commissioners v. FCC*, 525 F.2d 630 (D.C. Cir. 1976) (*NARUC I*). The case approved the FCC's definition of a new class of competitors free of common carrier regulation.

In *National Association of Regulatory Utility Commissioners v. FCC*, 533 F.2d 601 (D.C. Cir. 1976) (*NARUC II*), the Washington, D.C. Circuit Court continued the tendency observed in *NARUC I* to decide common carrier status by its own application of law to facts, with little deference toward FCC determinations. The court confirmed its *NARUC I* statement that the FCC did not have "any significant discretion in determining who is a common carrier." *NARUC II* marks a significant move toward an individualized approach to common carrier analysis that is not concerned with a firm's ability to charge monopoly prices to consumers.

NARUC v. FCC (NARUC I)

525 F.2d 630 (D.C. Cir.), cert. denied,
425 U.S. 992 (1976)

II. 30 MHz Allocation for Use by Private Mobile Service, Including a New Class of Entrepreneurial Operators Known as Specialized Mobile Radio Systems (SMRS)

The aspect of the 30 MHz allocation which is challenged is the authorization of a new category of entrepreneurial mobile operators who will share access to the allocated spectrum with private operators eligible under the Public Safety, Industrial and Land Transportation Radio Services. Private operations involve primarily dispatch services which the operator provides to himself, such as those provided by police departments and taxicab companies. Prior to the present Order, they have also included systems operated on a cooperative basis for the benefit of several affiliated users. The significant action taken under the present Order is the assimilation, with the above operations, of profit-motivated systems by an entrepreneur solely for the use of third party clients.

In authorizing the creation of these entrepreneurial Specialized Mobile Radio Systems (SMRS), the Commission seeks to deal with them precisely as it deals with the more traditionally private mobile operators. Applications of all private operators including SMRS, are to be processed, up to spectrum capacity, on a first-come, first-served basis. Believing that competition between many operators is the best way to hasten the development of improved technologies, the Commission seeks to treat SMRS, like all other private operators, as non-common carriers, and to pre-empt state regulation of entry.

The non-common carrier classification is the pivot upon which the Commission's scheme for regulating SMRS turns. It makes clearly inapplicable the stringent rate and service regulations of the Title II Common Carrier provisions. Also, it renders inapplicable certain provisions of Title III (Radio Licensing), which require a 30-day waiting period prior to the granting of any application and which guarantee the right to petition for denial of the application. Finally the classification as non-common carriers appears to have certain effects on the power of federal pre-emption, which power the Commission has sought to exercise here by barring state entry regulation.

A. Classification of SMRS as Non-Common Carriers

1. Statutory Definition of Common Carrier. For purposes of the Communications Act, a common carrier is "any person engaged as a common carrier for hire. . . ." The Commission's regulations offer a slightly more enlightening definition: "any person engaged in rendering communication service for hire to the public." However, the concept of "the public" is sufficiently indefinite as to invite recourse to the common law of carriers to construe the Act.

In seeking an applicable common law definition of common carrier, a good deal of confusion results from the long and complicated history of that concept. Originally, the doctrine was used to impose a greater standard of care upon carriers who held themselves out as offering to serve the public in general. The rationale was that by holding themselves out to the public at large, otherwise private carriers took on a quasi-public character. This character, coupled with the lack of control exercised by shippers or travellers over the safety of their carriage, was seen to justify imposing upon the carrier the status of an insurer.[53]

The late nineteenth century saw the advent of common carriers being subjected to price and service regulations as well. At first challenged as deprivations of property without due process, these early regulations were upheld on the basis of the near monopoly power exercised by the railroads, coupled with the fact that they "exercise a sort of public office" in the duties which they perform.[54] Subsequently, legislation has been upheld imposing stringent regulations of various types on entities found to be affected with a public character, even where nothing approaching monopoly power exists. In such cases as the Motor Carrier Act of 1935, relatively competitive carrying industries have been subjected to entry, rate and equipment regulations on the basis of the quasi-public character of the activities involved.

Whether the common carrier concept is invoked to support strict tort liability or as a justifying basis for regulation, it appears that the critical point is the quasi-public character of the activity involved. To create this quasi-public character, it is not enough that a carrier offer his services for a profit, since this would bring within the definition private contract carriers which the courts have emphatically excluded from it. What appears to be essential to the quasi-public character implicit in the common carrier concept is that the carrier "undertakes to carry for all people indifferently. . . ."

This does not mean a given carrier's services must practically be available to the entire public. One may be a common carrier though the nature of the service rendered is sufficiently specialized as to be of possible use to only a fraction of the total population. And business may be turned away either because it is not of the type normally accepted or because the carrier's capacity has been exhausted. But a carrier will not be a common carrier where its practice is to make individualized decisions, in particular cases, whether and on what terms to deal. It is not necessary that a carrier be required to serve all indiscriminately; it is enough that its practice is, in fact, to do so.

The requirement, that to be a common carrier one must hold oneself out indiscriminately to the clientele one is suited to serve, is supported by common sense as well as case law. The original rationale for imposing a stricter duty of care on common carriers was that they had implicitly accepted a sort of public trust by availing themselves of the business of the public at large. The common

---

53. This insurance obligation has never been unexceptioned, and has not extended to acts of God, damages resulting from warfare, or causes beyond the control of the carrier which are expressly excepted in the bill of lading. *Propeller Niagara v. Cordes*, 62 U.S. (21 How) 7, 23, 16 L.Ed. 41 (1858).

54. *Munn v. Illinois*, 94 U.S. (4 Otto) 113, 130, 24 L.Ed. 77 (1876). For an historical discussion of the idea that businesses affected with a public interest are subject, on that account, to governmental regulation, see McAllister, *Lord Hale and Business Affected with a Public Interest*, 43 Harv.L.Rev. 759 (1930).

carrier concept appears to have developed as a sort of *quid pro quo* whereby a carrier was made to bear a special burden of care, in exchange for the privilege of soliciting the public's business.

Moreover, the characteristic of holding oneself out to serve indiscriminately appears to be an essential element, if one is to draw a coherent line between common and private carriers. The cases make clear both that common carriers need not serve the whole public, and that private carriers may serve a significant clientele, apart from the carrier himself. Since given private and common carriers may therefore be indistinguishable in terms of the clientele actually served, it is difficult to envision a sensible line between them which does not turn on the manner and terms by which they approach and deal with their customers. The common law requirement of holding oneself out to serve the public indiscriminately draws such a logical and sensible line between the two types of carriers.

Finally, the holding out prerequisite to common carrier status is not without implicit support in the FCC Regulations themselves. In defining "public correspondence," the Regulations focus upon the element of being at the disposal of the public. Unlike "public correspondence," "private line service" is distinguished by its being set aside for the use of particular customers, so as not to be generally available to the public.[64] This public-private dichotomy is generally regarded as synonymous with the distinction between common carrier and non-common carrier operators.

*   *   *

We conclude that nothing in the record indicates any significant likelihood that SMRS will hold themselves out indifferently to serve the user public. While it is undisputed that they would be permitted so to hold themselves out if they desired, that is not sufficient basis for imposing the burdens that go with common carrier status. In so holding, we do not foreclose the possibility of future challenge to the Commission's classification, should the actual operations of SMRS appear to bring them within the common carrier definition.

Further, we reject those parts of the Orders which imply an unfettered discretion in the Commission to confer or not confer common carrier status on a given entity, depending upon the regulatory goals it seeks to achieve.[74] The common law definition of common carriers is sufficiently definite as not to admit of agency discretion in the classification of operating communications entities. A particular system is a common carrier by virtue of its functions, rather than

---

64. "Private line service. A service whereby facilities for communication between two or more designated points are set aside for the exclusive use or availability for use of a particular customer and authorized users during stated periods of time." 47 C.F.R. § 21.1 (1974).

74. The strongest statement of this sort is in the 1974 Order: "We are fully aware . . . that some of the entities we propose to license, i.e., entrepreneur-operated, common-user systems, could be licensed as common carriers and regulated under Title II of the Communications Act. However, our basic goal in this proceeding is . . . to make available to the land mobile service additional spectrum and to do this in a way that would promote the larger and more effective use of this spectrum. . . . In accomplishing this goal, we are free, we believe, to adopt whatever comprehensive regulatory scheme is best suited for the purpose. . . ."

because it is declared to be so. Thus, we affirm the Commission's classification not because it has any significant discretion in determining who is a common carrier, but because we find nothing in the record or the common carrier definition to cast doubt on its conclusions that SMRS are not common carriers.[76] If practice and experience show the SMRS to be common carriers, then the Commission must determine its responsibilities from the language of the Title II common carrier provisions.

NARUC v. FCC (NARUC II)

533 F.2d 601 (D.C. Cir. 1976)

*   *   *

The Commission argues that the two-way, non-video communications via cable, over which it has pre-empted state and local regulation, are not common carrier communications because they are carried on by entities (cable operators) previously adjudged to be non-common carriers.[26] However, it has long been held that "a common carrier is such by virtue of his occupation," that is by the actual activities he carries on. Since it is clearly possible for a given entity to carry on many types of activities, it is at least logical to conclude that one can be a common carrier with regard to some activities but not others. Deferring to the next section any final ruling on the Commission's holistic view of cable operations, we will proceed at this point to examine the particular activities over which the preemption is asserted, to determine if they fall within the common carrier concept as used in the statute.

. . . In a recent case of the same name as that now before the court, we set forth our understanding of the common carrier concept as invoked by the Communications Act.[29] We concluded that the circularity and uncertainty of the common carrier definitions set forth in the statute[30] and regulations[31] invite

---

76. The statements of the Order can be made to square with the view of this court, if they are read to mean that the Commission could have treated SMRS as common carriers by imposing on them requirements which would have made them common carriers. Without asserting that this was the Commission's meaning, it is clear that the Commission had discretion to require SMRS to serve all potential customers indifferently, thus making them common carriers within the meaning of the statute.

26. 49 F.C.C.2d at 1062. It has been held several times that cable systems, operating in the characteristic broadcast retransmission mode, are not common carriers. *United States v. Southwestern Cable Co.*, 392 U.S. 157, 169 n.29, 88 S.Ct. 1994, 20 L.Ed.2d 1001 (1968); *Philadelphia Television Broadcasting v. FCC*, 123 U.S.App.D.C. 298, 300, 359 F.2d 282, 284 (1966); *Frontier Broadcasting Co. v. Collier*, 24 F.C.C. 251, 254 (1958).

29. *National Ass'n of Reg. Util. Comm'rs v. FCC*, 173 U.S.App.D.C. 423, 425, 525 F.2d 640, 642 (5 Jan. 1976).

30. Under 47 U.S.C. § 153(h) (1970), a common carrier is defined as "any person engaged as a common carrier for hire. . . ."

31. Under 47 C.F.R. § 21.1 (1974), a communication common carrier is defined as "[a]ny person engaged in rendering communication service for hire to the public."

recourse to the common law of carriers. An examination of the common law reveals that the primary *sine qua non* of common carrier status is a quasi-public character, which arises out of the undertaking "to carry for all people indifferently. . . ." This does not mean that the particular services offered must practically be available to the entire public; a specialized carrier whose service is of possible use to only a fraction of the population may nonetheless be a common carrier if he holds himself out to serve indifferently all potential users. Nor is it essential that there be a statutory or other legal commandment to serve indiscriminately; it is the practice of such indifferent service that confers common carrier status. That is to say, a carrier will not be a common carrier where its practice is to make individualized decisions in particular cases whether and on what terms to serve.

. . . A second prerequisite to common carrier status was mentioned but not discussed in the previous *N.A.R.U.C.* opinion. It is the requirement formulated by the FCC and with peculiar applicability to the communications field, that the system be such that customers "transmit intelligence of their own design and choosing."

. . . Applying these two tests to the two-way, point-to-point, non-video communications over which the Commission here asserts its pre-emptive power, we conclude that a common carrier activity is involved. We are able to reach this conclusion, even though there is no evidence before us arising from any actual operations in the two-way, non-video mode, by examining the nature of the projected activity and the regulatory framework in which it is expected to operate.

. . . As to the first prerequisite of common carrier status, the regulations as originally promulgated by the 1972 Order establish a policy of "first-come, nondiscriminatory access." Although a binding requirement of such indifferent service is not necessary to confer common carrier status, it is an adequate substitute for evidence of actual operations, for we know what those operations will be if the FCC regulations are followed.

. . . It is true that this general commandment of indifferent service is modified by the Commission's acceptance, or even requirement, of certain types of priority treatment. The regulations themselves state that "[o]n at least one of the leased channels, priority shall be given part-time users. . . ." As the Commission explained, however, this measure was necessitated to prevent monopolization of the leased access bandwidth by entrepreneurs leasing bandwidth for extended periods. The requirement is thus designed to assure open access to all users, and it does not detract from the common carrier status of those subject to it.

. . . The Commission has also stated its tolerance, for the time being at least, of preferential rate structures whereby leased access channelling is made available to noncommercial users at reduced cost. While such sanctioned price discrimination is difficult to square with the common law notion of indifferent service to all willing customers, we hold that it is fundamentally consistent with the essence of the common carrier concept. As we stated in our previous *N.A.R.U.C.* opinion, the common denominator of common carriers is their quasi-public character. We stated at that time that an undertaking to carry for all indifferently "appears to be essential" to the quasi-public character. However, price discrimination in favor of non-commercial public, education, and governmental users presents no obstacle to the conclusion that a common carrier activity is involved. To the contrary, such action, at least if not carried to the point of excluding all commercial users, appears to enhance rather than detract from the enterprise's dedication to public purposes and affectation with the public interest.

With regard to the second common carrier prerequisite, the user's design and choosing of the intelligence to be transmitted, we have no difficulty determining from the very nature of the technology that in many if not most instances this requirement will be satisfied. Although the regulations require only a non-voice return capability, which would perhaps make possible transmissions of only a rudimentary sort, the content of the transmission (which may arise solely from the determination to transmit or not[45]) may nonetheless be under the customer's control. We therefore hold that any two-way use of cable in which the customer explicitly or implicitly[46] determines the transmission or content of the return message, satisfies this second prerequisite to common carrier status.

We therefore conclude that most, if not all, of the uses to which the two-way, non-video cable capability is likely to be put fall within the term "carrier" as used in 47 U.S.C. § 152(b). . . .

In 1982, Congress amended the Communications Act, adding 47 U.S.C. §332 to clarify the distinction between private carriers and common carriers.[1]

---

45. The most primitive uses of such return transmission technology would appear to involve the transmission of a single signal, to convey a pre-determined message. A burglar alarm system, conveying the message of illicit entry, seems to be one of the simplest uses for such technology.

46. A burglar alarm, involving the purchase of a service whereby the customer intends and expects a message to be sent at the occurrence of a particular event, is an example of implicit customer control.

1. 47 U.S.C. §332 (a) In taking actions to manage the spectrum to be made available for use by the private land mobile services, the Commission shall consider, consistent with section 1 of this Act, whether such actions will—

(1) promote the safety of life and property;

(2) improve the efficiency of spectrum use and reduce the regulatory burden upon spectrum users based upon sound engineering principles, user operational requirements, and market-place demands;

(3) encourage competition and provide services to the largest feasible number of users; or

(4) increase interservice sharing opportunities between private land mobile services and other services.

(b)(1) The Commission, in coordinating the assignment of frequencies to stations in the private land mobile services and in the fixed services (as defined by the Commission by rule), shall have authority to utilize assistance furnished by advisor coordinating committees consisting of individuals who are not officers or employees of the Federal Government.

(2) The authority of the Commission established in the subsection shall not be subject to or affected by the provisions of part III of title 5, United States Code, or section 3679(b) of the Revised Statutes (31 U.S.C. 665(b)).

(3) Any person who provides assistance to the Commission under this subsection shall not be considered, by reason of having provided such assistance, a Federal employee.

(4) Any advisory coordinating committee which furnishes assistance to the Committee under this subsection shall not be subject to the provisions of the Federal Advisory

Private carriers, licensed to the land mobile service, are not bound by the *NARUC* restriction to hold themselves out indiscriminately. As private radio carriers, §332 (c)(3) prohibits state regulation of their services. On the other hand, these carriers could be limited as to their ability to then interconnect with the public telephone network.

The *Telocator* decision, interpreting this statute, turns on a fairly technical distinction of who is in control of the carriage—the customers or the carrier, Millicom. Notice how Millicom in this instance differs from a traditional carrier. It can take advantage of the public switched network but it need not hold itself out indifferently to its customers.

The result of *Telocator* was nearly to obliterate the private/common carrier distinction established in *NARUC I* for private carrier licensees like SMRS licensees. In 1991, Fleetcall won approval to provide a radio-based network that interconnects with the public switched network, thanks to *Telocator*. Fleetcall's system parallels the cellular telephone service regulated by state PUCs and the FCC as common carriers but without the regulatory burdens of a common carrier.

TELOCATOR NETWORK OF AMERICA v. FCC

761 F.2d 763 (D.C. Cir. 1985)

*   *   *

This case is another episode in the long-running controversy about the allocation of radio spectrum between common carriers and private land mobile radio services. Telocator Network of America, the national trade association of

---

Committee Act.

(c)(1) For purposes of this section, private land mobile service shall include service provided by specialized mobile radio, multiple licensed radio dispatch systems, and all other radio dispatch systems, regardless of whether such service is provided indiscriminately to eligible users on a commercial basis, except that a land station licensed in such service to multiple licensees or otherwise shared by authorized users (other than a nonprofit, cooperative station) shall not be interconnected with a telephone exchange or interexchange service or facility for any purpose, except to the extent that (A) each user obtains such interconnection directly from a duly authorized carrier, or (B) licensees jointly obtain such interconnection directly from a duly authorized carrier.

(2) A person engaged in private land mobile service shall not, insofar as such person is so engaged, be deemed a common carrier for any purpose under this Act. A common carrier shall not provide any dispatch service on any frequency allocated for common carrier service, except to the extent such dispatch service is provided on stations licensed in the domestic public land mobile radio service before January 1, 1982.

(3) No State or local government shall have any authority to impose any rate or entry regulation upon any private land mobile service, except that nothing in this subsection may be construed to impair such jurisdiction with respect to common carrier stations in the mobile service.

the radio common carrier industry, seeks review of two orders of the Federal Communications Commission ("FCC"). The first order established the private carrier paging system ("PCPS") as a new license classification to operate within the private land mobile radio services. The second order granted a PCPS license to Millicom Information Services, Inc. ("Millicom").

The central legal issue is whether, within the meaning of the Communications Amendments Act of 1982, customers of Millicom's PCPS are "authorized users" of Millicom's land station. If, as the Commission held, Millicom is the sole "authorized user," Telocator's challenge fails. We hold that the Commission was correct and affirm its orders. . . .

FCC policy, since at least 1949, has been to provide spectrum for land mobile radio service to both private and common carriers. . . . Land mobile radio service includes three forms: (1) mobile telephone service,[1] (2) dispatch calling,[2] and (3) one-way signaling. This case involves the third service, one-way signaling, which is commonly referred to as "pocket paging" or "beeper" service. Pocket paging systems can be licensed to single entities or to multiple users in approved sharing arrangements that can take either a common or private carrier form. The FCC has approved private sharing arrangements, although similar in many respects to common carrier licensing, to promote competition and allow private users to make more efficient use of the spectrum. Unlike in the common carrier service, private radio service frequencies are generally nonexclusive and have no guarantee of protection from interference. . . .

Prior to the introduction of PCPS's, the FCC had established three types of private sharing arrangements. The first, cooperative use arrangements, involves licensing the base station to a sole licensee. The licensee can share the land station with other eligible persons as long as all use of the station comes under the licensee's control. . . .

The second form of shared use, multiple licensing arrangements, involves licensing the base station to two or more eligible users. . . . Unlike cooperative use arrangements, the users in multiple licensing arrangements are each licensees of the base station and individually have access to and control the transmitter. Each licensee is assigned "tone" signals for direct activation, over a telephone line, of the land station transmitter. This allows each licensee control of the transmitter exclusive of other licensees.

Specialized Mobile Radio Systems are the third form of shared use. This system is similar to multiple licensing arrangements except that the equipment owner is the licensee of the base station transmitter, and he provides the paging service on a commercial basis allowing each user access to and control of a station. *National Association of Regulatory Utility Commissioners v. FCC*, 525 F.2d 630 (D.C. Cir.), *cert. denied*, 425 U.S. 992, 96 S.Ct. 2203, 48 L.Ed.2d 816 (1976) ("NARUC").

---

1. Mobile telephone service involves two-way radio communications between a mobile radio and an ordinary telephone station.

2. Dispatch calling service involves two-way radio communications between base and land mobile stations or between a land mobile station and a landline telephone station not connected to the telephone system.

In July 1982, after a rulemaking proceeding, the FCC determined that the public interest would be served through the allocation of 40 channels in the 929–930 mega-Hertz ("MHz") band for one-way private paging services. *Second Report and Order, General Docket 80–183*, 91 F.C.C.2d 1214 (1982). The Commission set aside 30 of the channels for private noncommercial systems and 10 of the channels for the creation of PCPS's to operate as additional private services. The Commission felt that "this apportionment of channels [would] provide eligibles with the option of obtaining private carrier paging service from PCP licensees, while reserving adequate spectrum for those users who wish to build and implement their own systems." *Id.* at 1223. Later that same year, the FCC granted Millicom several licenses to operate as a nationwide PCPS on a for-profit basis. Millicom as the sole licensee exercises exclusive control of its base station. Eligible users gain access to the transmitter through the licensee either by an oral telephone communication to a Millicom operator or through a keyboard display terminal entry over the telephone lines directly to Millicom's METASAT-Sender Computer Interface. Brief of Intervenor Millicom at 10–11.[3] Telocator contends that these methods of access and the interconnection between the METASAT and the land stations violate the interconnection restrictions of 47 U.S.C. § 332(c)(1) (1982). . . .

Prior to the proposed creation of PCPS, common carriers had mounted an extensive campaign against expansion of private land mobile radio services. Eventually each of the share systems was implemented. *See, e.g., NARUC*, 525 F.2d 630 (court approval of Specialized Mobile Radio Systems). Litigation continued, however, over determinations whether various systems qualified under one of the private classifications and over what standard the FCC should apply in making those determinations. Courts applied the test developed in *NARUC*, which required a case-by-case analysis to determine whether a particular system fit within the common law definition of common carriage: indiscriminate offering of service to the public. *NARUC*, 525 F.2d at 641–642, 647.

In an effort to end the controversy, Congress, in late 1982, enacted 47 U.S.C. § 332(c)(1) (1982) to provide a "clear demarcation between private and common carrier land mobile services."

* * *

Shortly after the passage of section 332(c)(1), Telocator challenged the FCC's authorization of PCPS under the *NARUC* test as being in violation of the recently passed section 332(c)(1)'s interconnection requirements. . . . [T]he Commission held that the PCPS regulations were consistent with section 332(c)(1). *Id.* . . . PCPS's that do not allow the end-users to control the land station are not subject to the interconnection restrictions of the Act.

Telocator's challenges to the Commission rule establishing PCPS and to the grant of a license to Millicom turn upon the interpretation of section 332(c)(1) of

---

3. The subscriber's entry into the METASAT computer is formatted and routed to the "METALINK" computer. That computer then directs the message to a METAPLEX computer at the control point of the appropriate land station transmitter. The subscriber has no access to or control over this system. Joint Appendix ("J.A.") at 129a.

the Communications Amendments Act of 1982. The question, as already noted, is whether Millicom's customers are "authorized users" of Millicom's land station so that the interconnection restrictions apply. In pertinent part, section 332(c)(1) provides:

> private land mobile service shall include service provided by specialized mobile radio, multiple licensed radio dispatch systems, and all other radio dispatch systems, regardless of whether such service is provided indiscriminately to eligible users on a commercial basis, except that a *land station licensed* in such service *to multiple licensees or otherwise shared by authorized users* (other than a nonprofit, cooperative station) shall not be interconnected with a telephone exchange or interexchange service or facility . . .

47 U.S.C. § 332(c)(1) (1982) (emphasis added). Telocator contends that section 332(c)(1) applies to all private shared systems, that PCPS's are such systems, and that Millicom is, therefore, subject to the interconnection restriction.

We think this reading of the statute is too broad. By its terms section 332(c)(1) does not apply the interconnection restriction to all private land radio services but rather to those with land stations that are licensed to "multiple licensees" or are "otherwise shared by authorized users." The phrase "otherwise shared by authorized users" refers back to "land station" and not to the service as a whole. The interconnection restriction applies only to shared systems where the land station is controlled directly by the authorized users and not to every shared system merely because the end-users have access to the system through the licensee. Only the sole licensee—in this case Millicom—has control of the land station in a PCPS. To find that each end-user in a PCPS has control of the land station, we would have to make the unwarranted finding that the entire PCPS network constitutes the "land station" for purposes of a section 332(c)(1) determination. . . .

It is conceded that "multiple licensees" are persons who are licensed to operate the station or to control its operation. It is natural, though perhaps not inevitable, to suppose that the "authorized users," who are placed by the clause in parity with licensees, are also persons who by agreement are authorized to operate or control the station. If the broader meaning advanced by Telocator had been intended, presumably Congress would not have bothered to describe both multiple licensees and authorized users but would simply have applied the interconnection restriction to all private systems as defined in 47 U.S.C. § 153(gg) (1982), the broad, all encompassing, definitions section of the Communications Amendments Act of 1982 passed in conjunction with section 322(c)(1). If the more restricted version of the language which we have found natural is not the necessary interpretation, it is surely an allowable one, and the Commission is entitled to adopt it. . . .

. . . Section 332(c)(1) was thus not intended to limit the private carrier systems to existing configurations. That section allows the FCC, when faced with future technological and public policy advances, to create new systems that will make more efficient use of the spectrum. The only limitation is that systems with shared land stations are to be subjected to the interconnection restrictions. That is not the case here.

Millicom's customers cannot operate or control Millicom's base stations. The customers merely deliver the message to the Millicom intermediary—the employee or METASAT interface. When the land station transmitter becomes available, the intermediary ensures that the message is relayed. . . . Although the message is initially transmitted to Millicom over the telephone lines, at no time does Millicom relinquish to subscribers control of or grant direct access to its land stations. . . . Thus, under the reading we and the Commission give the statute, Millicom's land stations are not "shared by authorized users" and the system, therefore, is not subject to the interconnection restrictions of section 332(c)(1). We affirm the Commission's grant of a PCPS license to Millicom.

CONTENT REGULATION OF CUSTOMER'S SPEECH

In 1988 Congress amended Section 223(b) of the Communications Act to impose a ban on indecent as well as obscene interstate commercial telephone messages, known as dial-a-porn. In *Sable Communications of Calif. vs. FCC*, 492 U.S. 115 (1989), the Supreme Court upheld the prohibition on obscene communications but overturned the provision relating to indecent communications. The *Sable* case followed a series of attempts by the FCC to develop regulations limiting access to dial-a-porn services. After previous regulations were deemed violations of the First Amendment, FCC rules providing for access codes, along with credit card payments and scrambled messages, were upheld in *Carlin Communications v. FCC*, 837 F.2d 546 (D.C. Cir.), *cert. denied*, 488 U.S. 924 (1988).

In 1989 Congress responded to the *Sable* decision by amending Section 223 to regulate, but not ban, indecent intrastate as well as interstate commercial telephone messages. Section 223(c) requires carriers to implement reverse blocking if the carrier performs billing and collection services for the provider. Reverse blocking prevents access to adult message services unless a subscriber submits a written request for access to the carrier.

Pursuant to this change, the FCC readopted the following rules for access codes, credit card authorizations, and scrambled messages (*Dial-a-Porn Regulations*, 67 R.R.2d 1460 [1990]). The regulations also require carriers to implement the reverse blocking scheme and oblige dial-a-porn operators to notify their carriers that they intend to offer an indecent message service.

In *Dial Information Services Corp. v. Thornburgh*, 938 F.2d 1535 (2d Cir. 1991), *cert. denied* (1992), the Court of Appeals for the Second Circuit upheld the Commission's order against claims based on the First Amendment that its definition of indecent was vague, that voluntary blocking was the least restrictive means allowable, and that no greater restriction was permitted. The court disagreed, stating, "It always is more effective to lock the barn before the horse is stolen."

REGULATIONS CONCERNING INDECENT
COMMUNICATIONS BY TELEPHONE,
REPORT AND ORDER

5 F.C.C. Rcd. 4926 (1990)

By a Notice of Proposed Rulemaking in *Regulations Concerning Indecent Communications by Telephone,* Gen Docket No 90–64 (*NPRM*), 5 FCC Rcd 1011 (1990), the Commission sought public comment on proposed regulations to be adopted pursuant to Section 223 of the Communications Act of 1934, as amended (*The Act*), 47 USC §223. Section 223, *inter alia,* imposes penalties on those who knowingly make obscene communications by telephone for commercial purposes and on those who knowingly make available indecent communications by telephone for commercial purposes to persons under 18 years of age or to adults without their consent. The section establishes that it is a defense to prosecution for the defendant to restrict access to the prohibited indecent communications to persons eighteen years of age or older by complying with such procedures as the Commission may prescribe by regulation. The statute also requires telephone companies, to the extent technically feasible, to prohibit access to indecent communications from the telephone of a subscriber who has not previously requested access in writing.

*   *   *

In this decision we review the proposed rules and comments submitted in response to the notice of proposed rulemaking and adopt final rules under Part 64 to establish defenses to prosecution under Section 223(b). These rules provide that in order to establish a defense to prosecution under Section 223 of the Act, adult information service providers are required to utilize credit card authorization, access codes, or scrambling in order to limit access to consenting adults over the age of eighteen. In addition, adult information service providers are required to notify carriers identified in Section 223(c)(1) of the Act that they are providing the kind of service described in Section 223(b) of the Act. Where the providers subscribe to mass announcement services tariffed at this Commission, they must request of the carriers in writing that calls to the message services be subject to billing notification as adult message services. Finally, we codify that a common carrier shall not provide access to a communication specified in Section 223(b) from the telephone of any subscriber who has not previously requested in writing the carrier to provide access to such communication. These regulations are promulgated pursuant to the Congressional mandate in Section 223 and are a necessary underpinning of the statutory scheme, which imposes penalties for violations of the statutory and regulatory provisions.

*   *   *

Some parties contend that the statute and our regulations are unconstitutional. First, parties argue that the statute and proposed regulations are unconstitutionally vague because the terms "obscene" and "indecent" are not defined. Second, parties argue that the proposed regulations are more burdensome than is necessary to serve the government's interest.

With respect to the first question, we conclude that the First Amendment does not require that the terms "indecent" and "obscene" be defined in either the statute or the regulations. Many federal statutes prohibit obscene speech without defining the term, *see, e.g.*, 18 USC §1462 (interstate transportation of obscene material); 18 USC §1461 (mailing obscene material), because the Supreme Court has supplied a definition of "obscene" under federal law. *See United States v. 12 200-foot Reels of Film*, 413 US 123, 130 n. 7 (1973). Indeed, in the *Sable* case, the Supreme Court upheld the portion of the statute that prohibited obscene speech. We therefore conclude that the term "obscene" in the statute is not unconstitutionally vague.

The Supreme Court has also accepted the regulation of "indecent" speech under certain conditions, even though that term is not defined in the statute. *FCC v. Pacifica Foundation*, 438 US 726 (1978) (upholding prohibition of indecent broadcasts under 18 USC §1464 when there is a reasonable risk that children are in the audience). In the broadcasting context, the courts have upheld the Commission's definition of indecency as "the description or depiction of sexual or excretory activities or organs in a patently offensive manner as measured by contemporary community standards for the broadcast medium."

*   *   *

In the dial-a-porn context, we believe it is appropriate to define indecency as the description or depiction of sexual or excretory activities or organs in a patently offensive manner as measured by contemporary community standards for the telephone medium. . . .

The second issue raised by these commenters is whether voluntary blocking, as opposed to the reverse blocking required by the statute, is the least restrictive, effective alternative.[16] The statute requires telephone companies to block access to providers of indecent services if technically feasible, unless the customer requests access.

The First Amendment does not preclude Congress from imposing a burden on message providers. *See Sable v. FCC.* Regulations need not be so weak that they are completely useless. It was reasonable for Congress to conclude that its reverse blocking scheme would be considerably more effective than a voluntary scheme in preventing children from accessing indecent material. A voluntary blocking scheme would be far less effective in protecting children from exposure to indecent material because it is likely that most parents would not realize the

---

16. We use the term "blocking" to include both "voluntary blocking" and "reverse blocking." By "voluntary blocking" we mean the telephone company will, at the central office, prevent calls from going through to specified exchanges or numbers if the customer has requested this blocking service. By "reverse blocking," we mean the telephone company will, at the central office, prevent calls from going through to specified exchanges or numbers *unless* the customer has requested access. Subsection (c) of the statute requires telephone companies to institute reverse blocking where technically feasible if they provide billing and collection services to indecent message providers.

need for blocking until their children had already obtained access to indecent messages. Nor would neighbors or relatives where children are only occasional visitors recognize the need to, nor act to, have access blocked. It is reasonable, therefore, to implement a reverse blocking scheme that brings the potential problem to the attention of parents *before* the damage to children has occurred, rather than waiting until the damage has been done.

*   *   *

In California under a voluntary blocking approach, the number of people asking for blocking was quite small. If only 10 percent of phones are blocked, children will have ready access to indecent materials via phones in neighbors' and relatives' homes and in public places. A reverse blocking scheme is far more effective in preventing children from gaining access to indecent messages. In addition, a reverse blocking approach puts the burden on those who want access to messages, rather than on those who wish to protect their children. The burden is not great in either case—it requires merely writing to the telephone company to request access or blocking. Balancing all the interests, it is apparent that reverse blocking is an effective, not unduly restrictive, means of protecting children.

*   *   *

b. Defenses to Prosecution

In the *NPRM* the Commission proposed to readopt the regulations of the *Third Report and Order* and require that, in order to have a defense against prosecution under Section 223 for providing indecent material, a provider must utilize credit cards, access codes, or scrambling, and, where applicable, carrier billing notification. . . .

We find that the use of credit card validation, scrambling or access codes before transmission places a minimal burden on the information provider and consenting adult while helping to assure that access by minors is restricted. Nevertheless, we believe Congress could reasonably conclude that each of these is far from foolproof and can be counteracted by less than the "most enterprising and disobedient young [person]," *see Sable*, 109 S Ct at 2838. Accordingly, it is necessary to impose reverse blocking, where technically feasible, to achieve Congress's compelling interest in protecting children. We find that the proposed defenses are sufficiently varied that any information provider should be able to adapt at least one of the proposed defenses to its operation without unreasonable expense.

*   *   *

Regarding authorized access or identification codes, no commenter has suggested that the access code defense should be eliminated. The Providers Coalition's criticisms of the defense merely underscore what the Commission has already recognized and incorporated in the proposed regulatory scheme, *viz*, that no single defense to prosecution can serve the needs of all information providers and carriers. The efficacy of each defense will depend on the circumstances under which it is used, taking into account the technology utilized and the information service provided. In circumstances where the provider has an established pool of repeat customers the access code defense may prove particularly effective and minimally restrictive. In addition, access code systems have been utilized in the financial services sector as an effective means to restrict access to account holders only. The likelihood that access codes will become available to most minors is small; yet in the hands of an adult the code is a reasonably easy method of access and may even be useful to information providers as a method to encourage their repeat business. As one of several options, it may represent, for some, the least restrictive method to bar access to minors. . . .

In order to effectuate Congress's mandate that reverse blocking be implemented, it is necessary that either the carrier or the message provider determine whether the messages involved are indecent. There is nothing in the record to show that requiring adult information providers to inform the carrier offering them the commercial service described in Section 223(c)(1) of the nature of the communications they intend to offer imposes other than a minimal burden, or that it is not an essential adjunct to implementation of blocking by carriers. Placing the burden on the information provider to give notice of the provision of indecent communications resolves the issue raised by the Providers Coalition because carriers need not monitor communications where providers are required to declare the nature of the subject communication to establish a defense to prosecution. We disagree with AC&E's assertion that notification to the carriers results in self-incrimination. The fact that an indecent communication has been made by telephone for commercial purposes is insufficient to establish a violation of Section 223 of the Act; rather, liability results when these communications are made available to minors or non-consenting adults. Moreover, we do not believe that this issue will arise in the normal course. As a practical matter, a service provider generally will identify itself to the carrier as providing adult information only in those instances where the service provider has complied as well with the additional defenses set forth in our regulations. Having availed itself of the safe harbor provided by our Rules and the statute, there is little risk of prosecution under Section 223.

* * *

Several commenters argue that restrictions on indecent communications will have an adverse impact on the fight against AIDS by restricting open discussion of related issues by telephone. The proposed regulatory scheme does not restrict communications which are clinical discussions of AIDS or any other topic. Legitimate scientific or social endeavors such as community hotlines generally fall outside the definition of obscenity or indecency. . . . In addition, we note that the statute encompasses only those indecent or obscene communications which are produced for commercial purposes.

Questions

1. Under a reverse blocking scheme, either the carrier or the message provider must determine whether the messages are indecent. Absent a

notification requirement on the provider, would such an inquiry into the content of messages seem consistent with the definition of a common carrier? Conversely, does such an admission as to the content of the messages pose any risks to message providers?

2. Some states would prefer that the FCC implement reverse blocking for all pay-per-call services, not just those offering adult message services. Does this impose a lesser duty on the telephone company (telco) to inquire into the content of a message? Is this inconsistent with the definition of a common carrier? Should the carrier merely distinguish between commercial and noncommercial messages?

3. Did the FCC satisfactorily deal with the AIDS/community hotline issue?

4. If a telephone company finds the nonindecent offerings of a message service to be especially repugnant, can it deny access or billing services to the message provider? For example, must a telephone company provide service to a message provider that offers racial and ethnic hate speeches that offend the carrier and its customers?

5. In April 1990 Hughes Communications Satellite Services, Inc., terminated its transponder lease agreement with Tuxxedo Network, an R-rated adult movie pay-per-view service. Two weeks later Tuxxedo, its parent company (HDSN), and its officers were indicted for violating Alabama's obscenity law. Hughes evidently cut off the service in response to an earlier criminal obscenity indictment in Alabama involving GTE Spacenet (satellite provider), U.S. Satellite Corp., (uplinker), American Exxxstasy (X-rated back-yard-dish service), HDSN, and its officers. The FCC did not take action against Hughes, GTE, or U.S. Satellite for terminating the services. What does this inaction mean for carriers, programmers, and message services?

6. Congress is considering whether to allow telephone companies to provide video services over their fiber-optic lines. What form of service might be consistent with the common carrier definition? May a telephone company act like a traditional cable system operator by picking and packaging program services to offer subscribers?

3

FEDERAL/STATE JURISDICTION

PREEMPTION GENERALLY

LOUISIANA PUBLIC SERVICE COMMISSION v. FCC

476 U.S. 355 (1986)

* * *

JUSTICE BRENNAN delivered the opinion of the Court.

In these consolidated cases, we are asked by 26 private telephone companies and the United States to sustain the holding of the Court of Appeals for the Fourth Circuit that orders of the Federal Communications Commission (FCC or Commission) respecting the depreciation of telephone plant and equipment preempt inconsistent state regulation. They are opposed by the Public Service Commissions of 23 States, backed by 30 *amici curiae*, who argue that the Communications Act of 1934 (Act), 48 Stat. 1064, as amended, 47 U. S. C. §151 *et seq.*, expressly denied the FCC authority to establish depreciation practices and charges insofar as they relate to the setting of rates for intrastate telephone service.

Respondents suggest that the heart of the cases is whether the revolution in telecommunications occasioned by the federal policy of increasing competition in the industry will be thwarted by state regulators who have yet to recognize or accept this national policy and who thus refuse to permit telephone companies to employ accurate accounting methods designed to reflect, in part, the effects of competition. We are told that already there may be as much as $26 billion worth of "reserve deficiencies" on the books of the Nation's local telephone companies, a reserve which, it is insisted, represents inadequate depreciation of a magnitude that threatens the financial ability of the industry to achieve the technological progress and provide the quality of service that the Act was passed to promote. Petitioners answer that the Act clearly establishes a system of dual state and federal authority over telephone service. They contend that the Act vests in the States exclusive power over intrastate rate-making, which power, petitioners argue, includes final authority over how depreciation shall be calculated for the purpose of setting those intrastate rates.

* * *

I

The Act establishes, among other things, a system of dual state and federal regulation over telephone service, and it is the nature of that division of authority that these cases are about. In broad terms, the Act grants to the FCC the authority to regulate "interstate and foreign commerce in wire and radio communication," 47 U. S. C. §151, while expressly denying that agency "jurisdiction with respect to . . . intrastate communication service. . . ." 47 U. S. C. §152(b). However, while the Act would seem to divide the world of domestic telephone service neatly into two hemispheres—one comprised of interstate service, over which the FCC would have plenary authority, and the other made up of intrastate service, over which the States would retain exclusive jurisdiction—in practice, the realities of technology and economics belie such a clean parceling of responsibility. This is so because virtually all telephone plant that is used to provide intrastate service is also used to provide interstate service, and is thus conceivably within the jurisdiction of both state and federal authorities. Moreover, because the same carriers provide both interstate and intrastate service, actions taken by federal and state regulators within their respective domains necessarily affect the general financial health of those carriers, and hence their ability to provide service, in the other "hemisphere."

In 1980 and 1981, the FCC issued two orders that ultimately sparked this litigation. In the 1980 order the FCC changed two depreciation practices affecting telephone plant. *Property Depreciation*, 83 F. C. C. 2d 267, reconsideration denied, 87 F. C. C. 2d 916 (1981). First, the order altered how carriers could group property subject to depreciation. Because carriers employ so many individual items of equipment in providing service, it would be impossible to depreciate each item individually, and property is therefore classified and depreciated in groups. The order permitted companies the option of grouping plant for depreciation purposes based on its estimated service life (the "equal life" approach). This replaced the FCC's prior practice of requiring companies to classify and depreciate property according to its year of installation (the "vintage year" method). This change was made to allow depreciation to be based on smaller and more homogeneous groupings, which, the FCC concluded, would result in more accurate matching of capital recovery with capital consumption.

The 1980 order further sought to promote improved accounting accuracy by replacing "whole life" depreciation with the "remaining life" method. Under remaining life, and unlike the treatment under a whole life regime, if estimates upon which depreciation schedules are premised prove erroneous, they may be corrected in midcourse in a way that assures that the full cost of the asset will ultimately be recovered.

The third FCC-mandated change in plant depreciation was announced in a 1981 order, and involved the cost of labor and material associated with the installation of wire inside the premises of a business or residence. The new rule provided that this so-called "inside wiring" no longer be treated as a capital investment to be depreciated over time, but rather as a cost to be "expensed" in the year incurred. *Uniform System of Accounts*, 85 F. C. C. 2d 818.

*   *   *

II

Both petitioners and respondents characterize this litigation as one in which two different persons seek to drive one car, a condition the parties agree is unsatisfactory. Where the parties disagree is with respect to who ought to be displaced from the controls. In order to address the contentions, it is appropriate to consider not only the structure of the Act and how it divides authority, but also the nature and function of depreciation as a component of utility regulation.

Depreciation is defined as the loss in service value of a capital asset over time. In the context of public utility accounting and regulation, it is a process of charging the cost of depreciable property, adjusted for net salvage, to operating expense accounts over the useful life of the asset. Thus, accounting practices significantly affect, among other things, the rates that customers pay for service. This is so because a regulated carrier is entitled to recover its reasonable expenses and a fair return on its investment through the rates it charges its customers, and because depreciation practices contribute importantly to the calculation of both the carrier's investment and its expenses. See *Knoxville* v. *Knoxville Water Co.*, 212 U. S. 1, 13–14 (1909). See generally, 1 A. Priest, Principles of Public Utility Regulation (1969); P. Garfield & W. Lovejoy, Public Utility Economics (1964); 1 A. Kahn, Economics of Regulation (1970).

The total amount that a carrier is entitled to charge for services, its "revenue requirement," is the sum of its current operating expenses, including taxes and depreciation expenses, and a return on its investment "rate base." The original cost of a given item of equipment enters the rate base when that item enters service. As it depreciates over time—as a function of wear and tear or technological obsolescence—the rate base is reduced according to a depreciation schedule that is based on an estimate of the item's expected useful life. Each year the amount that is removed from the rate base is included as an operating expense. In the telephone industry, which is extremely capital intensive, depreciation changes constitute a significant portion of the annual revenue requirement recovered in rates; the parties agree that depreciation charges amount to somewhere between 10% to 15% of the intrastate revenue requirement.

In essence, petitioners' argument is that the plain and unambiguous language of §152(b) denies the FCC power to compel the States to employ FCC-set depreciation practices and schedules in connection with the setting of intrastate rates. In part, that section provides:

> [N]othing in this chapter shall be construed to apply or to give the Commission jurisdiction with respect to (1) charges, classifications, practices, services, facilities, or regulations for or in connection with intrastate communication service by wire or radio of any carrier. . . .

Petitioners maintain that "charges," "classifications," and "practices" are "terms of art" which denote depreciation and accounting, and thus that the question presented by these cases is expressly answered by the statute. They argue also that the legislative history shows on a more general level that §152(b) was intended to reserve to the States exclusive regulatory jurisdiction over intrastate service, especially intrastate ratemaking, and that given the importance of depreciation to ratemaking, to require state regulators to follow FCC depreciation practices would frustrate the statutory design of preserving the States' ratemaking authority over intrastate service. Petitioners maintain that to confer this power on the FCC would be, in effect, to write the jurisdictional limitation of §152(b) out of the Act.

Where petitioners focus on §152(b), respondents' principal argument is that this litigation turns on §220 of the Act, which they insist constitutes an unambiguous grant of power to the FCC exclusively to regulate depreciation. Their argument is that once the FCC has acted pursuant to that section, States are automatically precluded from prescribing different depreciation practices or rates. Section 220(b) states:

> The Commission shall, as soon as practicable, prescribe for such carriers the classes of property for which depreciation charges may be properly included under operating expenses, and the percentages of depreciation which shall be charged with respect to each of such classes of property, classifying the carriers as it may deem proper for this purpose. The Commission may, when it deems necessary, modify the classes and percentages so prescribed. Such carriers shall not, after the Commission has prescribed the [classes] of property for which depreciation charges may be included, charge to operating expenses any depreciation charges on classes of property other than those prescribed by the Commission, or after the Commission has prescribed percentages of depreciation, charge with respect to any class of property a percentage of depreciation other than that prescribed therefor by the Commission. No such carrier shall in any case include in any form under its operating or other expenses any depreciation or other charge or expenditure included elsewhere as a depreciation charge or otherwise under its operating or other expenses.

Respondents assert that their understanding of §220(b) is bolstered by other substantive provisions of §220. They note, for example, that under §220(g), once the FCC has prescribed the "forms and manner of keeping accounts," it is "unlawful . . . to keep any other accounts . . . than those so prescribed . . . or to keep the accounts in any other manner than that prescribed or approved by the Commission," and that subsections (d) and (e) of §220 provide for civil and criminal penalties for failing to keep accounts as determined by the Commission. Moreover, §220(h) permits the FCC in its discretion, if it finds such action to be "consistent with the public interest," to "except the carriers of any particular class or classes in any State from any of the requirements" under the section "in cases where such carriers are subject to State commission regulation with respect to matters to which this section relates." . . . In sum, the position of respondents is that "Congress clearly intended that there be one regime—rather than multiple regimes—of depreciation for each subject carrier. The FCC was given responsibility for establishing such a regime, and its depreciation decisions have to be respected unless and until it relinquishes authority to the states in individual instances. The states' interest is recognized but their role is confined to providing their 'views and recommendations.'"

Although respondents rely primarily on §220 to support pre-emption, they also urge as an alternative and independent ground the reasoning relied on by the Court of Appeals, namely that the FCC is entitled to pre-empt inconsistent state regulation which frustrates federal policy. It is in the context of this argument that respondents most forcefully contend that state regulators must not be permitted to jeopardize the continued viability of the telecommunications industry by refusing to permit carriers to depreciate plant in a way that allows for accurate and timely recapturing of capital. . . .

III

The Supremacy Clause of Art. VI of the Constitution provides Congress with the power to pre-empt state law. Pre-emption occurs when Congress, in enacting a federal statute, expresses a clear intent to pre-empt state law, *Jones* v. *Rath Packing Co.*, 430 U. S. 519 (1977), when there is outright or actual conflict between federal and state law, *e. g., Free* v. *Bland*, 369 U. S. 663 (1962), where compliance with both federal and state law is in effect physically impossible, *Florida Lime & Avocado Growers, Inc.* v. *Paul*, 373 U. S. 132 (1963), where there is implicit in federal law a barrier to state regulation, *Shaw* v. *Delta Air Lines, Inc.*, 463 U. S. 85 (1983), where Congress has legislated comprehensively, thus occupying an entire field of regulation and leaving no room for the States to supplement federal law, *Rice* v. *Santa Fe Elevator Corp.*, 331 U. S. 218 (1947), or where the state law stands as an obstacle to the accomplishment and execution of the full objectives of Congress. *Hines* v. *Davidowitz*, 312 U. S. 52 (1941). Pre-emption may result not only from action taken by Congress itself; a federal agency acting within the scope of its congressionally delegated authority may pre-empt state regulation. *Fidelity Federal Savings & Loan Assn.* v. *De la Cuesta*, 458 U. S. 141 (1982); *Capital Cities Cable, Inc.* v. *Crisp*, 467 U. S. 691 (1984).

*   *   *

The critical question of any pre-emption analysis is always whether Congress intended that federal regulation supersede state law. *Rice* v. *Santa Fe Elevator Corp., supra.* The Act itself declares that its purpose is "regulating interstate and foreign commerce in communication by wire and radio so as to make available, so far as possible, to all the people of the United States a rapid, efficient, Nationwide, and world-wide wire and radio communication service with adequate facilities at reasonable charges. . . ." 47 U. S. C. §151. In order to accomplish this goal, Congress created the FCC to centralize and consolidate the regulatory responsibility that had previously been the province of the Interstate Commerce Commission and the Federal Radio Commission under predecessor statutes. See generally McKenna, Pre-Emption Under the Communications Act, 37 Fed. Comm. L.J. 1, 12–18 (1985). To this degree, §151 may be read as lending some support to respondents' position that state regulation which frustrates the ability of the FCC to perform its statutory function of ensuring efficient, nationwide phone service may be impliedly barred by the Act.

We might be inclined to accept this broad reading of §151 were it nor for the express jurisdictional limitations on FCC power contained in §152(b). Again, that section asserts that "nothing in this chapter shall be construed to apply or to give the Commission jurisdiction with respect to (1) charges, classifications, practices, services, facilities, or regulations for or in connection with intrastate communication service. . . ." By its terms, this provision fences off from FCC reach or regulation intrastate matters—indeed, including matters "in connection with" intrastate service. Moreover, the language with which it does so is certainly as sweeping as the wording of the provision declaring the purpose of the Act and the role of the FCC.

In interpreting §§151 and 152(b), we are guided by the familiar rule of construction that, where possible, provisions of a statute should be read so as not to create a conflict. *Washington Market Co.* v. *Hoffman*, 101 U. S. 112 (1879). We agree with petitioners that the sections are naturally reconciled to define a national goal of the creation of a rapid and efficient phone service, and to enact a *dual* regulatory system to achieve that goal. Moreover, were we to find the sections to be in conflict, we would be disinclined to favor the provision declaring a general statutory purpose, as opposed to the provision which defines the jurisdictional reach of the agency formed to implement that purpose.

*   *   *

. . . We cannot accept respondent's argument that §152(b) does not control because the plant involved in this case is used interchangeably to provide both interstate and intrastate service, and that even if §152(b) does reserve to the state commissions some authority over "certain aspects" of intrastate communication, it should be "confined to intrastate matters which are 'separable from and do not substantially affect' interstate communication."

With respect to the present cases, respondents insist that the refusal of the States to employ accurate measures of depreciation will have a severe impact on the interstate communications network because investment in plant will be recovered too slowly or not at all, with the result that new investment will be discouraged to the detriment of the entire network.

*   *   *

The short answer to this argument is that it misrepresents the statutory scheme and the basis and test for pre-emption. While it is certainly true, and a basic underpinning of our federal system, that state regulation will be displaced to the extent that it stands as an obstacle to the accomplishment and execution of the full purposes and objectives of Congress, . . . it is also true that a federal agency may pre-empt state law only when and if it is acting within the scope of its congressionally delegated authority. This is true for at least two reasons. First, an agency literally has no power to act, let alone pre-empt the validly enacted legislation of a sovereign State, unless and until Congress confers power upon it. Second, the best way of determining whether Congress intended the regulations of an administrative agency to displace state law is to examine the nature and scope of the authority granted by Congress to the agency. Section 152(b) constitutes, as we have explained above, a congressional *denial* of power to the FCC to require state commissions to follow FCC depreciation practices for intrastate ratemaking purposes. Thus, we simply cannot accept an argument that the FCC may nevertheless take action which it thinks will best effectuate a federal policy. An agency may not confer power upon itself. To permit an agency to expand its power in the face of a congressional limitation on its jurisdiction would be to grant to the agency power to override Congress. This we are both unwilling and unable to do.

Moreover, we reject the intimation—the position is not strongly pressed—that the FCC cannot help but pre-empt state depreciation regulation of joint plant if it is to fulfill its statutory obligation and determine depreciation for plant used to provide interstate service, *i. e.*, that it makes no sense within the context of the Act to depreciate one piece of property two ways. The Communications Act not only establishes dual state and federal regulation of telephone service; it also recognizes that jurisdictional tensions may arise as a result of the fact that interstate and intrastate service are provided by a single integrated system. Thus, the Act itself establishes a process designed to resolve what is known as "jurisdictional separations" matters, by which process it may be determined what portion of an asset is employed to produce or deliver interstate as opposed to intrastate service. 47 U. S. C. §§221(c), 410(c). Because the separations process literally separates costs such as taxes and operating expenses between interstate and intrastate service, it facilitates the creation or recognition of distinct spheres of regulation. See *Smith* v. *Illinois Bell Telephone Co.*, 282 U. S. 133 (1930). As respondents concede, . . . it is certainly possible to apply different rates and methods of depreciation to plant once the correct allocation between interstate and intrastate use has been made,[4] . . . just as it is possible to determine that, for example, 75% of an employee's time is devoted to the production of intrastate service, and only one quarter to interstate service, and to allocate the cost of that employee accordingly. Respondents maintain that if the FCC and the States apply different depreciation practices to the same property, then the "whole purpose of depreciation, which is to match depreciation charges of the equipment with the revenues generated by its use," will be frustrated. But this is true and a concern only to the degree that the principles, judgments, and considerations that underlie depreciation rules reflect only "real world" facts, rather than choices made by regulators partially on the basis of fact and partially on the basis of such factors as the perceived need to improve the industry's cash flow, spur investment, subsidize one class of customer, or any other policy factor. What is really troubling respondents, of course, is their sense that state regulators will not allow them sufficient revenues. While we do not deprecate this concern, §152(b) precludes both the FCC and this Court from providing the relief sought.

* * *

[Note: In the remainder of the opinion, the Court finds that Section 220, concerning depreciation, must be read as subordinate to Section 152(b).]

---

4. Thus, these cases are readily distinguishable from those in which FCC pre-emption of state regulation was upheld where it was *not* possible to separate the interstate and the intrastate components of the asserted FCC regulation. See, *e. g.*, *North Carolina Utilities Comm'n* v. *FCC*, 537 F. 2d 787 (CA4), cert. denied, 429 U. S. 1027 (1976), and *North Carolina Utilities Comm'n* v. *FCC*, 552 F. 2d 1036 (CA4), cert. denied, 434 U. S. 874 (1977) (Where FCC acted within its authority to permit subscribers to provide their own telephones, pre-emption of inconsistent state regulation prohibiting subscribers from connecting their own phones unless used exclusively in interstate service upheld since state regulation would negate the federal tariff).

TAXATION AND THE POWER OF STATES

Sometimes a state regulation runs afoul of the Constitution's commerce clause because the federal government has preempted the field from state regulation. In these areas courts can limit state authority over interstate communications. In particular, when a state taxes an interstate activity, the commerce clause can be invoked. In *Goldberg v. Sweet*, 488 U.S. 252 (1989), the Supreme Court upheld a tax imposed by Illinois on interstate telephone calls. The court found that the 5 percent tax, which applied only to those interstate calls charged to an in-state service address, imposed no double taxation.

However, as Justice Stevens noted in a concurring opinion, "A call originating and terminating in Illinois that costs $10 is taxed at full value at 5%. A second call, originating in Illinois but terminating in Indiana, costs the same $10 and is taxed at the same full value at the same 5% rate. But while Illinois may properly tax the entire $10 of the first call, it (technically) may tax only that portion of the second call over which its has jurisdiction, namely the intrastate portion of the call (say, for example, $5). By imposing an identical 50 [cent] tax on the two calls, Illinois has imposed a disproportionate economic burden on the interstate call. . . . This argument, however, overlooks the true overall incidence of the Illinois tax. Although Illinois taxes the entirety of every call charged to an Illinois number, it does not tax any part of the calls that are received at an Illinois number but charged elsewhere."

Does the Illinois tax still burden interstate businesses that happen to use Illinois as a central base of operations? Does the tax encourage migration of businesses to "tax free" telecommunications zones?

NORTH CAROLINA UTILITIES COMMISSION v. FCC

537 F.2d 787 (4th Cir. 1976)

HASTIE, Senior Circuit Judge.

This controversy began with a petition in which several manufacturers and distributors of communications equipment asked the Federal Communications Commission (hereinafter, FCC or the Commission) to rule that state regulatory agencies are precluded from restricting or regulating the interconnection of customer-provided equipment to the customer's individual subscriber station and line in any way that conflicts with the Commission's regulation of the same subject matter. The petition recited that the North Carolina Utilities Commission had given public notice of a proposed rule to prohibit such connection of customer-provided equipment in that state, except for use exclusively with facilities separate from those used in intrastate communication. It also was alleged that the Attorney General of Nebraska had advised the Nebraska Public Service Commission that rulings of FCC did not control the attachment of customer-provided equipment to telephone facilities used for intrastate communication. The same opinion stated that approval of the state regulatory authority was necessary before a motel could lawfully connect its own internal communications equipment to its telephone subscriber station.

* * *

As the agency established by the Communications Act of 1934, 47 U.S.C. § 151, to administer the provisions of that statute, the Federal Communications Commission is empowered, in the language of section 1 of the Act, to regulate interstate and foreign commerce in communication by wire and radio "so as to make available . . . a rapid, efficient, Nation-wide, and world-wide wire and radio communication service with adequate facilities at reasonable charges. . . ." By comprehensive definition of "communication by wire", section 3 makes it explicit that the subject matter of the Commission's jurisdiction includes "all instrumentalities, facilities, apparatus, and services . . . incidental to . . . [interstate] transmission" by wire.

On the other hand, section 2 both restates the applicability of the Act to "all interstate and foreign communications by wire or radio" and specifies that it shall not "be construed to apply to or give the Commission jurisdiction with respect to '(b)(1)' . . . facilities, or regulations for or in connection with intrastate communication service . . . of any carrier. . . ."

Terminal equipment that is connected to a telephone subscriber's station and line does in fact connect with the national telephone network. Usually it is not feasible, as a matter of economic and practicality of operation, to limit the use of such equipment to either interstate or intrastate transmissions. In paragraph 26 of the decision from which these appeals have been taken, the Commission has described the underlying realities as follows:

> . . . exchange plant, particularly subscriber stations and lines, is used in common and indivisibly for all local and long distance telephone calls. There is no interstate message toll telephone service either offered or practically possible except over exchange plant used for both intrastate and interstate and foreign service. 45 F.C.C.2d 204, 215.

Although some appellants have expressed disagreement with this finding, we find no basis for challenging it.

It follows that the Commission's present assertion of jurisdiction over the interconnection of customer provided equipment to the nation-wide network unavoidably affects intrastate as well as interstate communication. And, by the same token, both would be restricted by any state action that prevented such interconnection. Thus, the language of sections 1 and 2 that both grants the Commission authority to regulate facilities of interstate communication and withholds authority to regulate facilities of intrastate communication creates the present dispute but, considered alone, does not resolve it.

In these circumstances it is relevant and helpful to consider other provisions of the Communications Act. By force of a heretofore unmentioned concluding clause of section 2(b), not only telephone companies with lines that extend interstate but also those local companies that provide interstate service solely through connection with the lines of telephone companies that are unrelated to them, are expressly made amenable to the regulatory provisions of sections 201 through 205 of the Act. All of the telephone companies parties to this suit are thus integrated into the national network and subject to the provisions of sections 201 through 205. More particularly, under section 201, charges and practices for and in connection with interstate service must "be just and reasonable". Section 202 makes unlawful any "unjust or unreasonable discrimination in charges, practices, classifications, regulations, facilities, or services. . . ." Section 203 requires carriers to file with the Commission their tariff schedules for interstate communication service "showing the classifications, practices, and regulations affecting such charges". Sections 204 and 205 prescribe the manner in which the Commission shall administer and implement the requirements of the preceding sections, approving or invalidating tariffs as may be appropriate. It is in connection with the Commission's efforts to discharge its responsibilities under sections 201 through 205 and the alleged frustrating effect of countervailing state action that this controversy about jurisdiction over the attachment of customer-provided equipment has arisen.

Historically, a telephone company's restrictions, requirements and other regulations concerning customer provided equipment have been published and effectuated through inclusion in interstate tariffs. Some years ago, tariffs published by American Telephone and Telegraph Co. (hereinafter AT&T), acting for itself and other concurring carriers throughout the nation, forbade the subscriber to connect to his line any device or equipment not furnished by the telephone company. As defendant in a consequent anti-trust suit by a manufacturer of a terminal device, AT&T successfully urged that the suit was premature because of the primary jurisdiction of FCC over the question of the lawfulness of the inclusion of this restriction in the controlling tariff. This led to a formal FCC proceeding for determination whether the tariff contained any unreasonable or unlawfully discriminatory restriction.

In its ensuing decision the Commission held that the tariff's blanket and unqualified prohibition of the interconnection of customer provided equipment was unreasonable and unjustifiably discriminatory, hence invalid under sections 201 and 202 of the Act. *Carterfone v. AT&T,* 1968, 13 F.C.C.2d 420, *reconsideration denied,* 14 F.C.C.2d 571. At the same time the telephone companies were authorized, without any particularizing directive, to file new tariffs regulating the use of customer-provided equipment. They did so, and the Commission reviewed the tariffs and permitted them to become effective. See *In the Matter of AT&T "Foreign Attachment" Tariff Revisions,* 1968, 15 F.C.C.2d 605, *reconsideration denied,* 18 F.C.C.2d 871.

The coverage of one of the approved new tariffs, F.C.C. No. 263, which, as subsequently amended, remains in effect, is relevant to the present dispute. It authorizes and regulates the connection and use of customer-provided terminal equipment with telephone company facilities for long distance message communication. It covers both data and voice transmitting and receiving terminal equipment, as well as mechanically attached accessories. Provision also is made for the connection of customer-provided communications systems with the interstate telephone network. At the same time, various safeguards are required. Thus, with few exceptions, the tariff provides that access to the telephone network must be through a telephone company supplied network control signalling unit, which serves as a protective interface. Far from surrendering jurisdiction over alternative means of access, the Commission postponed, pending further engineering and technical study, decision whether and what customer-provided signalling devices should be approved.

If, as North Carolina is formally proposing and the Attorney General of Nebraska has held to be permissible, state jurisdiction over intrastate communication facilities is exercised in a way that, in practical effect, either prohibits customer-supplied attachments authorized by tariff F.C.C. No. 263 or restricts their use contrary to the provisions of that or any other interstate tariff, the Commission will be frustrated in the exercise of that plenary jurisdiction over the rendition of interstate and foreign communication services that the Act has conferred upon it. The Commission must remain free to determine what terminal equipment can safely and advantageously be interconnected with the interstate communications network and how this shall be done.

. . . We have no doubt that the provisions of section 2(b) deprive the Commission of regulatory power over local services, facilities and disputes that in their nature and effect are separable from and do not substantially affect the conduct or development of interstate communications. But beyond that, we are not persuaded that section 2(b) sanctions any state regulation, formally restrictive only of intrastate communication, that in effect encroaches substantially upon the Commission's authority under sections 201 through 205.[6] In this view of the

---

6. To support their contentions about the intended effect of section 2(b), the opposing parties have cited particular statements made in Congressional committee reports, or on the floor during debate, or by witnesses during the 1934 Senate and House hearings on the then newly proposed federal communications legislation. These references certainly show concern that, as a result of the so-called *Shreveport* rate decision, *Houston, E. & W. Texas Ry. v. United States*, 1914, 234 U.S. 342, 34 S.Ct. 833, 58 L.Ed. 1341, the Interstate Commerce Commission had been able to deprive state authorities of almost all regulatory power over intrastate rail transportation. And there was rather general agreement that this should not be done by the new federal commission in the communications field. However, it is equally clear that such little particularization as appears in the various statements of state concerns focuses upon the desire of state authorities to regulate local telephone rates and charges. See the statements of Mr. Clardy and Mr. McDonald, both senior officers of the National Association of Railroad and Utilities Commissioners, Hearings on S.2910 before the Senate Committee on Interstate Commerce, 73d Cong., 2d Sess. 155, 156. Of course, rate making typifies those activities of the telephone industry which lend themselves to practical separation of the local from the interstate in such a way that local regulation of one does not interfere with national regulation of the other. Focusing upon this type of local regulation, members of Congress and the witnesses they heard did not discuss the impact, if any, of section 2(b) on the type of regulation we now are considering. However, one of the above mentioned industry witnesses, Mr. Clardy, did make this perceptive comment:

". . . [W]e now have a great deal of difficulty in saying what is interstate and what is intrastate property . . . because every exchange and every piece of machinery and all help and everything else, may at any moment be carried over exclusively, temporarily at least, into interstate business. There has got to be some new philosophy developed, perhaps, by this Commission to assist the State

interrelation of the provisions of the Act, the Commission's declaratory statement of its primary authority over the interconnection of terminal equipment with the national telephone network is a proper and reasonable assertion of jurisdiction conferred by the Act. *Cf. G.T.E. Service Corp. v. F.C.C.*, 2d Cir. 1973, 474 F.2d 724, approving an FCC ruling that prohibited telephone companies, including those that engaged primarily in local exchange service and participated in interstate service only through connection with other unrelated carriers, from engaging in the data processing business.

We are all the more confident of this because, elsewhere in the Act itself, Congress has recognized the existence of areas of common national and state concern and has provided a procedure under which national primacy is recognized, yet the Commission is authorized to receive and consider information, views and proposals from concerned state agencies that may aid it in reaching informed and wise decisions. More particularly, section 410(c) of the Act confers upon the Commission discretionary power to refer any matter "relating to common carrier communications of joint Federal-State concern, to a Federal-State Joint Board" of four state and three federal Commissioners for examination and for preparation of a recommended FCC decision. It even is required that the state members of a Joint Board shall participate, without vote, in the Commission's consideration of the Board's recommendation. We find it very difficult to square this Congressional design with the present contention that section 2(b) is intended to deprive the Commission of jurisdiction over the use of facilities that necessarily serve both interstate and intrastate communications. We think the Commission has acted properly in this case by resolving the challenge to its jurisdiction and at the same time proceeding separately, as it has, to utilize the Joint Board procedure as an aid to sound resolution of interconnection problems that emerge in this period of developing technology and increasing demand.

It also is significant that for many years FCC, rejecting the argument that section 2(b)(1) deprives it of control over terminal facilities and equipment used in connection with both interstate and intrastate communications, has repeatedly exercised such jurisdiction. As early as 1947, FCC directed telephone companies to file tariff regulations that would permit the connection of recording devices to telephone receivers under specified conditions. *Use of Recording Devices*, 11 F.C.C. 1033. For present purposes the significant circumstance is that in its opinion the Commission discussed and rejected a contention of the Bell Systems that "facilities which are used for interstate and intrastate services are excluded from the Commission's jurisdiction as 'facilities . . . for or in connection with intrastate communication', as that term is used in Section 2(b)(1) of the Communications

---

commissions in proper determination. . . ." Hearings on H.R.8301 before the House Committee on Interstate and Foreign Commerce, 73d Cong., 2d Sess. 73.

In our view, the legislative history of the Act furnishes no impressive guidance for our determination of the reach of section 2(b). In any event, we are satisfied that it is not inconsistent with the view that the purpose of section 2(b) is to restrain the Commission from interfering with those essentially local incidents and practices of common carriage by wire that do not substantially encroach upon the administration and development of the interstate telephone network.

Act". 11 F.C.C. at 1046. A subsequent opinion pointed out that "[w]ere the Commission to exercise its jurisdiction only where the telephone facilities in question were exclusively interstate in character, it would result in virtually complete abdication from the field of telephone regulation. . . ." *Katz v. A.T.&T.,* 1953, 43 F.C.C.1328, 1332, 8 Pike & Fischer Radio Reg. 919, 923.

* * *

Congress cannot have been unaware that for some 30 years FCC has viewed and treated section 2(b)(1) of the Act as imposing no bar to its exercise of jurisdiction over facilities used in connection with both intrastate and interstate telephone communications. Significantly, it was as recently as 1971 that Congress amended the Act by adding the present section 410(c) with its discretionary Joint Federal-State Board procedure that already has been discussed. We think it likely that Congress would have taken quite different action to restrict the Commission's jurisdiction and assure state primacy if, in its view, the Commission had long and repeatedly been exceeding its jurisdiction and impinging upon an area which Congress had intended for exclusive state control.

. . . One additional contention merits brief discussion. Some of the petitioners argue that the Commission's action in this case violates a jurisdictional limitation imposed by section 221 of the Act which provides in part:

> (b) . . . [N]othing in this Act shall be construed . . . to give the Commission jurisdiction, with respect to charges, classifications, practices, services, facilities, or regulations for or in connection with wire . . . exchange service, . . . even though a portion of such exchange service constitutes interstate or foreign communication, in any case where such matters are subject to regulation by a State commission or by local governmental authority.

For present purposes it suffices to point out that the legislative history indicates that this restriction is intended to do no more than to prevent the circumstance that a single telephone exchange serves an area that includes parts of more than one state from enlarging the jurisdiction of FCC over the business and facilities of that exchange.[11] To put the matter affirmatively, by force of section 221(b) a local carrier that serves a single multi-state exchange area is assured whatever degree of freedom from federal regulation section 2(b) provides for uni-state carriers and intrastate telephone business generally.

In sum, all of the foregoing considerations make appropriate for this case Judge (now Chief Justice) Burger's admonition that the communications "Act must be construed in light of the needs for comprehensive regulation and the

---

11. Mr. Rayburn, presenting the 1934 bill on the floor of the House, explained that section 221(b) "is designed to cover cases of cities located within two States, as Texarkana". 78 Cong.Rec. 10314. Similarly, on the Senate floor, Senator Dill, explaining the reach of the amendment, cited the uncertain status of metropolitan Washington and New York areas as essentially local exchanges that crossed state lines. 78 Cong.Rec. 8823. The Committee reports in both the Senate and the House are explicit in saying that section 221(b) is intended to enable state commissions "to regulate exchange services in metropolitan areas overlapping State lines". S.Rep. No. 781, 73rd Cong. 2d Sess., 5; H.R.Rep. No. 1850, 73rd Cong., 2d Sess., 7.

practical difficulties inhering in state by state regulation of parts of an organic whole". *General Telephone Co. of California v. F.C.C.*, 1969, 134 U.S.App.D.C. 116, 413 F.2d 390, 398, *cert. denied,* 396 U.S. 888, 90 S.Ct. 173, 24 L.Ed.2d 163.

The Commission's Memorandum Opinion and Declaratory Order are sustained as reasonable administrative action within its statutory jurisdiction.

WIDENER, Circuit Judge (concurring and dissenting):

I respectfully dissent from that part of the court's opinion which determines that the FCC has primary jurisdiction over the interconnection of customer-provided equipment to the subscriber's telephone terminal. Should the statutory jurisdictional hurdle be overcome, I would concur in the balance of the opinion. . . . I submit the intent of Congress was to establish a regulatory scheme for telephone companies, which envisioned a system of *divided jurisdiction,* Federal *or* State, rather than a system of *primary jurisdiction,* Federal *then* State, and that the jurisdiction of the State regulatory authorities was intended to be regulated by Congress, not by the whim of the Federal Communications Commission. While the power of Congress to regulate commerce under the Constitution has not been doubted since *Gibbons v. Ogden,* 9 Wheat. 1, 6 L.Ed. 23 (1824), that opinion itself points out that Congress may entirely legitimately manifest ". . . an intention to leave this subject entirely to the States until Congress should think proper to interpose." 9 Wheat. at 208.

No more reason exists for a federal regulatory commission to assert jurisdiction it does not have than exists for a federal court to do so. It should have ". . . no more right to decline the exercise of jurisdiction which is given than to usurp that which is not given." *Cohens v. Virginia,* 6 Wheat. 264, 404, 5 L.Ed. 267 (1821). The FCC here not only, or even principally, usurps the regulatory authority of the States; it usurps the right of Congress to provide for regulatory jurisdiction.

While the opinion of the court may seem to relegate the precise question of the statutory jurisdiction of the FCC to almost an afterthought, I think it is the most important and very nearly the only issue of real consequence in the case. Jurisdiction carries with it the right to regulate revenue—not only the amount, but who gets it, and its source. Depriving the States of jurisdiction deprives them of the right to regulate, which in turn deprives them of the right to distribute the burden of telephone service among the various classes of customers. As a practical matter, this assertion of federal primacy necessarily and directly affects the intrastate rates which may be charged, jurisdiction of which could not be more clearly reserved to the States. The result we arrive at, then, I suggest was never dreamed of by Congress.

Today, we allow the FCC to regulate only a facility mentioned in the statute as reserved for State regulation, but by approving the principle, we establish precedent of affirming FCC regulation of those matters mentioned in § 221(b) as reserved to the States. No reason would then exist for the FCC not to regulate "charges, classifications, practices, [and] services," other matters specifically reserved for State regulation by the same statute, and it must now be taken as the law that any continued State regulation of "charges, classifications, practices, [and] services" is by grace of the Federal Communications Commission, not by act of Congress, for we have approved the principle of FCC assertion of primary jurisdiction.

Questions

1. Why did the FCC want to set the depreciation schedules in the *Louisiana* case? Why did the states oppose the FCC?

2. How do the concepts of jurisdiction and preemption differ? Why does the FCC's preemption argument fail in the *Louisiana* case? Why does it succeed in the *North Carolina* case?

3. Three weeks after *Louisiana PSC* was decided, the FCC issued an order retaining authority to preempt state regulation of "enhanced services" (i.e., those services not commonly considered basic telephone services) without considering the Supreme Court's opinion (*Third Computer Inquiry*, Report and Order, 60 R.R.2d 603 [1986]). A number of PUCs successfully challenged this effort at preemption (*California v. FCC*, 905 F.2d 1217 [9th Cir. 1990]). The Ninth Circuit Court of Appeals, however, may not have strictly followed the Supreme Court. It adopted a D.C. Circuit Court ruling that " 'a valid FCC preemption order must be limited to [state regulation] that would *necessarily* thwart or impede' the FCC's goals" and that the Commission must prove "*with some specificity* that [state regulation] would negate the federal policy" (emphasis added) (*Id.* at 1243, quoting *NARUC v. FCC*, 880 F.2d 422, 430 [D.C. Cir. 1989]. See Note, "*California v. FCC:* A Victory for the States," 13 *Hastings Communications/Entertainment Law Journal* 233 [1991]). What must the FCC show to prevail in the future?

For other preemption cases decided since *Louisiana PSC*, see *Hawaiian Tel. Co. v. Hawaii PUC*, 827 F.2d 1264 (9th Cir. 1987), *cert. denied*, 487 U.S. 1218 (1988) (FCC separations order preempts conflicting state separations order) and *NARUC v. FCC*, 880 F.2d 422 (D.C. Cir. 1989) (FCC failed to prove that state regulation of telephone inside wiring would negate a valid federal policy to promote a competitive inside wiring market). See also *PUC of Texas v. FCC*, 886 F.2d 1325 (D.C. Cir. 1989); *Illinois Bell Tel. Co. v. FCC*, 883 F.2d 104 (D.C. Cir. 1989); and *California v. FCC*, 798 F.2d 1515 (D.C. Cir. 1986). By and large, the *Louisiana* depreciation decision signaled a shift to greater state hegemony in communications policy. But where a national policy, rather than a testing of power, is at risk, the FCC can continue to expect to receive more deference.

4. What procedure is used to deal with tensions arising from dual state and federal regulation? What happens when interstate and intrastate components cannot be separated?

4

STATUTORY REQUIREMENTS: "JUST AND REASONABLE"; "UNREASONABLE DISCRIMINATION"

NADER v. FCC

520 F.2d 182 (D.C. Cir. 1975)

*   *   *

American Telephone & Telegraph Company, the world's largest utility, derives its interstate revenue from several classes of communication service; 80% is from message toll telephone service (MTS), in which the user dials his call or is assisted by an operator and pays for the service on a per-call basis. A variant of MTS, Wide Area Telephone Service (WATS), which allows the customer to make direct dialed telephone calls anywhere within a specified service area at monthly rates, accounts for approximately 7% of AT&T's interstate revenue. MTS and WATS are essentially monopoly services in which AT&T does not face competition.

The other 13% of AT&T's interstate revenue accrues from private line service, which can consist of telephone, telegraph, audio and video program transmission and data transmission services. These services provide the customer with continuous communication between fixed points without the necessity of establishing a new circuit for each message. Unlike MTS and WATS, several specialized carriers, including MCI, compete against AT&T in this part of the market.

In November 1970, AT&T filed tariffs designed to produce an additional $545 million in earnings before taxes and to increase AT&T's interstate rate of return to 9.5%.[2] The filing increased rates on its monopoly MTS and WATS services, but not on its competitive private line services. On January 12, 1971, the Commission requested AT&T to postpone the effective date of its proposed $545 million increase, and granted permission to file tariffs increasing net earnings before taxes to $250 million. AT&T agreed and substituted a tariff which increased MTS rates by $175 million and reduced costs by $75 million. Tariffs for private line services again remained unaffected.

---

2. AT&T estimated that the rate increases would yield $385 million and result in cost savings of $160 million. 27 F.C.C.2d 149, 152 (1971).

* * *

Thus, to recapitulate, when the Commission commenced its docket 19129 investigation into AT&T's November 1970 proposed increases, it set forth the following procedures: Phase I would determine whether AT&T was entitled to a rate of return higher than the 7–7.5% found reasonable in 1967; Phase II would determine how Western Electric's earnings would affect the Commission's revenue decision; and Docket 18128, composed in part of Phase IB of docket 16258, would adjudicate the question of rate relationships among the various classes of interstate services and the cross-subsidization issue. . . .

On November 22, 1972, the Commission issued its final decision on Phase I, holding that AT&T's overall minimum fair rate of return should be 8.5%. 38 F.C.C.2d at 245. The Commission reviewed AT&T's 1971 operating results and concluded that the utility required an additional $145 million in interim relief to achieve the 8.5% return. *Id.* at 249–51.[5] Based on these results, the Commission struck as unlawful AT&T's original tariff filing designed to raise $545 million and authorized it to submit new tariffs that would provide an additional $145 million. *Id.* at 251. The Commission cautioned that this interim rate increase should be subject to the same accounting and refund order as the original $250 million interim adjustment, and that it expected the increase to be "consistent with sound ratemaking principles. . . ." *Id.* at 246, 251.

* * *

Under the principle that a utility is entitled to rates that allow it, under honest, economical, and efficient management, to achieve a fair overall return, *e. g.,* *Bluefield Water Works & Improvement Co. v. Public Service Commission,* 262 U.S. 679, 692–95, 43 S.Ct. 675, 67 L.Ed. 1176 (1923), the Commission set out in Phase I of Docket 19129 to determine what AT&T's rate of return on its interstate investment should be. Essentially, AT&T's rate of return is a composite of the return on the two components of AT&T's investment—debt and stockholder's equity. The Commission found that AT&T's cost of debt was 6.0% and that the cost of raising equity capital (the fair return on equity) was 10.5%. Finding that AT&T's capital structure consisted of 45% debt and 55% equity, the Commission arrived at an overall 8.5% rate of return through the following simple formula:

Item	Proportion of Capital (percent)	Cost Rate (percent)	Proportion of Total Cost (percent)
Debt	45	6.0	2.70
Total Equity	55	10.5	5.78

---

5. While the Commission authorized AT&T to file tariffs designed to achieve a return of 8.5%, the Commission established a range above this level—8.5–9%—which would not prompt a regulatory response. The Commission's goal was to thereby encourage AT&T to improve its efficiency and productivity. 38 F.C.C.2d 213, 245–46 (1972)

Total Cost (including convertible preferred)	8.48
Use	8.5

*   *   *

Since the Phase I rate of return investigation is an integral part of the investigation of AT&T's rates and charges, the Commission's responsibility is to determine what rate of return is "just and reasonable." 47 U.S.C. §§ 204, 205 (1970). In making this determination, there is a "zone of reasonableness" within which the Commission's determination must be upheld. *Permian Basin Area Rate Cases*, 390 U.S. 747, 767, 88 S.Ct. 1344, 20 L.Ed.2d 312 (1968), *citing FPC v. Natural Gas Pipeline Co.*, 315 U.S. 575, 585, 62 S.Ct. 736, 86 L.Ed. 1037 (1942). Consequently, a party who seeks to set aside such an order "carries the heavy burden of making a convincing showing that it is invalid because it is unjust and unreasonable in its consequences." *FPC v. Hope Natural Gas Co.*, 320 U.S. 591, 602, 64 S.Ct. 281, 288, 88 L.Ed. 333 (1944). Our function is not to impose our own standards of reasonableness upon the Commission, but rather to ensure that the Commission's order is supported by substantial record evidence and is neither arbitrary, capricious, nor an abuse of discretion. *See* 5 U.S.C. § 706(A), (E) (1970); *Goodman v. Public Service Commission*, 162 U.S.App.D.C. 74, 497 F.2d 661 (1974).

III. The Issues in No. 73–2051

Petitioner in 73–2051, Microwave Communications, Inc. does not challenge the validity of the Commission's rate-of-return determination in Phase I of Docket 19129. Rather, MCI, in a singularly unenlightening brief virtually devoid of authority, apparently complains that the Commission violated sections 204 and 205 of the Federal Communications Act, 47 U.S.C. §§ 204, 205 (1970), and abused its procedural discretion by allowing AT&T to implement the Phase I decision solely through increased rates for its monopoly MTS and WATS services. A brief review of the statutory scheme is necessary in order fully to comprehend the import of MCI's contention.

The common carrier provisions of the Federal Communications Act, as other regulatory agency statutes, place primary responsibility for initiating rate revisions upon the carrier, who must provide at least thirty days notice to the Commission and to the public and such information as the Commission may require. 47 U.S.C. § 203. Whenever a carrier initiates a tariff revision, the Commission, upon a complaint or on its own motion, may suspend the tariff for a maximum of three months while it investigates its lawfulness. 47 U.S.C. § 204. With respect to a validly filed carrier-initiated tariff revision, the Commission is not vested with any suspension power other than the three month provision of section 204. *See AT&T v. FCC*, 487 F.2d 864, 876–81 (2d Cir. 1973). If the Commission has not completed its investigation by the end of the suspension period, the tariffs become effective; but the Commission may make the increases subject to an accounting and refund order. Once the Commission has properly exercised the limits of its suspension power, the courts cannot further enjoin the effectiveness of the tariff. *See, e. g., United States v. SCRAP,* 412 U.S. 669, 697–98, 93 S.Ct. 2405, 37 L.Ed.2d 254 (1973).

Under section 204, the carrier has the burden of proving that the rates or practices being investigated are "just and reasonable." If, "after full opportunity for hearing," the Commission finds that the rates are not just and reasonable, 205(a) authorizes it "to determine and prescribe what will be the just and reasonable charge or the maximum or minimum, or maximum and minimum, charge or charges to be thereafter observed." Thereafter, the carrier may not "publish, demand, or collect any charge other than the charge so prescribed. . . ." 47 U.S.C. § 205. Rates prescribed by the Commission may be invalidated by the courts. *See, e. g., AT&T v. FCC, supra; Moss v. CAB,* 139 U.S.App.D.C. 150, 430 F.2d 891 (1970).

At the outset, we are confronted by MCI's apparent confusion over the scope of the Commission's and our authorities. MCI maintains that this court must enter a decree instructing the Commission to order AT&T to refund all rate increases collected since November 22, 1973, because AT&T has failed to carry its burden of proving that increasing rates solely for MTS and WATS was just and reasonable under section 204. *See* MCI's Br. at 55–56. However, section 204 applies only to carrier-initiated rate revisions; until the Commission has determined that a rate is not just and reasonable, its only recourse is to suspend the tariff for up to three months and to impose an accounting and refund order. *See, e. g., AT&T v. FCC, supra,* 487 F.2d at 872–73. Since this court cannot order the Commission to act in a manner contrary to the statutory scheme, even if we concluded that the Commission had somehow violated section 204 or had otherwise abused its discretion, we could only order the Commission to reopen its hearings; the rate increases would remain in effect until the Commission determined whether they were just and reasonable.

Moreover, we must reject any contentions based on section 204. The Commission has stated that AT&T has the burden of proving in Docket 18128 that its competitive services are not being cross-subsidized by its monopoly services. 27 F.C.C.2d at 155–56. As we have previously indicated, Docket 18128 is an exhaustive investigation into the ratemaking principles that should be applied in determining the rate relationships among the various classes of services that AT&T provides. By saying that AT&T has not met its burden in Docket 19129, MCI implies that Docket 18128 must be duplicated in Phase I to satisfy the statute. There is absolutely no merit to this contention. In effect, if MCI is relying on section 204, its objection is little more than a complaint concerning the Commission's procedures for disposing of its caseload. We have already recognized the great discretion afforded the Commission in its efforts to adjudicate complex issues. We do not detect any abuse of discretion or violation of section 204 in the Commission's decision to adjudicate the cross-subsidization issue in Docket 18128.

*   *   *

These cases and numerous others recognize that ratemaking is a complex and difficult task. Under the cost-of-service method of rate regulation applied here, not only must the Commission determine the allowable rate of return, but it must also determine whether: 1) the utility's investment is properly calculated and efficiently incurred; 2) the level of cash expenses is honestly, efficiently, and economically incurred; 3) the level of noncash expenses such as depreciation and other accruals is properly reflected in the rate calculation; and 4) the rates proposed or in effect actually cover these costs and produce a fair rate of return. *See generally, J. Bonbright, Principles of Public Utility Rates, supra,* 66–108. Additionally, the Commission must see that the rates themselves are not unjustly or unreasonably discriminatory.

Obviously, reaching a decision on each of the components that make up a rate is a time-consuming task, especially when the Commission undertakes to reevaluate the economic principles for making these determinations. If the Commission can effectuate its decision as it adjudicates each component of the rate, the public more rapidly receives the benefit of the protection inherent in the Commission's authorization to prescribe just and reasonable charges. Therefore, we believe that the Commission's Phase I order prescribing AT&T's rate of return was in the public interest, necessary for the Commission to carry out its functions in an expeditious manner, and within its section 4(i) authority.

Moreover, we do not believe that this conclusion is at all inconsistent with section 205 or any other provision of the Federal Communications Act. Clearly, there is no explicit statutory prohibition against prescribing a rate of return. Additionally, since the rate of return is one component of a charge, and the charges prescribed must properly reflect the allowable rate of return, the prescription of a rate of return is fully consistent with the prescription of charges. *Compare AT&T v. FCC, supra.* These factors convince us that within the power to prescribe charges is the power to determine and prescribe those elements that make up the charge.

The essential elements of a valid prescription order are a full opportunity to be heard and a finding that the action taken is just and reasonable. *AT&T v. FCC, supra,* 487 F.2d at 874, *quoting AT&T v. FCC, supra,* 449 F.2d at 450. There can be no doubt that AT&T had a full hearing on the rate-of-return issue and has not appealed that determination. Additionally, although the Commission did not use the just and reasonable terminology, it found that 8.5% was AT&T's "fair rate of return," 38 F.C.C.2d at 245, which to the Commission meant:

> the minimum required by Bell to enable it to attract capital at a reasonable cost and to maintain the credit of Bell; and to assure continued, adequate and safe interstate and foreign communications service to the public. . . .

Id. We think that this is the equivalent of just and reasonable.

ABC v. FCC

663 F.2d 133 (D.C. Cir. 1980)

TAMM, Circuit Judge:

*   *   *

This case involves AT&T's Transmittal No. 12793 to FCC Tariff No. 260, Series 7000 local channel and Type 7001 interexchange channel and station connection television service. This service offers one directional channel service to distributors of television programming. The service consists of three basic elements: local channels (television loops), which connect the point of program origination (e. g., television studio or sports stadium) to an AT&T television operating center (TOC); interexchange channels (IXC), which link the TOCs; and station connections, which transmit the signal from TOCs to local stations for broadcast to viewers.[2]

AT&T has offered two service categories from the beginning of the transmission service in 1948. Originally, customers could opt for either a monthly service in which they purchased at prescribed rates a minimum of eight hours service each day or the hourly occasional service with charges computed based on the amount of time purchased. In 1973, upon Commission acceptance of a stipulated tariff structure, *see American Telephone & Telegraph Co.*, 44 F.C.C.2d 525 (1973), AT&T changed the categories, giving purchasers the option of buying 24-hour "full-time" service for a minimum period of a month or using the occasional (now called "part-time") hourly rates.

In 1977, in response to Commission directives concerning cost principles, *see American Telephone & Telegraph Co.*, 61 F.C.C.2d 587 (1976) [hereinafter cited as *Docket 18128*], *aff'd in part and vacated in part sub nom. Aeronautical Radio, Inc. v. FCC*, No. 77–1333 (D.C.Cir. June 24, 1980), AT&T filed Transmittal 12793 to its Series 7000 tariff schedules. The filing retained the same basic categories that had been established in 1973 but extended to one year the minimum period for full-time service. The tariff also raised prices sharply for part-time service and both raised and lowered full-time rates. AT&T believed that the filing "provide[s] structures and rate levels which more closely reflect the costs incurred in the provision of full-time and part-time television services and . . . improve[s] the revenue/cost relationship for the total service category. Moreover, it is designed to meet the requirements of [*Docket 18128*]." Letter from W. E. Albert, AT&T, to Secretary, FCC, at 2 (Aug. 1, 1977) (Cover letter to Transmittal 12793). AT&T filed thirteen volumes of supporting cost data.

The major networks supported the filing. As users of the full-time service, they would benefit from the lower tariffs. Others were less satisfied. Independent television stations, sports networks, and other users of part-time service urged the Commission to reject the tariff. They objected violently to the proposed tariffs because their costs would increase substantially.

The Commission rejected the tariff, citing seven independent deficiencies in the filing. *American Telephone & Telegraph Co.*, 67 F.C.C.2d 1134 (1978). The Commission found that AT&T's full- and part-time service categories are "like communication services" within the meaning of section 202(a) of the Commu-

---

2. An example here may be helpful: if a station is broadcasting a football game in Dallas to viewers in Washington, D. C., the television signals would be transmitted via local channels from the stadium to the area TOC, via the IXC network from Dallas to Washington, and via station connections from the Washington IXC to the station that broadcasts the game to local fans.

nications Act, 47 U.S.C. § 202(a) (1976).[5] AT&T thus had the burden of introducing cost data to justify the differences in rates. The Commission rejected the tariff because AT&T did not offer the necessary data.

. . . Two independent findings supported the Commission's decision that AT&T's service categories are "like communication services." First, the Commission held that continued use of these categories violated its decision in *Sports Network inc. v. American Telephone & Telegraph Co.*, 25 F.C.C.2d 560 (1968), *aff'd sub nom. Hughes Sports Network, Inc. v. American Telephone & Telegraph Co.*, 25 F.C.C.2d 550 (Rev.Bd.1970), *aff'd*, 34 F.C.C.2d 691 (1972) [hereinafter cited as *SNI*]. In that case, the Hearing Examiner found that the monthly and occasional interexchange channels were like services whose rate structure was unduly discriminatory under 47 U.S.C. § 202(a). Second, the Commission determined that full- and part-time services were not "different in any material functional respect." *American Trucking Associations, Inc. v. FCC*, 377 F.2d 121, 127 (D.C.Cir. 1966), *cert. denied*, 386 U.S. 943, 87 S.Ct. 973, 17 L.Ed.2d 874 (1967). This finding of functional equivalency requires a proponent of two services to justify any difference in costs for those services.

*   *   *

Petitioners claim that the Commission erred in using the functional equivalency test in determining whether full- and part-time services are "like." They assert that this standard is vague and inconsistent with criteria used in other Commission decisions. Furthermore, they point to various factors mentioned in similar decisions made by other governmental agencies and allegedly ignored by the Commission and contend that this relevant information would have been available to the Commission had it held a hearing on the question. We believe that the functional equivalency test is a proper criterion for likeness, that the proceeding before the Commission produced adequate airing of the relevant factors, and that the Commission's determination of likeness under this test is supported by substantial evidence.

. . . Section 202(a) prohibits "unjust or unreasonable discrimination in charges" in the provision of "like communication services." 47 U.S.C. § 202(a). Under this provision, the Commission first determines whether the services are "like." This question is decided on a case-by-case basis. *Western Union International, Inc. v. FCC*, 568 F.2d 1012, 1018 n.11 (2d Cir. 1977), *cert. denied*, 436 U.S. 944, 98 S.Ct. 299, 56 L.Ed.2d 785 (1978); *American Telephone & Telegraph Co. (WATS)*, 70 F.C.C.2d 593, 613–14 (1978).

. . . A standard means for determining "likeness" is the functional equivalency test. Under this test as developed by the Commission, the inquiry centers on whether the services are "different in any material functional respect." *American Trucking Associations, Inc. v. FCC*, 377 F.2d 121, 127 (D.C.Cir. 1966), *cert. denied*, 386 U.S. 943, 87 S.Ct. 973, 17 L.Ed.2d 874 (1967). The test looks to the nature

---

5. This provision states in relevant part: "It shall be unlawful for any common carrier to make any unjust or unreasonable discrimination in charges, practices, classifications, regulations, facilities, or services for or in connection with like communication service, directly or indirectly, by any means or device . . ." 47 U.S.C. § 202(a) (1976).

of the services offered to determine likeness; the perspective of the customer faced with differing services is often considered a significant factor. *See American Telephone & Telegraph Co. (WATS)*, 70 F.C.C.2d 593, 609 & 614 (1978).

. . . Despite petitioners' assertions, the functional equivalency test includes the proper elements necessary for making a determination of likeness under section 202(a). By looking to the nature and character of the services in question, the test focuses the initial inquiry under section 202(a) on the similarity of the services. Considerations of cost differentials and competitive necessity are properly excluded and introduced only when determining whether the discrimination is unreasonable or unjust. *See Western Union International, Inc. v. FCC*, 568 F.2d 1012, 1029 n.15 (2d Cir.1977), *cert. denied*, 436 U.S. 944, 98 S.Ct. 2854, 56 L.Ed.2d 785 (1978).

Having found the functional equivalency test to be the proper standard, we further believe the Commission had substantial evidence to support its finding. The Commission noted that "[i]t is apparent from an examination of the face of AT&T's tariff and this filing that full time and part time users receive the identical transmission service."[13] *American Telephone & Telegraph Co.*, 67 F.C.C.2d 1134, 1167 (1978). The Commission found, and AT&T conceded, that customers regarded the full- and part-time service as the same, with cost considerations being the sole determining criterion. *Id.* Moreover, cost was the only reason some major customers such as the networks preferred full-time service. Indeed, the substantial use of the part-time service by the networks demonstrated that they believed the services to be functionally equivalent. *Id.* at 1168.

We find this evidence substantially supports the Commission's view that the services are functionally equivalent. Customers apparently view the two services as the same, making their decisions about service solely on the basis of price. This customer perception, in conjunction with petitioners' failure to demonstrate that the two services in fact satisfy different communications requirements, provides substantial support for the Commission's determination that the services are like.

Having made this showing, the Commission shifted the burden to AT&T to justify the discrimination. In a decision not on review before this court, the Commission found that AT&T did not meet this burden. It therefore rejected the tariff on this ground

* * *

AT&T must now submit a new tariff for its Series 7000 service. The ruling in this proceeding in no way prohibits AT&T from maintaining its present part- and full-time service categories. It must now demonstrate, however, in the new filing that the discrimination between these categories is not unjust or unreasonable under 47 U.S.C. § 202(a) (1976).

---

13. Petitioners argue that part-time and full-time service users do not receive identical service because each service category has its own "dedicated" facilities. This argument misses the point; both categories offer the exact same service, albeit over differently dedicated facilities. The dedication argument is relevant in determining whether the discrimination is unjust or unreasonable.

AD HOC TELECOMMUNICATIONS USERS COMMITTEE v. FCC

680 F.2d 690 (D.C. Cir. 1982)

GINSBURG, Circuit Judge:

Petitioners and intervenors in this case provide, use or are otherwise interested in the availability of long distance telephone services known as Outward WATS and Inward WATS. They challenge a Federal Communications Commission (FCC or Commission) decision that each of these WATS services is "like" ordinary long distance telephone service for purposes of 47 U.S.C. § 202(a), which prohibits unjust or unreasonable discrimination in charges "for or in connection with like communication service." The Commission emphasizes that its determination does not mandate elimination or alteration of WATS services. Rather, the FCC explains, if its decision is affirmed, "any rate discrimination or preference between [WATS and ordinary long distance service] must be clearly shown to be justified in accordance with applicable Commission rules and orders, and if not, the discrimination or preference must be eliminated." Petitioners and intervenors contend that, in making the "likeness" determination at issue, and adhering to it on reconsideration, the Commission failed to apply any ascertainable standard. They further assert that, in face of overwhelming record evidence to the contrary, the FCC's decision characterizing WATS and ordinary long distance as "like service[s]" was arbitrary and capricious.

The Commission purported to apply its judicially-approved "functional equivalency" test in arriving at the "likeness" determination before us for review. But the Commission's explanation slips from the grasp and, in the shape presented to us, does not satisfy the demands of cogent decisionmaking. Because the "functional equivalency" test is an important, still-evolving Commission approach, we do not believe it appropriate to cut off at this juncture the FCC's opportunity to define comprehensibly the path it is taking. Accordingly, we vacate the Commission's orders and remand for a more precise determination of the "likeness" *vel non* of the services at issue.

I.

The American Telephone and Telegraph Company (AT&T) operates a nationwide telecommunications system and offers several forms of long distance communication including ordinary long distance service and two distinct WATS services. Long Distance Message Telecommunications Service (MTS) is the familiar nationwide long distance service. It has two-way capability (placing and receiving calls) and may be accessed from almost any telephone at any time. It provides virtually world-wide service. Operator assistance is available for special service features, including collect, credit card, conference, person-to-person, and third-party-billed calls. Subscribers are provided a detailed bill which itemizes the charges for each call period.

Wide Area Telecommunications Service (WATS), on the other hand, is a one-way-only calling or receiving service covering specified geographical areas. The WATS services in question are of two kinds: Outward WATS and Inward WATS (the latter commonly called "800" Service).

Outward WATS, first introduced in 1961, permits high-volume users to place direct-dialed calls anywhere within a designated service area at a fixed monthly rate. Outward WATS calls proceed over a unidirectional access line from the subscriber's phone to a specifically equipped WATS central office. At this location the calls are switched onto the interstate long distance telephone network, known as the public switched network, the same network over which regular long distance calls travel. At the WATS central office a screening and blocking function occurs which accepts only calls to the designated geographic area covered by the subscription. Outward WATS customers subscribe to coverage selected from among five service areas within the United States, none of which includes the subscriber's home state.[3] These areas may be viewed as five concentric circles of increasing size. The larger the size of the service area selected, the higher the rate charged.

Inward WATS (800 Service), first introduced in 1967, operates in a manner essentially the reverse of Outward WATS. It permits the subscriber to receive direct-dialed calls, originating from within the selected service area, on a collect basis at a fixed monthly rate. Inward WATS calls first traverse the public switched network and then are blocked and screened at the terminating WATS office serving the subscriber. Inward WATS also requires the use of separate access lines to carry the calls from the central office to the subscriber. The special WATS access lines cannot be used for placing or receiving any other type of calls.

The fixed monthly fees for both WATS services are prepaid. If WATS services of either character are used in excess of the time periods paid for, additional charges are billed. The itemized billing statement characteristic of MTS is not a feature of either WATS service.

On September 26, 1977, the Commission released a Notice of Inquiry in which it solicited comments on the question whether Outward WATS or Inward WATS constitutes service "like" MTS within the meaning of section 202(a). *American Telephone & Telegraph Co. (WATS)*, 66 F.C.C.2d 224, 226 (1977) (*Notice of Inquiry*). The Commission also solicited comments on the specific standards or criteria it should rely upon in making "likeness" determinations. *Id.* After evaluating the numerous responses received, the Commission discarded differences in service it deemed "irrelevant" and concluded that both WATS services are "like" MTS for section 202(a) purposes. *American Telephone & Telegraph Co. (WATS)*, 70 F.C.C.2d 593 (1978) (*Like Services Decision*).

The Commission stated that, in reaching its decision, it employed the "functional equivalency" test, which focuses on whether the services under consideration differ in any material functional respect. *Id.* at 604. The FCC concluded here that "no difference exists between the services in terms of [the] communication functions performed for the subscriber." *Id.* at 605. The Commission

---

3. Intrastate WATS service is generally available for subscribers whose intrastate toll calling volumes warrant such subscription. *See id.* at 595 n.4.

asserted that it arrived at this conclusion after examining, through review of comments submitted by subscribers, customer perception of the various services, which the FCC "believe[s] to be a major test of functional equivalency." *Id.* at 609 (footnote omitted). The Commission also pointed to the undisputed fact that the transmission of MTS and WATS calls from end-to-end within the public switched network is essentially identical. *Id.* at 605. Based on its "like service" finding, the FCC ordered AT&T either to demonstrate the lawfulness of its discriminatory charges or to eliminate them. *Id.* at 614–15.

On July 15, 1980, the Commission released a Memorandum Opinion and Order in *American Telephone & Telegraph Co. (WATS),* 79 F.C.C.2d 10 (1980) (*Like Services Reconsideration*), denying petitions for reconsideration of the *Like Services Decision.* The Commission reaffirmed its position that both WATS services are functionally equivalent to MTS service because they use the same interstate network and "offer the same telephone calling capability from the standpoint of the customer." *Id.* at 12. the Commission also responded to the charge that its "likeness" finding with respect to WATS and MTS conflicted with its earlier determination in *American Telephone & Telegraph Co.,* 59 F.C.C.2d 671 (1976), *recon.,* 64 F.C.C.2d 538 (1977), that Inward and Outward WATS were not like services. The two inquiries were discrete, the FCC maintains. The earlier ruling occurred in the context of a section 201(b) just and reasonable rate determination. There, the Commission made no section 202(a) "like service" determination. It did not compare WATS and MTS; it found only that "Inward and Outward WATS, as offered by AT&T, were different service classifications" which must be cost-justified and priced independently. 79 F.C.C.2d at 13.

II.

Court opinions have consistently recognized that the "functional equivalency" test is an appropriate method for determining "likeness" within the meaning of Section 202(a). . . . This test, initially stated and developed by the Commission, focuses on whether the services in question are "different in any material functional respect." *American Broadcasting Cos.,* 663 F.2d at 138; *American Trucking Associations,* 377 F.2d at 127. "The test looks to the nature of the services offered to determine likeness; the perspective of the customer faced with differing services is often considered a significant factor." *American Broadcasting Cos.,* 663 F.2d at 139.

The Commission here, purporting to apply the functional equivalency test, determined that both Outward WATS and Inward WATS are services "like" MTS. In reaching this conclusion, the FCC relied dominantly on its view of customer perception of the three services and on transmission technology. The Commission did not separately apply the functional equivalency test to compare Outward WATS and MTS on the one hand, and Inward WATS and MTS on the other. Rather, the FCC, in this proceeding, essentially lumped together Outward and Inward WATS and swiftly declared WATS and MTS functional equivalents. But the failure to attempt distinct comparisons of each WATS service with MTS is not easily reconciled with the Commission's prior determination that Inward and Outward WATS "are functionally different and . . . serve different subscriber communication needs." *American Telephone & Telegraph Co.,* 59 F.C.C.2d at 685;

see supra note 4. And it is far from apparent that users' perceptions support the FCC's blending of the two distinct WATS services. It may be that the Commission settled for blurred analysis because it was reaching for more than a clearly focused "like service" determination would permit it to achieve.

In remanding this proceeding to the Commission, we affirm our prior declarations that the functional equivalency test, with customer perception as a linchpin, is an appropriate standard for determining section 202(a) "likeness." Recognizing that it is the Commission's responsibility to elaborate the functional equivalency test, we state these few guides for sharpened analysis. First, the Commission should not blend discrete services in its application of the test. Second, the perceptions of users of each service under examination should be evaluated. Finally, alleged differences in the services compared should be considered. The Commission may well conclude, after consideration, that particular differences do not bear on "functional equivalency," but it should state comprehensively the reasoning upon which it relies to discard a difference as "irrelevant."

III.

Without attempting further suggestion of the inquiry and analysis the Commission might pursue on remand, we note some problematic facets of the opinion concurring in the result. That opinion initially embraces the functional equivalency test, then proceeds to define it virtually out of existence. Despite faint qualifications here and there, the opinion concurring in the result maintains that two services are not "like" unless they are, for all practical purposes, "identical." We are told, with the aid of Webster's, that there will be no "equivalency" unless "two things are 'identical.'" Concurring op. at 801. But emphasis on equivalence in derogation of function misses the mark. The focus of the test should be practical, oriented to customers: what function or need do customers perceive to be satisfied by the services under examination? If customers perceive that two services perform the same function, price will govern choice. Sensibly, the functional equivalency test should be allowed to yield a determination that these services are "like," whether or not they are "identical," and we so hold.

In elaborating its notion of the "functional equivalency" test, the opinion concurring in the result tenders a subset analysis as a central element. It suggests that if one service is only a subset of the other, the two are not readily classified as "functionally equivalent," or "like." For, "in order to be functionally equivalent, the two services must possess virtually all the same qualities of (and be capable of being employed for the same uses as) the other while neither possesses significant qualities (or uses) the other lacks." Concurring op. at 804. Applying this analysis to the instant case, the opinion concurring in the result indicates that because WATS service cannot do everything MTS is able to do, neither WATS service can be "like" MTS. *Id.* at 804–805.

The proffered subset analysis turns sharply away from our Circuit's most recent precedent in point. In *American Broadcasting Cos.*, this court, approving the FCC's functional equivalency determination, upheld a Commission decision that AT&T's full- and part-time television broadcast service categories were "like communication service" under section 202(a). Plainly, part-time video transmission service is a subset of full-time service, and the opinion concurring in the result so acknowledges. Concurring op. at 805. Equally beyond debate, a full-time service user could not substitute part-time service and receive the same "package of benefits, rights, restrictions, duties, facilities and services . . ." *See id.* at 804. Since the opinion concurring in the result would hold that the word "service" as it is used in section 202(a) means "entire package," and nothing less, and generally describes subsets as unlike the larger package, we find the tendered analysis dissonant with *American Broadcasting Cos.* Our decision, in contrast, like the one in *American Broadcasting Cos.*, continues genuine approval of the Commission's "functional equivalency" test and allows for further development and refinement of the Commission's approach to "like service" determinations.

Conclusion

Because the Commission has not adequately explained why it determined that, in the context of 47 U.S.C. § 202(a), both Outward WATS and Inward WATS provide communication service "like" MTS and, particularly, has not clarified a critical concept it claims to employ—customer perception of functional equivalency—we vacate the orders on review and remand for such further proceedings, consistent with this opinion, as the Commission may wish to pursue.

It is so ordered.

QUESTIONS

1. Who has the burden or proving that rates are "just and reasonable" under §204? If the FCC determines that certain rates do not meet the "just and reasonable" standard, may the FCC prescribe its own rate schedule? Are rates subject to court review? See §205.

2. In *Nader*, where does the court find the FCC's authority to prescribe an allowable rate of return? What factors must the FCC consider in determining the rate of return?

3. Why did the court say that MCI was confused in *Nader?*

4. In *NARUC v. FCC*, 737 F.2d 1095 (D.C. Cir. 1984), the court held that the Commission's decision to recover non–traffic-sensitive costs from carriers on a usage-sensitive basis was not inherently discriminatory under §202(a). Does the language of §202 grant the FCC this type of discretion?

5. How does the Commission determine whether tariffed services are "like communications services" for the purposes of §202(a)? What factors does the test consider? If the Commission finds that services are "like," is the carrier banned from discriminatory pricing of those services?

6. Why did the court remand the FCC's "likeness" determination in the *Ad Hoc Telecommunications Users* decision? Should the FCC be required to compare Inward WATS and Outward WATS separately with MTS? What should be the result under the functional equivalency test?

7. The FCC decided to abandon the administrative approach and adopt a market-based strategy to determine whether WATS was merely a form of market segmentation and price discrimination. The Commission ordered AT&T to eliminate the resale restrictions in its WATS and MTS tariffs, thus creating a potential arbitrage opportunity for resellers. If WATS was really just volume-discounted MTS, then resellers could purchase WATS lines and use them to resell MTS-like services. Their profits would be the price gap between AT&T's WATS and MTS services. In response to the ruling, AT&T raised its WATS rates. The increase, however, was constrained by AT&T's fear that it would alienate its largest customers. As a result, arbitrage opportunities remained and were exploited by a number of resellers such as Allnet. MCI and Sprint also took advantage of the price gap and leased WATS lines to expand their networks into areas they had not previously served. How do resellers operate to constrain the prices of AT&T?

8. How does the FCC attempt to justify its prior determination that Inward and Outward WATS are not "like" services in the *Ad Hoc* case? Is this convincing? Must "like" services be virtually identical?

9. In its *Tariff FCC No. 12*, AT&T attempted to offer integrated service packages of different, individually tariffed services. The services and the amount of the package were to be arrived at through negotiation between AT&T and its customers, each of which is a large corporation. The package rate was lower than the price the customer would pay if it purchased each service separately. AT&T's prices matched the offerings of nondominant carriers. The FCC declared the initial tariffs unlawful but allowed refiled tariffs to go into effect. On review, the Court of Appeals for the D.C. Circuit remanded the FCC's summary analysis but concluded that the "FCC (one way or another) will undoubtedly permit AT&T to compete effectively against its competitors in the large user market" (*MCI Telecommunications Corp. v. FCC*, 917 F.2d 30 [D.C. Cir. 1990]). And it held that AT&T could formulate a proposed tariff based on negotiations with a potential customer. But price differences must not be the basis for declaring services "unlike," concluded the court, "otherwise, the very discrimination Section 202 attempts to prevent would be the grounds for finding that section inapplicable." Do you agree that "unlike" prices is not a fair basis for discrimination?

10. Today, most national television programming is carried via satellite. Supposing satellite operators were subject to Title II regulation—would such an operator be bound by the "likeness" determination made in *ABC v. FCC*? Do you think competition between terrestrial carriers and satellite carriers would diminish the need for the ban on discriminatory pricing?

11. Consider these hypotheticals; which cases support your result? Will the FCC be able to preempt state regulation in cases 1–2? Do the activities proposed in cases 3–6 violate Title II?

1. A state PUC wants to regulate office switchboard equipment.

2. A state wants to regulate the depreciation rate of desks used by operators to assist with interstate and intrastate calls.
3. AT&T wants to give a 10 percent discount rate to UCLA if the school agrees to place all its long-distance calls with AT&T.
4. AT&T refuses to allow a dormitory to have an Outward WATS line because of sharing.
5. Calling Plan Z–100 offers 10 percent off Inward WATS (800) service for nonprofit corporations.
6. Plan A, a subset of Plan A–100, offers part-time data transmission flow. A100 is a full-time data transmission network.

5

DOMINANT/NONDOMINANT CARRIERS; FORBEARANCE

THE COMPETITIVE CARRIER PROCEEDING

In a series of decisions beginning in 1979, the FCC reinterpreted congressional intent underlying the Communications Act in light of the structure of the modern telecommunications industry, giving less consideration to traditional statutory or common law definitions of common carriers. Instead, the FCC focused on a firm's competitive impact on its relevant market as the factor determining whether or not to regulate.

In *Competitive Common Carrier Service*, First Report and Order, 85 F.C.C.2d 1 (1980) (*First Report*), the Commission classified carriers in terms of "market power"—that is, each firm's ability to restrict output and increase unit price above cost, or artificially below cost, in its market. The FCC defined firms exerting market power as "dominant carriers," subjecting them to full regulation under Titles II and III of the act.

The *First Report* classified firms capable of exerting limited or no market power as "nondominant carriers" and subjected them to streamlined regulation or, in some instances, no regulatory controls. Nondominant carriers were required to file only limited tariff schedules, and these schedules were held to be presumed lawful until successfully challenged. Any competitor challenging the nondominant firm's tariff was required to demonstrate competitive injury greater than the harm to the public from the loss of the offending service. Why did the FCC approve lighter regulation of nondominant carriers? It found that market forces sufficed to keep prices, terms, and conditions within the statutory requirements of "just, reasonable, and nondiscriminatory."

It also held that the focus of the Commission's inquiry should not be on the business functions of the firm, as had been the case under the earlier statutory analysis and at common law, but rather on the firm's ability to exert market power, which requires an economic analysis. A nondominant common carrier could fit within the statutory and common law concept of a common carrier, but if it exerted no market power, it would not be subject to full FCC regulation.

COMPETITIVE CARRIER RULEMAKING, FIRST REPORT AND ORDER

85 F.C.C.2d 1 (1980)

*   *   *

The policies we now adopt were initially proposed in our *Notice of Inquiry and Proposed Rulemaking*, 77 F.C.C.2d 308 (1979) (hereafter *Notice*), in which we proposed to modify our rules to reflect changes in the industry over the last decade. We stated that with the emergence of many competitive telecommunications firms a new approach to reflect the nature of such firms would allow these companies and the overall telecommunications industry to satisfy consumer demands more effectively than the undifferentiated set of rules theretofore applied.

The proposals in the *Notice* emanated from two basic principles. First, in order to retain business with prices above total costs a firm must possess market power and some firms in this industry do not. Similarly, in order to recoup losses incurred by pricing below costs, either immediately or even over the long term, market power is also required. Indeed, market power is often defined as the ability to maintain prices at levels unrelated to the costs of the good or service in question.

Second, enforcement of a system of regulation of business conduct imposes costs. These costs can be identified in two classes. There are the less significant administrative costs of compiling, maintaining, and distributing information necessary to comply with agency licensing and reporting requirements. More significant costs, however, are inflicted on society by the loss of dynamism which can result from regulation. Indeed, regulation sometimes creates what can only be called perverse incentives for the regulated firms.

The Averch-Johnson effect, *i.e.*, rate of return regulation creates incentives that may distort the input choices of a regulated firm away from production at minimum cost, is one example.[7] The filing of public tariffs is another. Effective competition is clearly curtailed when firms are required to give advance notice of innovative marketing plans and have those initiatives be subject to public comment and regulatory review. . . . The posting of prices and the legal obligation to refrain from "unjust or unreasonable discrimination," 47 U.S.C. §202(a), may result as well in artificially stabilizing prices to the consumer's eventual disadvantage.

The initial set of proposals contained in the *Notice* were directed only toward reducing, but not eliminating these costs. We examined the application of the rules under review to determine whether these costs were outweighed by benefits accruing to the public from their continuation. We found that some firms did not possess the economic attributes which appear necessary to engage in the conduct the rules were designed to help prevent.

---

7. H. Averch and L. Johnson "Behavior of a Firm under Regulatory Constraint," 52 *American Economic Review*, 1053–69, (Dec. 1962).

Recognizing that the industry to which our rules have been applied had changed, we reevaluated the appropriateness of continuing the same regulatory program developed under different circumstances. We tentatively concluded that our system of regulation imposed significant costs on carriers and their customers, which in the case of some firms were not outweighed by their benefits. We therefore proposed to eliminate certain of these rules imposed on those carriers and create a presumption of lawfulness applicable to their rates.

To implement our proposal, we proposed to distinguish between carriers on the basis of their dominance or power in the marketplace and apply different regulatory rules to each. A carrier would be labelled dominant if it has substantial opportunity and incentive to subsidize the rates for its more competitive services with revenues obtained from its monopoly or near-monopoly services. We recognized that the power to keep prices above full costs not only meant the firm could violate the "just and reasonable rate" mandate of the Act, but also that it could inefficiently invest in new or additional facilities and still produce enough revenue to recoup these wasteful costs. We therefore proposed to continue to regulate these carriers essentially as we do today so that the Commission could insure that they did not exploit their market power to the detriment of the public.

In contrast the firms labelled dominant, we identified a class of firms not possessing the market power necessary to sustain prices either unreasonably above or below costs. We referred to such firms as non-dominant. As proposed in the *Notice*, the regulatory requirements imposed upon non-dominant carriers would be substantially reduced or even eliminated. Because these carriers generally lack the market power to charge rates or impose conditions of service that would contravene the Act, we would consider their tariff filings to be presumptively lawful. They would no longer be required by our rules to submit extensive economic data to support their tariff filings and they would only have to provide 14 days' notice to the public of proposed tariff changes.[10] Nor would we generally suspend their tariff filings unless a petitioner could make a strong showing of substantial and irreparable injury to competition, thereby harming the public.

*   *   *

A non-dominant carrier would also be able to institute or discontinue service more easily under our proposed procedures. Upon grant of initial Section 214 authorization we would also grant a non-dominant carrier blanket authority for unlimited expansion of circuits into its authorized geographic service areas. It would only be required to report additions of circuits 30 days after this service

---

10. Under our current rules, 47 C.F.R. §61.58, all carriers must provide at least 90 days' notice of tariff filings involving a change in rate structure, a new service offering or rate increase; and 70 days' notice for all other tariff filings with the exception of filings involving such matters as editorial changes or corrections or the imposition of termination charges for which carriers need only give 15 days' notice. If a petitioner raises a substantial question that warrants more extensive consideration, the 14 day notice period can be extended as provided in Section 61.58(d) (which permits the Chief, Common Carrier Bureau to defer the effective date of any tariff filing made on less than 90 days' notice) so that action can be taken prior to the effective date. (*Notice*, para. 58).

date. Conversely, in recognition that ease of exit is a necessary part of a truly competitive market, it could discontinue a service 30 days after notice to its customers and the Commission if no showing were made that a reasonable substitute service is not available.

Although, as noted, the Commission determined that a carrier possesses market power if it has the ability to cross-subsidize its services unlawfully, it did not promulgate any final standards or procedures to identify dominant firms. Instead, we requested commenting parties to focus on what criteria they believed would be useful in determining whether a carrier has market power or when it has achieved dominance. However, after reviewing in some detail the current industry structure and the state of competition between and among the various telecommunications carriers, we tentatively decided to classify AT&T, the independent telephone companies, and Western Union as dominant.

*   *   *

We have carefully and thoroughly weighed the positions and arguments of all commenting parties. On the basis of this review and our own analysis discussed in the Notice we have decided (a) to adopt and make final our proposal to classify carriers either as dominant or non-dominant depending upon their power to control prices; and (b) to employ regulatory regimes more precisely designed to account for the attributes of firms in each denomination as proper and warranted by the public interest.

We will consider a carrier to be dominant if it has market power (*i.e.*, power to control price).[14] We find that AT&T and the independent telephone companies come within the definition of dominant carriers. Moreover, due to what are perhaps transitory factors, especially shortages of the supply of facilities relative to the demand, Western Union, domestic satellite carriers (Domsats), Domsat resellers, and the miscellaneous common carriers (MCCs) possess market power sufficient to justify continuing the application of the current regulatory system to them. As to these carriers, a continuing assessment of the costs and benefits of imposing the dominant-carrier regulatory requirements clearly is warranted. We will be receptive to the presentation of evidence that circumstances have evolved in a manner which permits the easing of the regulatory requirements to which any carrier or class of carriers is subject. Indeed, it may be that several of these carriers could qualify for our streamlined procedures since they may become subject to sufficient potential competition to assure good performance without detailed government intervention.

All other carriers will be classified as non-dominant and, as such, brought within the streamlined tariff filing and facilities authorizations procedures pro-

---

14. In this regard, the Commission suggested several factors for discussion including: a carrier's share of the market for a particular tariffed service; whether a carrier is effectively rate regulated; whether the market for a particular service is workably competitive; the number of carriers involved in providing a particular service or practical substitutes for the service; and the relative size of carriers as measured by customer base, plant investment, R&D capability, overall company revenues; corporate structures such as affiliation with other carriers or non-regulated companies; and standing in the financial community.

posed in the Notice and finalized here. We find several changes to these rules are warranted, however, especially in the case of those governing facilities authorizations. These will further reduce the regulatory burdens for non-dominant carriers. First, non-dominant carriers will only be required to report circuit additions in their authorized service areas on a semi-annual basis, rather than every 30 days as originally proposed. Second, initial carrier certification under Section 214 will be conferred for the continental United States unless the applicant asks otherwise. Finally, non-dominant carriers will not be required to submit the annual financial information proposed in Appendix D of the Notice.

We now turn to a discussion of this new scheme itself, focusing on our legal authority to adopt a two-tiered regulatory structure, the criteria we have used to determine dominance, and the objections raised against the specific rules for non-dominant carriers.

* * *

It is, of course, well established that the Commission has "broad discretion in choosing how to regulate." *AT&T v. FCC*, 572 F.2d at 26. As the Supreme Court has long recognized, the dynamic and rapidly changing nature of the communications industry requires "that the administrative process possess sufficient flexibility to adjust itself to these factors." *FCC v. Pottsville Broadcasting Co.*, 309 U.S. 134, 138 (1940). *See also, United States v. Southwestern Cable Co.*, 392 U.S. 157 (1968); and *National Broadcasting Co. v. United States*, 319 U.S. 190 (1943). Indeed "regulatory practices and policies that will serve the public interest today may be quite different from those that were adequate for that purpose in 1910, 1927 or 1945 . . ." *Washington Utilities & Transportation Comm. v. FCC*, 512 F.2d at 1157, and thus, "one of the most significant advantages of the administrative process is its ability to adapt itself to new circumstances in a flexible manner. . . ." *FCC v. National Citizens Committee for Broadcasting*, 436 U.S. 775, 811 (1978).

This broad power to fashion rules appropriate to the problems confronted is perhaps even more expansive in the area of agency regulation of rates. *Aeronautical Radio, Inc. (ARINC) v. FCC*, No. 77–1333 (D.C. Cir. June 24, 1980) (pet. for rehearing pending). Slip Op. at 13 and cases cited there. The Supreme Court has repeatedly recognized that agencies operating under statutes similar to the Communications Act have been vested with a "legislative" power regarding rates. *Permian Basin Area Rate Cases*, 390 U.S. 747, 776 (1968), *quoting, Los Angeles Gas & Electric Co. v. Railroad Comm'n*, 289 U.S. 287, 304 (1933). While this power is not unbounded *cf. FCC v. RCA Communications, Inc.*, 346 U.S. 86, 90 (1953), it is broad enough "to make the pragmatic adjustments which may be called for by particular circumstances." *Permian Basin*, 390 U.S. at 777, *quoting, FPC v. Natural Gas Pipeline Co.*, 315 U.S. 375, 586 (1942). This power specifically has been held to encompass agency programs involving circumstances not dealt with in the organic statute.

* * *

[W]e have determined that our "ultimate purpose," as defined in Section I of the Act "to make available, so far as possible, to all the people of the United States a rapid, efficient . . . communication service with adequate facilities at reasonable charges . . .", 47 U.S.C. §151, requires the action we take today. So long as our regulation imposes costs on some firms, and thus on the public, not exceeded by the benefits generated thereby, the provision of communications service by those firms can never be as "efficient" nor can the charges be as "reasonable" as they might be in the absence of such artificial costs.

It is equally well-established that Section 4(i) of the Act, 47 U.S.C. §154(i), provides us with the statutory basis to enact regulations and adopt policies codifying our view of the public interest. *FCC v. National Citizens Committee for Broadcasting*, 436 U.S. at 793. Indeed, it has been held that Section 4(i) of the Communications Act enhances the general "legislative discretion" in ratemaking relied upon by the Supreme Court in *Permian Basin. Nader v. FCC*, 520 F.2d 182, 203 (D.C. Cir. 1975). We recognize that this view must be based on "permissible public interest goals" and otherwise be "reasonable", *FCC v. National Citizens Committee for Broadcasting*, 436 U.S. at 794, but we believe our decision to regulate dominant and non-dominant carriers differently comes well within this standard. Our experience to date is replete with evidence that competition in the telecommunications industry is a relevant factor in weighing the public interest. *See, e.g., FCC v. RCA Communications, Inc.*, 346 U.S. 86 (1953); *Specialized Common Carrier Services*, 29 F.C.C. 2d 870 (1971), *recon.* 31 F.C.C. 2d 1106 (1971), *aff'd sub nom. Washington Utilities and Transportation Commission v. FCC*, 512 F. 2d 1142 (9th Cir.), *cert. denied*, 423 U.S. 836 (1975); *Bell Telephone Company of Pennsylvania v. FCC*, 503 F. 2d 1250 (3d Cir. 1974), *cert. denied*, 411 U.S. 1026 (1975); *NARUC v. FCC*, 525 F. 2d 630, 640, (D.C. Cir. 1976), *cert. denied*, 425 U.S. 992 (1977), *United States v. FCC*, No. 77–1249 (D.C. Cir. March 7, 1980). The new regulatory scheme adopted today will enhance competition by reducing the degree of unnecessary regulation imposed upon non-dominant carriers. We believe this will allow them to respond to consumer demand by providing innovative services at the lowest reasonable prices as market needs can be discerned.[36] By maintaining our regulatory oversight of dominant carriers, we do not intend to hinder their accomplishment of these same goals, but only insure that they do not exploit their market power unlawfully.

Not only is our action permissible, but we believe that it would defy logic and contradict the evidence available to regulate in an identical manner carriers who differ greatly in terms of their economic resources and market strength.[37] The Commission has often taken this fundamental incongruity into account in fashioning its regulations and reaching its decisions. Ten years ago, for example, this was our underlying premise in adopting rules requiring carriers to submit support material and economic data to justify their tariff filings:

---

36. As discussed in the *Notice* (paras. 51–54), marketplace forces should be sufficient to insure that the rates of competitive non-dominant carriers are reasonable and not unjustly discriminatory. Indeed, unregulated markets that are structurally sound do satisfy consumer demand at reasonable prices. *See, e.g.,* J. Quirk and R. Saposnik, *Introduction to General Equilibrium Theory and Welfare Economics* (1968).

37. As we pointed out in the *Notice*, AT&T and the independent telephone companies dominate the industry, providing virtually all of the interstate and local telephone service and accounting for the bulk of private line and terminal equipment revenues. . . .

The information needed . . . will vary widely with, among other things, the nature of the rate filed, the size of the market it applies to, and the revenue it will generate. We do not expect that every rate filed by every carrier will require exactly the same amount of supporting information. It is not correct to state that every tariff filing must be supported by detailed cost projections and elaborate statistical studies. Large carriers filing rates for sizeable service offerings, would be expected to support their filing with the most comprehensive and reliable data that they can produce. For such carriers, statistical studies should be used wherever such studies can offer substantial improvements in study reliability. A point-to-point microwave carrier, on the other hand, with small revenues, only one service, and few customers would not be required, nor would it need, elaborate studies to support its rates.

At least since the advent of competitive entry in the telecommunications market we have in fact recognized that the structure and market power of AT&T have required different regulatory treatment from that accorded firms not similarly situated.

* * *

Perhaps the most detailed instance of our adopting particularized rules applicable to AT&T is our Final Decision in Docket 18128. There, in recognition of its ability to cross-subsidize rates for competitive services to the detriment of both competitive and monopoly service customers, we adopted a specific costing methodology applicable only to AT&T.

* * *

Thus, the classification scheme we now establish is by no means a radical departure, as some assert; if anything, it merely codifies our practice of adjusting our regulation to the realities of this industry and the marketplace. Clearly, by adopting this scheme in the face of the record here, we effectuate our statutory responsibilities rather than abrogate them.

* * *

Our goal throughout this rulemaking proceeding has been to establish a set of criteria to enable us to determine whether there are certain firms which could not rationally engage in the activities proscribed by the operative provisions of Title II of the Communications Act, *viz.* Sections 201–205 and 214. For convenience, we have referred to such firms as non-dominant. We have found that application of our current regulatory procedures to non-dominant carriers imposes unnecessary and counterproductive regulatory constraints upon a marketplace that can satisfy consumer demand efficiently without government intervention. In this section we develop a test to classify carriers as either dominant or non-dominant. We start by defining dominant carriers as carriers that have market power (*i.e.*, power to control price). Non-dominant firms, therefore, are those which do not possess power over price. Our analysis leads us to conclude that the specialized common carriers (also referred to as terrestrial microwave carriers) and the resale carriers (excluding the resellers of satellite transmission facilities) are not dominant. Therefore, we revise our tariff and Section 214 procedures for these carriers.

*   *   *

In the *Notice*, we proposed a definition of dominance that we felt would enable us to identify carriers that are subject to sufficient competitive pressure so that their performance is, and can be presumed to continue to be, in the public interest, without detailed governmental oversight and intervention. That definition of dominance was one of market power. We reasoned, based upon the well-established teachings of modern welfare economics, that a firm without market power does not have the ability or incentive to price its services unreasonably, to discriminate among customers unjustly, to terminate or reduce service unreasonably or to overbuild its facilities. The comments on these findings generally have been supportive and have acted to strengthen our tentative beliefs.

Consistent with the *Notice*, we define a dominant carrier as a carrier that possesses market power. Market power refers to the control a firm can exercise in setting the price of its output. A firm with market power is able to engage in conduct that may be anticompetitive or otherwise inconsistent with the public interest. This may entail setting price above competitive costs in order to earn supranormal profits, or setting price below competitive costs to forestall entry by new competitors or to eliminate existing competitors. In contrast, a competitive firm, lacking market power, must take the market price as given, because if it raises price it will face an unacceptable loss of business, and if it lowers price it will face unrecoverable monetary losses in an attempt to supply the market demand at that price.

We have focused on certain clearly identifiable market features in order to determine whether a firm can exercise market power. Among these are the number and size distribution of competing firms, the nature of barriers to entry, and the availability of reasonably substitutable services. The presence of certain features, such as barriers to entry, may allow a firm to exercise market power.

An important structural characteristic of the marketplace that confers market power upon a firm is the control of bottleneck facilities. A firm controlling bottleneck facilities has the ability to impede access of its competitors to those facilities. We must be in a position to contend with this type of potential abuse. We treat control of bottleneck facilities as prima facie evidence of market power requiring detailed regulatory scrutiny.

Control of bottleneck facilities is present when a firm or group of firms has sufficient command over some essential commodity or facility in its industry or trade to be able to impede new entrants. Thus bottleneck control describes the structural characteristic of a market that new entrants must either be allowed to share the bottleneck facility or fail.

In this part we analyze the telecommunications industry to determine the carriers that have market power. While we must identify, for regulatory purposes, whether carriers are dominant or non-dominant, it is performance of the marketplace in satisfying consumer demand that is our overriding concern and not the performance of individual carriers *per se*. Thus our classification of carriers or their individual service offerings is not designed to help or hinder any one particular firm or industry, but rather is designed to enable consumers to derive the best attainable service from each component of the telecommunications industry, given the state of technology as we know it today.

Our analysis, for purpose of exposition, is segmented into the following categories: telephone companies, Western Union, domestic satellite carriers (Domsats), miscellaneous common carriers (MCCs, also referred to as video terrestrial microwave carriers), specialized common carriers (SCCs, also terrestrial microwave carriers) and resale and value added carriers.

[Note: The opinion hereafter reviews the status of each type of carrier.]

COMPETITIVE CARRIER: THE CONCLUSION

Extending the economic analysis of the Communications Act in the *First Report*, the Commission in its *Further Notice of Proposed Rulemaking*, 84 F.C.C.2d 445 (1981) determined that congressional intent underlying the act was to ensure universal service by limiting the market power of dominant carriers. Title II regulation of nondominant carriers could well contradict Congress's goals and be economically counterproductive and so should be removed.

The Commission considered two basic methods of market power analysis: the "definitional" and "forbearance" approaches. Under a definitional approach, the outcome of a market power economic analysis determines whether a company is a common carrier. Under a forbearance approach, a firm may be a common carrier, but its market power determines whether it will be subject to full Title II regulation. Only dominant common carriers would be covered by Title II tariff regulation.

By following the forbearance approach, the FCC could assert its jurisdiction over dominant carriers to protect consumers from monopoly prices but unleash nondominant carriers from regulatory restraints. In *Competitive Common Carrier Service*, Second Report and Order, 91 F.C.C.2d 59 (1982), the Commission affirmed its tentative conclusion of the *First Report*, holding that it has the discretionary authority to forbear from applying Title II regulation when doing so would promote the public interest.

Concluding that it need not use all of its Title II regulatory tools for all common carriers when the costs of regulation exceed any public interest benefits, the FCC chose to promote price competition among nondominant carriers by eliminating traditional tariff requirements, allowing nondominant carriers to contract with consumers as a tariff substitute. The key concept in the *Second Report* is "permissive forbearance." Invoking that concept allowed the Commission to permit nondominant carriers to effectively cancel their tariffs.

Price regulation was found to be unnecessary because nondominant carriers will theoretically price between their own cost and the regulated costs of dominant carriers. Under the permissive forbearance approach in *Second Report*, the FCC found that certain nondominant carriers (specifically, resellers of basic terrestrial communications services) could be permitted, but not required, to cancel their tariffs and structure their businesses on a private contractual basis. Entry regulation under §214 was also relaxed. Permissive forbearance was extended to virtually all nondominant carriers, including MCI and GTE Sprint, by *Competitive Common Carrier Service*, Fifth Report and Order, 98 F.C.C.2d 1191 (1984).

Although permissive forbearance apparently distances the Commission from contact with the marketplace, the complaint process produces information the FCC can use to take action against any supranormal price charged by a nondominant carrier. Exit and entry regulation was also found subject to forbearance because of the already high telecommunication service penetration (in contrast to the low penetration levels when the Communications Act was passed in 1934) and the continued regulation of dominant telephone companies. The FCC refused to forbear from imposing on nondominant carriers the duty to serve the public on reasonable request.

By *Competitive Common Carrier Service*, Sixth Report and Order, 99 F.C.C.2d 1020 (1985), the Commission had deregulated a long list of telecommunications services, termed "forborne carriers." In *Fourth Notice of Proposed Rulemaking*, the Commission proposed that forborne carriers discontinue filing tariffs to avoid suggesting an FCC "stamp of approval" on their rates. In the *Sixth Report*, the Commission adopted this proposal. It emphasized that it was not abdicating its oversight responsibility with respect to the forborne carriers, especially because it maintained the complaint process and all authority to reimpose tariff requirements on forborne carriers. But the Commission had shifted from *permissive* forbearance to *mandatory* forbearance.

MCI TELECOMMUNICATIONS CORP. v. FCC

765 F.2d 1186 (D.C. Cir. 1985)

GINSBURG, Circuit Judge:

Petitioner MCI Telecommunications Corporation (MCI) challenges a Federal Communications Commission (FCC or Commission) directive, captioned the *Sixth Report and Order*, issued in the Commission's long-evolving *Competitive Carrier* rulemaking. The *Sixth Report* (1) requires all non-dominant common carriers of interstate telephone service, including MCI, to cancel their tariffs on file with the Commission within six months of the effective date of the order, and (2) declares that the Commission will not accept tariff filings from the non-dominant carriers in the future.

*   *   *

I. Background

A. Regulatory Proceedings

In 1979, the FCC commenced its *Competitive Carrier* rulemaking, a proceeding shaped with a view toward gradual deregulation of the non-dominant common carrier interstate telephone industry. The Commission's initial *Notice* observed that non-dominant companies—those lacking market power—had no ability to charge supra-competitive rates or to engage in predatory pricing. *Notice*, 77 F.C.C.2d at 334. The FCC sought comments on a broad range of options, and its *First Report*, issued in 1980, announced streamlined regulations for non-dominant common carriers. *First Report*, 85 F.C.C.2d at 30–49.[2]

In its 1981 *Further Notice*, the Commission focused on whether to undertake "definitional" or "forbearance" deregulation. The definitional approach entailed classifying certain non-dominant carriers of communication services as noncommon carriers. Because Title II of the Communications Act, 47 U.S.C. §§201–224 (1982), applies only to common carriers, this approach would have exempted non-dominant carriers from all Title II regulation. *See Further Notice*, 84 F.C.C.2d at 463–70. The forbearance approach involved abstaining from applying to non-dominant carriers certain Title II procedural requirements while maintaining the basic substantive requirements that carriers charge "just and reasonable" rates and not engage in "unreasonable discrimination." 47 U.S.C. §§ 201–202 (1982); *see Further Notice*, 84 F.C.C.2d at 471–91.

In its *Second Report*, released in 1982, the Commission adopted a forbearance position, *Second Report*, 91 F.C.C.2d at 61–62, which *permitted* resellers of basic services who owned no transmission facilities to cancel tariffs filed with the Commission and to convert to service on a private contract basis. *Id.* at 73. In subsequent 1983 and 1984 orders, the Commission extended permissive forbearance first to specialized common carriers (including MCI) and all resellers, *Fourth Report*, 95 F.C.C.2d at 557, and later to domestic satellite carriers providing domestic interstate service, miscellaneous common carriers, carriers providing domestic, interstate, and interexchange digital transmission networks, and affiliates of exchange carriers providing interstate interexchange services. *Fifth Report*, 98 F.C.C.2d at 1209–10.

B. Sixth Report

The *Sixth Report*, target of MCI's petition for review, changed the permissive forbearance arrangement to a mandatory one. Under the previous orders, "forborne" carriers could elect to continue offering service pursuant to filed tariffs, or to cancel their filed tariffs and convert to private contracts. Many new entrants apparently chose not to file tariffs, but the vast majority of existing forborne carriers opted to maintain their services under the tariff system. The Commis-

---

2. Under the streamlined regulations, non-dominant carrier rates were presumed lawful, *First Report*, 85 F.C.C.2d at 33, and new rates could be filed on 14-day (rather than the previously required 90-day) notice. *Id.* at 37.

sion's *Fourth Further Notice* requested comment on whether forborne carriers should be required to cancel their tariffs and convert to a carrier-customer individual contract system. *Fourth Further Notice,* 49 Fed.Reg. at 11,857.

In the *Sixth Report* the Commission replied to the comments of numerous parties. The principal arguments confronting the FCC were these: (1) the Commission lacks authority to abolish tariffs, *Sixth Report,* 50 RAD.REG.2d at 1393; (2) the abolition of tariffs would eliminate the repository of information consumers need to detect discriminatory practices, *id.* at 1394; (3) conversion to private contracts would impose an excessive burden on carriers, *id.* at 1394–95; and (4) there are less drastic alternatives, *id.* at 1395–96.

The Commission responded first that it found in section 203(b)(2) of the Communications Act, 47 U.S.C. § 203(b)(2) (1982), "express authority to exempt carriers from tariff filing requirements where appropriate." *Sixth Report,* 57 RAD.REG.2d at 1398. Consumers would benefit in several ways, the Commission reported. Dropping tariff filings would eliminate delay and opportunities for collusive pricing tactics. Furthermore, the absence of filed tariffs could be expected to stimulate the development of customer-specific and innovative service offerings. *Id.* at 1399–400. The Commission acknowledged that carriers "might perceive some increased administrative burdens, at least initially," *id.* at 1400, but it considered this prospect outweighed by the positive features of detariffing non-dominant carriers. Sufficient information would be available to consumers, the FCC said, because carriers seeking to preserve their competitive position "will make their rates and other information, formerly contained in tariffs, available to the public." *Id.* at 1401. for these reasons, the Commission declared that forborne carriers henceforth would be prohibited from filing tariffs and that forborne carriers with tariffs on file would be required to abolish those tariffs and convert to private contracts within six months. . . .

II. Discussion

*   *   *

B. Statutory Authority

"[T]he starting point for interpreting a statute is the language of the statute itself." *Consumer Product Safety Commission v. GTE Sylvania, Inc.,* 447 U.S. 102, 108, 100 S.Ct. 2051, 2056, 64 L.Ed.2d 766 (1980)[.]

*   *   *

Section 203(a) of the Communications Act provides:

> *Every* common carrier, except connecting carriers, *shall,* within such reasonable time as the Commission shall designate, file with the Commission and print and keep open for public inspection schedules showing all charges for itself and its connecting carriers . . . and showing the classifications, practices, and regulations affecting such charges.

47 U.S.C. § 203(a) (1982) (emphasis added). "Shall," the Supreme Court has stated, "is the language of command," *Escoe v. Zerbst,* 295 U.S. 490, 493, 55 S.Ct.

818, 820, 79 L.Ed. 1566 (1935); "[a]bsent a clearly expressed legislative intention to the contrary," courts ordinarily regard such statutory language as conclusive. *GTE Sylvania*, 447 U.S. at 108, 100 S.Ct. at 2056; *see, e.g., Amalgamated Transit Union v. Donovan*, 767 F. 2d 939, 944 (D.C.Cir. 1985).

The FCC counters with a further statutory provision, section 203(b)(2) of the Communications Act, 47 U.S.C. § 203(b)(2) (1982), and contends that its "plain meaning" permits the Commission to order the forbearance at issue. *See Sixth Report*, 57 RAD.REG.2d at 1398 (section 203(b)(2) "gives the Commission the express authority to exempt carriers from tariff filing requirements where appropriate"). Section 203(b)(2) provides:

> The Commission may, in its discretion and for good cause shown, *modify* any requirement made by or under the authority of this section either in *particular instances* or by general order applicable to *special circumstances or conditions* except that the Commission may not require the notice period . . . to be more than ninety days.

The words "modify . . . in particular instances or by general order applicable to special circumstances or conditions" suggest circumscribed alterations—not, as the FCC now would have it, wholesale abandonment or elimination of a requirement. *See, e.g.*, BLACK'S LAW DICTIONARY 905 (5th ed. 1979) ("modify" defined as "[t]o alter; to change in incidental or subordinate features; enlarge, extend; amend; limit, reduce"). Our resistance to the uncommon meaning the Commission currently reads into its "particular instances" and "special circumstances" modification authority is strengthened by precedent closely in point.

* * *

Counsel for the Commission conceded at oral argument that the FCC has arrived at its fully expanded view of section 203(b)(2) rather lately. By contrast, shortly after the Commission opened its *Competitive Carrier* inquiry, the agency stated in *Western Union Telegraph Co.*, 75 F.C.C.2d 461 (1980):

> There can be no question that tariffs are essential to the entire administrative scheme of the Act. They serve as a kind of "tripwire" enabling the Commission to monitor the activities of carriers subject to its jurisdiction and to thereby insure that the charges, practices, classifications, and regulations of those carriers are just, reasonable, and nondiscriminatory within the meaning of Sections 201 and 202 of the Act. The importance of tariffs and the requirement that common carriers—*all common carriers—must offer all of their communications services to the public through published tariffs* is well established. *See Armour Packing Company v. United States*, 209 U.S. 56, 28 S.Ct. 428, 52 L.Ed. 681 (1908).

* * *

In short, at least until 1980, the Commission shared, indeed fostered, the judicial perception of the statutory tariff-filing requirement for common carriers. The requirement could be modified by administrative action, the FCC once understood, but not removed in gross by agency order. We hold that the Commission's prior comprehension of the meaning section 203 will bear was correct, and that the FCC's new view departs from any plausible reading of the statute's text.

As a second line of argument in support of the *Sixth Report*, the Commission asserts general authority to forbear from full Title II common carrier regulation in order to adapt its superintendence to changing circumstances as "the public interest" indicates. The FCC relies principally on four decisions to back up the asserted general authority: *Wold Communications, Inc. v. FCC*, 735 F.2d 1465 (D.C.Cir. 1984); *Computer & Communications Industry Association v. FCC*, 693 F.2d 198 (D.C.Cir 1982), *cert. denied*, 461 U.S. 938, 103 S.Ct. 2109, 77 L.Ed.2d 313 (1983); *Western Union Telegraph Co. v. FCC*, 674 F.2d 160 (2d Cir. 1982); and *Philadelphia Television Broadcasting Co. v. FCC*, 359 F.2d 282 (D.C.Cir. 1966). These decisions lack the breadth that the FCC attributes to them. They provide no warrant for erasing the congressional instruction in section 203(a) that *every* common carrier *shall* file tariffs.

Wold Communications upheld the Commission's decision to allow the sale of certain discrete satellite transponders on a noncommon carrier basis. The FCC isolates and quotes this court's statement that "the public interest touchstone of the Communications Act, beyond question, permits the FCC to allow the marketplace to substitute for direct Commission regulation in appropriate circumstances." 735 F.2d at 1475. The "appropriate circumstances" in *Wold* included the Commission's representation that it had made "a modest adjustment" and had not "displaced regulated common carrier service as the dominant mode." *Id.* at 1468. The "limited departure from the status quo" approved in *Wold, id.* at 1469, concerned "noncommon carrier offerings," *id.* at 1474, and did not implicate, as this case does, "unfettered discretion to regulate or not [ ] regulate common carrier services." *Id.* at 1475 (quoting *Computer & Communications Industry Association*, 693 F.2d at 212).

Computer & Communications Industry Association held reasonable "[t]he Commission's finding that enhanced services and CPE [customer premises equipment] are not common carrier communications activities within Title II." 693 F.2d at 209. Similarly, *Western Union* upheld the Commission's decision to detariff terminal equipment, based on the FCC's reasonable conclusion that the sale or lease of that equipment was not a communications service. 674 F.2d at 165. *Philadelphia Television* also involved regulation—there of community antenna television (CATV)—of noncommon carrier activity:

> [The Commission's] holding that CATV systems are not common carriers thus comes before us in a context of regulation . . . under different provisions of the Communications Act. In a statutory scheme in which Congress has given an agency various bases of jurisdiction and various tools with which to protect the public interest, the agency is entitled to *some leeway* in choosing which jurisdictional base and which regulatory tools will be most effective in advancing the Congressional objective.

359 F.2d at 284 (emphasis added).

In this case, the services provided by the non-dominant carriers remain common carrier services. Indeed, at an earlier stage of the *Competitive Carrier* rulemaking the Commission apparently rejected a definitional approach. *See Second Report*, 91 F.C.C.2d at 61–62 & n. 7. Therefore, decisions that depend on classification of the service or operation in question as outside the common carrier context will not travel the distance the Commission would take them.

Finally, the Commission urges that the *Sixth Report* orders an altogether rational regulatory reduction because "competitive marketplace forces in almost all cases will be sufficient to assure just and reasonable rates." Brief for Respondents at 51.

However reasonable the Commission's assessment, we are not at liberty to release the agency from the tie that binds it to the text Congress enacted. Significantly, the Commission's search for support leads it to decisions upholding the exemption of certain airline, railroad, and trucking services from tariff filing requirements—cases in which Congress had supplied explicit deregulatory authority.

* * *

Perhaps most tellingly, Congress has armed the FCC, in the Record Carrier Competition Act of 1981, Pub.L. No. 97–180, § 2, 95 Stat. 1687, with authority of the kind the Commission would exercise here without statutory change. In the Record Carrier legislation Congress instructed:

> The Commission shall, to the *maximum extent feasible,* promote the development of fully competitive domestic and international markets in the provision of record communications service, so that the public may obtain record communications service and facilities (including terminal equipment) the variety and price of which are governed by competition. In order to meet the purposes of this section, the Commission *shall* forbear from exercising its authority under [Title II of the Communications Act] as the development of competition among record carriers reduces the degree of regulation necessary to protect the public.

47 U.S.C. § 222(b)(1) (1982) (emphasis added); *see RCA Global Communications, Inc. v. FCC,* 758 F.2d 722 (D.C.Cir.1985).

But Congress has not given the FCC new instruction for the case at hand. As the Second Circuit stated in *AT&T Special Permission:*

> In enacting Sections 203–05 of the Communications Act, Congress intended a specific scheme for carrier initiated rate revisions. A balance was achieved after a careful compromise. The Commission is not free to circumvent or ignore that balance. Nor may the Commission in effect rewrite this statutory scheme on the basis of its own conception of the equities of a particular situation.

487 F.2d at 880 (footnote omitted). In sum, if the Commission is to have authority to command that common carriers not file tariffs, the authorization must come from Congress, not from this court or from the Commission's own conception of how the statute should be rewritten in light of changed circumstances.

Conclusion

For the reasons stated, we vacate the Commission's decision prohibiting common carriers from filing tariffs. In so ruling, we do not reach the question whether the FCC's earlier permissive orders are invalid. We note that the

Commission could further streamline the regulation of non-dominant carriers without encountering any contrary congressional prescription. *See Sixth Report*, 57 Rad.Reg.2d at 1395–96. But to proceed in the manner ordered by the *Sixth Report*, the Commission, in our view, must obtain leave of Congress. We may interpret the FCC's authority generously, but we are not positioned to confer upon the agency "unfettered discretion to regulate or not regulate common carrier services." *Computer & Communications Industry Association*, 693 F.2d at 212. . . .

Questions

A brief history of how the communications market opened to the other common carriers may be helpful. It began with the FCC's approval of an application to construct a microwave relay to provide private line service between St. Louis and Chicago submitted by a small unknown applicant, known today as MCI (*Microwave Communications, Inc.*, 18 F.C.C.2d 953 [1969] [MCI]). As *Telecommunications Reports*, a trade journal, aptly noted at the time, "The domestic telecommunications business will never be the same." By July 1970 the FCC had received over 1,700 "special service" microwave applications. These were nonswitched services—basically, pairings of points selected by the customer and linked by the special service provider. In May 1971 the Commission ruled: "[T]here is a public need and demand for the proposed facilities and services and for new and diverse sources of supply" (*Specialized Common Carriers*, First Report and Order, 29 F.C.C.2d 870 [1971], *aff'd sub. nom Washington Utilities and Transportation Commission v. FCC*, 513 F.2d 1142 [9th Cir. 1975]). Glen Robinson, who served as an FCC commissioner in the 1970s, analyzed the effect this way:

> The FCC's "original intent" in the *Specialized Common Carrier Services* decision, which authorized competitive private line services, was the subject of much controversy in the mid-1970s and early 1980s. Emerging private line carriers sought to give it a capacious interpretation and AT&T a narrow one. Interpretation of what the FCC had meant in 1971 was crucial to the Justice Department's antitrust suit against AT&T, as well as to private actions by MCI and others. This debate over intent recalls Robert Browning's response to an inquiry into the meaning of one of his early poems: "When I wrote that only God and Robert Browning knew what it meant; now only God knows." If God knew what the FCC meant in 1971, He didn't say; neither did the FCC. It seems that what the FCC originally had in mind was specialized services tailored to distinctive service needs of particular customers, as opposed to the homogenized services provided by MTS and WATS. It should follow that the specialized carriers could not demand that AT&T provide interconnection arrangements to allow the new carriers to provide service directly competitive with MTS-WATS. But this was never precisely stated in the FCC's decision. (Robinson, "The

Titanic Remembered: AT&T and the Changing World of Communications," 5 *Yale Journal on Regulation,* 517, 523–524 [1988]).

The next step was MCI's tariff filing to offer the Execunet services. Bernard Strassburg, an FCC official at the time, described the situation:

In both the MCI proceeding and the specialized common carriers proceeding, MCI had explicitly represented to the Commission that it was not seeking authority to compete with AT&T's message toll service and wide area telephone service—AT&T's regular switched voice long distance services. Based on these representations of the limited nature of MCI's proposed service offerings, there was no need for the Commission in those proceedings to address the multiplicity of difficult economic and public policy questions that competition with MTS and WATS so obviously raised. . . .

In the event that MCI had proposed Execunet service to the FCC while I was bureau chief . . . I would have advised MCI that its facility authorizations and FCC policies precluded such a service. If MCI chose to pursue the matter further, I would have recommended that the Commission take appropriate action to prevent MCI from providing Execunet service. (Henck and Strassburg, *A Slippery Slope: The Long Road to the Breakup of AT&T,* 168 [1988]).

The D.C. Circuit, however, disagreed and held that the services could be offered because they were not specifically excluded in its facility authorization (*MCI Telecommunications Corp. v. FCC,* 561 F.2d 365 [D.C. Cir. 1977], *cert. denied,* 434 U.S. 1040 [1978] [*Execunet I*]; *MCI Telecommunications Corp. v. FCC,* 580 F.2d 590 [D.C. Cir], *cert. denied,* 439 U.S. 980 [1978] [*Execunet II*]). For additional discussion see Brock, *The Telecommunications Industry: The Dynamics of Market Structure* (1981).

1. In the *First Report,* the FCC claims that the new classifications are "by no means a radical departure." Do you agree? Upon what mechanism does the FCC rely to ensure that rates are reasonable and nondiscriminatory? How does the new scheme promote the public interest?

2. What factors should the FCC consider to determine if a carrier has market power? What condition constitutes prima facie evidence of market power? What does it mean for tariff filings by nondominant carriers to be presumptively lawful?

3. Who are dominant carriers today? Who are nondominant carriers? What is a specialized common carrier? miscellaneous common carrier? resale common carrier? value-added carrier?

4. Why did the FCC adopt the forbearance approach to deregulation in the *Second Report?* Why did it adopt mandatory forbearance in the *Sixth Report?*

5. Why did most forborne carriers choose to file tariffs while "permissive" forbearance was in effect? Why did MCI challenge the validity of mandatory forbearance? Why did the courts uphold MCI's challenge?

6. An ongoing struggle exists over whether dominant carriers can offer customer-specific pricing plans to prevent the loss of large business accounts to nondominant carriers who may lawfully offer such discounted plans. In 1989 the FCC rejected AT&T's Holiday Rate Plan on narrow factual grounds (*AT&T Communications Tariff FCC No. 15*, Memorandum Opinion and Order, 65 R.R.2d 433 [1988]; Subsequent Order, FCC 88–471 [November 1989]). AT&T offered the discount plan in 1988 in response to an off-tariff discount offer made by MCI to Holiday Corp. A second Tariff 15 plan, matching MCI's bid to Resort Condominiums, Inc., was also found to be discriminatory because AT&T offered the specific discounts only after MCI had underbid AT&T and the client had disclosed it. Thus, while the tariff was ostensibly available to like customers, the tariff only emerged in response to a competitor, not as a general offering (*AT&T Communications, Tariff FCC No. 15*, Memorandum Opinion and Order, 69 R.R.2d 1102 [1991]).

The FCC has allowed discriminatory pricing where there is a showing of "competitive necessity," (*Private Line Rate Storage and Volume Pricing Practices*, 97 F.C.C.2d 923 [1984]), but Tariff 15 failed to meet that standard. What is notable is that the FCC failed to prohibit AT&T from matching competitors' bids by offering discounts not available to its other customers. Would such discount offerings violate §§201–202? Have market conditions changed enough to justify such plans? Does the FCC have the authority to approve such plans?

For a discussion of the justification of customer-specific offerings under the competitive-necessity doctrine, see Larson, Monson, and Nobles, "Competitive Necessity and Pricing in Telecommunications Regulation," 42 *Federal Communications Law Journal* 1 (1989).

STREAMLINED REGULATION FOR AT&T

As the 1990s began, the FCC sent out its call for a comprehensive investigation of the state of competition in the interstate long-distance market. The FCC decided that increasingly vigorous long-distance competition should lead to a new policy of streamlined regulation for AT&T[1] (*Competition in the*

---

1. Price-cap regulation replaced rate-based regulation for AT&T in 1989. Basically, price-cap regulation groups related services, such as residential and small-business services, into "baskets." Then a price range with upper and lower bands is established for each service group. AT&T is allowed to respond to competition by adjusting its rates for individual services without FCC approval so long as it stays within the pricing bands. Price-cap regulation is discussed in detail in the next chapter.

Interstate Interexchange Marketplace, Report and Order, CC No. 90–132, 69 R.R.2d 1135 [1991]).

The Commission based its policy shift on several characteristics of the long-distance market. First, BOCs provide equal-access service to approximately 300 interexchange carriers. Second, AT&T maintains about a 65–70 percent share of the market. Even more important than market share analysis, though, are the substantial supply capabilities of AT&T's competitors; MCI, Sprint, and others have the ability to take on new customers should AT&T behave anticompetitively. And restraining AT&T's competitiveness may actually harm the competitiveness of the market.

The FCC concluded that the high-end, business-services marketplace is the most competitive long-distance market. Large business customers are more sophisticated and have greater bargaining power than the average customer; MCI and Sprint combined serve about one-third of the business-services market; and AT&T's rates under price-cap regulation have been well below the ceiling rate. As a result, the Commission applied streamlined regulation to AT&T's "basket" (i.e., group) of business services. Maximum streamlined regulation eliminates the price-cap ceiling and the upper and lower rate bands (i.e., the range in which rates may fall), for the individual service categories. AT&T is also permitted to change its rates effective on fourteen days' notice for business users without cost support. (Does the FCC have legal authority to ease regulations under Title II?)

The Commission further concluded that all interexchange carriers, including AT&T, should be allowed to make single-customer service offerings to meet unique needs. The "carrier contract" offerings, also referred to as "Tariff 12" filings, could be negotiated through a contract system but must be generally available to similarly situated customers.

As to 800 services, the Commission concluded the market lacked full competition due to the technical limitations on number portability. Portability means that a customer with an 800 number from AT&T can use the same 800 number if it contracts with Sprint. Without number portability, a customer who switches carriers must change its 800 number. Also, if a customer wants the number to spell a particular name with the seven-digit number, it must subscribe to the carrier to whom that number has been assigned. Since AT&T services approximately 80 percent of the market, most of the numbers are assigned to AT&T. The company was forbidden from bundling 800 services (i.e., linking them with other services) in contract-based tariffs, although it grandfathered existing bundled arrangements. Once portability is achieved, the restriction on 800 number bundling can be relaxed.

The FCC has also proposed to implement streamlined regulation for international message telephone services in 1993. Although barriers to competition are being dismantled as MCI and Sprint continue to obtain operating agreements with foreign nations, not enough time has elapsed to have sufficiently diminished the 90 percent market share held by AT&T in

1988. In addition, the Commission remains concerned that the competing carriers will be taken advantage of, or "whipsawed," by foreign postal, telephone, and telegraph organizations under a streamlined system.

The AT&T streamlining decision found the business-service market competitive, but the FCC did not go so far as to declare AT&T "nondominant." And it rejected a more radical proposal to allow AT&T tariff changes to go into effect on one day's notice or to allow AT&T to declare itself a private carrier. Commissioner Ervin Duggan dubbed the approach "cautious incrementalism."

Questions

1. Does allowing AT&T to meet competitive forces through contract carriage signal more like a major swing away from Title II?

2. How does "carrier contract" differ from the approach unsuccessfully tried in Tariff 15?

6

PRICE CAPS

INTRODUCTION TO PRICE CAPS

Given the deficiencies of rate-of-return regulation, the FCC and state regulators have considered alternative approaches. Chief among these are price-focused regulations, or price caps. This regulatory approach, a fundamental change from the current system, simulates competition without the presence of competing firms by limiting what is charged. Under price caps, regulators apply rules so that the average price of a basket of services remains the same. Prices of individual services within a basket may rise or fall.

This scheme permits a phone company to change its prices as it wants in order to meet competition or bring user charges more into line with costs. But so long as the prices of basic services stay within the established range, regulatory approval of price changes is guaranteed. This approach lets a phone company revise its rate structure without facing delays.

There are two features to keep in mind when analyzing price caps. Both encourage efficiency: productivity index and profit sharing.

The *productivity index* is part of an annual adjustment made to price caps to account for the rate of inflation. Rather than just adding the full inflation increase to the price cap, the company first subtracts a productivity index. The adjustment is necessary because telecommunications costs historically have grown more slowly than overall inflation due to technological progress. The productivity index tends to be high where the particular price cap involves a usage-based service, because costs per message unit have declined about 2.5 percent per year. For non–usage-sensitive prices such as basic local service, the index would be less or none at all, resulting in a higher inflation increase. The index pressures companies to meet or exceed anticipated increases in productivity: If the company beats the index target, it keeps the rewards of its efforts.

Setting a productivity index is a critical step in price cap regulation. If the index is set too high, the adjustment formula may allow no room for profits, undermining the financial health of the company. Increases in productivity are not inevitable; productivity growth can drop off for unexplained reasons, as happened between the 1960s and 1970s in the entire world economy. But if the index is set too low, technological developments may lead to rapid productivity gains and cause profits to be unacceptably high. So price caps

Long-Distance Market Shares

	Market Share			
	AT&T	MCI	Sprint	Others
1989	68%	12%	8%	12%
1984	87%	5%	3%	5%

Cost of a Thirty-Minute Direct-Dial Phone Call in 1989

	10:00 a.m.			8:00 p.m.		
Call	AT&T	MCI	Sprint	AT&T	MCI	Sprint
Washington, D.C., to Seattle	7.50	7.35	6.98	5.02	4.95	3.37
Los Angeles to San Francisco	6.91	6.72	6.52	5.38	5.29	5.31
Chicago to Dallas	7.20	6.75	6.69	4.82	4.65	3.10

require a *sharing rule*, the second distinctive feature of this form of regulation. Some fraction of any deviation in profits outside a predetermined range, say a 12 percent to a 14 percent return, would be translated into price relief for consumers (if profits exceed the range) or for the company (if profits fall below the range).

In the articles that follow, the FCC demonstrates its willingness to consider, and subsequently adopt, price-cap regulation for AT&T.

POLICY AND RULES CONCERNING RATES
FOR DOMINANT CARRIERS
(PRICE CAPS), FIRST REPORT AND ORDER

4 F.C.C. Rcd. 2873 (1989)

*   *   *

B. Background and Summary of Order

1. Synopsis of Historical Dominant Carrier Regulation

The Communications Act of 1934 (Act) charges this Commission with regulating "so as to make available . . . to all the people of the United States a rapid, efficient, Nationwide, and worldwide . . . communication service with adequate facilities at reasonable charges. . . ." We attempt to carry out this mandate within the context of the regulatory structure established under the Act, which provides for dual regulation of telephone companies by this Commission and the individual states.[7]

---

7. 47 USC §152. Pursuant to this regulatory structure, telephone company costs are appor-

The Act provides this Commission with various powers and tools to use in regulating the recovery of costs apportioned to the interstate jurisdiction. The courts consistently have found that the Act grants us broad discretion to employ these tools in a flexible manner, in accordance with prevailing circumstances and conditions. With regard to the ratemaking process, the courts have determined that there is no single method or formula that agencies must use to satisfy the requirements in Title II of the Act and other similar statutes that rates be just and reasonable, and not unreasonably discriminatory. Instead, courts evaluate the end result of particular regulatory methodologies to determine whether they produce rates that fall within a "zone of reasonableness," an area bounded at the lower end by investor interests in maintaining financial integrity and access to capital markets and at the upper end by consumer interests against non-exploitative rates.

Since this Commission was created in 1934, we have revisited and altered the mix of our regulatory policies and rules on many occasions. At the present time, we employ a regulatory system known as rate base, or rate of return, regulation to ensure that the rates for AT&T and LEC interstate services remain within the zone of reasonableness. This approach requires not only that we establish a carrier's allowable rate of return, but also whether: (1) its investment and cash expenses are properly calculated and efficiently incurred; (2) the level of non-cash expenses such as depreciation and other accruals is properly reflected in rate calculations; and (3) the rates proposed or in effect cover these costs and produce a fair rate of return.

This elaborate approach is often thought of as "traditional" regulation. In fact, we did not begin to develop this system until the mid-1960s. Prior to that time, there were no explicit criteria for determining whether Bell System rates were just and reasonable. Instead, we followed a policy of "continuing surveillance" of Bell System earnings levels to ensure that rates remained within the zone of reasonableness. This process operated without regular formal proceedings of any kind, and rate adjustments occurred only if this Commission or Bell System representatives initiated "discussions looking toward appropriate rate changes whenever the level of . . . total interstate earnings . . . appeared to warrant such action."

---

tioned between the state and the interstate (federal) jurisdictions in accordance with rules adopted by this Commission after consultation with the states. 47 USC §§221(c), 410(c). Such costs are thereafter recovered according to applicable federal or state regulatory policies. The apportionment process is commonly referred to as "jurisdictional separations," and the procedures governing apportionments are incorporated into Part 36 of this Commission's Rules. See 47 CFR §36.1 *et seq.* These rules cannot be changed unilaterally. Rather, proceedings regarding apportionments must be referred to a Federal-State Joint Board comprised of four state commissioners appointed by the National Association of Regulatory Utility Commissioners and three federal commissioners appointed by the Chairman of this Commission. 47 USC §410(c). The Joint Board makes recommendations for this Commission's consideration. *Id.* No changes in jurisdictional apportionments are adopted or proposed in the instant proceeding. At the present time, approximately 84.6 percent of AT&T's total company non-access costs, and approximately 30 percent of LEC regulated costs, are apportioned to the interstate jurisdiction.

During the period when the "continuing surveillance" policy was in effect, a voice occasionally was raised in complaint that the Bell System's costs and rates might be too high, but only once during this period did this Commission initiate a comprehensive investigation of such matters. This inquiry in the late 1930s cost millions of dollars and occupied approximately 300 researchers for several years. The staff's efforts culminated in the preparation of a voluminous report on Bell System costs and operations, but allegations of inflated costs and rates— and substantial cost shifting between unregulated Western Electric and regulated telephone company operations—were never documented to the Commission's satisfaction. Ultimately, no action was taken on the report's major recommendations, and the investigation produced no significant changes in Commission or Bell System procedures.

The use of "continuing surveillance" to assure just and reasonable rates occurred during a period when the Bell System faced little or no competition in the domestic interstate telecommunications market. The absence of competition resulted in large measure from the formidable barriers to entry into telephone markets, including substantial scale economies that operated to the advantage of the incumbent Bell System. These barriers may not have been so great as to impart to the telephone industry the status of a "natural monopoly," but they formed a distinct boundary between that industry and other industries. And, they existed during a time of technological stability.

In the 1950s and 1960s, technological developments began to lower economic barriers to entry into the telephone business and to put pressure on the boundary between telephone companies and other firms. The development of microwave technology rendered scale economies insignificant at the "high" end of the telephone market. As a result, entities using large amounts of telephone service, which generally had been telephone company customers, could operate their own telephone systems and, potentially, compete against their former suppliers. The development of satellite technology as a cost-effective method of transmitting messages transformed firms with satellite expertise into potential entrants into the telephone field. Previously unrelated firms, such as aerospace companies and the Bell System, thus came into competitive interaction. Rapid development of digital electronics and transistor technology blurred the line between computers and communications. Computer systems took on the characteristics of telephone systems—*i.e.*, switches linked by transmission lines—while, at the same time, telephone companies were adopting computer technology for use in communications systems and expanding their operations into the domain of computer firms.

This Commission was not unmindful of the pressures and changes generated by technological developments. In the face of such developments, and often following the lead of the courts, we embarked on two paths of regulatory change.

The first path consisted of a series of proceedings in which we addressed the impact of technological advances that made it possible for companies outside the Bell System to provide telecommunications equipment and services. The second path consisted of a series of proceedings in which we abandoned the "continuing surveillance" policy and began to construct the regulatory system currently relied upon to regulate dominant carriers. In retrospect, it is easy to see how the two paths of regulatory change were related in major part, with the second coming as a response to the first. Permitting entry into certain segments of telecommunications allowed competition to develop in part, but not all, of that market. New competitors called upon this Commission to police the boundary between the competitive and less competitive portions of the market, and to arbitrate disputes among all competitors. Issues that had been left largely to telephone companies during the period of "continuing surveillance," such as rate structure, became crucial competitive variables. The allocation of telephone company costs among competitive and less competitive services became a subject of intense controversy.

With regard to both paths, this Commission's efforts were devoted to structuring regulatory policies that affirmatively promote competition, that rely on competitive forces as an effective means of assisting us in achieving our statutory goals, or that attempt to emulate the operations of a competitive market. The public interest rationale for applying this competition-based regulatory model is readily understandable. Companies subject to competition are forced to operate in ways that generally result in just, reasonable, and non-discriminatory rates. Although firms operating in a competitive environment simply are attempting to maximize their profits, the various means each uses to achieve this result—innovating, enhancing efficiency, providing quality services—benefit consumers individually and society as a whole.

* * *

Throughout most of the 1970s, we conducted extensive and complex investigations of the Bell System's rate base and cost allocation systems, and of its tariffed rates. In a repeat of our rate base investigation in the 1930s, no significant disallowances of carrier investment resulted from these inquiries.

2. The Rate of Return System

Our experiences in travelling the second path of regulatory change, in which we developed the existing rate of return structure, illuminate the difficulties of administering rate of return regulation under any circumstances. In theory, rate of return is intended to replicate competitive market results. However, there are many differences in the manner in which rate of return regulation and competitive forces operate. Competition holds each firm to "normal" profit levels as a result of a dynamic process that operates over time—a firm strives to maximize profits and secure advantage over other firms by responding to consumer demand effectively. Under rate of return, however, "normal" profit levels are established in advance by regulatory fiat. The dynamic process that produces socially beneficial results in a competitive environment is strongly suppressed. In fact, rather than encourage socially beneficial behavior by the regulated firm, rate of return actually discourages it.

The distorted incentives created by rate of return regulation are easily illustrated. In a competitive environment, where prices are dictated by the market, a company's unit costs and profits generally are related inversely. If one goes up, the other goes down. Rate of return regulation stands this relationship on its head. Although carriers subject to such regulation are limited to earning a particular *percentage* return on investment during a fixed period, a carrier seeking to increase its dollar earnings often can do so merely by increasing its *aggregate* investment. In other words, under a rate of return regime, profits (*i.e.*, dollar earnings) can go up when investment goes up. This creates a powerful incentive for carriers to "pad" their costs, regardless of whether additional investment in necessary or efficient. And, because a carrier's operating expenses generally are recovered from ratepayers on a dollar-for-dollar basis, and do not affect shareholder profits, management has little incentive to conserve on such expenses. This creates an additional incentive to operate inefficiently. Moreover, in situations in which carriers providing more than one service face competition for one or more of such services, rate of return regulation enables carriers to distort the competitive process by manipulating their reported cost allocations.

A system that establishes such incentives is unlikely to encourage efficiency. Moreover, administering rate of return regulation in order to counteract these incentives is a difficult and complex process, even when done correctly and well. This is so primarily for two reasons. First, such regulation is built on the premise that a regulator can determine accurately what costs are necessary to deliver service. In practice, however, a regulator may have difficulty obtaining accurate cost information as the carrier itself is the source of nearly all information about its costs. Furthermore, no regulator has the resources to review in detail the thousands of individual business judgments a carrier makes before it decides, for example, to install a new switching system.

The second inherent difficulty associated with administering rate of return regulation relates to its requirement that determinations be made about how to allocate a carrier's costs among services that often are provided jointly or in common. Such determinations tend to become more economically problematic as they become more detailed. The history of this Commission's experience in this area over the past several decades reflects the difficulty of implementing cost allocation systems. We recently have been able to implement rational and effective allocation systems for the purpose of allocating costs between regulated and nonregulated activities. It must be recognized, however, that even though cost allocation systems deter anticompetitive activity and assist in its detection, these results may be obtained at a high cost to society. This is so because a cost allocation system can present a strong deterrent to anticompetitive activity and, at the same time, be so detailed and rigid that it imposes on a carrier a complex and inflexible rate structure, one that may have little relation to consumer demand. If such a rate structure is deployed in a competitive environment, it may result in distorted consumption decisions, distorted production decisions, and distortions of the competitive process.

Our experiences administering rate of return regulation lead us to conclude that this methodology has certain inherent flaws. As explained above, this type of regulation presents carriers with certain incentives—to pad their rates and forego efficient innovation, for example—that are perverse when viewed from a public interest perspective. These incentives would exist even if technology and industry boundaries were to remain stable, and the existence of such incentives alone provides sufficient justification to seek alternative regulatory approaches that are better suited than rate of return to achieving the consumer-oriented goals of the Communications Act.

We have every reason to expect, moreover, that the telecommunications industry will continue to be marked in the future by the same steady technological advancement it has demonstrated in the past. This will lead to greater competition than at present and a continuing shift in the boundaries between the competitive and less competitive segments of the telecommunications marketplace. Notwithstanding this technological change and growing competition, we could continue our current practice of implementing cost allocation systems that present strong deterrents to anticompetitive activity associated with those boundaries, but it will become increasingly difficult to obtain these benefits while concomitantly holding to a minimum the costs such deterrents impose on society. We conclude, therefore, that it is prudent to implement regulatory systems that are better able than rate of return to operate effectively in an environment marked by competition and technological change.

Our concerns about rate of return regulation are shared by many state, federal, and foreign bodies with experience in the telecommunications arena. The National Telecommunications and Information Admin. (NTIA) has evaluated the rate of return approach and found it wanting in many respects. Both NTIA and the United States Dep't of Justice are participating in this proceeding, and both are supportive of the price cap approach, particularly as we have proposed to apply it to AT&T. Regulators in the United Kingdom have administered price cap regulation successfully since 1984. Furthermore, the flight from the rate of return approach by state regulators continues unabated. Only 20 of the 42 states in which AT&T offers service currently regulate AT&T pursuant to a regulatory structure like that employed by this Commission, and the number of states applying some form of incentive regulation to LECs is increasing.

3. The Incentive System

The attractiveness of incentive regulation lies in its ability to replicate more accurately than rate of return the dynamic, consumer-oriented process that characterizes a competitive market. In general, such regulation operates by placing limits on the rates carriers may charge for services. In the face of such constraints, a carrier's primary means of increasing earnings are to enhance its efficiency and innovate in the provision of service. Because cost padding and cross-subsidization do not justify higher prices under this system—but instead lower profits—the incentives to engage in such activity are limited. The system also is less complex than rate of return regulation and easier to administer in the long run, which should reduce the cost of regulation.

Because cost allocation requirements do not play as central a role under incentive regulation as they do under rate of return, incentive regulation represents a more effective method of policing shifting industry boundaries than rate of return. The restraints on price increases become less significant when competition develops because competitive forces hold prices down. Indeed, a system of pricing restraints offers a means of determining what sectors of the market are becoming competitive, as this will be revealed when carriers voluntarily price below authorized pricing levels. Our ability to obtain such information will enable us to determine more accurately under incentive regulation than we can under rate of return what, if any, further movement should be made regarding regulation of particular dominant carriers. More important, the pricing limitations offer consumers strong protection against attempted exercises of market power.

The incentive regulatory approach adopted for tariff review purposes in this Order for AT&T and proposes for the LECs operates according to the following model. A carrier's services are grouped together in accordance with common characteristics, and the weighted prices in each group are adjusted annually pursuant to formulas designed to ensure that rates are based on the cost of providing service. The formulas provide for adjustments similar to those carriers make to their rates under the current system. For example, all carriers currently adjust their rates in accordance with changes in their input costs. Our formulas accomplish the same result, measuring such changes with reference to the Gross National Product Price Index (GNP-PI), a recognized, government-administered index that reflects broad-based input cost changes experienced by dominant carriers more accurately than the more commonly known Consumer Price Index. We also will continue under price caps the current policy of adjusting rates for known cost changes, such as those caused by regulatory decisions, that are beyond a carrier's direct control. For example, AT&T's rates will be adjusted to reflect regulatory changes, such as changes in the level of access charges, as is the case today.

Our incentive system also requires that we add another component to our formula limiting aggregate price increases. Although the GNP-PI already reflects productivity gains for the economy as a whole, it does not reflect the degree of productivity gains experienced by the telecommunications industry historically. A number of studies demonstrate that the telecommunications sector has been more productive than the economy as a whole. In evaluating how large to make the productivity factor, we have examined a number of long term historical studies of pre-divestiture Bell System productivity and concluded that, on a long term basis, productivity has been approximately 2.1 percent per year higher than the general economy. Data from the more recent period, *i.e.*, the 1970s and 1980s, have tended to be slightly higher than the number suggested by the long term studies. Our own analysis of AT&T's price changes during the post-divestiture period indicates that AT&T's productivity differential since 1984 has been approximately 2.3 percent per year. Because we are sufficiently impressed with evidence of the more recent trend in telecommunication productivity indicating a productivity level slightly above the long term view, and because we wish to err, if we must, on the side of consumers, we have decided that AT&T's productivity factor under our plan should be 2.5 percent per year.

For the LECs, we similarly found that the available data suggest a long term historical productivity differential of slightly over 2 percent per year above the general economy, with a slightly higher differential in the more recent period. Unlike for AT&T, however, we are unable to corroborate to the same degree the LECs' productivity experience since divestiture. Because of this and possible variations in individual LEC productivity around the industry average, we tentatively have decided to proceed with a 2.5 percent productivity factor, while proposing other adjustments to LEC aggregate prices in order to ensure just and reasonable rate levels.

The downward pressure on rates exerted by the 2.5 percent productivity offset assures that consumers will be as well off under caps as they likely would have been under rate of return. Because our goal is to make consumers better off under price caps than they likely would be if we continued rate of return regulation, however, our plan requires carriers to meet goals that exceed the historic productivity of the telephone industry. In addition to the 2.5 percent adjustment noted above, carriers would be required to lower rates by another 0.5 percent—an amount we refer to as the Consumer Productivity Dividend— in order to ensure that consumers receive a guaranteed, up-front share of the additional efficiencies flowing from the improved incentives created by price cap regulation.

In effect, the price cap rate adjustment formula establishes a rule of thumb to use in evaluating a carrier's performance for tariff review purposes: a benchmark. The rates filed by carriers are self-initiated, but the relationship of those filed rates to the price cap formula will trigger various types and levels of Commission scrutiny. If a carrier achieves results superior to this benchmark as a result of its own initiative, it is permitted to keep the resulting profits, at least for a while. If a carrier claims that it cannot achieve the benchmark, we will suspend its tariff revisions and examine its proferred justification. Suspension and investigation is a reasonable response to such an event because the benchmark is based in part on a measurement of carriers' past performance, calculated on a long run basis, and failure to achieve that level of performance is legitimate grounds for inquiry. After the fourth year of the plan, the mark is subject to adjustment as a result of our comprehensive review of the price cap system, which will be conducted in light of the information the carrier reveals about itself in the course of operating pursuant to the plan.

In addition to lower rates, consumers will receive other benefits as a result of incentive regulation implemented through price caps. First, for example, they will receive assurances of rate stability that do not exist under existing regulation. These assurances result from banding limitations that mark the boundaries of potential annual price changes that would be permitted without triggering detailed investigation through the tariff process. Second, price cap regulation should spur innovations that result in consumers enjoying a wider range of high quality services at cost-effective prices. This spur to innovation should occur because, quite simply, carriers operating under price caps can make more money in the short term than under existing regulation if they respond to consumer demand for more and better services. And these are just the direct consumer benefits. The incentives for greater efficiency and innovation established by price caps should provide indirect benefits for society as a whole. Increased productivity will make the telecommunications industry more competitive both at home and abroad. In addition, a system that promotes efficiency and innovation has the indirect effect of lowering the cost of non-telecommunications goods and services because telecommunications services are a significant and growing input of the economy generally.

In general, caps will be applied to all of a carrier's existing services. Such application ensures that price cap regulation provides the greatest amount of consumer benefit and protection. Existing rates have been subject to the tariff review process, often involving exacting scrutiny, and represent the best and most practical place to initiate the new system. Although some existing rates currently are under investigation, this presents no legal barrier to their use in initiating price cap regulation. The Communications Act specifically contemplates that rates subject to investigation shall take effect, and this has occurred on many occasions during this Commission's history. Investigations will continue to be initiated and resolved under price cap regulation, as appropriate, just as they are today under rate of return regulation. Nothing in the price cap plan prevents us from ordering adjustments, including refunds, in the event that a rate subject to investigation is found to be unlawful after the initiation of price cap regulation and we fully intend to exercise our authority in such instances.

Implementing price cap regulation primarily through the tariffing process eliminates any need to make wholesale revisions in our existing rules. Our plan presents no threat to policies and programs designed to benefit low-income households or rural America, such as the Link-Up America program and geographically averaged long distance rates. In order to ensure that our proposal does not disturb telecommunications regulation by the states, no changes to jurisdictional separations rules or procedures have been proposed.

The plan we adopt today for AT&T, and our proposal for regulating LECs through price caps, are structured to ensure the continuation of the high quality telephone service Americans currently enjoy. All existing Commission procedures and reporting requirements relating to the monitoring of service quality are retained, and our LEC proposal outlines and seeks additional comment on methods of strengthening these procedures and reporting requirements.

It is important to note as a general matter that many forces constrain a carrier's ability to degrade its quality of service. First, cutting back on quality does not necessarily increase profits because permitting the network to deteriorate would result in larger blocking percentages, poorer transmission clarity, and longer down-time for switches and lines—all of which ultimately reduce the number of completed calls and, therefore, a carrier's revenues. A second practical restraint is that quality declines manifest themselves readily. No customer needs special training to detect an increase in busy signals, wrong numbers, or static on the line. And as this Commission demonstrated in the post-divestiture period when such complaints were made, we can respond swiftly and effectively to customer complaints about quality. A third restraint is that competition in the long distance market has turned quality into an important selling point, indicating that AT&T could permit quality to decline only at peril to its market position. We conclude that the combination of these practical restraints, and our ongoing monitoring efforts, will ensure that quality of service does not decline under price cap regulation.

*   *   *

As adopted in this Order, AT&T services used primarily by residential customers are placed in their own basket. Separating such services in this manner ensures that residential customers will receive a larger proportion of expected AT&T future productivity achievements than would be guaranteed under the proposal in the *Further Notice* or under existing regulation.

We also have grouped AT&T's remaining services into two baskets, according to an evaluation of the degree of competition AT&T faces in the provision of such services. All of these services are targeted primarily toward business customers. The record reflects a consensus that AT&T faces varying degrees of competition for such services, and that they should be separated accordingly. We are persuaded by this record showing and, consequently, we have created a separate basket for 800 services, in which AT&T retains substantial market power. All other AT&T business services—those provided in what the majority of commenters agree is the most competitive segment of the telecommunications market—are grouped together in what constitutes the third "service basket" contained in our plan. Grouping services in this fashion provides greater assurances than exist under existing regulation or the plan proposed in the *Further Notice* that AT&T will not raise prices for services for which it retains substantial market power and use revenues generated thereby to fund price decreases for other, more competitive services.

Because these changes in the structure of the baskets in our price cap plan significantly reduce AT&T's ability to shift costs among its various services, they also enable us to place upper and lower banding limitations on service categories, as opposed to the rate-element-by-rate-element approach proposed in the *Further Notice*. The upper band constitutes a service category price ceiling which AT&T must establish substantial cause to pierce. The lower band constitutes a price "floor." AT&T may propose service category rate decreases lower than 5 percent, but such a proposal must be accompanied by cost materials demonstrating that the proposed reduction is not predatory.

The plan proposed in the *Further Notice* for applying price cap regulation to the LECs was identical to the plan proposed for AT&T in most respects, and the LEC proposal generated the largest and most critical response to the *Further Notice*. This is not surprising. As we stated in the initial *Notice*, applying price cap regulation to LECs raises difficult and complex issues. This is not because of any weakness in the theory of incentive regulation as it is applied to the LECs. Rather, such difficulties arise in the context of implementation.

We are not persuaded by arguments that price caps cannot be applied to the LECs because implementing this alternative regulatory system entails making predictions. If a need to make predictions were a basis for finding a regulatory process fatally flawed, we would have to abandon rate of return immediately because it is based almost entirely upon predictions. As noted previously, under rate of return regulation this Commission is required to make predictions almost on a daily basis about all aspects of dominant carrier operations, from their construction proposals to the estimates of future costs and demand that form the basis for carriers' proposed tariff revisions. We have good reason to be confident that our 2.5 prediction in this Second Further Notice is a reasonable one because it is based on long term, statistically sound data.

At the same time, we do lack the same degree of corroboration for that prediction we we have obtained for AT&T through an evaluation of its post-divestiture productivity performance. Although the record contains data and other evidence relating to LEC productivity during this relatively brief period (1984–88), including several studies submitted by interested parties, such evidence is not as meaningful as similar evidence for AT&T for numerous technical reasons. In addition, the evidence in the record does not preclude possible variability of individual LEC productivity around the industry average. Therefore, in keeping with our determination that the public interest will best be served by implementing caps in a cautious manner, we propose to modify our price cap plan for LECs by adding to it a "backstop" designed to address this uncertainty about LEC productivity. Our primary proposal for this backstop is a mechanism we refer to as an automatic stabilizer. This mechanism will work in conjunction with the price cap formula to adjust LEC rates whenever it appears that rates may fall outside the zone of reasonableness for tariff review purposes. We also seek comment on a potential alternative to the stabilizer, which would consist of a detailed review of the LEC price cap system initiated two years after the first LEC price cap tariffs take effect. We are not proposing to add either suggested "backstop" to the AT&T plan because the record evidence of its productivity does not reflect the same uncertainty as it does with regard to the LECs.

*   *   *

STATEMENT OF COMMISSIONER JAMES H. QUELLO

I believe that this action is in the public interest and long overdue. The Commission, after exhaustive inquiry and comprehensive analysis, has taken a first step in imposing a new form of regulation upon AT&T, the sole interexchange carrier still considered dominant. While initiating an incentive scheme of regulation for AT&T, I believe we could have reasonably gone farther to enhance competition and benefit the public.

I am not convinced that we needed to impose floors limiting AT&T's flexibility to lower its prices. After all, we should not be in a position of limiting public benefits which result from falling prices. Nor should we be handicapping AT&T's ability to compete in markets in which there is intense and growing competition.

I am reluctantly supporting the imposition of floors at this time out of an abundance of caution and in the spirit of collegial compromise. I hope and expect that it will soon become apparent that such restraint is unnecessary and counterproductive.

With respect to the Further Notice of Proposed Rulemaking considering the imposition of price caps for the local exchange carriers, I continue to favor a structure which will provide some significant, tangible consumer benefits from the start. I would welcome a manifestation of good faith from the local exchange carriers in the form of rate reductions in the initial price cap tariff filings. While I am not wedded to any particular structure for this rate reduction, I do expect a sincere effort on the part of the carriers to bring something to the table. The timetable for implementation of price caps for the local exchange carriers presupposes that we will have rules in place well in advance of July 1, 1990. It will require the best efforts of the carriers and the Commission to ensure that those rules can be written in a timely fashion.

Again, I believe that incentive regulation holds the promise of benefiting ratepayers and shareholders alike. The care we take in implementing such regulation is crucial in realizing that promise.

PRESS STATEMENT OF
COMMISSIONER PATRICIA DIAZ DENNIS

The AT&T price cap train is leaving the station. I have climbed aboard, but with some concern. I concur in adopting this item because I support this grand experiment to give dominant telephone companies an incentive to lower their costs.

The problem is that the route is circuitous and tickets are expensive. Price caps for AT&T is a second-best solution which results in more, not less, regulation. Rather than eliminating rate of return regulation, we are keeping much of it as a check on the reasonableness of the price caps method. And we are adding (as we must) service quality checks. Added to this are complex and intrusive mechanisms which will be a burden to AT&T and the Commission—and which guarantee full employment for communications lawyers and consultants. In addition to new reporting requirements on service quality, the item creates an elaborate structure that will have to be defined, refined and monitored: baskets; bands that will be subject to weighting and indexing; "new" services; and service "restructuring." These and other regulatory measures, including cost support requirements in some instances, make this item far from the ideal "better form of regulation" which the price caps mechanism was intended to be.

Rather than take this more expensive train today, I would have preferred to take a more direct one tomorrow—but I am not sure it will ever make it out of the roundhouse. I have been saying for some time that we need to reanalyze the state of competition in the interexchange market. (*See, e.g.*, Separate Statement of Commissioner Patricia Diaz Dennis in the AT&T ONA proceeding, FCC 88–382, released Dec. 22, 1988.) The Commission first classified AT&T as dominant almost a decade ago. Telecommunications technology, regulation and competitors have changed markedly since then. Anecdotal evidence shows (and the item assumes) that there are now markets in which AT&T is "less than" dominant. A comprehensive and detailed analysis of competition would give the Commission a much firmer basis for tailoring our method of regulating AT&T, whether rate base or price cap. If we found markets in which AT&T were nondominant, we could deregulate to the maximum extent possible under the Communications Act. At least, we could give a nondominant AT&T more pricing flexibility, as this item attempts to do. An analysis of current competition would be difficult work, but it could be the little engine that pulls us over the mountain of regulation and delivers our trail full of high-quality, low-priced communications services to the good American public on the other side.

For LECs, I agree that price caps appears to be a better method of regulation. I hope that the LEC train leaves as scheduled. Whether we need to send that train off on a different track or toward a different destination will be answered after the further rulemaking.

I am willing to go along on the ride with price caps for AT&T, but I fear the journey will not be smooth. I am concerned, first, that some of AT&T's existing rates are an inadequate starting point for price caps. The Commission does not know whether sufficient competitive pressure exists on AT&T to drive its rates into the zone of reasonableness. Nor can we say that regulation has brought all of AT&T's existing rates into the zone of reasonableness.

Secondly, the possibility of AT&T's shrinking the evening and night/weekend discounts for MTS has generated (and will likely continue to generate) controversy. I would not presume such potential changes reasonable. Instead, I would subject them to the usual tariff filing requirements of cost support or similar justification.

Finally, although price caps does not directly raise the issue, I am pleased that the item recognizes geographic rate deaveraging would raise important social and equity issues. I plan to address this issue and others in a separate concurrence upon release of the item. . . .

THE FUTURE OF PRICE CAPS

The FCC's price-cap scheme went into effect for AT&T in 1989, nearly two years after it was first proposed. Price caps should provide cost incentives for AT&T to produce more efficiently, thereby avoiding the Averch-Johnson Effect. According to Averch and Johnson, the two economists who first described the perverse incentives of rate-of-return regulation, carriers have an incentive to adopt inefficient, capital-intensive strategies when the allowed rate of return exceeds the cost of capital and to adopt inefficient, labor-intensive approaches when the cost of capital exceeds the allowed rate of return.

Price caps help eliminate management's disincentive to minimize operating costs, commonly known as the "X-inefficiency," by passing savings on to the company as well as the rate base. Price caps also encourage innovation and discourage cross-subsidization by reducing the economic incentives to engage in such conduct. Administrative savings for the regulator also come into play.

In 1990 the FCC adopted mandatory price caps for the interstate operations of the eight largest local exchange carriers (LECs)—the seven Bells and GTE—and a price-cap option for smaller companies. Those not adopting price caps were made subject to a lower prescribed rate of return.

Recall, the FCC has only limited jurisdiction over LECs, with PUCs exercising jurisdiction over all intrastate services. The Commission's jurisdiction covers LEC offering of 1) switched access to long-distance carriers, 2) special-access tariffs provided to the private line providers, and 3) other interstate matters such as LEC corridor service between two states. (For example, Chesapeake and Potomac Telephone Co., an LEC, services areas of Virginia, Maryland, and the District of Columbia, which is a corridor for interstate service. Such corridor situations exist between other states as well.)

The four baskets the FCC adopted for the LECs track the above-mentioned services. The baskets are common line (relating to a local telephone company's offering of "carrier common line" access); traffic-sensitive switched services; private line services; and an interexchange basket to account for the corridor services. Carrier common line access charges, discussed in Chapter 9, are the per-minute charge imposed by local phone companies on long-distance companies for access to their local exchanges to complete calls.

Traffic-sensitive switched service includes services such as LEC-provided operator and directory assistance. Private line services, also discussed in Chapter 9, are dedicated lines made available to larger users.

The FCC also adopted a 3.3 percent productivity index for the LECs. The LECs following this option must begin sharing earnings with ratepayers when earnings go 1 percent above the rate of return established for them. LECs opting for a higher offset of 4.3 percent will be subject to less-stringent sharing rules. The plan also has a lower-end adjustment mechanism to ensure that the price-cap scheme corrects itself if the productivity factor proves too demanding for a given company.

Since the FCC has jurisdiction only over interstate LEC behavior, it is up to each state to consider whether more flexible regulation is appropriate. Several states have considered alternatives to rate-of-return regulation. In the article following the 1990 price cap order, one state regulator gives her views on the subject generally. After that is an excerpt from a study on regulatory alternatives adopted in a few states and in Great Britain. Finally, a more radical approach, recommended by the former chairman of the FCC and others, is presented with a response.

Price caps also raise a constitutional issue that deserves brief mention. Suppose a carrier could show it was unable to recoup its costs under the capped price. Would the price cap then in effect be an unconstitutional "taking" under the Fifth Amendment, permitting the carrier to exceed the established cap as a matter of constitutional right? Suppose, on the other hand, the capped price yielded extraordinary profits for the carrier. Would failure to return a portion of the excess amount to a "taking," this time from the consumer?

POLICY AND RULES CONCERNING RATES
FOR DOMINANT CARRIERS
(PRICE CAPS), SECOND REPORT AND ORDER

5 F.C.C. Rcd. 6786 (1990)

This Report and Order adopts a new system of regulating the interstate common carrier services of the Nation's largest local exchange carriers (LECs). These companies, providing the critical telecommunications link between customer's premises and the interexchange networks, have until now been regulated under a "cost-plus" system of regulation, in which rates the LECs can charge for services are based on costs plus a return on invested capital. By our action today, the "cost-plus" system of regulation will be replaced for the largest of the LECs on Jan. 1, 1991, with an incentive-based system of regulation similar to the system we now use to regulate AT&T. Incentive regulation will reward companies that become more productive and efficient, while ensuring that productivity and efficiency gains are shared with ratepayers.

In designing an incentive-based system of regulation for the largest LECs, our objective, as with our price caps system for AT&T, is to harness the profit-making incentives common to all businesses to produce a set of outcomes that advance the public interest goals of just, reasonable, and nondiscriminatory rates, as well as a communications system that offers innovative, high quality services. To accomplish this objective, the plan we adopt for LECs modifies the tariff review process to set a ceiling, or cap, on the prices LECs can charge for their interstate offerings. The price cap is subject to an annual adjustment that ensures prices will drop in real, inflation-adjusted terms. LECs that can outperform the productivity level embedded in the annual adjustment mechanism are rewarded with the ability to retain reasonably higher earnings than would be available under the former regulatory system. Depending upon their achieved returns, their ratepayers share in those earnings. Those LECs able to decrease prices beyond the required level can retain an even greater amount of earnings.

Price caps regulation of LECs, as we have designed it, is intended to produce rates within a zone of reasonableness. Higher earnings will be shared with, or returned to, ratepayers. The checks and balances built into the system ensure that, with periodic review and adjustment, price cap regulation can serve as a long term mode of regulation for the LECs subject to it. In this respect, we review price cap regulation no differently than many of the state governments and foreign administrations that have adopted incentive-based regulation for LECs' intrastate operations or their foreign equivalents, as a permanent method of regulation.

While the price cap system we adopt for LECs is similar in many respects to the one that we use to regulate AT&T, the differences in the markets involved, the difficulties in designing a single regulatory structure to apply to multiple companies, and a desire to safeguard regulatory programs promoting universal service, have required us at this initial stage to adopt an even more cautious and careful approach to the redesign of our regulatory processes than we did with AT&T. As with the AT&T plan, the LEC price cap system essentially operates through the tariff review process to ensure rates are within the parameters our price cap rules require. However, the LEC system also contains additional safeguards, such as sharing of profits, that represent both a limited departure and logical outgrowth from the AT&T plan.

B. Summary of the Plan

The *Second Further Notice* proposed an interstate access price cap mechanism composed of three elements—a measure of inflation, a productivity offset, and exogenous costs. We retain that basic adjustment mechanism, including the measure of inflation the Commission proposed[3] and a specific list of exogenous cost changes that are generally beyond the control of the companies involved and the product of regulatory decisions. Also as proposed, we decide not to employ the basic cap mechanism for non-traffic sensitive common line services.

---

3. The measure of inflation will be the same as in the AT&T price cap system, the Gross National Product Price Index.

The mechanism we adopt for common line service embraces the philosophy that local exchange carriers should split the benefits in growth in minutes per line for common line service with their ratepayers. This philosophy balances demand-inducing incentives to improve and diversify network offerings, with the recognition that under rate of return, carriers have had somewhat limited incentives to influence growth in demand. We modify the prior proposal in response to concerns expressed by commenters that the specific equations used to determine carrier common line rates produced an unintended windfall to carriers. The equations have been revised to ensure that half the benefits of demand growth are reflected in the resulting reductions in carrier common line charges. In addition to removing the unintended windfall created by the prior common line formula, we conclude that the previously proposed 3 percent productivity offset, which included a Consumer Productivity Dividend (CPD) of .5 percent, is too low given the recent performance of the largest LECs in the provision of interstate access. Therefore, for the interstate access activities of the LECs subject to price cap regulation, we will mandate a price cap that requires a higher 3.3 percent productivity gain each year including the CPD, or if a LEC chooses, a 4.3 percent productivity gain including the CPD. Selection of a higher productivity offset, *i.e.*, lowering prices beyond the mandated level, will permit the LEC to retain a larger share of its earnings.

We respond in two ways to concerns about the validity of the productivity offset as to the industry as a whole and as to individual LECs. First, we will limit mandatory application of the price cap system to the eight largest LECs—the seven Regional Bell Operating Companies (RBOCs) and General Telephone and Telegraph Co. (GTOC). The data we have collected as a basis for our selection of a 3.3 percent productivity offset is directly applicable to these largest carriers. For mid-sized and smaller LECs, price cap regulation will be optional. This decision addresses the concern that mid-sized carriers, those just below the largest eight in size, might not be able to generate productivity gains of the same magnitude as the largest LECs.

Our second response to concerns about the validity of applying a single productivity offset to a number of LECs is the adoption of sharing and adjustment devices. The mechanisms we adopt here ensure that ratepayers share further in the benefits a price cap system can produce. If a LEC whose rates are at or below the price cap an outperform the 3.3 percent productivity offset embedded in the price cap, thereby earning a higher profit, the LEC will be entitled to retain all of its earnings up to 100 basis points (or 1 percent) above the 11.25 percent unitary rate of return established for rate of return carriers. When using a 3.3 percent productivity offset to establish prices, LECs must share with their customers 50 percent of their earnings between 100 and 500 basis points (1 to 5 percent) above the 11.25 percent level, and share (or credit their customers with) 100 percent of their earnings above 16.25 percent, or 500 basis points above 11.25 percent. Based on the 11.25 percent rate of return we select in the companion item we adopt today, this mechanism allows LECs whose productivity performance exceeds the 3.3 percent productivity offset to potentially earn up to an effective equivalent of a maximum 14.25 percent rate of return.[6]

---

6. Since LECs must share 50 percent of their regulated earnings between 12.25 percent and

If a LEC decides to lower its set prices further by using a higher productivity offset of 4.3 percent, the LEC can retain more of its earnings if it subsequently is able to earn higher profits through improved efficiency. In this case, the LEC can retain all of its earnings up to 200 basis points (or 2 percent) above 11.25 percent. LECs would share with their customers 50 percent of their earnings between 200 and 600 basis points (2 to 6 percent) above 11.25 percent, and share 100 percent of their earnings above 17.25 percent, or 600 basis points above 11.25 percent. In electing to lower prices further to a level reflecting a higher 4.3 percent productivity offset, a LEC thus enables itself to reach an effective equivalent of a maximum 15.25 percent rate of return.[7]

This sharing mechanism for carriers whose rates are at or below the price cap provides strong financial incentives for carriers to improve productivity to the maximum extent possible, while providing ratepayers with additional upfront benefits of productivity gains in the form of price decreases. If a carrier manages to produce significantly higher returns, those are returned to ratepayers in the form of prospective downward adjustments in the price cap. This plan eliminates certain disincentives posed by the previous plan for an automatic stabilizer device that was proposed to control high earnings of LECs under price caps. Such a stabilizer would have created permanent downward adjustments to the cap each time earnings rose above a specified level. As such, it would have created some of the same disincentives as our present rate of return system—cost padding—in order to avoid triggering the stabilizer.

We retain a lower end adjustment mechanism with modifications, in order to ensure that the plan automatically corrects itself should our selection of a productivity factor for the industry turn out to be too high for a given company. Should a LEC's earnings drop below the lower end figure established, that LEC is entitled to a prospective automatic upward adjustment to its cap. The lower trigger point will be located 100 basis points (1 percent) below 11.25 percent.

The price cap forms the cornerstone of the new regulatory system, at once protecting ratepayers as a group from high prices and providing carriers with the incentive to increase productivity. However, since a cap on aggregate prices can result in some offerings being priced relatively high, while others are priced relatively low, we adopt further ratepayer protections in the form of baskets, service categories, and pricing bands. Baskets are broad groupings of LEC services, each subject to its own cap. Service categories are subdivisions of baskets. Pricing bands permit prices for service categories to move on a streamlined basis no more than plus or minus 5 percent per year, adjusted for the change in the price cap.

Together, the cap and pricing bands form a "no-suspension" zone within which rates for LEC access services can be changed on a "streamlined" basis, *i.e.*, on 14 days' notice, with a presumption of lawfulness. If filed rates are at a level above or below the pricing bands, or above the cap, more burdensome tariff

---

16.25 percent, and return all earnings above 16.25 percent, LECs may keep only 14.25 percent once sharing is completed.

7. In this case, LECs retain 50 percent of the earnings between 13.25 percent and 17.25 percent, for a total of 15.25 percent.

review requirements are used to evaluate the LECs' rates, and longer notice periods apply.

While the baskets continue to be defined by the interstate access structure contained in our Part 69 Rules, we have decided to expand the number of baskets of services from three to four. The first three baskets will be common line services, traffic sensitive services, and special access services. The fourth basket is created for those LECs that offer interexchange services. As previously proposed, these offerings would have been included in the basket containing special access offerings. Inclusion of these very different services into one basket raised issues concerning the flow-through of exogenous costs that can be solved by separating the interexchange activity from interstate access. Furthermore, since these services compete with the offerings of interexchange carriers, we have decided to apply the productivity factor we use for AT&T: 3 percent. Since our short term productivity study did not include a separate evaluation of the productivity of these services, we believe it would be ill-advised to apply a higher productivity requirement to the LECs' interexchange offerings than we apply to AT&T.

Service categories are used in two of the four baskets to limit streamlined price movement. In the traffic sensitive basket, we create three service categories: (1) local switching; (2) local transport; and (3) information. In the special access basket, we have decided to modify the service category proposal, reducing the number of categories from nine to four. Our decision is based on consideration of the small, and in some cases, shrinking amount of certain special access services offered by LECs. By grouping similar services together, we believe we have effectively prevented opportunities for the LECs to engage in pricing discrimination or anticompetitive practices. The four categories we adopt are: (1) voice grade/WATS/metallic/telegraph; (2) audio/video; (3) high capacity/Digital Data Service; and (4) wideband data/wideband analog.

*　　*　　*

Also as proposed, LECs subject to price cap regulation will use July 1, 1990 rates as a basis for their first price cap filing. Those rates were subject to scrutiny as part of the annual access filing and review process, and have thus recently been retargeted to earn the authorized rate of return. In the companion item we adopt today, we lower the authorized return. Price cap LECs will be required to flow through the effects of that adjustment to their price cap levels and rates as part of their initial filing.

Companies that are required to enter price caps, or that volunteer for price caps, are required to do so on an "all or nothing" basis; all affiliates, except average schedule affiliates, must enter the price cap system. Our "all or nothing" rule is intended to prevent cost shifting to affiliates that are regulated under rate of return from affiliates that are subject to price caps. In addition, price cap "volunteers" and their affiliates that currently participate in National Exchange Carrier Association pooling arrangements must remove themselves from the pools before entering price caps. To accommodate this requirement, we have slightly modified the exit rules for depooling carriers. We also decide to permit voluntary elections into caps on an annual basis.

The tariff review standards we adopt are the same as those we now use for AT&T. Tariff transmittals containing only price changes that are within the cap and pricing bands are filed on short notice. Only those transmittals that contain within-cap and within-band price changes to existing services are presumed lawful for tariff review purposes. Any filings that include rate changes below the bands must be accompanied by an average variable cost showing and are filed on 45 days' notice. Any filings proposing above-band rates are filed on 90 days' notice and must be accompanied by a showing that substantial cause exists to justify an above-band rate. Any above-cap filings are also filed on 90 days' notice and must be accompanied by a detailed cost showing that will enable the Commission to determine compliance with statutory requirements of just and reasonable rates that are not unjustly discriminatory. These latter two types of filing carry with them a heavy burden of justification and a strong likelihood of suspension. New services, defined as those that expand a ratepayer's range of choices, are filed on 45 days' notice and must be accompanied by a showing demonstrating that the new service will generate net revenues for the LEC over a specified period of time. Restructured services, those that simply redefine existing offerings, are also subject to 45-day notice requirements, and are not presumed lawful. We have decided that Open Network Architecture services, and other services that require fundamental changes in the structure of our access charge rules, raise pricing issues that can best be resolved in other proceedings.

To enhance our ability to evaluate the price cap system and to ensure that the incentives created in the plan operate in the public interest, we are retaining our existing monitoring and expanding our collection of service quality information. By doing so, we can measure the success of our regulatory program and ensure continued high quality service to ratepayers. Furthermore, we find that periodic reviews of our regulatory system are essential to keep it on track. We therefore adopt, as part of the price cap package, the proposal to undertake a comprehensive performance review of the system after the end of the third year. The review, to be completed during the fourth year of the plan, will evaluate all aspects of LEC performance, and make any adjustments to the plan that are warranted.

* * *

C. Rationale for Adoption of Incentive Regulation

The basic rate of return mechanisms that form the foundation of our current system of regulation were originally designed for the regulation of public utilities decades ago. When rate of return was applied by the Commission to interstate telephone operations in the 1960s, the regulatory environment in which it was introduced was vastly different from today. In 1965, rate of return needed to be applied only to one telephone services provider—AT&T. One company essentially provided most local service, intrastate and interstate toll service, international service, virtually all research and development for the industry, as well as the manufacture of equipment through its Western Electric subsidiary.

Today, we operate in a much more complex environment. The divestiture of the seven RBOCs from AT&T not only brought into being eight entities where formerly there was one, but also compelled the establishment of a uniform, tariffed system of charging interexchange carriers for access to the local networks for the origination and termination of messages. For the first time, the Commission had to apply its rate of return mechanisms directly to 1400 providers of access—the independent LECs and the RBOCs. Moreover, as the *Second Further Notice* discussed, the once-sharp boundaries between communications and data processing became blurred. Advances in transmission technology, geometric advances in microchip technology, and an improved ability to manage and utilize the spectrum, caused previously unrelated industries to come into competitive interaction. As domestic markets evolved, so did markets at the international level. LECs today are involved in a broad range of international activities, a movement that will surely continue given the movement toward the liberalization of world markets. At the same time, international entities are actively involved in U.S. markets, particularly in the provision of telecommunications equipment. Finally, our own pro-competitive policies provide an environment for increased competition for a wide variety of telecommunications goods and services.

In sum, the telecommunications environment LECs face has changed radically since the mid-1960s. And while we have made improvements in our ability to administer rate of return rules, the basic, underlying regulatory structure lying at the heart of our Rules remains unchanged. We are also concerned that, particularly for the largest LECs, the system of regulation we currently employ does not serve to sharpen the competitiveness of this important segment of the industry at a time when markets for telecommunications goods and services are becoming increasingly competitive, both nationally and internationally. We are aware of the extensive debate currently in progress over the relative competitiveness of U.S. industries in comparison to those of Western Europe and the Far East. We do not intend to ignore an opportunity to reshape our regulatory system in a manner that benefits us in the international marketplace while also improving the productivity of the LEC industry and benefiting ratepayers.

*   *   *

Some parties have sought to equate pricing flexibility with the ability to engage in predation against the newly formed alternative access industry, or to engage in cross-subsidization to the detriment of particular classes of customers. We believe that the limited amount of pricing flexibility available to LECs under our incentive regulation plan will not grant a license to LECs to engage in predation or cross-subsidization. Indeed, our decision not to streamline price cuts below a certain level, and to require more detailed cost information for those price cuts, is testimony to our commitment to police any LEC attempts to engage in predation or cross-subsidization. Moreover, segregating LEC access services into four baskets defeats any LEC attempts to finance a predatory rate level by contemporaneously increasing rates for other services. And, since aggregate prices in these baskets cannot rise above the price cap ceiling, it should be difficult for LECs to engage in the classic predation scenario of lowering prices to predatory levels today in an effort to raise them to monopoly levels once competition is defeated. Our Section 208 complaint process remains available as a further check against possible predation. Thus, we remain committed to ensuring that rates are just, reasonable and nondiscriminatory.

*   *   *

D. Regulatory Alternatives

In the course of debating the relative merits of price cap and rate of return regulation, a number of parties have asked the Commission to consider alternatives to price cap regulation. Several parties ask that we instead focus on ways of improving rate of return regulation. Some commenters unite behind the proposition that regulatory lag is a better alternative than incentive regulation.

Although improvement in rate of return methods is one possible course to follow in reforming current regulatory practices, it is not the best approach. We recognize that a number of state regulatory commissions have opted to improve rate of return regulation in redesigning their regulatory structures. Nevertheless, only a few states now continue to regulate intrastate LEC activities pursuant to traditional rate of return practices. The majority of states have authorized significant reforms to their regulatory systems, as part of an effort to improve efficiency incentives, increase flexibility, reduce administrative burdens, and benefit consumers.

*   *   *

II. The Price Cap Plan

A. The Price Cap Index

The Price Cap Index (PCI) is designed to limit the prices carriers charge for service. By employing a regulatory system that shifts our focus to prices while permitting retention of some reasonably higher earnings, we provide carriers an incentive to become more productive, and to offer new services. To provide a quantitatively achievable incentive for the LECs, the price cap mechanism includes components that reflect historical LEC productivity, and then requires them to out-perform historical trends. These factors are the productivity offset and the Consumer Productivity Dividend. The establishment of an objective productivity hurdle that applies to prices in each year of the plan provides the LECs an incentive to be more productive, since an improved productivity performance above the amount required by the formula permits them to generate and retain higher earnings.

The PCI contains three components. The first two, a measure of inflation less a productivity offset, represent the amount by which carrier productivity has historically exceeded productivity in the economy generally. The value attached to the PCI is further permitted to move up or down in response to specific exogenous cost changes. Exogenous cost changes are generally outside the carrier's managerial control and are often the product of this Commission's own regulatory actions.

In broad terms, the PCI is the first test of whether a carrier's tariff filings qualify for streamlined review. By setting price limits that are defined by changes in input costs, the formula controls aggregate rates charged by carriers from fluctuating beyond a "zone of reasonableness." . . .

PRICE CAPS WITH A CONSUMER BENEFIT MECHANISM: A WORKABLE APPROACH FOR AT&T

Gail Garfield Schwartz

*   *   *

Price caps are most appropriate in a "mixed" market, that is, in a situation where some competition of a variable nature exists and some monopoly power remains. In a situation where competition is vigorous and widespread, no economic regulation at all is desirable. In a natural monopoly situation price caps *might* be superior to RORR[1] in the degree that they induce efficiencies and cost savings that would be passed on to the ratepayer, but they will not *necessarily be so*. Price caps would be a carrot, but lacking competition, the monopolist would fear no stick. The stick is essential: economists have long recognized the possibility that, where competition is weak and firms hold market power, management efficiency may be lacking. This is why it is in the mixed case that a price cap approach is most promising.

Furthermore, price caps are more questionable in a monopoly situation than in a mixed situation because the extent to which caps will ensure that some consumers are not harmed (or that all consumers benefit to some degree) will be determined by the structure of the caps themselves. In the absence of competition, a system of price caps that would adequately protect consumers (and competitors, to ultimately benefit consumers) may significantly reduce the practical advantage of caps over RORR. A very loose price cap regime exacerbates the classic regulator's challenge: how to keep a monopolist from setting excessive markups for services where demand is least elastic, i.e., where customers are most captive. Particularly where a monopolist or its parent holding company can engage in some unregulated activities using the same equipment and personnel that are used in the regulated portion of the business, the incentive to do this is large. The only reason to allow a monopolist this freedom is that arguably, long-run efficiencies may be realized. However, short-run unfairness to some consumers may also result. To prevent unfair pricing, an extremely complex system of caps would be needed. Such a system would not necessarily encourage efficiency more than RORR.

In the mixed situation, the existing competition, while not sufficient to fully control a dominant firm's residual market power, would complement price caps. For competitive services, price caps can be less specific and fine-grained; for less competitives services, they can be more tightly structured. If competition varies geographically, flexibility can be allowed while averaged pricing is either encouraged or guaranteed.

Gail Garfield Schwartz is the Deputy Chairman of the New York State Public Service Commission. Jeffrey H. Hoagg assisted in the preparation of this article. Reprinted from *Telematics*, vol. 5, no. 6 (June 1988) with the permission of Prentice-Hall Law & Business.

1. Rate of Return Regulation

For these reasons, the adoption of price caps with consumer benefit mechanism does seem a viable policy at this time for AT&T. For the same reasons, a price cap regime does not seem appropriate for the largely monopoly interstate service of the LECs. To gain the advantages sought, a "cap" approach for LECs would require a cap on *revenues* that allowed *price flexibility* within that revenue cap—thus risking either discriminatory pricing or a very complex pricing mechanism. At this time, there is simply not enough competition demonstrated with regard to LEC interstate services to make the choice.

*   *   *

Pure Price Caps vs. Consumer Benefit Mechanisms

"Pure" price caps denote the case where there exists no vestige of ROR regulation; indexed caps would be the sole mechanism relied upon to establish dominant carrier prices. In the pure case there are two key mechanisms intended to pass the benefits of future cost reductions through to ratepayers. The first of these mechanisms is direct pass-through of reductions that are basically outside the carrier's control, (e.g., reductions in access costs in the case of AT&T). Naturally, this is expected.

The second is a productivity adjustment factor which might reflect either generalized productivity experience or more industry-specific experience. This would be an imperfect instrument at best. It would always lag, reflecting history rather than reflecting actual cost efficiencies as they occur. Thus, it could depart significantly from realized efficiencies.

It is unrealistic to think that this mechanism would be an adequate substitute for competition, or even RORR, in assuring that consumers share in realized efficiencies. It seems that most supporters of caps are actually relying on competition to do this, so the core of the debate revolves around the intensity and nature of competition. On the one hand, many supporters of price caps contend that fully effective competition exists in virtually all AT&T's markets. If so, price caps would not improve efficiency much, since AT&T already has the most effective incentive for efficient behavior—the discipline of competition. Yet the company argues that consumers have much to gain by sharing in the increased efficiencies price caps will automatically induce. Either the degree of competition AT&T currently faces is being exaggerated, or the benefits consumers would receive from caps is overstated.

We can only guess at the carrier's probable behavior under price caps. Certainly it is doubtful that all the interstate long distance markets are competitive enough to guarantee that all ratepayers would receive a sufficient share of the total benefit "pie" under a pure price cap system. We cannot be assured even that some ratepayers would realize lower prices. Prices may stick at or near the level of the cap as a result of the fact that AT&T may have greater economies of scale and scope than its competitors; these competitors may not be able to lower prices below the cap, and AT&T would therefore not have to do so.

This uncertainty clearly poses a threat to popular acceptance of the price cap scheme. It argues persuasively in favor of a mechanism to ensure that prices adequately reflect both initial costs and cost trends. Two possible mechanisms are discussed.

*   *   *

The first possibility is to impose periodic rate of return review upon price caps. This would guarantee that, within a reasonable time period, efficiencies are translated into price cuts if earnings exceed a suitable norm. It would also permit, at the end of each period, an adjustment to price caps if justified by rising costs as reflected in subnormal earnings.

To avoid unduly reducing the carrier's incentives for efficiency, which are inversely related to the frequency of earnings review, the determination of an appropriate review period is critical. The more frequent the review, the smaller may be the total benefits of price cap regulation, but the greater the ratepayers' assured share of those benefits. The less frequent the review, the greater may be the total benefits, but the smaller the consumers' share. For example, a three-year period might offer a fair and reasonable balance between the short-run and long-run interests of the firms and of the consumers. The carrier's incentives to innovate and cut costs will not be dampened by early reductions of profits, and the consumers would not be forced to wait an undue time to realize their share of the gains.

*   *   *

An alternative consumer benefit mechanism is the sharing between company and consumers of profits above a threshold level. The ability to realize profits above a target norm ensures that carriers will pursue efficiency improvements. Ratepayers are assured of regular and consistent benefits when costs fall. In New York, such sharing has been established for New York Telephone Co., Rochester Telephone Co., Continental Telephone Co., and AT&T Communications.

Opponents of this mechanism might argue that it would inhibit cost-cutting behavior. However, the argument has not been found compelling in other situations. In fact, the earnings "share" going to ratepayers could be viewed as a tax paid by the carrier directly to this group. It is not generally argued that taxes of this sort reduce a firm's incentive for *efficient operation*, although it can, of course, affect the output decisions of the firm. If there is reasonable assurance that this is a stable regulatory environment, the carrier should not be unduly deterred from striving for maximum cost efficiency by the fact that it can keep only a part of the resulting benefits.

*   *   *

Price Cap Adjustment Factor

While much attention has been focused on the proper formulation of a price cap adjustment factor, the prior question of whether and under what circumstances an adjustment factor is appropriate seems to have received little discussion. The adjustment factor is unnecessary in a price cap regime that includes any consumer benefit mechanism. Periodic price cap review associated with the implementation of the consumer benefit mechanism would sidestep all the problems raised by the proposed adjustment factor.

In the "pure" price cap proposals, one role of the adjustment factor is to adjust cap levels to reflect changes in the general price level. However, this is a regulatory device which would work against the efficiency incentives that are central to any price cap system's superiority over RORR. Insulating carriers from the risk that rising price levels cannot be passed on to consumers has no counterpart in unregulated industries. In the larger economy, no sector is totally immune from general price level changes, and the more competitive the sector, the less the immunity. It is difficult to justify singling out the telecommunications sector for insulation, because this is the antithesis of the goal of the sector: to gain the benefits of competition. Neither AT&T nor its competitors should be granted immunity from the risks associated with inflation, as indexation of price caps could well do.

The other role of the proposed adjustment factor is to reflect productivity trends in the industry. However, the question arises whether this would be the most appropriate mechanism in light of expectations of continued declining costs and the significant efficiency gains anticipated from price caps. If these are as great as expected, a price cap fixed in nominal terms between periodic reviews could more accurately reflect these trends and work no hardship on the carrier.

In sum, an adjustment factor is not necessary in price caps with periodic earnings review or sharing of excess earnings, either of which is preferable to a price index. With either consumer benefit mechanism, the carrier is protected over the long run from capital confiscation due to inflation. Over the shorter run, the carrier isn't artificially insulated from risks associated with changing price levels, and therefore faces increased pressure for efficiency.

Conclusion

There is good reason to adopt a price cap approach for AT&T, with a consumer benefit mechanism. It is likely that consumers would benefit by comparison to what they experience under RORR. While shareholders may also gain more than they would under RORR, this is acceptable if consumer benefits are realized.

As for the LECs, it is premature to apply the price cap scheme to them, as they are not sufficiently competitive. Overall, the downside risk to ratepayers of capping prices for LEC monopoly access services outweighs the benefits that might occur in the few markets where alternatives to LEC network access exist. To prevent bypass, banded or tapered access charges could be permitted. Other forms of price flexibility for LEC interstate services could also be explored, including experimental deregulation of access prices where vigorous competition is established.

THE IMPACT OF REGULATION AND PUBLIC POLICY ON TELECOMMUNICATIONS INFRASTRUCTURE AND U.S. COMPETITIVENESS

Shooshan & Jackson, Inc. (1989)

[R]egulatory reform is especially important because the existing regulatory structure does not provide adequate incentives for investment. Telecommunications infrastructure in the United States is owned by private firms rather than by government entities and is funded by private investment rather than by government subsidies. Since investments are not centrally directed, investment in the public network is not automatic. A regulatory and legislative environment that provides firms with the greatest incentives to bring new products and services to *all* customers (large and small businesses, residential customers) would allow the U.S. to maintain its leadership position in telecommunications. At the same time, the regulatory system must be designed so that it offers incentives for the firm to act in the public interest and also protects consumers against potential monopolistic abuse.

With regard to modernizing the telecommunications infrastructure, the most "effective" legislation or regulation is that which achieves the three following policy objectives: (1) the introduction of competition along with pricing flexibility for established firms which allows those firms to respond to competition while at the same time protecting consumers and competitors from unfair practices; (2) the opportunity and the incentive for regulated firms to upgrade and modernize their networks; and (3) the opportunity for these firms to recover the costs of embedded plant in response to a changing environment.

State Level

According to a recent survey, 26 states have enacted some form of deregulation legislation since 1983. Of these 26 states, nine are in the Northeast-Midwest region: Connecticut, Illinois, Indiana, Iowa, Michigan, Minnesota, Missouri, Vermont and Wisconsin. For purposes of this discussion, deregulation legislation is defined as legislation which either withdraws regulatory authority from the state regulatory commission or provides the state regulatory commission with the authority to deregulate telecommunications services and/or products using any number of standards: presence, nature or degree of competition; market power or share; or a threshold number of alternate providers.

Some state regulatory commissions have used this regulatory flexibility to enter into agreements with telecommunications providers. While these plans have several different names (social contract, price caps, incentive regulation), they are "first steps" toward improving incentives to modernize telecommunications infrastructure, and as such, may serve as models for future policy.

Nebraska

Nebraska's comparatively radical approach towards the deregulation of its telecommunications firms has brought the state widespread attention. The 1986 Nebraska deregulation statute is unique because it mandated that all telecommunications services and companies be removed from state rate regulation, and permitted the Public Utility Commission *no* discretion regarding the nature of deregulation. The PUC does, however, continue to regulate the quality of service.

The existence and degree of competition were not at issue in enacting this legislation. However, with the exception of local telephone franchises, all barriers to entry into telecommunications markets were removed. In order for local exchange service to be removed from rate regulation, rate increases may not exceed a certain amount over a specified period of time. For basic local exchange service to be deregulated, 60 days notice is required. If a certain percentage of customers complain, or if rates rise by more than 10 percent, the PUC must review the rates. For services other than basic local exchange, companies are required to file rate lists for services with 10 days notice to the PUC, but the PUC has no power to veto or review the lists.

As a result of deregulation, telecommunications firms in Nebraska can use all available resources to compete successfully with new entrants into the industry, while still maintaining reasonable rates and quality of service. For example, US West recently announced plans to introduce commercial videotex in Omaha by October, 1989. Omaha was chosen as the first site for the service offering because, according to US West Chairman Jack MacAllister, "Nebraska offers the most freedom from regulation of any state in the country."

*   *   *

Vermont

Earlier this year, the Vermont Public Service Board (PSB) ratified a reform which will enable it to enter into agreements with the local exchange service provider, New England Telephone (NET), regarding the provision of telecommunications service in the state. Dubbed "social contract," the reform itself is the product of several years of negotiations between government and industry. The concept of a social contract was introduced by Louise McCarren in 1985 (PSB Chairman at the time), and endorsed by the legislature in 1987.

*   *   *

The initial plan was first rejected with suggested modifications by the Board late last summer. As now modified and adopted by the PSB, the Vermont social contract will further infrastructure development with the additional benefit of yielding savings and rate stability for state ratepayers.

Specifically, the contract provides for rate stability for basic and residential service through 1991 (which can, subject to approval by the Board, be extended through 1992). In "exchange," New England Telephone will be able to introduce (or withdraw) new services and products (those not spelled out in the agreement) after a 15-day notice period. Not only will new services be made available without regulatory delay, but ratepayers will benefit from stable rates.

As part of this agreement with the state, New England Telephone has promised to invest $284 million over the next two years in telecommunications equipment and facilities, an investment which will benefit telecommunications infrastructure.

New York

Another type of agreement is the so-called "New York Plan." Under an agreement reached with the New York Public Utility Commission, New York Telephone agreed to freeze basic telephone rates until 1991 in return for pricing flexibility for competitive services. The phone company was permitted to earn a higher rate-of-return, but required to share one-half of its earnings above 14 percent equally with state ratepayers (similar agreements were reached with Rochester Telephone and ALLTEL).

The New York Plan, however, falls short of major reform in regulation that may be required to encourage the risky investments needed to modernize the telecommunications infrastructure. The New York Plan has the same asymmetrical incentives as traditional rate-of-return regulation. Upside potential is limited, because the company must reduce rates to "share profits" with ratepayers if its innovations are successful. Upside potential could be further limited if regulators disallow expenses associated with unsuccessful innovations. On the other hand, the telephone company has no protection on the downside since the rates it charges for monopoly services are frozen while the rates it charges for competitive services are constrained by competition.

* * *

A Case Study in Price Caps: British Telecom. British Telecom (BT), the dominant British telecommunications carrier, has operated under price cap regulation since 1984. The analysis below focuses on the British Telecom experience, partly in order to judge the success of this regulatory scheme and partly to see whether or not it would be desirable to implement such regulatory reform in the U.S.

Prior to 1984, British Telecom (BT) was a government-owned enterprise. The firm was privatized at the same time that price cap regulation was implemented. A major objective of adopting price caps for BT was to ensure that, as a private firm, it would be an attractive investment opportunity.

The price-based regulatory scheme required BT to set tariffs so that the tariff index could be increased by the retail price index (RPI) minus a certain percentage (X) in any given year. The formula (RPI-X) would be applied to a basket of services (excluding public telephones and including domestic long distance) so that BT would enjoy pricing flexibility over a broad range of services. In the version of the plan adopted, three percentage points are to be subtracted from annual changes in the RPI for the five-year term from 1984 to 1989 to reflect the potential for cost reduction and changes in demand. This figure was negotiated between British Telecom and the British Department of Trade and Industry. In addition, BT agreed not to raise residential line rentals by more than two percentage points per year over the retail price index.

By constructing the formula in this way, customers could be sure that overall rate increases would not exceed the rate of inflation since the retail price index acts as a constraint on average prices in the basket of services. Rate elements are weighted according to their estimated revenues from the past year. The inflation rate is calculated based on the retail price index in the past year. If prices are not increased by the maximum level, the shortfall can be applied in future periods. If the rate of inflation is less than three percent, BT has a year in which to reduce rates, provided no other price increases are affected.

The Office of Telecommunications (OFTEL) is responsible for the regulation of British Telecom, and that regulation is extensive. Performance indicators are closely monitored so that service quality will not deteriorate. Reduction in quality is regarded as equivalent to an increase in price, and will be treated in the same manner. In fact, BT must pay a fine if there are delays in installation or repair. According to OFTEL, quality of service has remained constant since the plan was implemented.

Since a common fear associated with price cap regulation is that the firm will earn excessive profits, BT's rate-of-return and profitability have also been closely monitored. Essentially, the regulatory system supervised by OFTEL focuses first on price, and then monitors profits to ensure that they are reasonable.

If BT's profits should become unreasonable in the future, price caps will most likely be adjusted for the next term. In this manner, OFTEL's price-based regulatory scheme provides an implicit constraint against BT's earning excessive profits. Indeed, BT has not raised its prices as much as it could have under the price cap plan, to avoid generating excessively high profits.

The British experience with regulatory reform suggests that price caps could be successfully implemented in the U.S. It is particularly encouraging that BT did not raise its rates as much as it was able to under the price cap plan. This regulation innovation is superior to the traditional rate-of-return approach, since it both encourages modernization and protects consumers. BT has invested heavily in new technology, particularly digital public switches. For the year ending March 31, 1987, capital expenditure totalled £2.1 billion. Stock market capitalization on March 31, 1987 increased to approximately £15 billion from £7.8 billion at the time of flotation. The specifics of a price cap plan could, of course, be adjusted as regulators gain more experience with the approach. . . .

BACK TO THE FUTURE: A MODEL FOR TELECOMMUNICATIONS

Mark S. Fowler, Albert Halprin, and James D. Schlicting

*   *   *

Telecommunications services—both local and long distance—traditionally have been included among the core of industries falling within the public utility paradigm. The view that telecommunications is a "natural" monopoly has been defended with a number of arguments, such as: (1) simple economies of scale in the provision of a standardized service dictate that one firm should provide that service; (2) aggregate investment costs can be minimized if the planning for the installation and expansion of capacity is done on a system-wide basis; (3) the demand for higher standards of service necessitates centralized responsibility and control; and (4) no company is likely to assume the responsibility of providing a truly national network—one that enables almost everyone at any moment to reach anyone else in the most isolated part of the country—unless it has a monopoly status.

*   *   *

The past thirty years have made it clear that the public utility paradigm does not apply, and perhaps should never have been applied, across-the-board to the entire telecommunications industry. The persistence of potential competitors, plus the development of new technologies, has effectively undermined the notion

---

Reprinted by permission of the *Federal Communications Law Journal*, vol. 38, no. 145 (1986).

that outside companies can never become effective competitors of the telephone companies. Open entry was first introduced into the markets for customer premises equipment (CPE) and interexchange private line services. As open-entry policies actually led to entry by non-telephone company firms, competitive pressures increased on telephone companies, highlighting the inefficient practices that were part and parcel of public utility regulation. As a result, regulation of the rates and conditions for telephone products and services had to be relaxed, allowing the benefits of competition to be realized by the American consumer. The public utility paradigm had collapsed with respect to large segments of the telecommunications industry.

*   *   *

These significant recent changes in telecommunications regulation suggest that the time has come to replace the traditional public utility paradigm of government regulation with a competitive industry paradigm. The effects of the recent injection of competition into significant segments of interstate telecommunications, the benefits flowing from deregulation in other industries formerly regulated as public utilities, and the promise of new technologies on the brink of realization all demonstrate the necessity for changing our model for telecommunications. Unless mistaken regulatory approaches either retard or limit the industry's potential, telecommunications should become a largely competitive marketplace in which competition drives prices to costs and lowers costs to the minimum, in which products and services are provided whenever end users are willing to pay the necessary costs of production, and in which only minimal subsidies, if any, are necessary to maintain universal service to every consumer who wishes telephone service. Realization of these efficiency benefits of competition will provide greater value in the future for every telecommunications dollar.

The benefits of competition in the markets for CPE and interexchange communications are clearly evident today. It is indisputable that the market for telecommunications equipment is vigorously competitive, with numerous well-financed ventures holding significant market shares.

It is also apparent that the interexchange market is well on the way to complete competition. The majority of Americans now have a choice of long-distance carriers.[47]

*   *   *

Besides precipitating changes towards more rational pricing of telecommunications products and services, the advent of a competitive marketplace will leave

---

47. . . . The commission is committed, however, to taking all actions needed to ensure a level playing field for competition in this market. . . . For example, the Commission has addressed a number of transitional problems resulting from the presubscription process under which customers select their primary interexchange carrier before conversion of their telephone company central office to equal access. In particular, the Commission found that the routing to AT&T of all traffic from customers who fail to presubscribe was unreasonable and discriminatory. It mandated instead a uniform *pro rata* allocation plan that became effective May 31, 1985. . . .

no companies with sufficient market power to present a significant danger of anticompetitive behavior. Whenever a firm attempts to engage in improper cost-shifting or to discriminate against competitors, it will run serious risks of losing customers and revenues. Regulation to constrain such acts simply will be unnecessary.

The significant increase in technological and financial innovation caused by competition in telecommunications may also in fact resolve the chief fairness issue in telecommunications today, ensuring that everyone who desires telephone service can obtain it at an affordable price. Competition may drive prices and costs so low that no need will exist for subsidies for telephone service to any American consumer. If a need for subsidy exists, the amount will be reduced to a bare minimum. As a matter of economic theory, the most efficient way of providing such subsidies is directly through general revenue funds.

*   *   *

The day of full competition across the telecommunications market has not yet arrived, however. Local exchange service and even access for interexchange telecommunications service still are generally provided on a monopoly basis. Moreover, in an increasingly competitive interexchange market, AT&T retains a predominant market share and some significant market power. As a result, it is clear that the concerns that led to traditional public utility regulation of telecommunications services still apply to the local exchange market and, to a lesser degree, to the interexchange market.

*   *   *

The transitional marketplace is asymmetric, with some firms having significant market power and other firms having little. This marketplace poses substantial problems for the industry and its regulators. The entry of nondominant firms into formerly monopolistic telecommunications markets has been pressuring, and will continue to pressure, telephone companies to align prices with costs in various areas and thus to discontinue several traditional public utility pricing practices. Regulators have thus far allowed telephone companies to implement certain competitive measures in response. But as competition continues to develop, telephone companies will have to implement several additional responses with the approval of regulators.

*   *   *

Perhaps the key objective for public interest regulation in the transitional marketplace should be to stimulate use of the public switched network to the efficient levels that would be attained in a competitive marketplace. The public switched network is a critical national resource that has been underutilized because of inefficient pricing, limitations on the permissible activities of important players in the market, and limitations on access to the network by competitive service providers. Regulators should therefore seek to allow dominant carriers some pricing flexibility, to adjust the regulatory measures used to prevent possible anticompetitive behavior by dominant carriers, and to encourage implementation of an open network architecture.

A new policy of dominant carrier pricing flexibility should serve to increase use of the public switched network. As competition enters new markets, existing companies should be allowed to innovate in pricing so as to recover their joint or common costs and fixed costs by the more efficient methods that are required in competitive markets. Subsidies necessary to preserve universal service should be limited to those subscribers who could not afford telephone service if they were required to pay the full costs of such service, and should be structured so as to cause the least distortion in the economic signals given by the market for both the relative costs incurred in providing new services and the prices reflecting the individual preferences of consumers.

The removal of costly structural safeguards increases utilization of the public switched network by allowing more efficient provision of telecommunications goods and services by dominant firms. Thus, regulation has been moving, and should continue to move, from an era of structural safeguards to an era of open network architecture and other nonstructural safeguards. Implementation of open network architecture should increase use of the public switched network by opening the network to new enhanced services providers, who will thereby be assured access to the local exchange network as nearly equal as possible to that of the local exchange carriers themselves. Those providers will be able to compete with dominant carriers in offering sophisticated services that employ the basic regulated services as underlying building blocks.

VI. Accelerating the Transition to a Competitive Industry Paradigm—A Proposal

The fast-paced technological and market changes of recent years show no signs of abating. The telecommunications industry is evolving so rapidly that a competitive industry paradigm should be considered the most appropriate model for the entire industry in the relatively near future. The task of regulators is to ensure that the transition to a competitive marketplace is completed quickly, effectively, and at the least cost to consumers. As explained above, this transition should, at a minimum, be based on a continued commitment to universal service and the implementation of a regime of open network architecture that permits: (1) open entry by potential competitors both free of regulatory burdens and protected against anticompetitive conduct by telephone companies, and (2) pricing flexibility that permits telephone companies to respond competitively to such entry.

The more specific questions concerning how best to manage this transition are not susceptible to easy answers. It can be argued, for instance, that some of the Commission's regulatory actions in the interexchange market that were designed to promote competition during transition, such as highly discounted access pricing for OCCs and restrictions on competitive pricing responses by AT&T, in fact have encouraged entry by uneconomic providers and uneconomic construction of excess capacity. If this is true, the gradualist approach to deregulation of interexchange markets will have resulted in substantial, unnecessary costs for society that never would have been incurred in a truly competitive marketplace. Moreover, this approach will have directly increased consumer costs by requiring regulated firms to charge higher prices to protect competitors during the transition.

These considerations are especially relevant now because of recent developments in the provision of local exchange and access services. Such services, although not competitive now, are showing the same characteristics of supporting competition that appeared earlier with respect to CPE and interexchange services. Recent developments, such as advances in bypass technologies and shared telecommunications services, suggest that the time has come for an open entry approach to the provision of local exchange and access services. This article therefore puts forward a proposal to initiate discussion by industry participants, regulators and other policymakers, and academics on alternative approaches to the transition that might allow the swifter realization of the benefits of competition at lower costs to society.

Under this proposal, a three-year trial of total deregulation of telecommunications would be implemented in states willing to undertake such experiments. Regulation of telecommunications goods and services would be largely suspended, including all entry/exit regulation, all rate-of-return regulation of individual service prices, and all structural regulation imposed by regulators or under the *MFJ*. Competition and business freedom for the local exchange companies would be given an opportunity to bring their benefits to all sectors of the industry.

These trials would be subject to certain conditions. They would require implementation of an open network architecture for all telecommunications services—interexchange access, enhanced services, and local exchange service—to ensure that potential competitors of the telephone companies have a meaningful opportunity to provide those services as or more efficiently than the telephone companies. This comprehensive policy of equal access to the local exchange, an extension of this nation's historic practice of requiring carriers to interconnect with their competitors, would constitute the final stage in the evolution of the concept of equal access traced above.

These trials also would require a continued commitment on the part of regulators and telephone companies to maintenance of universal service. This commitment would be fulfilled most importantly through the rapid introduction of the positive forces of competition into the marketplace, which could well serve as the most effective mechanism for maintaining universal service by driving down costs to the absolute minimum. Local telephone companies are unlikely to find it in their economic interest to price local service at a level that causes any significant number of subscribers to drop off the network.[153] They instead are likely to have increased incentives to experiment with alternative rate structures and service options to continue affordable telephone service for the poor. For

---

153. This is so, at least in part, because the marginal cost of attracting new subscribers or retaining existing subscribers in areas that are already wired for telephone service is relatively small. Feeder cables to individual neighborhoods generally provide substantial excess capacity for the addition of new subscribers. In fact, it is common to bring the telephone wires to homes before the telephone company knows whether individual occupants want service. *See* BELL TELEPHONE LABORATORIES, ENGINEERING AND OPERATIONS IN THE BELL SYSTEM 289–90 (1983).

example, various local measured service alternatives to unlimited flat-rate calling could be tried, such as providing dial tone and a specified quantity of local calling for a flat monthly fee, plus a usage charge for additional calling. During these trials, this Commission and the state commissions would have to monitor developments carefully to ensure that universal service is not jeopardized. If telephone penetration levels dropped to any significant degree, corrective measures would have to be taken.

Under the terms of this proposal, any state or the federal government would remain free to regulate (*i.e.*, set a price and limit entry for) any service it was willing to subsidize from general tax revenues. The states may well determine to continue their regulation of local exchange service rates for residential and, perhaps, small business users, the services over which the local telephone companies are most likely to retain significant market power in the short term. Because these services are currently priced below cost in most instances, continued regulation will bring with it a need for external funding.

The proposal advanced here would require that any continuation of below-cost provision of local exchange services for residential and small business customers be funded from the government's general tax revenues. Other approaches have been proposed. For instance, in California, a tax has been imposed on gross revenues received from the provision of intrastate, interexchange telecommunications services to collect monies for a state-administered Universal Service Fund. Similarly, various proposals for state deregulation by "social contract" contemplate that the local telephone companies will have to increase rates or maintain rates at uneconomically high levels for their other services in order to recover any shortfall in local exchange service rates until such time as political and economic developments permit those rates to recover all costs of those services.[156] The approach suggested here brings at least two advantages over these alternative methods of financing telephone subsidies. First, it avoids the economic distortions in resource allocation that have so long plagued telephone pricing. The manifold economic efficiency benefits of competition detailed above otherwise would be lost or severely compromised; allocation of investment among various telecommunications services would be distorted; and telephone companies, still needing a source of subsidy from other services, would be forced to price certain services above relevant costs, inducing uneconomic bypass by larger customers and leaving a dwindling customer base to pay the substantial fixed costs of the public switched network. Second, this approach makes clear the true costs of maintaining low residential service rates allowing an explicit public policy judgment on the appropriate level of subsidy. Until recently, the false impression has prevailed that low residential service rates were costless.

---

156. Under "social contract" proposals, deregulation would take place through an agreement between state authorities and individual telephone companies. The companies would be required to limit local rate increases according to some external index, such as the Consumer Price Index, and to make specified capital investments during the contract period to maintain and upgrade their networks. In return, the companies would be freed from the burdens of rate-of-return regulation for all services and would be subject to minimal regulation, at most, of particular services. Obviously, the details of any social contract could vary widely depending on the concerns of state regulators and the telephone companies in different states.

If, nevertheless, such subsidies for local exchange services are to be borne by other competitive telephone services, there appear to be advantages to allowing the local telephone companies to determine where to obtain the subsidy and how to target this assistance to needy end users, subject to the absolute requirement that universal service be maintained. Attempts by regulators to find sources for these subsidies are likely to result in significant distortions from competitive cost-based pricing that will lead to a marked misallocation of resources and "uneconomic bypass" of those extra charges by end users of the burdened services. By contrast, the telephone companies, who ultimately will feel the effects of the distorted pricing in an otherwise competitive marketplace, will be constrained to structure the subsidies so as to minimize any damaging distortions of the competitive marketplace. In particular, the companies should be best able to target the subsidies only to those who need them in order to afford telephone service, to ensure that the subsidies are only as large as necessary, and to obtain the subsidies from services in inverse relation to those services' demand elasticities. By contrast, the social contract approach of limited prices on all basic local exchange service would result in a high percentage of the subsidy benefits going to recipients who have no need for them. It appears unlikely that the social benefits of this subsidy will outweigh the cost of the inefficiencies required to generate it.

Regulation of any services during trial deregulation would, of course, require measures to ensure that the providers of those services do not engage in anticompetitive conduct. This task could be accomplished through the continued application of various nonstructural safeguards, including most prominently the employment of minimal cost allocation measures and accounting safeguards to prevent cross-subsidization of competitive services by those services characterized by short-run or long-run market power. This would ensure that neither taxpayers nor ratepayers will bear a disproportionate share of any joint and common costs of regulated and unregulated services. . . .

BACK TO THE FUTURE: A COMMENT

Edythe S. Miller

*   *   *

"Back to the Future" seems to be an attempt to tie current FCC precepts and practices to the past; to picture them as no more than the outgrowth and continuation of actions of previous commissions—in effect, a linear progression in world view and decision-making. The attempt fails. Current commission decisions, plotted against those of the past, reveal not extrapolation but discontinuity. Taking the broad view, and despite the substantial unevenness of past commission decisions, there is little doubt that the effort in the past was to

Ms. Miller was a member of the Colorado Public Utilities Commission. Reprinted from *Telematics*, vol. 4, no. 3 (March 1987) with the permission of Prentice-Hall Law & Business.

regulate—admittedly a difficult task given the nature of the communications beast. In contrast, the self-assigned thrust and mission of the present commission is to deregulate. This is a distinction with a profound difference; a difference that is one of kind, and not simply of degree.

*   *   *

[The authors] propose "a three-year trial of total deregulation of telecommunications . . . in states willing to undertake such experiments" under which regulation, including controls on entry and exit and on rate of return, would be "largely suspended." At the same time, the imposition of structural safeguards also would be abjured. The transition to competition would be accomplished while maintaining a commitment to universal service and within a framework of "open network architecture" based on free entry and pricing flexibility.

The Deregulator's Creed

The program the authors propose is in accord with the deregulatory spirit that has gripped this nation in recent years. Viewed from a broader perspective, that ethic is part of a program to constrict severely the overall role of government in the economy; in the vernacular of the age, to "get government off our backs." To this end, the program has encompassed not simply economic deregulation, but tax and expenditure decreases, a general reduction in government programs, services, and planning, the selling off of government owned assets, and an increase in the incidence of user fees.

Despite certain doctrinal differences among proponents of this view, they share allegiance to a common underlying theme. The theme is privatization; the approval—more accurately, the celebration—of voluntary exchange and private contract effectuated through the "free market." The ideology reserves legitimacy for private sector activity only. Public sector operations, for the most part, are viewed as transgressions.

The ethic borrows from the economic orthodoxy to construct an economic model in which all markets are simple and free of restraint. Markets are caused to "clear" by increases and decreases of prices at the margin. The theory rests on a host of simplifying assumptions about the nature of human beings, of markets, and of social systems. Moreover, not only does it not adjust for the lack of accordance of its assumptions with reality; it prides itself on them.

. . . In fact, the concept of the "free market" as used in traditional economics is highly metaphorical. Not only can no physical location, meeting place, or geographic boundaries be specified, but most markets in modern industrialized societies are not free. They are constrained in a variety of ways by many factors, among which is the ability of certain of the market participants to use their economic strength to fetter market forces. In the real world, as opposed to the ideal world of orthodox economic theory, markets are not uniformly neutral mechanisms for allocational efficiency and distributional equity. They are not simply controlling, but are themselves controlled.

*   *   *

The "Theory of Contestable Markets," recently developed by a group of economists closely associated with the predivestiture Bell system, is a variant of the traditional theory that is widely used to justify deregulation of telecommunications. It is the implicit foundation of many current state telecommunications deregulation legislative efforts and is explicitly relied upon by the authors of "Back to the Future." It holds that a "free market," even if it allows entry only of a hit-and-run variety, and *even if the entry does not in fact occur,* will intimidate an established firm sufficiently to drive prices to cost, prevent monopoly profits and cross-subsidization, and ensure productive efficiency and innovation. According to the theory, in the absence of legal barriers to entry it will be in the interest of rational monopolists to act as if they had competitors in order to forestall entry, and act in that interest they will.

*   *   *

[R]eality differs from the models in many important respects. It should be evident that the applicability of the traditional model even to nonindustrial societies is questionable. But it is even clearer that when we introduce such intricacies as modern corporations, our banking system, labor organizations, financial instruments, the state itself—to say nothing of human characteristics that vary widely from the "rational economic man" assumed in the economics literature—the applicability of the model to the real world becomes problematic.

Questions

1. How does price-cap regulation differ from rate-based regulation? What important assumptions underlie each regulatory approach?

2. What factors are included in the price-cap formula? How accurate are the figures? What is the best way to deal with the uncertainties? Is the FCC's solution satisfactory?

3. Why are services grouped in baskets? What is the function of the upper band? the lower band? What events trigger the tariff review process?

4. Why does Commissioner Quello question the wisdom of imposing price floors on AT&T? Do you agree?

5. Why might Commissioner Dennis think price caps result in more regulation for AT&T than rate-based regulation? What are her other concerns? How would she prefer to deal with AT&T?

6. How would the price-cap scheme function under the FCC's proposed streamlined regulations for AT&T discussed *supra?*

7. How do Ms. Schwartz's views differ from those of the Commission? How do they differ from those of Commissioner Dennis?

8. Consider the different state price-cap and social-contract schemes in the Shooshan and Jackson article. Which scheme seems more likely to provide long-term price savings for consumers? new service offerings? infrastructure modernizations? Does one scheme appear to balance these interests better than the others?

9. Can the parties—the PUC and the telco—deal at arm's length while negotiating a social contract? What is the best alternative for the parties if an agreement is not reached? Who bears the risk of a bad agreement on either side?

10. What is Chairman Fowler's more radical approach? How will competition be promoted and AT&T's power be controlled under his plan? How does he propose to deal with the problems of subsidies and universal service?

11. What is Ms. Miller's response to Chairman Fowler's proposal? What is the "theory of contestability"? See Baumol, Panzar, and Willig, *Contestable Markets and the Theory of Industry Structure* (1982) and Landes and Posner, "Market Power in Antitrust Cases," 94 *Harvard Law Review* 937 (1981).

7

DIVESTITURE OF THE BELL SYSTEM

NOTE ON THE BREAKUP OF AT&T

The most significant regulatory event in telecommunications in the last twenty-five years has got to be the breakup of the Bell system. As discussed at the outset of this book, competing long-distance providers and equipment manufacturers played a large part, demanding changes in the way AT&T did business. For the company's part, its previous exclusion from the growing computer industry made business as usual unacceptable to it as well. The result was the separation of the local exchange companies of AT&T from the rest of the Bell System. This freed AT&T, as part of the bargain, to enter the computer field.

The breakup is an ongoing issue because under its terms the judge supervising the divestiture, U.S. District Judge Harold Greene, must undertake a review every three years to see whether the decree should be modified in any way. In the articles and cases that follow, the breakup of the AT&T system is reviewed, and the judge's initial decision and subsequent orders are examined.

UNITED STATES v. WESTERN ELECTRIC

552 F.Supp. 131 (D.D.C. 1982)

*   *   *

On January 8, 1982, the parties to these two actions filed with the District Court for the District of New Jersey a stipulation consenting to the entry by the Court of the "Modification of Final Judgment" filed therewith. On the same day, they attempted to file in this court a dismissal of the AT&T action pursuant to Rule 41(a)(1)(ii), Federal Rules of Civil Procedure. This Court ordered that the dismissal be lodged, not filed, and, in accordance with that order and the provisions of the Tunney Act, the dismissal has not yet been effected. . . .

In their settlement proposal, the parties proposed that the Court enter the following judgment with respect to both lawsuits.

Section I of the proposed decree would provide for significant structural changes in AT&T. In essence, it would remove from the Bell System the function of supplying local telephone service by requiring AT&T to divest itself of the portions of its twenty-two Operating Companies which perform that function.

The geographic area for which these Operating Companies would provide local telephone service is defined in the proposed decree by a new unit, the "exchange area." According to the Justice Department, an exchange area "will be large enough to comprehend contiguous areas having common social and economic characteristics but not so large as to defeat the intent of the decree to separate the provision of intercity services from the provision of local exchange service." . . .

The Operating Companies would provide telephone service from one point in an exchange area to other points in the same exchange area—"exchange telecommunications"[37]—and they would originate and terminate calls from one exchange area to another exchange area—"exchange access."[38] The interexchange portion of calls from one exchange area to another exchange area[39] would, however, be carried by AT&T and the other interexchange carriers, such as MCI and Southern Pacific Co.[40]

The proposed decree sets forth general principles governing the configuration of the Operating Companies which AT&T would be required to divest. Under the proposal, AT&T would be required to endow the companies with sufficient personnel, facilities, systems, and rights to technical information to enable them to provide exchange telecommunications and exchange access services. These personnel, systems, facilities, and rights would be drawn from the Operating Companies and from AT&T and its other affiliates. AT&T would be permitted to choose to transfer some of these elements directly to the new Operating Companies and to place others in a central entity jointly owned by them.

AT&T would be required by the proposed decree to formulate a plan of reorganization which complied with these principles, and to submit the plan to the Department of Justice within six months after the Court approved the decree. The plan would not be effective without the Department's approval.

After divestiture, the new Operating Companies would be required to provide, through a centralized body, a single point of contact for national security and emergency preparedness. They would be permitted to use this or a similar central body to provide those services, such as administration and engineering, which "can most efficiently be provided on a centralized basis." In addition, until September 1987, AT&T, Western Electric, and Bell Laboratories would have to provide on a priority basis, all research, development, manufacturing, and other support services necessary to enable the Operating Companies to fulfill the requirements of the proposed decree.

---

37. Also referred to herein as intraexchange service. This may roughly be equated with local telephone service.

38. That is, they would provide local access to interexchange carriers.

39. In general, this is the service commonly known as long distance service.

40. The Operating Companies must also provide access services to link their subscribers with companies providing information services. This category of service, discussed in Part VI, *infra.* includes information retrieval, automatic telephone answering services, and electronic publishing.

Section II of the proposed decree would complement these structural changes by various restrictions which are said to be designed (1) to prevent the divested Operating Companies from discriminating against AT&T's competitors, and (2) to avoid a recurrence of the type of discrimination and cross-subsidization that were the basis of the AT&T lawsuit.

The first group of these provisions would require the divested Operating Companies to provide services to interexchange carriers equal in type, quality, and price to the services provided to AT&T and its affiliates. In addition, they would be prohibited from discriminating between AT&T and other companies in their procurement activities, the establishment of technical standards, the dissemination of technical information, their use of Operating Company facilities and charges for such use, and their network planning. The Justice Department has indicated that it intends these provisions to be "construed broadly to encompass all potential areas of favoritism, subtle as well as overt, that may arise in relationship between the divested BOCs and AT&T and its competitors."

*   *   *

The second type of restriction imposed upon the Operating Companies is said to be intended to prevent them from engaging in any non-monopoly business so as to eliminate the possibility that they might use their control over exchange services to gain an improper advantage over competitors in such businesses. Thus, the Operating Companies would not be permitted (1) to manufacture or market telecommunications products and customer premises equipment; (2) to provide interexchange services, (3) to provide directory advertising such as the Yellow Pages; (4) to provide information services; and (5) to provide any other product or service [that] is not a "natural monopoly service actually regulated by tariff." The Operating Companies would have the authority, however, to engage in what are called the "inherent" functions of procurement, engineering, marketing, and management.

Section III of the agreement provides that the decree would be binding on AT&T and the Operating Companies and their successors and that it would not constitute any evidence against, in admission by, or an estoppel against AT&T or the Operating Companies.

*   *   *

The proposed reorganization of the Bell System raises issues of vast complexity. Because of their importance, not only to the parties but also to the telecommunications industry and to the public, the Court has discussed the various problems in substantial detail. It is appropriate to summarize briefly the major issues and the Court's decisions which are central to the proceeding.

A. The American telecommunications industry is presently dominated by one company—AT&T. It provides local and long-distance telephone service; it manufactures and markets the equipment used by telephone subscribers as well as that used in the telecommunications network; and it controls one of the leading communications research and development facilities in the world. According to credible evidence, this integrated structure has enabled AT&T for many years to undermine the efforts of competitors seeking to enter the telecommunications market.

*   *   *

The key to the Bell System's power to impede competition has been its control of local telephone service. The local telephone network functions as the gateway to individual telephone subscribers. It must be used by long-distance carriers seeking to connect one caller to another. Customers will only purchase equipment which can readily be connected to the local network through the telephone outlets in their homes and offices. The enormous cost of the wires, cables, switches, and other transmission facilities which comprise that network has completely insulated it from competition. Thus, access to AT&T's local network is crucial if long distance carriers and equipment manufacturers are to be viable competitors.

AT&T has allegedly used its control of this local monopoly to disadvantage these competitors in two principal ways. First, it has attempted to prevent competing long distance carriers and competing equipment manufacturers from gaining access to the local network, or to delay that access, thus placing them in an inferior position vis-a-vis AT&T's own services. Second, it has supposedly used profits earned from the monopoly local telephone operations to subsidize its long distance and equipment businesses in which it was competing with others.

For a great many years, the Federal Communications Commission has struggled, largely without success, to stop practices of this type through the regulatory tools at its command. A lawsuit the Department of Justice brought in 1949 to curb similar practices ended in an ineffectual consent decree. Some other remedy is plainly required; hence the divestiture of the local Operating Companies from the Bell System. This divestiture will sever the relationship between this local monopoly and the other, competitive segments of AT&T, and it will thus ensure— certainly better than could any other type of relief—that the practices which allegedly have lain heavy on the telecommunications industry will not recur.

B. With the loss of control over the local network, AT&T will be unable to disadvantage its competitors, and the restrictions imposed on AT&T after the government's first antitrust suit—which limited AT&T to the provision of tele- communications services—will no longer be necessary. The proposed decree accordingly removes these restrictions.

The decree will thus allow AT&T to become a vigorous competitor in the growing computer, computer-related, and information markets. Other large and experienced firms are presently operating in these markets, and there is therefore no reason to believe that AT&T will be able to achieve monopoly dominance in these industries as it did in telecommunications. At the same time, by use of its formidable scientific, engineering, and management resources, including partic- ularly the capabilities of Bell Laboratories, AT&T should be able to make significant contributions to these fields, which are at the forefront of innovation and technology, to the benefit of American consumers, national defense, and the position of American industry vis-a-vis foreign competition.

All of these developments are plainly in the public interest, and the Court will therefore approve this aspect of the proposed decree, with one exception. Electronic publishing, which is still in its infancy, holds promise to become an important provider of information—such as news, entertainment, and advertising—in competition with the traditional print, television, and radio media; indeed, it has the potential, in time, for actually replacing some of these methods of disseminating information.

Traditionally, the Bell System has simply distributed information provided by others; it has not been involved in the business of generating its own information. The proposed decree would, for the first time, allow AT&T to do both, and it would do so at a time when the electronic publishing industry is still in a fragile state of experimentation and growth and when electronic information can still most efficiently and most economically be distributed over AT&T's long distance network. If, under these circumstances, AT&T were permitted to engage both in the transmission and the generation of information, there would be a substantial risk not only that it would stifle the efforts of other electronic publishers but that it would acquire a substantial monopoly over the generation of news in the more general sense. Such a development would strike at a principle which lies at the heart of the First Amendment: that the American people are entitled to a diversity of sources of information. In order to prevent this from occurring, the Court will require, as a condition of its approval of the proposed decree, that it be modified to preclude AT&T from entering the field of electronic publishing until the risk of its domination of that field has abated.

C. After the divestiture, the Operating Companies will possess a monopoly over local telephone service. According to the Department of Justice, the Operating Companies must be barred from entering all competitive markets to ensure that they will not misuse their monopoly power. The Court will not impose restrictions simply for the sake of theoretical consistency. Restrictions must be based on an assessment of the realistic circumstances of the relevant markets, including the Operating Companies' ability to engage in anticompetitive behavior, their potential contribution to the market as an added competitor for AT&T, as well as upon the effects of the restrictions on the rates for local telephone service.

This standard requires that the Operating Companies be prohibited from providing long distance services and information services, and from manufacturing equipment used in the telecommunications industry. Participation in these fields carries with it a substantial risk that the Operating Companies will use the same anticompetitive techniques used by AT&T in order to thwart the growth of their own competitors. Moreover, contrary to the assumptions made by some, Operating Company involvement in these areas could not legitimately generate subsidies for local rates. Such involvement could produce substantial profits only if the local companies used their monopoly position to dislodge competitors or to provide subsidy for their competitive services or products—the very behavior the decree seeks to prevent.

Different considerations apply, however, to the marketing of customer premises equipment—the telephone and other devices used in subscribers' homes and offices—and the production of the Yellow Pages advertising directories. For a variety of reasons, there is little likelihood that these companies will be able to use their monopoly position to disadvantage competitors in these areas. In addition, their marketing of equipment will provide needed competition for AT&T, and the elimination of the restriction on their production of the Yellow

Pages will generate a substantial subsidy for local telephone rates.[376] The Court will therefore require that the proposed decree be modified to remove the restrictions on these two types of activities.

D. With respect to a number of subjects, the proposed decree establishes merely general principles and objectives, leaving the specific implementing details for subsequent action, principally by the plan of reorganization which AT&T is required to file within six months after entry of the judgment. The parties have also made informal promises, either to each other or to the Court, as to how they intend to interpret or implement various provisions. The Court has decided that its public interest responsibilities require that it establish a process for determining whether the plan of reorganization and other, subsequent actions by AT&T actually implement these principles and promises in keeping with the objectives of the judgment. Absent such a process, AT&T would have the opportunity to interpret and implement the broad principles of the decree in such a manner as to disadvantage its competitors, the Operating Companies, or both, or otherwise to act in a manner contrary to the public interest as interpreted by the Court in this opinion.

For that reason, the Court is requiring that the judgment be modified (1) to vest authority in the Court to enforce the provisions and principles of that judgment on its own rather than only at the request of a party; and (2) to provide for a proceeding, accessible to third party intervenors and to the chief executives of the seven new regional Operating Companies, in which the Court will determine whether the plan of reorganization is consistent with the decree's general principles and promises.

E. For the reasons stated in this opinion, the Court will approve the proposed decree as in the public interest provided that the parties agree to the addition of the following new section:

VIII. Modifications

A. Notwithstanding the provisions of section II(D)(2), the separated BOCs shall be permitted to provide, but not manufacture, customer premises equipment.

B. Notwithstanding the provisions of section II(D)(3), the separated BOCs shall be permitted to produce, publish, and distribute printed directories which contain advertisements and which list general product and business categories, the service or product providers under these categories, and their names, telephone numbers, and addresses.

Notwithstanding the provisions of sections I(A)(1), I(A)(2), I(A)(4), all facilities, personnel, systems, and rights to technical information owned by AT&T, its affiliates, or the BOCs which are necessary for the production, publication, and

---

376. The decree also provides for another method of subsidizing these rates. It permits the Operating Companies, under the supervision of state and federal regulators, to levy access charges upon long distance carriers and those companies that provide information services. These charges may, if the regulators desire, be set at levels which will subsidize for local telephone rates.

distribution of printed advertising directories shall be transferred to the separated BOCs.

C. The restrictions imposed upon the separated BOCs by virtue of section II(D) shall be removed upon a showing by the petitioning BOC that there is no substantial possibility that it could use its monopoly power to impede competition in the market it seeks to enter.

D. AT&T shall not engage in electronic publishing over its own transmission facilities. "Electronic publishing" means the provision of any information which AT&T or its affiliates has, or has caused to be, originated, authored, compiled, collected, or edited, or in which its has a direct or indirect financial or proprietary interest, and which is disseminated to an unaffiliated person through some electronic means.

Nothing in this provision precludes AT&T from offering electronic directory services that list general product and business categories, the service or product providers under these categories, and their names, telephone numbers, and addresses; or from providing the time, weather, and such other audio services as are being offered as of the date of the entry of the decree to the geographic areas of the country receiving those services as of that date.

Upon application of AT&T, this restriction shall be removed after seven years from the date of entry of the decree, unless the Court finds that competitive conditions clearly require its extension.

E. If a separated BOC provides billing services to AT&T pursuant to Appendix B(C)(2), it shall include upon the portion of the bill devoted to interexchange services the following legend:

> This portion of your bill is provided as a service to AT&T. There is no connection between this company and AT&T. You may choose another company for your long distance telephone calls while still receiving your local telephone service from this company.

F. Notwithstanding the provisions of Appendix B(C)(3), whenever, as permitted by the decree, a separated BOC fails to offer exchange access to an interexchange carrier that is equal in type and quality to that provided for the interexchange traffic of AT&T, the tariffs filed for such less-than-equal access shall reflect the lesser cost, if any, of such access as compared to the exchange access provided AT&T. . . .

Questions

1. What was gained or lost as a result of the breakup? Was the breakup avoidable?

2. Gerald Faulhaber argues:

> The lesson should be crystal clear: Regulation will not solve these problems; regulation *is* the problem. . . . And so corporation heads, congresspersons, regulators, and judges have all tried their hand at solving this dilemma. With each attempt to cut the Gordian knot, the putative problem-solver, be it John

deButts, Tim Wirth, or Judge Greene, has become part of the problem, yet another player in a regulatory game of unimaginable complexity. . . . It is now time to start taking people away from the problem. It is time to rely on the first and last resort of the American economic system: Let the market decide. (Faulhaber, *Telecommunications in Turmoil*, 174–175 [1987]).

Should the industry be completely deregulated?

3. What political forces and events of the 1970s may have influenced the breakup? Why was competition so vigorously promoted during the 1980s?

4. Why did AT&T want to settle the case? Why did the Justice Department settle?

5. What did the court say was the key to AT&T's power to restrain competition? How did AT&T allegedly wield this power to thwart competitors?

6. Logically, aren't the BOCs the best-suited market participants to compete with AT&T in the long-distance market? And aren't the BOCs and AT&T naturally the most formidable competitors for local exchange service? What effect would this have on the OCCs? See Faulhaber, *supra*, note 2, at 128–134.

Why haven't companies from the computing industries, such as IBM, established a stronger presence in the communications market? Would they be subject to regulation? Does this depend on the services offered? Would it be necessary to separate structurally their communications and noncommunications activities? Do these heavyweights pose a sufficient competitive threat to justify total deregulation of AT&T or the BOCs?

7. Why did the decree allow AT&T to enter the computer and information markets? What is the exception? Are any of these activities inconsistent with the definition of a common carrier? See the definition of electronic publishing in the opinion. Why was AT&T allowed to offer "electronic directory services" after the decree was modified? The American Newspaper Publishers Association, a powerful special interest group, vigorously lobbied against AT&T's entry into electronic publishing. The newspaper lobby cited the First Amendment's free press guarantee to oppose AT&T's entry. What First Amendment arguments could AT&T make in its favor?

8. In what activities were the BOCs allowed to participate under the decree? What restrictions were placed on the BOCs? Why are different restrictions applied to the BOCs and AT&T?

9. What services are the BOCs allowed to provide to subsidize local rates? Why would local rates need subsidization?

10. Who has the authority to modify and enforce the judgment? Should the discretion of one judge supersede the expertise of an entire agency (i.e., the FCC)? A broad range of proposals has been offered with respect to the nation's need to establish a coherent national telecommunications policy. See Dempsey, "Adam Smith Assaults Ma Bell with His Invisible Hands: Dives-

titure, Deregulation, and the Need for a New Telecommunications Policy," 11 *Hastings Communications/Entertainment Law Journal* 527 (1989); Brotman, "Executive Branch Communications Policymaking: Reconciling Function and Form with the Council of Communications Advisers," 42 *Federal Communications Law Journal* 51 (1989); Faulhaber, *Telecommunications in Turmoil* (1987).

11. What is the interplay between communications and antitrust law? Is the MFJ court judge a "super regulator" or just a judge enforcing an antitrust decree?

8

LINE OF BUSINESS RESTRICTIONS

THE DECREES

UNITED STATES v. WESTERN ELECTRIC

592 F. Supp. 846 (D.D.C. 1984)

* * *

HAROLD H. GREENE, District Judge.

The Regional Holding Companies,[1] have requested the Court to waive the "line of business" restrictions in section II(D) of the decree so that they may pursue ventures other than the provision of local telephone service. These motions raise the question whether and the extent to which these companies shall be permitted to engage in new business enterprises—perhaps the most important issue to have arisen since the AT&T Plan of Reorganization was approved last year.[2]

Section II(D) of the decree mandates that

> After completion of the reorganization . . . , no [Operating Company] shall, directly or through any affiliated enterprise:
>
> 1. provide interexchange telecommunications services or information services;
> 2. manufacture or provide telecommunications products or customer premises equipment (except for provision of customer premises equipment for emergency services); or
> 3. provide any other product or service, except exchange telecommunications and exchange access service, that is not a natural monopoly service actually regulated by tariff.

---

1. The twenty-two Operating Companies, the successors of the local affiliates of the Bell System, provide local telecommunications services and certain other services and products pursuant to the decree. Each of these local companies is now a subsidiary of one of seven Regional Holding Companies established by Part IV(A)(6) of the Plan of Reorganization. The Plan itself was approved by the Court on July 8, 1983. *United States v. Western Electric Co.*, 569 F.Supp. 1057 (D.D.C.1983), *aff'd sub nom. California v. United States*, —U.S. —, 104 S.Ct. 542, 78 L.Ed.2d 719 (1983).

2. As one party has put it, resolution of this issue may represent the "'second phase' restructuring of the American telecommunications industry." Department of Justice Memorandum of April 5, 1984, at 56.

Section VIII(C) provides for the removal of these restrictions under certain circumstances. Motions filed by the Regional Holding Companies or their affiliated Operating Companies request permission to engage in enterprises ranging from real estate investments to foreign business ventures, and the Court is advised that additional motions, for further diversification, will follow. Some of the proposed enterprises are related and some are unrelated to the telecommunications business.[3]

*   *   *

History of the Restrictions

In deciding requests for waivers under section VIII(C), the Court must determine whether the petitioning Regional Holding Company has made "a showing" that "there is no substantial possibility that it could use its monopoly power to impede competition in the market it seeks to enter." The parties disagree not only on the factors the Court may consider in making its section VIII(C) determination; they also disagree on the question whether that section establishes the exclusive standard for a removal of the line of business restrictions.

The Regional Holding Companies argue that such removal is contingent entirely on the anticipated antitrust consequences of their entry into a particular market; that the Court is not free to consider other provisions of the decree; and that when the pending waiver requests are considered in light of the proper standard, all of them must be granted without conditions. The Department of Justice and others maintain, however, that many, if not all, of the requests should be denied, if only because the Regional Holding Companies have failed to demonstrate that their entry into the markets they seek to penetrate is not likely to impede competition. Beyond that, these parties argue that the Court should refrain from taking a restricted view of its responsibilities but should measure the potential effect of entry on the decree's overall objectives.

The key remedy adopted in the decree for the elimination of anticompetitive conditions within the telecommunications industry was the divestiture of the Operating Companies from AT&T. As a regulated monopoly, AT&T had both the incentive and ability—through cross subsidization and various discriminatory actions related to interconnection—to use its control over the local exchange

---

3. The following waiver requests have been filed thus far: (1) Bell Atlantic's motion of January 26, 1984 to enter the equipment leasing market; (2) BellSouth's motion of January 27, 1984 to provide certain software programs and related services; (3) Pacific and Nevada Bell's motion of February 8, 1984 to enter into foreign business ventures; (4) Nynex's motion of February 15, 1984 to provide office equipment and related services; (5) BellSouth's motion of February 24, 1984 to bid on a request for proposal issued by NASA to provide communications services and equipment; (6) US West's motion of March 20, 1984, to provide real estate services and to engage in real estate transactions and investments; (7) Ameritech's motion of March 23, 1984 to provide computers and computer-based services to developers and tenants as part of shared-service arrangements for multi-tenant buildings; (8) Ameritech's motion of April 26, 1984 to provide consulting services to foreign telecommunications systems; and (9) NewVector's motion of April 20, 1984 to construct and operate a cellular radio system in the Gulf of Mexico (NewVector is a wholly-owned subsidiary of US West).

facilities to foreclose or impede competition in the several competitive or potentially competitive markets.[6] The functional separation of the Operating Companies from AT&T was designed to eliminate the potential for such anticompetitive behavior.

In order to prevent the occurrence or reoccurrence of anticompetitive conduct by the Operating Companies—each of which retains in its particular area a monopoly over local telecommunications service and thus has the potential for using its monopoly power to discriminate against others—the decree imposes several restrictions upon their activities. In fact, as originally drafted, the decree flatly prohibited these companies from engaging in any business other than that of supplying local telephone service.[7]

The Court rejected such a blanket restriction, reasoning that the mere theoretical ability to engage in anticompetitive conduct did not constitute a sufficient basis for prohibiting the companies from entering all competitive markets. In the Court's view, the test was to be a pragmatic one. The Operating Companies were different from AT&T—largely because of their smaller size and relative lack of complexity[8]—and they were therefore to be barred from competitive markets on a less rigid basis.

After examining the restrictions set forth in section II(D) of the proposed decree in light of that standard, the Court rejected two of these restrictions— that on marketing of customer premises equipment and that on the publication of the Yellow Pages—and it approved the remainder of the restrictions. In so doing, the Court further noted that

> It is probable that, over time, the Operating Companies will lose the ability to leverage their monopoly power into the competitive markets from which they must now be barred. This change could occur as a result of technological developments which eliminate the Operating Companies' local exchange monopoly or from changes in the structures of the competitive markets. In either event, the need for the restrictions upheld in Subparts A through C will disappear. . . .

---

6. *E.g.,* long distance service, equipment manufacture and sale.

7. The Department of Justice argued that such a rigid restriction was justified because the companies would have the incentive and the ability to leverage their monopoly power in the local exchange market to impede competition in the competitive markets by two types of behavior—subsidizing their prices in such markets with profits earned in the monopoly market, and restricting their competitors' access to the local distribution networks. This, of course, was the same type of anticompetitive conduct that was at issue in the *AT & T* case.

8. *United States v. Am. Tel. & Tel. Co.,* 552 F.Supp. 131, 187 (D.D.C.1982), *aff'd sub nom. Maryland v. United States,* 460 U.S. 1001, 103 S.Ct. 1240, 75 L.Ed.2d 472 (1983). On August 23, 1982, in denying the Department of Justice's motion for reconsideration of the Court's ruling permitting the Operating Companies to market customer premises equipment, the Court noted, *inter alia,* that the Operating Companies "will be relatively small, geographically dispersed corporations. They will be limited to a narrow range of products and services, . . . [and they] will also lack the ability to use various components and affiliates in the pursuit and concealment of anti-competitive conduct." Slip opinion at 3.

552 F.Supp. at 194–95.

Accordingly, the Court required the parties to incorporate into the decree a mechanism by which the line of business restrictions could be removed, and it stated that

> the removal of the restrictions should be governed by the same standard which the Court has applied in determining whether they are required in the first instance.

552 F.Supp. at 195.

The parties accepted the section II(D) and section VIII(C) modifications required by the Court. It was also understood that the restrictions would be removed altogether if the rationale therefor became outmoded by technical developments or changes in competitive conditions. On that basis, the Department of Justice was required to report to the Court every three years concerning the continuing need for the retention of the restrictions.

It is in light of this history that the issues now before the Court must be analyzed.

II. Cross Subsidization

In one respect, the risk that a Regional Holding Company will use its monopoly power for anticompetitive purposes becomes more remote as the market it seeks to enter becomes increasingly unrelated to and independent of local exchange service. That is so because products or services in unrelated fields are not dependent upon interconnection to the companies' monopoly bottleneck facilities, and discriminatory access therefore cannot injure the manufacturers or sellers which compete with them. However, competition can be impeded as readily in another way—by cross subsidization, that is, by a subsidy to a new, competitive line of business with profits earned from or assets held by the existing, regulated monopoly line of business.

As long as a Regional Holding Company is engaged in both monopoly and competitive activities, it will have the incentive as well as the ability to "milk" the rate-of-return regulated monopoly affiliate to subsidize its competitive ventures and thereby to undersell its rivals in the markets where there is competition. For that reason, caution with respect to "outside" activities is always warranted, particularly in the case of wholesale diversification because the larger the scale and the greater the diversity of a company's activities, the more difficult it is to detect and to remedy cross subsidization between the various affiliates. Compare also note 8 *supra*. Indeed, widely diversified Regional Holding Companies could enjoy greater opportunities to cross subsidize than did the Bell System which, under the 1956 consent decree, was limited to a relatively narrow range of products and services.

Cross subsidization may take a variety of forms. One such practice would be the misallocation of common costs. To the extent that a Regional Holding Company used the same facilities, equipment, and personnel to serve both its regulated and its unregulated activities, it would have the ability to overallocate the costs assigned to the former in order to maximize the amount that would be passed on to the ratepayers (who have no choice but to pay).[12] Not only would this improper assignment of costs burden the ratepayers; it would also enable the company profitably to charge less for its competitive products and services than do its rivals who enjoy no such subsidy.

A Regional Holding Company could also subsidize its competitive ventures by transferring assets[13] from its regulated affiliates to its unregulated affiliates at less than their cost or below their market value.[14] Such a practice would not only adversely affect the ratepayers who ultimately fund the research and development costs of the transferred assets,[15] but it would, once again, impede fair and effective competition in the competitive market: this cross subsidization would give the company's unregulated enterprise an obvious and improper advantage over its competitors. Conversely, a regulated affiliate could "purchase" assets from the unregulated affiliate at a price above their market value and pass on the extra costs to the ratepayers.[16]

In addition to cross subsidization, a Regional Holding Company could impede competition in markets unrelated to telecommunications by exploiting the marketing advantages stemming from its local exchange monopoly. The company

---

12. Nynex's proposal for an office equipment venture illustrates this problem. Under that company's proposal, over 75 percent of the employees of its Business Information Systems Company (BISC) subsidiary will be located in a sales division that will also serve as the sales agent for its telephone exchange services. Under this arrangement, Nynex could easily manipulate the common costs of the BISC and Operating Companies so that the ratepayers would subsidize the office equipment business.

13. *E.g.*, property, facilities, financial resources, technical information, and contractual services.

14. An asset would be undervalued for competitive purposes, if the Operating Company was "paid" less by its unregulated affiliate than it would cost another entity to purchase the same asset.

15. An affiliate which develops an asset in its regulated market in anticipation of its potential use in the competitive market would have the incentive to add features or capabilities beyond those required for the provision of local telephone service in order to enhance the asset's market value. As a result, the ratepayers would subsidize the unregulated businesses by paying for "extras" which benefit only those businesses. Indeed, the ratepayers might bear the entire risk of researching and developing these assets because a Regional Holding Company would transfer from its regulated to its unregulated affiliate only those projects which turn out to be successful. Conversely, if the unregulated affiliate developed an asset and sold it to the Operating Company at the full cost of development, a cross subsidy would occur if the asset possessed features or capabilities beyond those required for the provision of the local telephone service.

16. This pattern would be similar to what was called the "procurement" portion of the government's case against AT & T. The government argued that the combination of vertical integration and rate-of-return regulation tended to generate decisions by the Operating Companies to purchase equipment produced by Western Electric which was more expensive or of lesser quality than that produced by the general trade. The Operating Companies could afford to make such seemingly irrational decisions, it was said, because they could always reflect the extra cost of the equipment in their rates without suffering a diminution in overall revenues. See *United States v. Am. Tel. & Tel. Co.*, 524 F.Supp. 1336, 1373 (D.D.C.1981).

would have a unique advantage over its competitors if, for example, it "bundled" its regulated monopoly services with its competitive products or services, or if it advertised, and in fact provided to its customers in the competitive market, more timely telecommunications service, preferential access, or both.[17]

In response to these concerns, the Regional Holding Companies argue primarily that cross subsidization is not a competitive issue but a regulatory cost allocation matter for which regulatory sanctions and penalties already exist. In addition, they contend that, even if they did engage in such anticompetitive conduct, the appropriate remedy would be a new antitrust action, not a refusal to grant a waiver. These arguments are entirely without merit.

The cross subsidization of competitive activities with profits earned from a regulated enterprise constitutes precisely the kind of conduct the decree was intended to curb, and for which the decree contains—in a denial of a section VIII(C) waiver request—a very precise remedy. There is therefore no reason or basis for turning elsewhere when such practices are threatened by organizations subject to the provisions of the decree.

That remedy, moreover, is preferable to a regulatory one. Cost misallocations and improper transfer pricing in interaffiliate sales have proved difficult, if not impossible, to detect.[19] It is for that reason that regulatory oversight has not been in the past,[20] nor is it likely to be in the future, an adequate check against them; it is for that reason that section VIII(C) was incorporated in the decree; and it is for that reason, too, that the burden was placed on the Operating Companies to demonstrate the absence of an anticompetitive effect. By contrast, in a new antitrust action or in a regulatory proceeding the proponent of a restriction would have the burden of proof. In short, the prevention of cross subsidization and other anticompetitive practices is an appropriate and significant ingredient in any decision under section VIII(C).

It does not follow from what has been said that all waiver requests must or will be denied. As noted below (Part VII *infra*) some of the problems discussed above can be alleviated by the imposition of conditions or safeguards upon the grant of waivers. It is also apparent, however, that such safeguards or conditions alone are not likely to be adequate to resolve legitimate concerns in this sensitive field, where claims of cross subsidization have contributed to a massive restructuring of the entire telecommunications industry, and where considerable caution is warranted to avoid yet another upheaval.

Thus, what plainly needs to be done is to avoid a headlong rush by the Regional Holding Companies into diversification programs which, for the reasons

---

17. Such practices are especially likely to occur if the regulated and unregulated services are marketed by a single sales staff.

19. There is no formula for allocating common costs among services, and, even if there were, the fact is that the Regional Holding Companies alone possess all the relevant cost information and have a great deal of discretion in the treatment of such costs.

20. The crux of the government's case against AT & T was that regulation had failed to safeguard competition from a powerful firm, engaged in both regulated monopoly and unregulated services, which had the incentive and the ability to use its regulated monopoly to impede competition in potentially competitive markets.

stated, would offer them too many opportunities for anticompetitive conduct. The Court will therefore require that the entry of these companies into competitive markets proceed at a measured pace. . . .

Additionally, as will now be seen, immediate, widespread diversification of the Regional Holding Companies would be at odds with other fundamental purposes of the decree.

*   *   *

V. Provision of Local Telephone Service

Under the decree, the Operating Companies' basic responsibility is to provide local telephone service to the public. The Plan of Reorganization, in turn, established the Regional Holding Companies for the primary purpose of serving the Operating Companies and facilitating their telecommunications functions. This is evident from the description in that plan of the structure and the responsibilities of these companies and from section III of the decree itself. As will now be seen, the vast and diverse programs the Regional Holding Companies are formulating, and the priorities the companies seem to be assigning to these programs, constitute a serious threat to their obligations under the decree and the implementing documents.

As evidenced both by the pending waiver requests and by reports of their intentions,[59] the Regional Holding Companies are expending significant managerial and other resources to discover and analyze new business opportunities. Moreover, some of these companies candidly state that they regard the telephone business as of limited interest to them and the fate of the rate-payers as of little significance in the context of the decree. Thus, US West proclaims that the "Operating Companies owned by US West are in the telephone business rather than US West" and that "US West does not itself intend to be a telephone company." Ameritech similarly asserts that, "[w]hile protecting ratepayers may be a worthy goal in the abstract, it is one that should be left to the regulators and the legislators to pursue as they see fit." And Bell Atlantic argues that its waiver requests must be granted even if diversification into new business will raise the company's cost of capital and divert the attention of its management from providing telephone service, because in its view the effect of diversification on the ratepayers "is extraneous to the Decree" and is therefore not a legitimate criterion for adjudging applications under section VIII(C).

---

59. US West is "trying to get into *all* the unregulated areas." "The First Year of a New Era in Telecommunications: A Look at 1984," *Telephony*, Jan. 16, 1984 at 52 (MCI App. B13); "Ameritech clearly wants to rid itself of the trappings of a telephone company," "AT & T Breakup Clears New Lines," *Advertising Age*, Jan. 23, 1984 at M10, M11 (MCI App. B36); Bell Atlantic plans "some very fast diversification 'very soon after one one eighty four.'" "Bells, Bells, Bells," *Forbes*, Nov. 21, 1983, pp. 286, 288 (MCI App. B44); " 'Telephone' is far too limiting" for Pacific Telesis. *Id.*; BellSouth wants to be in the long distance business in the next five years. "Bell Firms' Entry into Long Distance Is Opposed by U.S.," *Wall Street Journal*, February 24, 1984, at 40 (MCI App. B66); and Southwestern plans to become a "nationwide cellular player." "Ma Bell's Kids Fight for Position," *Fortune*, June 27, 1983, at 62, 67 (MCI App. B6).

The more the Regional Holding Companies diversify, the less central their telecommunications functions will obviously become to their corporate existence. To the extent that these companies perceive their new, unregulated businesses as more exciting, or more profitable than the provision of local telephone service to the American public—as they obviously do—it is inevitable that, should they be permitted to embark upon such business enterprises on a significant scale, their managerial talent and financial resources will be diverted from the business of providing such service. As a consequence, both the quality and the price of that service are bound to suffer. . . .

Some parties allege that the attention the Operating Companies are presently giving to outside ventures has already had the effect of diminishing their interest in telephone service,[64] impairing the quality of service and increasing telephone rates. Some of the problems with local service reported in the press have been overstated. Nevertheless, the Regional Holding Companies themselves concede that complaints over installation, maintenance, and service have increased, and that appears plainly to be true.

*   *   *

The Regional Holding Companies assert that all these problems and fears are outweighed by the benefits they would derive from diversification, *i.e.,* their ability to attract more capital and to increase revenue. In each of the waiver requests, the moving company argues that diversification will enhance its financial viability by reducing its overall risks. Diversified growth companies, it is said, are more attractive to securities investors and for that reason they are able to sell their stock at a higher price-earnings ratio, lowering their cost of equity capital. It follows, according to that line of reasoning, that a Regional Holding Company which is successful in diversifying could pass on its savings from lower capital costs to the ratepayers. These arguments are erroneous in every respect. . . .

There is no reason why the "efficiency and dynamism" of Ameritech, Pacific Bell's "flood of ideas," and the energies of the other Regional Holding Companies could not be directed toward improving local telephone service rather than pursuing extraneous ventures. Much can and should be done through the application of new technology, administrative efficiency, and marketing techniques to reduce the cost of telephone service, to improve its quality, and to make new features available to the public. If the Regional Holding Companies were determined to bring about such developments, they might well reap substantial benefits, and continue to attract the talent they seek.

One needs only to contemplate the advances made in the customer premises equipment market and the variety of telephone equipment now available on store shelves in the wake of divestiture and hence of competition to realize that,

---

64. MCI complains that its request to BellSouth for specific traffic data made in July of 1983 was still outstanding at the time of the April 11, 1984 hearing on the pending requests, eight months later. Transcript of hearing at 30. Yet, according to the Department of Justice, BellSouth had approximately 36 employees available for work on its "outside" NASA proposal. Transcript of hearing at 71.

where there is a will, there are ample opportunities for technological and other advances in the telecommunications markets themselves. The Regional Holding Companies are only limited in the services they can provide; they are not limited to any particular technology in providing those services.

. . . The principal substantive purpose of the divestiture was to promote competition and hence to create conditions which will reduce the cost and improve the quality and reliability of the telephone service. For the reasons stated, the diversion of energy, talent, capital, and other resources by the Regional Holding Companies to pursue outside ventures on a substantial scale at this early stage has the potential for threatening the basic objective of the decree. The Court will therefore carefully scrutinize requests for waivers in accordance with the guidelines discussed below, to ensure that, if approved, they will not frustrate the implementation of the decree, the plan of reorganization, or the principles underlying the divestiture.

This does not mean that the Court will not allow the Regional Holding Companies to engage in other activities, particularly if such activities would tend to increase competition. However, if there is to be a "second phase" restructuring of the telecommunications industry (see note 2 *supra*), it will evolve only in a deliberate, cautious manner, with every step tailored to ensure that the public's telephone service does not suffer, but improves in quality and price.

The Court will now consider the broad categories of the waiver requests.

VI. Interexchange Service

Considerable concern has been expressed by a number of parties that the Regional Holding Companies plan to enter the interexchange market. These concerns are not without basis. Only one Regional Holding Company has thus far explicitly sought a waiver that would permit it to enter into the interexchange market,[86] but several others have expressed a similar desire. See, *e.g.,* statement of Ameritech's Chairman William Weiss that the company wants to enter long-distance market and that the court-ordered restraints against such entry are "artificial" and "over time will fall away." Similarly, Pacific Telesis has stated that it expects to connect all major California cities by optics by 1986.

To approve these plans and applications would be to contravene the decree's prohibitions in the most direct and obvious way. Indeed, even to leave open the possibility of Regional Holding Company entry into this market would have negative implications, for if the companies perceive themselves as future long distance competitors they will have incentives to spend ratepayer funds for long-distance network construction and to position themselves for successful entry by discriminating against other carriers in interconnection any be delaying their achievement of equal access.

---

86. See BellSouth's motion of March 26, 1984 to provide services and equipment to NASA. BellSouth states that it intends to enter the long distance business itself in the next five years. "Bell Firms' Entry into Long Distance Is Opposed by U.S.," *Wall Street Journal,* February 24, 1984 at 40 (MCI App. B66).

It is therefore important that the Court state its position clearly. The Court will not even consider the substantive merits of a waiver request seeking permission to provide interexchange services until such time as the Regional Holding Companies lose their bottleneck monopolies and there is a substantial competition in local telecommunications service. That is not now. The BellSouth motion for a waiver with respect to the NASA contract is therefore denied.

Similar considerations govern the appropriateness of entry of the Regional Holding Companies into the information services and equipment manufacturing markets. No significant technological or structural changes have occurred in these markets to justify a relaxation of these line of business restrictions, and no requests for waivers in these markets will be considered unless and until such changes have taken place.

VII. Safeguards and Conditions

For the reasons stated, the pending waiver requests, and presumably the requests which are bound to follow, present such anticompetitive and other problems that the Court could grant them only with safeguards which would minimize these problems. The Department of Justice has suggested several safeguards of a structural nature which, as noted *infra*, the Court has carefully considered. . . .

. . . The Court has considered these proposals in light of the objections filed by the Regional Holding Companies, and it has concluded that the following four conditions are adequate and will be required.

First. It is generally agreed that if the Regional Holding Companies conducted competitive activities through separate subsidiaries, intracompany transactions would become more apparent and thus cross subsidization and other anticompetitive conduct could more easily be prevented or rectified. The Regional Holding Companies themselves appear to acknowledge that such structural measures are a necessary safeguard. Accordingly, while, as a general matter, the Court is not eager to require the establishment of separate subsidiaries, that measure is warranted in this situation, and it will be required.

Second. The use of the Operating Companies' financial resources or credit to finance new ventures creates an obvious potential for anticompetitive cross subsidization. It also tends to jeopardize the financial soundness of the Operating Companies for purposes unrelated to their own enterprises. The Court will therefore approve waiver applications only if they incorporate provisions which will ensure that subsidiaries of the Regional Holding Companies engaged in competitive enterprises obtain their own debt financing on their own credit and that no entity affiliated with the Regional Holding Company will guarantee the debt in a manner that would permit a creditor, on default, to have recourse to the assets of an Operating Company.

Third. In order to prevent cross subsidization by widely diversified holding companies to implement the decree's equal access provisions and to protect the nation's telephone service from injury due to lack of attention or the absence of a sound financial base the Court will require that the bulk of the investments of the Regional Holding Companies remain in decree-related activities. Accordingly, the Court will not, for the present, grant line of business waivers for activities the total estimated net revenues of which exceed ten percent of a Regional Holding Company's total estimated net revenues.

Fourth. Each Regional Holding Company seeking a waiver will be required to agree in its application that the monitoring and visitorial provisions of section VI of the decree apply to its proposed competitive activities. This will enable the Department of Justice to monitor compliance with the order granting the waiver and to report to the Court in the event that there are violations.

In the view of the Court, these safeguards are adequate to protect the integrity of the decree in the respects discussed in this Opinion. Some of the additional conditions proposed by the Department of Justice would involve the Court too deeply in the internal operations of the Regional Holding Companies; others would not be readily enforceable; and still others are unnecessary in view of the unambiguous requirements of the decree. . . .

UNITED STATES v. WESTERN ELECTRIC

673 F. Supp. 525 (D.D.C. 1987)

* * *

X. Conclusion

The purpose of the decree in this case is not to assist one company or another, nor is it to promote abstract antitrust theory or divestiture as part of some broad ideological scheme. Rather, it is the decree's purpose to allow consumers to reap the benefits of competition in telecommunications that competition has generated for a hundred years or more in a myriad of other fields. It is with that basic philosophy in mind that the Court has approached the present set of motions, requests, and reports.

A. Core Restrictions

Although it may be difficult to recall this now, the fact is that for thirty years prior to 1984, the Congress, the courts, the Federal Communications Commission, and state regulators wrestled with the problem of what to do about the Bell System monopoly, its arrogance in dealing with competitors and consumers, and its power to shut out competition. One Department of Justice lawsuit was filed and aborted; regulators issued edicts that were largely ignored; Congress investigated but could not come to a decision; and a second federal lawsuit and several private actions were filed in the courts where they remained pending for a number of years. In the meantime, competitors languished and the American ideal of free and fair competition remained absent from the telecommunications industry. When ultimately the decree that governs this case was negotiated between the parties and approved by the Court, it resolved the problem of claimed monopolistic conduct in telecommunications by going to its root.

That root was the control by the Bell System of the local telephone switches—in which it had a monopoly—and its simultaneous presence in several other markets (long distance, telecommunications manufacturing, and information services)—in which it had competitors. The competitors in each of these markets were suffering from an insuperable disadvantage: they could reach their ultimate customers only by connecting their circuits and products to the Bell System's local switches, the only technologically available avenue to the homes, offices, and factories of America where the individual telephone instruments are located. It followed that these competitors were at the mercy of the Bell System's managers, who could with ease discriminate against them by such practices as delaying interconnections, providing inferior connections, charging exorbitant prices, or refusing to attach competitors' products altogether. The Bell System was also able to subsidize its competitive products with funds syphoned off from the monies paid in by the ratepayers, thus to undercut the prices charged by independent firms and drive them out of business.

The quite predictable result was that no independent long distance, manufacturing, or information company ever really got off the ground: for practical purposes, the Bell monopoly remained just that. Since exhortations, regulations, and orders requiring a cessation of the Bell System's activities had proved fruitless, the remedy adopted in the decree, as simple as the problem itself, had but two basic aspects: first, the divestiture from AT&T of its local monopoly affiliates (thus forcing AT&T's other enterprises, all competitive, to stand or fall on their own); and second, an order prohibiting the new owners of the local bottlenecks—the Regional Companies—from engaging in the competitive long distance, manufacturing, and information services markets (so as to make it impossible for them to duplicate the Bell practices, now that *they* controlled the bottlenecks).

These simple yet drastic measures have already begun to bear fruit for the benefit of competition and of the users of the telephone. Contrary to much popular belief, the overall trend with respect to telephone rates is down,[328] and the cost of telephone instruments is down dramatically.[329] More importantly, competition has brought about innovations in telephone features on a scale and variety unknown before divestiture.[330] While complaints about that divestiture

---

328. Long distance rates have declined in the last three years by roughly thirty percent. Local rates are not affected by the decree because, for technological reasons, they have had to remain in the monopolistic control of the Regional Companies which . . . were able initially to raise these rates. However, as a consequence of greater public and regulatory awareness and resistance, local rates rose only slightly during the current year, while long distance rates continued their substantial decline. Indeed, state regulatory commissions turned local rate increase requests in the first half of 1987 into rate reductions totalling $92.6 million. *Communications Week*, August 24, 1987, at 30.

329. When the Bell System monopoly had full control, it refused to sell its telephones to consumers, or to permit anyone else to sell them, preferring to charge rentals in the neighborhood of $5–7 per month or more, for a total in, say thirty years, of over $2,000. Today, telephone instruments can be purchased in retail stores everywhere for $25–30 and up. Even if new instruments were purchased from time to time, the total cost would still be far below the unending rental fees.

330. There are now on the market at reasonable prices such by now commonplace features as residential telephones that are able to memorize dozens or hundreds of different phone

and the ensuing inconveniences have by no means ceased, an understanding is beginning to emerge that these temporary dislocations are a necessary price for what the newly competitive marketplace can achieve.

It is the attempted destruction of that careful design that the motions now before the Court are all about. Almost before the ink was dry on the decree, the Regional Companies began to seek the removal of its restrictions. These efforts have had some success, in that they have tended to cause the public to forget that these companies, when still part of the Bell System, participated widely in anticompetitive activities, and that, were they to be freed of the restrictions, they could be expected to resume anticompetitive practices in short order, to the detriment of both competitors and consumers. Regional Company claims of wishing only to participate with others in long distance and other restricted businesses on a level playing field obscure the fact that there is no level playing field when one of the participants holds an unassailable franchise on the goal lines that no one else may touch without its permission.

By direction of the decree itself, the restrictions placed on the Regional Companies may be removed only if these companies demonstrate that "there is no substantial possibility that they could use their monopoly powers to impede competition in the markets they seek to enter." The decree rests on the premise that the incentive and the ability to act anticompetitively existed in 1984 when that decree was entered, and the question before the Court therefore is only whether events in the three years since then have changed that situation. Essentially three types of changes are claimed to have occurred.

First, it is argued that the local monopoly bottlenecks have been either wiped out or substantially eroded. However, by the finding of the Department of Justice's own expert, these bottlenecks are still so pervasive that only one in one million telephone users is able to bypass them to communicate with his ultimate customers on his own; the remaining 999,999 users remain strictly dependent for local connections upon the Regional Company monopolies. Second, it is said that there are now seven Regional Companies instead of one nationwide Bell System. While that is certainly true, it is not a new development; it was foreseen and even mandated by the very decree that requires a *future* change in circumstances before the line of business restrictions may be removed. Moreover, in

---

numbers; telephones that repeat the last number called until it is no longer busy; cellular phones for business and emergency use; cordless phones; instruments that can be instructed by voice (*e.g.,* in an automobile) to call a certain individual, office, or number; and many others.

Parallel with the development of equipment that provides greater accessibility to the telephone user, devices are being produced and marketed that, in a sense, operate in the opposite direction: some of them display the caller's number before the receiver has been lifted; others provide a distinctive ring when a call is received from a number previously designated as worthy of priority consideration; still others automatically block calls from persons with whom the phone's owner does not wish to speak. For the first time since the invention of the telephone, these devices are returning control to the instrument's owner from every salesman, unwelcome relative, or even crackpot who may decide to call at any hour of the day or night.

It is surely not a coincidence that these features, and many more, have become available since the Bell monopoly was ended by divestiture and competition began to reign in the telecommunications marketplace.

terms of monopoly power, the combined Regional Companies more or less equal the Bell System. Third, suggestions have been made that, unlike at the time of the entry of the decree, federal regulation can now prevent anticompetitive abuses. But FCC regulation, far from being more stringent than before, is today actually less so, for reasons of reductions in staff and changes in regulatory philosophy, among others. And although new and possibly stricter regulations have been discussed, they have not thus far been adopted; they are not even in final form; and they will not become effective, if at all, until next year or the year after that. Their ultimate impact on anticompetitive activities is therefore entirely speculative.

The Court has accordingly concluded—it could not but conclude—that no significant changes have occurred with respect to the core restrictions—long distance, manufacturing, and the sale of information services—that would justify a radical change in the decree.

When the law and the facts are thus examined dispassionately, it becomes readily apparent that there is less to the Regional Company contentions than meets the eye. Indeed, had it not been for the drumbeat of a wide-ranging public relations campaign, no one would have seriously entertained the proposition that a solution arrived at after a thirty-year struggle, that had caused a major and wrenching change in the structure of the industry and the habits of most American telephone users, should be jettisoned in substantial part after a mere three years, particularly when the changes that have occurred in the interim in the power of those who control the local switches are insignificant.

If the interexchange and manufacturing motions were granted, the telecommunications industry would be back where it was when these struggles began. The Regional Companies would have the same incentives as well as the same means for discrimination, manipulation, and cross-subsidization that the Bell System possessed before the break-up.

Once before, in 1956, an antitrust suit against the Bell System was aborted precipitously by a Department of Justice decision, and that step laid the groundwork for many years of turmoil and travail in the industry, the courts, the regulatory commissions, and the Congress. That history must not be repeated. This Court cannot and will not lend its authority to so self-defeating an enterprise. It is therefore denying all the requests for the removal of the core restrictions of the decree.

B. Transmission of Information and Catch-All Restriction

At the same time, the Court is ordering the removal of two other restrictions where this will yield significant benefits without serious risk of harm to competition.

First. The wide-ranging yet diffuse "catch-all" restriction on the entry of the Regional Companies into all non-telecommunications markets is being repealed outright. Experience has shown that no substantial purpose is being served by requiring the Regional Companies to petition the Court whenever they wish to enter a business having no direct relationship to telecommunications, and where the risk of anticompetitive activity is relatively small. Indeed, the Court has to date granted over 160 "waivers" of this restriction and refused none. Although some danger of improper cross-subsidization remains, the benefits from a removal of this restriction outweigh that danger in this circumstance. Elimination of the restriction will also have the beneficial effect of permitting the Regional Companies hereafter to make decisions with respect to substantial segments of their business without day-to-day involvement or supervision by the Court.

Second. One of the core restrictions of the decree prohibits the Regional Companies from providing information services. The Court is retaining that restriction insofar as it involves the generation of information content, for the same reason that it is retaining the other core restrictions. If the Regional Companies had the authority to sell information in competition with other providers of these services, their control of the networks essential to the distribution of that information would give them the same ability to discriminate against competitors as they have with regard to interexchange services and the manufacture of telecommunications equipment.

That does not mean, however, that the public must be deprived of the revolutionary changes that are possible if information, instead of being transmitted only by current methods,[338] can also be made available to vast numbers of consumers instantaneously by means of the telephone network. Other nations—France in particular, but also Japan and Great Britain—have experimented with such an innovative use of the telephone system, with some considerable success. The French Teletel system—which may for present purposes serve as a rough guide in this regard—has some three million subscribers and is used to supply to these subscribers immediate access to about 4,000 independent services supplying specific information upon request in such fields as banking and brokerage, shopping (availability and price), travel (schedules and reservations), tickets to entertainment and sporting events, employment availability, language instruction, governmental notices, schedule of meetings of associations, reprints of newspaper and magazine articles, and others.

The Court has concluded that the apparently competing interests—prevention of monopolization of information services versus broad availability of such services to the public—can be reconciled by severing for decree purposes the generation of information content (which will remain prohibited to the Regional Companies) from the transmission of information services (which the Regional Companies will be allowed to provide).

The Court will accordingly lift so much of the information services restriction as prevents the Regional Companies from constructing and operating a sophisticated network infrastructure that will make possible the transmission, on a massive scale, of information services originated by others, directly to the ultimate consumers.[341] No one can know with certainty whether this revolution-

---

338. *E.g.*, by contacting a public library, through the mails, or by advance subscription to one of the existing information services.

341. In order to receive this information in usable form, these consumers will not require, as now, a complex PBX to unscramble and receive it, or even a full-fledged computer terminal; they will only need to have what is called a "dumb terminal"—a relatively inexpensive instrument that could be sold both by the Regional Companies and by more conventional retailers.

ary means of transmitting useful, readily-available information will find acceptance in this country to the same extent as it has elsewhere. But the Court believes that it should do what it legitimately can to foster the availability of such a service.

The decisions made herein continue to advance the objectives of the decree as the Court understood them when it approved that decree in 1982, and in its rulings since then: (1) the establishment in the telecommunications industry of conditions of fair competition, freed from the heavy hand of monopoly; (2) the protection of the goals of universal service and of reasonable rates for those who could not otherwise afford telephone service; and (3) the encouragement of innovation, to the end that the full benefits of a sophisticated telecommunications industry be made available to all segments of the American public in this Information Age.

THE TRIENNIAL REVIEW PROCESS

The 1987 *United States v. Western Electric* decision constituted the first triennial review of the MFJ. Based on a 1,200-page study by independent consultant Dr. Peter Huber, the U.S. Department of Justice recommended to Judge Greene that manufacturing, information service, and new business restrictions be eliminated. The DOJ also suggested that the BOCs be allowed to enter competitive long-distance markets on a case-by-case basis. Greene dashed the hopes of the BOCs and ignored the DOJ's suggestions by largely following his 1984 decision.

Greene concluded that three years after the MFJ, the competitive environment had not changed sufficiently to prevent the BOCs from using their power over local bottlenecks (in this case, the local telephone loop needed to initiate and complete any call) to give them an anticompetitive advantage. Consequently, the BOCs still may not enter manufacturing or long-distance markets.

However, Greene granted some concessions. The BOCs could act as a conduit for information services (i.e., they were allowed to transmit, but not generate, computerized information). Also, the BOCs no longer need comply with the complicated permission process necessary for nontelecommunications ventures (e.g., purchase of real estate). Finally, the BOCs are no longer required to run their nontelephone activities in separate subsidiaries.

AT&T was relieved that seven potentially formidable competitors were kept out of the interexchange market. For AT&T, the triennial review assured market stability.

In 1988 Judge Greene modified the decree to allow the BOCs to develop information-service transmission systems so long as they preserve the distinction between content and conduit. The judge also permitted the regionals to enter the voice storage and retrieval markets, but he maintained other prohibitions on the information-service offerings. See 1988–1 CCH Trade Cases §57, 619 (D.D.C. 1988).

In *United States v. Western Electric*, 900 F.2d 283 (D.C. Cir. 1990), the court of appeals generally upheld the judge's determinations of the triennial review. It reversed and remanded the judge's ruling on information services, finding that the judge should have applied Section VIII(C) of the decree, which required a BOC to show that there is no "substantial possibility that it could use its monopoly power to impede competition," rather than Section VII, which, based on common law principles, allowed the district court to approve uncontested modifications to the MFJ, even without proof of a change in market conditions, so long as they are in the public interest. The appeals court ordered the district court to

> bear in mind the *flexibility* of the public interest inquiry: The court's function is not to determine whether the resulting array of rights and liabilities "is one that will *best* serve society," but only to confirm that the resulting "settlement is 'within the *reaches* of the public interest'" (*U.S. v. Bechtel Corp.*, 648 F.2d 660, 666 [9th Cir. 1981] [quoting *U.S. Gillette Co.*, 406 F. Supp. 713, 716 (D.Mass. 1975)] [emphasis added] 900 F.2d at 309).

On remand in 1991, Judge Greene reluctantly dropped the information-services restriction (*United States v. Western Electric*, 767 F. Supp. 308 [D.D.C. 1991]). The judge stated: "[W]ere the court free to exercise its own judgment, it would conclude without hesitation that removal of the information-services restriction is incompatible with the decree and the public interest." But the burden of proof as dictated by the court of appeals led the court to remove the restriction. The court also felt it was bound to defer to the Justice Department's endorsement of the repeal (*Id.* at 327–330). The district court's stay of the order to remove the restriction was speedily overturned by the court of appeals in an interim decision.

Questions

1. In the 1984 *Western Electric* case, the RHCs argued that antitrust law provides adequate remedies to deal with potential cross-subsidization violations. Do you agree? If the communications market is not substantially competitive, how satisfactory is an antitrust remedy? Given the Justice Department's past record in these cases, how effective is this remedy likely to be? Who bears the burden of proof?

2. An antitrust suit is a post hoc remedy, whereas the decree embodies a prophylactic rule. If successful, how long until the antitrust remedy is granted? Could an injunction be obtained to preclude alleged continuing violations while the suit is pending?

3. Were you surprised by the remarks made by the RHCs regarding their lack of concern for ratepayers' interests? What type of duty does an RHC owe its ratepayers? Is it different from the duty owed by a BOC?

4. Who is likely to benefit the most by RHC diversification into noncommunications ventures? Who bears the risks?

5. What safeguards did the court impose in 1984 to protect ratepayers? Why did the court abandon some of them in 1987? Is the public harmed by the court's unwillingness to release the RHCs?

9

ACCESS AND BYPASS

NOTE ON ACCESS CHARGES

As we observed at the outset, there has been a movement to greater cost-based pricing of local and long-distance phone calls. In general, local rates have been subsidized by long-distance users. Prices that are lower than justified by the costs have helped keep the local exchange a monopoly; prices that are higher have helped create the competitive long-distance market.

The subsidy from long-distance to local was and continues to be accomplished by manipulation of the access charges the local-exchange carrier can impose for access to its local loop. This access charge is called the carrier's carrier charge or the carrier common line (CCL) charge. In the 1980s the FCC enabled phone companies to move to greater cost-based pricing of long-distance service by the introduction of the subscriber line charge (SLC), added to every phone bill regardless of the number of long-distance calls made. The charge was accompanied by reductions in the per-minute CCL charge, which was reflected in lower per-minute charges to customers. The changes were made to discourage long-distance companies from bypassing the local exchange to avoid the unrealistically high access charge imposed on calls handled by the local-exchange carrier.

Large customers had already been given special treatment through "special access" tariffs for private lines (see Figure 9.1). These access tariffs are lower than those charged public switched network customers. Indeed, private lines are a form of bypass, but one offered by the long-distance company itself.

Because local exchanges offer basically two services—transport and access—lost revenues from the latter can strain the former. The subscriber line charge was an attempt to compensate for the inequities between large and small users of long-distance, thereby stemming the bypass flow.

Some do not view the revenue flow from long-distance customers and carriers to local users as a subsidy because the supposed subsidizing parties derive substantial benefits from a universally available local distribution network. Furthermore, it is hard to determine what the precise cost of access is, just as all costing in the phone industry involves a degree of guesswork; the word "subsidy" is too value-laden, some believe. The worries about bypass that led to changes in the way access is charged may be overstated.

FIGURE 9.1 Accessing Long Distance Networks

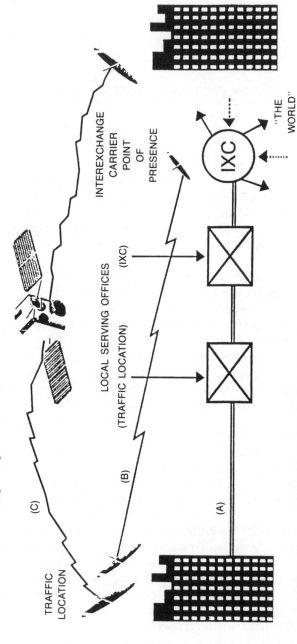

A - Special Access to IXC (Service Bypass)
B - Direct Connect to IXC (Facility Bypass) via Microwave
C - End-to-End Private Satellite Network (Facility Bypass)

Source: Weisman, "The Proliferation of Private Networks and Its Implications For Regulatory Reform," 41 *Federal Communications Law Journal* 331, 336 (1989).

Bypass never materialized to the extent feared by the local-exchange carriers, justifying a slower expansion of the SLC than had been called for in the early 1980s, when the FCC first addressed the bypass issue.

LONG DISTANCE NETWORK SERVICES

Phyllis E. Hartsock
NTIA Telecom 2000 (1988)

* * *

Declining Long Distance Rates

One of the biggest benefits to consumers with the advent of competition has been significant reductions in the price for domestic long distance calling, as follows:

AT&T Domestic Long Distance Reductions

May 1987	6.4%
Jun 1985	5.6%
Jun 1986	11.8%
Jul 1987	4.8%
Jan 1988	3.5%

Much of the domestic price decline has been attributed to decreased access charges paid by AT&T, with savings passed through to customers, as required by the FCC. It is difficult to ascertain the extent to which price declines may reflect other factors. Along with the decreased long distance prices there has also been an increase in volume of usage. It is likely that such network stimulation occurs when consumers realize calling is less costly. Therefore, the latest price decrease may induce further network usage. Moreover, when AT&T reduces its rates, competitors typically follow suit, attempting to undercut those rates just enough to capture a greater market share. Thus, all long distance customers benefit as AT&T's rates decline.

Price reductions have not been as significant internationally as domestically, but nevertheless have been occurring, perhaps on the order of 10 percent annually. U.S. international telephone service revenues earned by carriers grew from $589 million in 1975 to $2 billion by 1986. Traffic volume grew from 42 million messages to 500 million messages over that same period. As in the domestic arena, the trend is to see both rate reductions and increased traffic volumes.

The trend toward decreased prices for interLATA and international calls is not reflected in the intraLATA market. There, prices have tended to remain relatively stable in recent years, although they are beginning to show some decline. This result seems consistent with the lesser degree of competition in that market, as competition is a primary force in driving rates downward.

In fact, the FCC recently reported that in the states' interLATA markets, AT&T's rates were about 16 percent lower when competitive forces were at work. In that report, the FCC also indicated that intraLATA toll rates were about 3–4 percent lower where there is facilities-based competition. It may be that as more states authorize intraLATA toll competition, consumers will see more price reductions there as well.

There are those who argue that long distance price reductions benefit only a limited segment of the population—those choosing to make such calls. Some feel benefits accrue mostly to businesses with high volume long distance usage. This view may fail to consider the whole picture. Even those who do not generally make long distance calls benefit to the extent others can reach them. Additionally, individuals benefit both as employees of companies and as consumers to the extent that businesses are more likely to operate on a broad geographic scale. For example, many people now enjoy use of 800 (toll free) lines to order goods, engage in financial transactions, or make hotel reservations. Accordingly, the benefits from reduced long distance rates are widespread.

*   *   *

Expansion and Upgrading of Long Distance Plant

Seeking to capture a greater market share in the future, many competitors are expanding or upgrading their networks and installing fiber optic transmission facilities. As of year end 1987, fiber capacity in service by major service providers was as follows:

InterLATA Fiber-Optic Networks

Company	Route Miles	Fiber Miles
US Sprint	17,000	323,000
AT&T	19,000	456,000
MCI	6,317	223,894
NTN	7,979	156,421
Lightnet	5,300	127,200

This new fiber capacity is significant in ensuring that long-distance competition remains robust. While fiber installation may be expensive initially, it is expected to produce lower costs in the long run. The fact that numerous companies are installing so much fiber suggests they do anticipate increased network stimulation justifying this level of capital investment. Once such capacity is built, it will be put to use, even if some companies are not successful and sell their businesses. Others buying such capacity would most likely begin with a new, lower basis, facilitating their operation of a profitable venture.

New service developments and plans for expanded networks have generally resulted in significant capital spending by facilities-based providers. AT&T, for example, announced plans to spend as much as $2.5 billion on digital expansion both in 1988 and 1989. MCI had planned to spend $750 million on its network in 1987, as well as another $300 million by 1990. Such spending suggests not only that the industry is vital and profitable presently, but also that it is expected to remain so in coming years.

Increased Efficiency and
Declining Cost Differences for Competitors

Competition has served as a spur to greater marketplace discipline and cost accountability, contributing to lower prices for consumers. There have been extensive cost cutting efforts, including employee layoffs, as companies have sought to operate more efficiently in the competitive marketplace. Despite the cost cutting moves, there appears to be a limit to the extent to which competitors can undercut AT&T's rates—typically the tactic to date. Whereas cost savings to customers from using a competitive carrier may have initially been 20 to 40 percent less than AT&T's rates, the differential now is more likely to be in the 5 percent to 10 percent range.

Access charges may account for as much as 50 percent of long distance costs. With the declining access cost differential (as equal access is implemented), it is increasingly difficult for competitors to offer huge discounts from AT&T's rates. Actual transmission costs, where scale economies are most feasible, account for roughly 7–10 percent of costs—providing only a narrow margin in which companies can reflect cost differentials.

Ability to compete effectively therefore is coming to depend largely on marketing skills, quality of service, or provision of special features or options. An example of current day marketing strategy is US Sprint's effort at product differentiation by advertising itself as the "fiber optic" provider of long distance transmission. Whatever the particular tactic, consumers are likely to benefit as companies seek ways to compete with each other to capture more dollars.

* * *

Payments by Competitors for Local Distribution

With the advent of long distance competition, competitors had won the right to connect their services with the local network for distribution to subscribers. A resulting dispute, which still continues to some extent, was over the appropriate level of compensation competitors should pay to the local operating companies for access. The FCC authorized a payment plan known as ENFIA (Exchange Network Facilities for Interstate Access), set forth in AT&T tariffs. Because competitors typically had lesser quality interconnection than AT&T, ENFIA rates were set at a level below that paid by AT&T for local connection.

With the changing market structure, certain traditional pricing policies were no longer supportable. When AT&T still had a virtual monopoly over both local and long distance services, a system of cross-subsidies came into existence: long-distance rates were kept artificially high, so local rates could be kept low. Once AT&T found itself subject to competition in the long distance market, however, continuation of the cross-subsidy became unsustainable. As AT&T sought to compete and to maintain its market share, it desired to lower long distance rates and reduce the subsidy to local loop costs.

The FCC overhauled this traditional cross-subsidy arrangement contemporaneous with the restructuring of the Bell System pursuant to the AT&T consent decree. The FCC's 1983 *Access Charge Decision* planned a gradual shift in cost burdens, to decrease substantially the long distance subsidy to local loops costs. Under the FCC's plan, there are two types of access charges for use of the local network: (1) that representing fees paid by toll carriers (and presumably passed on to their customers) and (2) the subscriber line charge (SLC) paid directly by the end user.

This payment system began in 1984 for businesses and in 1985 for residential customers, and SLC increases were scheduled for subsequent years. In 1987, the FCC scheduled future increases in the SLC. With each increase in the SLC, there are decreases in the carriers' subsidy to local loop costs, which could be reduced to about eight or nine percent by 1989. With each reduction in the carriers' access charges, the FCC also required AT&T to pass cost savings through to the public, greatly contributing to the long distance price reductions discussed above.

Equal Access for AT&T Competitors

The equal access provisions of the AT&T consent decree have significantly improved the competitive environment for long distance carriers. Under that decree, which divested AT&T of its local service operations, the Bell Companies were required to provide long distance competitors the same quality interconnection afforded AT&T. The decree envisioned conversion of all Bell Operating Company central offices to equal access by September 1, 1986, with the possible exception of those serving 10,000 or fewer lines, or those not equipped with stored-program switches.

Other local exchange companies are also subject to equal access requirements, although such requirements are not identical to those governing the Bell companies. Under a consent decree signed in conjunction with GTE's acquisition of Sprint, GTE is obligated by 1990 to provide equal access in central offices serving more than 10,000 lines. The FCC has required other local exchange carriers to offer equal access to all interstate toll carriers within three years of a "reasonable request."

As of year end 1988, nearly 84 percent of Bell Company lines (81 million network access lines) had been converted to equal access. This meant that subscribers using such lines could choose their primary long distance carrier with easy 1+ dialing, and that competitors had the benefit of interconnections of comparable quality to that provided AT&T. By the end of 1989, it is expected that 94.6 percent of the Bell Companies' lines will have been converted to equal access; and by 1990, 97 percent of their lines. As of year end 1987, about 64 percent of independent company lines were converted, with 74 percent conversion expected by year end 1988.

Selection of a primary long distance carrier, under the FCC's regimen, requires an affirmative choice by subscribers. Companies were required to provide ballots to telephone customers, on a market by market basis, enabling them to select their primary carrier. Some subscribers failed to make such a selection, although they still desired to make long distance calls. An issue therefore arose over distribution of the default traffic for customers failing to return ballots. Originally, any default traffic was automatically assigned to the customer's current carrier. As this was typically AT&T, other carriers contended AT&T received an unfair advantage, skewing competition. The FCC thereafter decided to apportion default traffic among the facilities-based toll carriers on a proportionate basis. . . .

LOCAL NETWORKS

Terry Monroe
NTIA Telecom 2000 (1988)

Local telephone service is provided by 22 Bell Operating Companies (BOCs), serving approximately 80 percent of the 84 million U.S. households with telephone service; 14 General Telephone Companies (GTE) with about 8 percent of households; and approximately 1400 other "Independent" companies serving the remainder of households. According to a recent Fortune survey of the top 50 utilities, the BOCs and GTE accounted for eight of the top ten positions, with combined assets of $180.6 billion and operating revenues (for both telephone and nontelephone operations) of $85.2 billion.

Prior to the AT&T divestiture in 1984, local service was defined as a call between any two points within a single "exchange" or "zone." Exchanges varied in size, from a few hundred subscribers in some rural areas, to millions of subscribers in large urban areas. As of 1986, there were 19,400 exchanges in the United States, of which the BOCs served 7,623, while the Independents accounted for 11,777 exchanges.

With the AT&T consent decree, 164 court-approved "Local Access and Transport Areas" (LATAs) were established. Today, local calls within the serving area of a BOC are also referred to as intraexchange, *intra*LATA calls. Within their local service area, the "local exchange carriers," (LECs) provide a myriad of services in addition to basic exchange service. For example, all may provide long distance (i.e., toll) service between exchanges within their LATAs (interexchange, *intra*LATA toll). In addition, these carriers offer "transport" services, which allows the movement of information within the LATA. Transport services can be further divided into three categories: point-to-point, point-to-multipoint, and multipoint-to-multipoint. The first two are generally provided through dedicated (i.e., private) lines and are used primarily by business customers. Multipoint-to-multipoint services are most commonly associated with basic local telephone service, used by both business and residential customers.

In addition, local exchange carriers provide access to long distance carriers. Access is most commonly provided through the public switched network. At certain usage levels, however, it may be more economical for customers to utilize a direct, nonswitched facility to connect premises to a long distance carrier. Such access may be obtained either from the LEC (referred to as "special" access) or as in the case with transport services, the customers could choose to lease or build facilities separate from the local exchange carrier.

Local calling continues to represent a substantial majority (approximately 90 percent) of the total number of calls made by subscribers. Local service subscribers, in turn, are basically divided into two groups: residential and business, with the former accounting for 71 percent of access lines. For residential subscribers, basic exchange service traditionally has meant paying one rate for the ability to make an unlimited amount of local calls per month (i.e., flat rate service). Today, however, an increasing number of subscribers are also provided the option of measured service. Measured service is generally more available in urban areas, where the equipment necessary to measure local calls is more prevalent. Measured service offers a lower "dial tone" charge, with additional charges levied for each local call above a certain number per month. Those additional charges are based either on a per call basis (often referred to as "message rate service") or a per minute basis.

* * *

As of March 1988, 92.9 percent of the 91 million households in the United States had at least one telephone, while 94.6 percent of households have access to a telephone either at home or elsewhere. Both figures are at their highest levels since the Census Bureau began collecting such data as part of the Current Population Survey. In addition, since the first data were collected in November 1983, nearly one million households previously without telephone service have been added to the network.

Local telephone rates, after increases in the first two years following the AT&T divestiture, generally have stabilized and in some instances declined in the past year. In 1987, for example, state commissions considered only $93.4 million in revenue increases for local telephone companies, compared with $7.32 billion in 1984. This trend continued into the first six months of 1988, with state commissions considering only $14.7 million in revenue increases.

Equally important is that fact that the level of requests granted has declined significantly. In 1984, for example, telephone companies were granted revenue increases of $3.9 billion, or 53%, of the total considered by state commissions. In 1987, however, the level of rate reductions and refunds ordered by state commissions resulted in a net reduction in intrastate revenues of $460 million. The reductions and refunds continued through the first six months of 1988, with a net reduction totaling $298 million.

One explanation for the lower rate requests and higher level of reductions is the recent change in the federal tax law, which lowered the corporate income tax rate from 46 to 34 percent. The National Association of Regulatory Utility Commissioners (NARUC) estimates the tax savings to AT&T and the local telephone companies resulting from federal tax reform to be $6 billion per year.

In a few instances, states have used the tax savings to allow the local operating companies to reduce their depreciation reserve deficiencies. The more common response, however, has been to require the local operating companies to adjust their rates to reflect the changes in the corporate tax rate (for many states, current revenue requirements were established when the tax rate was 46 percent).

* * *

Current estimates are that the nationwide average for flat rate residential local telephone service (including the subscriber line charge) is $16.61 per month. Including the cost of optional services (e.g., touch tone dialing, inside wiring maintenance plan) and long distance services, the average monthly residential bill is estimated to be approximately $40.00–$45.00. By comparison, in 1983, the year prior to divestiture, the average bill for similar service was estimated at $35.00–$40.00 monthly.

Lower priced, measured service alternatives also are available in most states, at an average monthly rate of $9.35 (this includes a package of 50 "free" calls per month). Measured rate service for low-usage subscribers (charge for each call) averages approximately $7.00 per month. The growing availability of measured service options has meant lower monthly local service bills for many subscribers. Local telephone rates for rural subscribers continue to remain lower generally than in urban areas.

In addition, the FCC, in conjunction with the states and local telephone companies, has established "lifeline" programs designed to help low-income and disadvantaged individuals afford telephone service. Twenty-five states and the District of Columbia have qualified for full assistance under the FCC's "lifeline" plan, which provides for a waiver of the federal subscriber line charge (currently at $2.60 per month), as long as states lower local rates by a concurrent amount. Recently, the FCC expanded its lifeline assistance to encourage households currently without telephone service to join the network by providing a $30 credit towards the costs of installation. Thirty-one states and the District of Columbia have been certified under the "Link Up America" program. Assistance is limited to those individuals who can meet a "means" test (such as eligibility for food stamps or Medicaid) and verify their eligibility for benefits under such programs. Funding for the federal contribution to these programs comes from interexchange carriers. In its first six months of operations, "Link Up America" made it possible for 13,995 low-income households to obtain telephone service, based on the results of four pilot programs (Arkansas, District of Columbia, Texas and West Virginia).

Thus, despite substantial changes in the structure of the telephone industry over the past twenty years, the following table shows that, compared to other "essential" commodities such as food, housing, fuel, utilities, and medical care, local telephone service during that period has remained an excellent value for most consumers.

Indexes for Selected Commodities

Commodity	Index
Fuel (home oil, piped gas & electricity)	471.6
Medical Care	467.8
Housing	375.4
Food and Beverages	326.9
Local Telephone Service	203.7

Indexes: 1967 = 100 (unadjusted)
(As of September 1987)
Source: U.S. Department of Labor

*   *   *

In the early years of the telephone industry, telephone companies recovered the total costs of providing local telephone service directly from subscribers of that service. Local exchange plant and equipment costs (also referred to as "fixed costs") were allocated between the interstate and intrastate service based upon the relative usage of local facilities for each type of call. Beginning in 1952, however, measures of relative use were weighted so as to assign an increasing share of local fixed costs to interstate service. This process accelerated in the 1960s and by 1981, the "separations and settlements" process had apportioned on average over 26 percent of the costs of local exchange plant and equipment to the interstate service, although interstate usage nationwide was only about 8 percent. This burden borne by toll subscribers increased at the same time that the costs of interstate service were declining because of advances in the under- lying technology.

Another factor that contributed to artificially low residential rates was the long-term depreciation schedules prescribed by regulators for local fixed plant and equipment. By recovering telephone company investment in plant and equipment over many years (e.g., 30–40 years), ratepayers were required to bear only a small burden of depreciation costs each year. So long as technology remained stable, this was not a problem.

The political unpopularity of rate increases, moreover, made it easier for regulators to shift some of the costs of residential service to business customers, who were heavily dependent on service from the local operating companies. Consequently, in addition to subsidies between local and long-distance, there were subsidies flowing among various classes of customers for each service.

As a result of these practices, increases in the price of residential local telephone service through the early 1980s remained well below both increases in the CPI and the wage rate for U.S. workers. Over a 30-year period (1950– 1980), the price of residential local telephone service fell in real dollar terms. In 1950, the average monthly charge for residential service in current dollars was $4.29. In 1980, the charge had risen in current dollars to $8.61. However, when the 1950 rates are adjusted to account for the actual purchasing power of money in 1980, the average monthly charge for phone service in 1950 would have been $14.58, or almost $6 *greater* than in 1980. (See Table 4.) Expressed another way, by 1980, the average worker had to work less than 1½ hours per month to pay for his local telephone service, compared with six hours in 1940.

One benefit of low-priced residential local service was that it helped the United States achieve the goal of "universal service." As the goal of universal service was being achieved, however, the *costs* of providing local service were increasing. By 1982, the Congressional Budget Office estimated the local loop revenue requirement (wiring connecting subscribers to central offices) was $24 billion. When the costs of CPE and inside wiring were added, subscriber plant costs in 1982 totalled $39 billion while industry revenues were $80 billion. On a per line basis, the fixed plant costs of providing service were estimated at more than $25.00 per month, while local rates were on average less than half that amount. As a result of the separation procedures previously discussed, interstate customers were asked to bear a disproportionate share of local costs through higher long distance rates. By 1984, this interstate subsidy of local service was estimated at $11 billion per year, or 14 cents per minute for each interstate call.

Rapid advances in technology and increased competition, however, made continuation of the traditional cost allocation and pricing policies infeasible. It was thought that without changes to bring rates closer in line with actual costs, large volume customers might bypass the public switched network, which in turn, would leave the local operating companies unable to recover their substantial fixed costs through existing rates. As a result, prices could increase substantially for those remaining subscribers (mostly residential and small business) on the public network. FCC actions in the early 1980s were, in part, a response to this concern.

Divestiture and Competition

At the same time the FCC was reexamining its pricing and cost allocation policies, the AT&T antitrust suit was being settled, with AT&T agreeing to divest itself of its 22 operating companies. In the wake of the AT&T divestiture, local operating companies requested significant rate increases from state public utility commissions. In the first six months of 1984, state commissions considered revenue increases totalling six billion, of which little over one-half ($3.1 billion) was granted by state commissioners. For the year, state commissioners granted companies $3.9 billion (53 percent) of the $7.3 billion they considered. Consumers, in turn, saw their telephone bills for local service increase on average by 17.1 percent in 1984.

Much of the blame for these rate increases was linked to the AT&T divestiture. It is possible that in the confusion and uncertainty surrounding divestiture, and its projected impact on the BOCs, the magnitude of rate increases was greater than normally might have been expected. It is true that some of the direct changes associated with divestiture affected local rates, although not to the degree imagined. For in addition to divestiture, there were other charges occurring which also had a short-term impact on local rates.

1. Loss of CPE and Toll Revenues

Perhaps the major revenue loss for the BOCs resulting from divestiture came about with the transfer of customer premises equipment back to AT&T. Prior to divestiture, the BOCs earned significant revenues from the leasing of telephone instruments to residential and business customers, which helped to keep down monthly local service rates. Southwestern Bell, for example, estimates that leased equipment contributed $1.14 billion to its revenues in 1983. NYNEX estimates that it lost approximately $500 to $550 million in revenues with divestiture.

Divestiture also resulted in the loss of toll revenues associated with the provision of certain long distance services. While much of this revenue loss was made up through the imposition of access charges on long distance carriers, it was often not sufficient to fully recover the revenues associated with long distance service. NYNEX and Southwestern, for example, each experienced a decrease in toll revenues of approximately $500 million in 1984, even after accounting for interstate and intrastate access charges.

2. Depreciation

Another factor which appears responsible in part for the increases in local service rates is the FCC's 1980 decision to change depreciation methods for interstate investment. It was the Commission's intent to allow for quicker recovery of capital investment which would reflect more accurately the *economic* life of telephone plant and equipment. Because of the early retirement of existing plant in the 1970s, due primarily to the rapid conversion from electromechanical to electronic switching, the industry's depreciation reserve (i.e., the accumulation of annual depreciation expense) was estimated at $21 billion by 1983.

By reforming its depreciation standards, the FCC sought to reduce the current reserve deficiency as well as provide incentives for future capital investment embodying new technologies, which, in the long run, would enable the local operating companies to more efficiently manage their networks and reduce their costs. In the short run, however, this faster recovery of capital investment would mean higher monthly rates for customers.

In its 1983 *Preemption Order*, the Commission extended its depreciation policy to the states, preempting inconsistent state depreciation regulations for intrastate ratemaking purposes. As a result of this decision, many operating companies asked for, and won, higher depreciation rates for intrastate services from their state commissions, with a resulting increase in local rates. On May 27, 1986, however, the U.S. Supreme Court held that the FCC cannot require the states to use FCC-prescribed depreciation rates. As a result of that decision, many states have extended intrastate depreciation schedules and reduced annual depreciation charges, although some (e.g., Illinois) continue to support accelerated depreciation.

3. Jurisdictional Cost Allocation

A second FCC decision which directly affected local service rates was the change in the jurisdictional allocation of local fixed plant costs used for both interstate and intrastate communications. Concerned that an increasing share of these costs was being shifted to the interstate sector, the FCC in 1982 temporarily froze the percentage of fixed costs allocated to the interstate jurisdiction (also known as the "subscriber plant factor" [SPF]) at 1981 levels pending further examination of the separations process by a Federal-State Joint Board (comprised of four state and three FCC commissioners).

Late in 1983, upon the recommendation of a Joint Board, the FCC extended the cap on interstate cost allocations until January 1, 1986, to be followed by a transition period during which a 25 percent interstate allocation would be implemented in four equal steps. In high cost areas (i.e., current allocation is above 25 percent), this transition meant that the level of costs allocated to interstate service would diminish, thereby increasing pressures to raise local rates. Recognizing this potential for significant local rate increases, the FCC ordered the new allocation factor to be supplemented with direct assistance to those areas (in many cases rural) with total fixed local exchange costs in excess of the national average. One year later, after the Joint Board's reconsideration, the Commission ordered the transition to the 25 percent allocation formula to be implemented in eight steps.

Statistics of Communications Common Carriers,
Telephone Development by States

State	*Percent of Households with Telephone Service*	
	March 1987	*March 1988*
United States	92.5	92.9
Alabama	87.2	88.4
Alaska	88.3	87.2
Arizona	89.1	90.5
Arkansas	87.0	83.6
California	94.3	94.7
Colorado	93.2	95.1
Connecticut	97.9	96.5
Delaware	96.5	97.2
District of Columbia	91.2	93.3
Florida	91.2	93.0
Georgia	87.5	91.5
Hawaii	94.8	95.3
Idaho	90.9	92.9
Illinois	94.0	94.3
Indiana	91.3	91.4
Iowa	95.5	94.5
Kansas	95.5	95.3
Kentucky	87.4	89.5
Louisiana	86.9	86.8
Maine	94.2	94.3
Maryland	96.2	96.4
Massachusetts	96.7	97.3
Michigan	94.1	94.4
Minnesota	95.8	97.3
Mississippi	82.6	83.8
Missouri	91.5	93.0
Montana	91.4	91.4
Nebraska	95.0	96.4
Nevada	92.1	91.8
New Hampshire	94.0	96.5
New Jersey	94.3	94.3
New Mexico	89.1	85.9
New York	93.3	93.0
North Carolina	89.7	90.1
North Dakota	97.8	96.7
Ohio	93.4	94.0
Oklahoma	88.5	89.6
Oregon	91.1	89.4
Pennsylvania	96.0	96.1
Rhode Island	95.1	95.4
South Carolina	89.0	88.3
South Dakota	92.2	92.2
Tennessee	89.3	91.7
Texas	90.4	87.8
Utah	93.2	93.0
Vermont	95.8	95.9
Virginia	92.9	94.7
Washington	93.2	93.4
West Virginia	88.7	87.9
Wisconsin	96.2	95.9
Wyoming	93.3	93.6

Source: Federal Communications Commission.

As a result of freezing the interstate allocation in 1982, local operating companies have not been able to shift an increasing share of subscriber plant costs to interstate ratepayers. In a 1985 report, the staff of the D.C. Public Service Commission concluded that the costs to be recovered through the intrastate jurisdiction would be $5.1 million (or $1.24 per month per line) greater because of the FCC's action. In addition, they estimated that the transition to a 25 percent allocator (at the time, D.C.'s allocator was 43.8 percent) would impose an additional total monthly cost of $2.80 per access line. Over the eight years of the allocator phase down, this would result in a yearly access line increase of 35 cents.

While the institution of the 25 percent allocation factor will lower the burden on interstate ratepayers in low-cost areas, subscribers may be asked to bear more of the local fixed costs in high-cost areas which will lose some of their interstate subsidies. Through its high-cost assistance fund, however, the FCC seeks to minimize the potential for significant increases in intrastate cost allocation, and thus, increases in local rates. Finally, there is the issue of those areas with high local costs, but low interstate usage (and thus a small interstate allocation). In those cases, as the interstate allocation rises to 25 percent, these areas actually could see a reduction in their local service revenue requirements.

4. Access Charges

The FCC action which perhaps has received the most attention over the past few years has been the imposition of access charges—commonly referred to as "subscriber line charges"—on residential and business customers. Access charges are intended to replace the traditional practice of recovering a portion of local fixed costs from interstate services. . . .

ADJUSTMENTS TO SLCs AND CCLs

Establishing the appropriate SLC was a challenge, both as an economic and a political matter. Too low an SLC would make it impossible to bring the CCLs down to where they no longer encouraged bypass. Too high an SLC—say, a "flashcut" to $11—and customers would see their phone bills doubled with no increase in service. While the FCC considered a flashcut approach, Congress made it clear that such high SLCs, no matter what the economic justification, would be unacceptable. So a phased-in SLC approach was adopted.

The FCC and the PUCs, through the Federal-State Joint Board, originally envisaged a system where the CCLs would be pooled and averaged so that areas with lower costs of providing access—densely populated areas where subscriber loops are shorter—could subsidize rural areas, where common line costs are higher. With standardized CCLs, it was presumed that long-distance charges would be averaged nationally. The National Exchange Carrier Association was established to file CCL tariffs and administer these funds (as well as the collected SLCs), and local-exchange carriers (LECs) joined this "NECA pool."

Lowering the CCL had two other important consequences beside the potential effect on bypass. First, the per-minute cost of long-distance declined, increasing overall demand. Thus, more people used long-distance than before, widening the pool for CCL collection. (The increased revenues of the interexchange carriers also formed a source of money to fund "Link Up America," a scheme to increase phone installations among poorer persons.) Second, as CCLs became a less dominant part of the per-minute long-distance charge, LECs in areas with lower CCL costs were permitted to leave the NECA pool, subject to paying transitional support payments to high-cost areas that needed the protection of CCL averaging by the pool. Freed of the cost-averaging of the NECA pool, those LECs could price CCL more closely to its actual costs, thereby discouraging bypass in those areas.

The following orders effectuate this complex balancing act. As you read them, ask: Does the FCC have an adequate economic model for determining the appropriate SLC charge? Or is it based more on a politically acceptable level of charges, gradually implemented? Does the FCC distinguish between economic and uneconomic bypass in its analysis? Why did the FCC introduce "Link Up America"—a program somewhat unrelated to the access-charge controversy—in this intricate proceeding?

MTS AND WATS MARKET STRUCTURE, REPORT AND ORDER

2 F.C.C. Rcd. 2953 (1987)

* * *

Background

In an order adopted in 1983 (*Access Charge Order*), this Commission adopted a comprehensive system of tariffed charges, generally known as the access charge plan, for the recovery of LEC costs associated with the origination or termination of interstate calls.[7] We concluded that the access charge plan would achieve the long standing goals of that proceeding, namely, preserving universal service, promoting economic efficiency, eliminating service pricing discrimination, and deterring uneconomic bypass.

---

7. The framework of this plan consists of a system of tariffed charges pursuant to which LECs recover most of their costs apportioned to the interstate jurisdiction through the process of jurisdictional separations. MTS and WATS Market Structure, *Third Report and Order*, CC Docket No. 78–72, 93 FCC 2d 241 (1983) (hereinafter the *Access Charge Order*). . . .

One aspect of the access charge plan provided that a major portion of common line costs,[8] specifically loop costs, allocated to the interstate jurisdiction would be recovered directly from telephone subscribers through monthly flat-rate charges called subscriber line charges.[9] In response to concerns about the impact of subscriber line charges on residential and single-line business subscribers, we deferred implementation of such charges on these subscribers pending the completion of a number of proceedings. These proceedings included an examination of subscriber line charges and the transition mechanism for implementing them, assistance programs for low income households, and assistance measures for subscribers in high cost study areas. We also issued a Further Notice of Proposed Rule Making requesting recommendations from the Joint Board regarding the implementation of residential and single-line business subscriber line charges, exemptions or targeted assistance for low income subscribers, and more effective mechanisms to meet the needs of high cost LECs for additional assistance.

In November 1984, the Joint Board issued its recommendations regarding these various issues. The recommendations took the form of a three-part plan. First, limited residential and single-line business subscriber line charges of $1.00 per line per month would be implemented in June 1985, with an increase to $2.00 in June 1986. Second, the Joint Board proposed guidelines for a limited federal lifeline program that would provide a 50% reduction in subscriber line charges, when matched by an equal amount of state local exchange lifeline assistance, to customers qualifying under a state-established program that was means-tested and subject to verification. The Joint Board also recommended an expedited study to establish broader lifeline measures to assist low income households. Third, the Joint Board recommended retargeting the federal high cost assistance measures to provide additional assistance to telephone subscribers served by LECs with fewer than 50,000 access lines and those with particularly

---

8. Common line costs (*i.e.,* exchange plant costs) encompass, among other things, all equipment costs and related expenses associated with connecting a subscriber's premises with a LEC switch. This equipment includes the protection block and drop wire at such premises, and the line (*i.e.,* loop) between the premises and the switch. . . .

Although only roughly 10 percent of all calls are interstate, approximately 27 percent of the local loop costs are assigned to the interstate jurisdiction.

9. Our initial plan provided that most of these loop costs, which were being paid by subscribers through higher charges on long distance usage, would ultimately be recovered directly through subscriber line charges. In order to avoid the potentially disruptive effects of immediately implementing full subscriber line charges, we provided that in 1984, the first year of the plan, LECs would have to charge a minimum flat fee of $2.00 per line per month for residential subscribers and $4.00 per line per month for business subscribers. We also established a five-year transition schedule for recovery of all interstate loop costs directly from end users, except for the additional loop costs associated with high cost assistance, customer premises equipment (CPE), and inside wiring, which were to be recovered by LECs from interexchange carriers (IXCs) on the basis of a charge per minute of use known as the carrier common line (CCL) charge. . . .

high loop costs.[15] Finally, the Joint Board recommended that subscriber line charges remain at $2.00 until the completion of a further Joint Board proceeding to study the effects of subscriber line charges, including the effect on universal service, bypass, and economic efficiency. . . .

* * *

On July 2, 1986, we issued the *Further Notice* asking the Joint Board to examine the effects of (1) subscriber line charges, (2) the federal lifeline assistance program, and (3) the present measures to assist high cost telephone companies, on the primary goals of the access charge proceeding and interexchange competition. The *Further Notice* stated that the lifeline program and high cost assistance measures were integral parts of a cohesive package, and therefore must also be examined as part of the review of subscriber line charges. In addition, the *Further Notice* sought the Joint Board's recommendations on possible modifications to the current provisions for mandatory nationwide pooling of common line costs and revenues.[18]

In seeking public comment for our consideration of these issues, the *Further Notice* also requested discussion on whether the three-part plan initially recommended by the Joint Board and adopted by this Commission has furthered the primary goals of this proceeding, and what further steps should be taken to achieve these goals. Specifically, the *Further Notice* asked for comments on: (1) whether subscriber line charges should be increased (and if so, to what level and on what schedule), modified in some fashion, or remain unchanged at their present level; (2) whether the federal lifeline assistance program and high cost assistance measures presently in place reflect a properly targeted response to the need for assistance to low income subscribers and subscribers in high cost areas, and whether these programs should be modified, and in what manner; and (3) what alternatives may be available to the current mandatory pooling mechanisms used to recover the interstate allocation of NTS exchange costs.

* * *

15. High cost assistance measures contained in Part 67 of the Commission's rules allocate an additional percentage of loop costs to the interstate jurisdiction in the case of LECs with study area loop costs that are higher than the national average of such costs. 47 C.F.R. §67.631 (1986). These measures reduce the intrastate cost allocation and, consequently, permit local service rates to be lower than they otherwise would be. In short, the high cost assistance program permits eligible local exchange carriers to recover a higher percentage of their revenue requirement from interexchange carriers rather than through local rate increases. . .

18. In the *Access Charge Order*, we prescribed a nationwide mandatory pool for the interstate allocation of common line costs. . . . In accordance with Part 69 of our Rules, these costs are assigned to the common line element and recovered in part from end users through subscriber line charges and in part from interexchange carriers through a nationally uniform CCL charge. *See* 47 C.F.R. §§ 69.601–69.610 (1986). This system of tariffed end user and CCL charges is administered by NECA on behalf of all LECs.

Summary of Joint Board's Major Findings and Recommendations

A. Subscriber Line Charges

1) Findings. The Joint Board concluded that implementation of subscriber line charges has had no adverse effect on universal service. The Joint Board found that (1) the nationwide telephone penetration rate has increased since the initial implementation of subscriber line charges, (2) the number of households without telephones has declined during this period from 7.4 million to 6.8 million, (3) subscribership levels among low income groups and the elderly have remained stable, and (4) subscribership among the elderly exceeds the national average.

The Joint Board also concluded that implementation of subscriber line charges has permitted the more rational recovery of NTS costs and has increased the economically efficient use of the public switched network. Specifically, the Joint Board found that the implementation of subscriber line charges has reduced switched access and interstate long distance rates, which, in turn, has generated substantial increases in interstate long distance calling. The Joint Board also stated that the economic benefits generated by subscriber line charges extend beyond the telecommunications sector, bringing a wide range of indirect economic benefits to the nation, including reduced overall price levels and increased employment.

The Joint Board further concluded that implementation of subscriber line charges has substantially reduced the extent of pricing discrimination between switched and special access service by moving switched access prices closer to the true economic cost of providing that service. This reduction in the loading of loop costs onto switched access service rates, the Joint Board concluded, will help reduce the threat of uneconomic bypass.

Finally, the Joint Board concluded that modest increases in subscriber line charges, in addition to furthering the goals of this proceeding, also will permit: (1) a more comprehensive lifeline assistance program designed to increase telephone subscribership among low income Americans; and (2) a limited restructuring of the current mandatory common line tariff and pooling system. These recommendations are discussed *infra.*

2) Recommendations. The Joint Board recommends that the cap on subscriber line charges for subscriber line residential and single-line business customers be increased to $2.60 on June 1, 1987, $3.20 on September 1, 1988, and $3.50 on April 1, 1989. The Joint Board also recommends that subscriber line charges on embedded Centrex lines be increased to $4.00 on June 1, 1987, $5.00 on September 1, 1988, and $6.00 on April 1, 1989. The increase to a maximum of $3.50 for residential and single-line business subscribers represents the Joint Board's final recommendation for nationwide implementation of subscriber line charges. Additionally, as noted above, each of these rate levels is a ceiling. Thus, a LEC may assess the full level of the authorized subscriber line charge only to the extent that the company's study area interstate loop costs equal or exceed that level. Accordingly, for some users the subscriber line charge will not reach the $3.50 ceiling. The Joint Board recommends that this Commission require LECs to flow through the proposed subscriber line charge increases in the form of reductions in the CCL charge. It specifically recommends that the first increase be applied to reduce the originating CCL charge, and thus limit the bypass threat on the originating end of the call; and that the further increases be applied to reduce both the originating and terminating CCL charges taking into account potential bypass threats. The Joint Board also recommends that AT&T Communications (AT&T) be directed to flow through to consumers, in the form of interstate rate reductions, the savings it will realize as a result of reductions in the CCL charge.

* * *

B. Lifeline Assistance

1) Findings. The Joint Board concluded that the existing lifeline assistance program is a sound response to concerns about the level of telephone subscribership among low income groups. Pursuant to this program, qualifying subscribers are exempted from subscriber line charges, up to the current full level of $2.00 monthly, when this assistance is matched by state benefits provided to such subscribers pursuant to a qualified state plan.

16. Although the Joint Board endorsed the structure and benefits of the existing lifeline assistance program, it concluded that high, initial service installation and connection charges appear to be the primary barrier to subscribership among low income groups. Thus, the Joint Board found that more could be done to address this problem directly, thereby not only preserving, but also increasing, universal telephone service.

2) Recommendations. The Joint Board makes two recommendations regarding federal lifeline assistance. First, the Joint Board recommends a program of federal assistance to qualified low income households that would help defray the one time charges for commencement of service. This program, which has been described as a program to "Link Up America," would offset one half of the charges for commencing telephone service, up to $30, for qualifying households. The program also would encourage LECs to offer deferred payment schedules for these charges by paying a LEC's interest costs, on an amount up to $200, when it provides for a deferred payment schedule and does not charge interest to qualified subscribers. The Joint Board recommends that this interest payment be set at the rate paid on ten year Treasury bills.

Second, the Joint Board recommends that the current federal lifeline assistance program be increased to correspond with the proposed subscriber line charge increases. Federal assistance would be available to match state contributions on any amount up to the full subscriber line charge of $3.50. Thus, with full state matching assistance, a total of $7.00 in benefits would be available per month to qualifying subscribers under this program upon full implementation of the federal subscriber line charge—$3.50 in federal assistance and $3.50 in reduced charges for local service.

The Joint Board recommends that the subscriber line charge waiver and Link Up America programs be funded by charges assessed on IXCs.

The existing subscriber line charge waiver program requires that a state or a local exchange carrier obtain Commission certification of its state assistance plan, which must be means tested and subject to verification, before federal benefits are made available. The Joint Board recommends that state Link Up America plans, or plans submitted by states' delegatees, be similarly certified before federal benefits are made available. The Joint Board recommends that Link Up America assistance be available for a single telephone line at the principal place of residence. It further recommends the following eligibility criteria for beneficiaries of this assistance:

a. Applicant must have lived at an address where there has been no telephone service for at least three months prior to the date that assistance is requested;
b. Applicant must not have received this assistance within the last two years;
c. Applicant must not be a dependent for federal income tax purposes, unless he or she is more than 60 years of age;
d. Applicant must meet the requirements of a state established income test.

The Joint Board recommends that the first two criteria be verified, for example, through telephone company records. The last two criteria may be self-certified.

C. High Cost Assistance

1. Findings. Existing high cost assistance measures permit LECs in study areas where loop costs are higher than the national average to allocate costs to the interstate jurisdiction over and above the basic interstate allocation. This assistance is designed to reduce the intrastate cost allocation and thereby keep local service rates lower than they otherwise would be in high cost areas. The Joint Board found that this rationale for providing high cost assistance remains valid and that such assistance is a sound means of fostering universal service.

2. Recommendation. The Joint Board recommends retargeting the high cost assistance measures provided to high cost telephone companies. This recommended retargeting would provide an additional interstate expense allocation to small and medium size LECs and less assistance to larger LECs, specifically, LECs with over 200,000 access lines. The Joint Board recommends that the retargeted assistance be recovered from IXCs through flat-rate charges calculated according to the same methodology as lifeline assistance.

D. Common Line Pooling

1. Findings. This Commission currently requires all LECs to participate in a single common line tariff and pooling arrangement administered by NECA. The Joint Board observed that the initial decision by this Commission to prescribe this arrangement was driven in large measure by concerns that LEC-specific CCL charges might result in the deaveraging of interstate long distance rates. This would have occurred, the Joint Board stated, due to the significant common line cost differences among LECs that prevailed in 1984 when the access charge plan initially was implemented. The Joint Board also noted that the Commission, although it prescribed mandatory pooling as a means of resolving these concerns, recognized that the effects of pooling were not entirely beneficial; and the Commission specifically stated that pooling limits LEC cost recovery flexibility, establishes economically inefficient cost/price distortions, and reduces LEC incentives to contain costs. The Joint Board stated that the Commission, despite these concerns, concluded that a common line tariff and pooling arrangement covering the CCL rate was necessary at that time. The Joint Board also found, however, that increasing the ceiling on subscriber line charges to $3.50 would reduce variations in common line cost recovery needs so as to substantially alleviate the possibility that pooling modifications would result in interstate long distance rate deaveraging.[29]

2. *Recommendations.* The Joint Board recommends that the existing common line tariff and pooling system be modified to permit LECs to withdraw from the NECA tariff and pool and file common line tariffs based on their own costs. Pursuant to the Joint Board's recommendations, LECs that withdraw from the NECA pool would be required to contribute long term support (LTS) to LECs that remain in the NECA pool, thus enabling pooling companies, which generally will be small high cost companies, to tariff a CCL charge equal to the charge that would result if all LECs remained in the pool. The Joint Board also recommends that four years of transitional support payments (TRS) be provided to qualifying LECs that withdraw from the pool. Such LECs must be net recipients from the pool in 1988 and must withdraw from the NECA tariff and pool in accordance with a schedule that provides the largest companies one opportunity and smaller companies two opportunities to leave the pool and qualify to receive TRS. TRS will be paid by those nonpooling companies that were net contributors to the pool in 1988. TRS recipients will not pay LTS to pooling companies during the transition period.

Since the Joint Board's recommended pooling modifications are predicated upon implementation of proposed increases in subscriber line charges, it recommends that these modifications be implemented on April 1, 1989, the date it has proposed for the final increase in subscriber line charges. The Joint Board

---

29. . . . LECs recover their common line costs through two separate charges: (1) subscriber line charges, which are flat-rate charges assessed on end users on a monthly basis; and (2) the CCL, which is a usage charge assessed on interexchange carriers such as AT&T on a per minute basis. Almost all common line costs not recovered through subscriber line charges are presently recovered through the CCL charge. Therefore, the higher the amount of common line costs recovered through subscriber line charges, the lower the CCL charge will be. When the access charge plan was implemented initially, the ceiling on subscriber line charges was $1.00, leaving the bulk of common line costs to be recovered through the CCL charge. Due to varying common line cost recovery requirements among LECs, CCL rates would have varied significantly in the absence of pooling, particularly in rural areas where costs tend to be significantly higher than the national average. This generated concern that interexchange carriers would deaverage their rates in response to widely varying CCL charges assessed by LECs, a situation that would force rural and other high cost subscribers to shoulder inordinately high common line cost recovery burdens. As a result, this Commission ordered all LECs to participate in a pooling arrangement administered by NECA that produces a nationwide, uniform CCL charge. . . . 314–315. The Joint Board concluded, however, that if the ceiling on subscriber line charges is increased to $3.50, potential CCL rate disparities among LECs will not be significant enough to cause carriers like AT&T to deaverage their interstate rates. The Joint Board reasoned that a smaller percentage of the NTS pool recovered through CCL charges coupled with increases in switched access minutes should generate study area specific CCL charges which are not substantially different in magnitude so as to encourage bypass.

recommends that transitional support be available only to net recipients that leave the pool on certain dates. In order to qualify to receive TRS, large companies must notify NECA by August 1, 1988 of their intention to withdraw from the NECA pool. The Joint Board proposed that smaller companies be given an additional opportunity, in June 1989 as well as in August 1988, to announce their intention to withdraw from the pool while still qualifying for TRS. The Joint Board also recommends that withdrawal from the pool be on an "all or nothing" basis. Specifically, a LEC withdrawing one of its study areas must withdraw all of them, and a holding company withdrawing one of its LECs must withdraw them all. Finally, the Joint Board recommends that this Commission prescribe the continuation of AT&T's current practice of maintaining a nationwide averaged rate schedule for its Message Telecommunications Service (MTS).

The Joint Board further recommends that this Commission initiate proceedings in order to: (1) consider what, if any, adjustment should be made to its recommended pooling modifications to ensure that they do not inadvertently and unreasonably affect the marketability of small LECs; and (2) conform existing Part 69 Rules governing the administration of NECA and the operations of the NECA common line pool.

Discussion

The Joint Board has recommended a carefully integrated plan of action for resolving a variety of issues concerning common line cost recovery. These recommendations are designed to further all four of the long standing goals of this proceeding—preserving universal service, promoting economic efficiency, eliminating service pricing discrimination, and deterring uneconomic bypass— and to achieve a proper balance among these goals. We hereby adopt these recommendations with minor modifications as well as the analysis and reasoning on which they are founded.

Adoption of these recommendations, particularly the proposed modest increases in subscriber line charges, represents a significant step toward the achievement of cost-based telecommunications pricing. As we stated at the time our access charge plan was initially adopted, cost-based telecommunications pricing is well worth achieving because a pricing structure in which most non-traffic-sensitive, common line costs are recovered through usage-based charges poses a substantial danger to the long term viability of our Nation's telecommunication system.[32] Artificially high telecommunications service pricing encourages a wide range of activity directed toward no other end than the avoidance of such prices. This not only diverts investment away from productive enterprise, it increases the possibility that users, particularly large users, will abandon the public switched network for less efficient alternatives that are less costly only because switched access services are offered at artificially high price levels.

---

32. . . . The Joint Board observed that approximately 62 percent of the interstate NTS common line revenue requirement is presently being recovered through the usage-based CCL charge. . . .

In adopting the access charge plan, we expressed the belief that movement toward cost-based pricing, including implementation of subscriber line charges, would produce significant, tangible benefits for large and small telecommunications customers and for the nation as a whole. The Joint Board's study of data concerning the impact of the existing $2.00 subscriber line charge confirms this belief. Part of these data—a study prepared by Wharton Econometrics and funded by AT&T—state that the $2.00 charge has increased the Gross National Product by $6 billion, contributed to the creation of 10,000 new jobs, reduced overall price levels by 0.1 percent, and reduced the federal deficit by $1.9 billion. While some may challenge the precision of these data, the trends they indicate are consistent with our experience and confirmed by a study by this Commission's Office of Plans and Policy, which also is part of the record in this proceeding, concluding that each dollar of the current subscriber line charge produces $1.30 in benefits, and that these benefits will continue to grow. These benefits have been reflected in the approximately 30% reduction in interstate long distance rates that has been achieved since the 1984 implementation of subscriber line charges. Equally important, all of these benefits have been achieved without any countervailing negative impact on universal service. As noted by the Joint Board, telephone subscribership nationwide has increased since implementation of subscriber line charges, and the number of households without telephone service has declined.

We adopt herein the Joint Board's recommendation that subscriber line charges increase in three increments, $.60, $.60, and $.30, however, we adopt them with minor modifications in the proposed schedule.[36] The first $.60 increase will be implemented on July 1, 1987, instead of June 1, 1987. This will provide a full 45 days notice for the flow through tariff to be filed by AT&T. The second step, *i.e.*, the second $.60 increase, will be implemented on December 1, 1988, rather than September 1, 1988. This will enable the members of the Joint Board to perform more extensive monitoring and analysis of the impact of the first $.60 increase.

We share the Joint Board's belief that additional benefits will be realized through the adoption of its recommendations, including increased telephone subscribership levels, efficiency gains,[37] reduced bypass incentives, and decreased

---

36. Although the increase in subscriber line charge will decrease the amount that interexchange carriers will pay to the LECs in the form of CCL charges, the Joint Board found that even with full implementation of its proposed increases in subscriber line charges, interexchange carriers will be paying approximately 50 percent of the total interstate revenue requirement associated with costs incurred by LECs that are unrelated to usage of the network by IXCs. The Joint Board also noted that IXCs will continue to pay 100 percent of the interstate revenue requirement associated with costs incurred by LECs that are directly caused by IXC network usage. We agree with the Joint Board that the substantial costs IXCs would be paying under this proposal adequately address concerns the IXCs pay a "fair share" of the interstate revenue requirement.

37. One measure of the economic efficiency gains achieved in part through subscriber line charges is reflected in the growth in switched access minutes of use since implementation of such charges. Since the implementation of subscriber line charges, from 1984 to 1986, there has been a two year growth rate of 21.52 percent in interstate switched access usage, measured to include MTS and WATS (including both open and closed-end WATS) minutes. . . .

service price discrimination. It is important to underscore the fact that these benefits are obtainable as a direct result of the implementation of subscriber line charges. In other words, absent future subscriber line charge increases, it is not possible to secure the major benefits attributable to other components of the Joint Board's unified package of recommendations.

This is most clearly demonstrated by examining the common line pooling modifications we are adopting. Without increases in subscriber line charges, most companies—particularly large "net recipients"—would have to remain in the pool because withdrawing would greatly increase their vulnerability to uneconomic bypass activity because their study area specific CCL charges after withdrawal would be significantly higher than the current averaged CCL rate. The Joint Board's carefully tailored pooling modifications, which retain the benefits of the present pool while eliminating the drawbacks, will not work unless large "net recipients" leave the pool. If they do not leave the pool, the few low cost companies that could withdraw from the pool will have little or no incentive to do so because the amount of their mandatory long term support payments to the NECA pool very likely would equal their current pool contributions. Increasing subscriber line charges on residential and single-line business lines to a maximum of $3.50 makes it possible for a sufficient number of LECs to withdraw from the pool, so that the needed changes can result. A subscriber line charge less than this amount would not induce large company receivers to leave the pool and would not reduce CCL charges among nonpooled LECs sufficient to ensure continuation of averaged rates.

Implementation of these pooling modifications is critical to achieving the benefits we seek to obtain through adoption of the Joint Board's package of recommendations. First, these modifications will provide telephone companies additional opportunities to reduce the threat of uneconomic bypass. By withdrawing from the pool, low cost companies will be able to charge a CCL rate that is closer to their own, lower, cost of service—rather than the higher nationally averaged (pooled) CCL rate—thereby reducing bypass incentives in their service areas. This ability to charge cost-based access rates is particularly significant because many of the lowest cost companies serve densely populated states where bypass alternatives are most readily available. Second, all companies that withdraw from the pool will have increased incentives to lower their costs. Under the current pooling system, telephone companies have little incentive to lower their costs because the benefits of such reductions are shared by all members of the pool. Once it withdraws from the pool, however, a LEC will be able to retain the savings it achieves through cost-cutting activity. Such activity can be passed on to all users of the network in the form of lower rates. Third, the small high cost companies that remain in the full common line pool will continue to be supported through the long-term support mechanism. We believe that this long-term support mechanism is necessary to ensure that such companies are not required to charge inordinately high CCL rates for access to their networks. The long-term support mechanism allows these carriers to maintain the nationwide averaged CCL rate that would have existed had the mandatory full common line pool been retained. This should avoid unnecessary pressures for bypass in high cost areas, preserve toll averaging, and encourage competitive providers of interstate switched services to enter such markets.

This package of recommendations also will help ensure the continuation of nationally averaged interstate long distance rates. Although common line cost recovery requirements will continue to vary among telephone companies even after the implementation of a $3.50 subscriber line charge, CCL rate disparities among telephone companies will be small enough to make it unlikely that interexchange carriers will need to deaverage their interstate long distance rates. This limitation in CCL rate disparities is accomplished primarily through increased subscriber line charges and a corresponding increase in switched access minutes of use which lower the amount of common line costs each telephone company must recover through its CCL charge. Finally, another mechanism limiting CCL rates disparities will be long-term support, which will allow all companies remaining in the pool to charge an average CCL equivalent to the national averaged rate of all companies.

The Link-Up America lifeline program also is made possible by subscriber line charge increases. We expect that this program will be fully financed by a portion of the revenues generated by increases in interstate toll traffic that result from increased use of interstate services attributable to long distance rate reductions made possible by subscriber line charge increases. We view this component of the Joint Board's recommendations as particularly important because the national telecommunications policy is to preserve universal service, and the Link Up America program is specifically designed to help bring onto the public switched network the approximately five million low income households presently without telephone service. While we do not ordinarily propose or support subsidy programs, the preservation of universal service is a fundamental goal of this Commission. We believe that this program is an appropriate means to achieve our universal service goal, and will help assure that no group of Americans are "locked out" of the information age. We encourage all states to participate in this new program.

*   *   *

Increasing subscriber line charges also will provide local telephone companies with substantial relief from the threat of uneconomic bypass. This relief will occur because subscriber line charge increases will lower all telephone company CCL rates, which, as noted above, are the driving force behind uneconomic bypass activity. Residential and small business customers will greatly benefit as a result of the reduced bypass activity because large users will remain on the switched network, thereby lowering the per minute charge for switched access services.[46]

---

46. The movement of large amounts of traffic off the public switched network as a result of bypass would cause long distance rates paid by residential and small business customers to increase dramatically. This would occur because switched access rates take the form of a charge that is assessed per minute of use. The charge is computed by dividing total switched access costs by total switched access minutes. To a significant degree, the costs in this equation are fixed but the minutes are not. Therefore, the movement of traffic (*i.e.*, minutes) off the switched network as a result of bypass would cause the number of minutes in the equation to decline, while costs would remain about the same—resulting in a higher per minute charge. Because

However, as has been discussed in the *Recommended Decision*, even with the present level of subscriber line charges, there still exists a significant threat of bypass of the public switched network. The threat can be explained in terms of potential revenue losses to the LECs. We know that a very small percentage of a telephone company's customers often represent the source of a much larger percentage of the company's switched access revenues. Since the switched access costs are relatively fixed, regulators must assure that the large users, which represent a significant amount of revenues, are not driven off the network due to uneconomic reasons. In particular, the GAO Bypass Study concludes that 16 to 29 percent of large telephone customers already are using alternative transmission facilities that bypass the switched network, and reports that as many as 53 percent of large telecommunications customers plan to initiate or increase their bypass activities in the future.

Additionally, the Huber Report finds that the amount of presently "installed capacity of non-LEC short-haul, medium capacity, point-to-point, transmission alternatives now exceeds the in-use capacity of equivalent RBOC services." This is the type of capacity which is commonly used for bypass. The report also estimated that the number of business lines served directly by local telephone company switches (*i.e.*, end offices) is less than the number served by private branch exchanges (PBXs). In other words, a business user's dial tone is more likely to be generated by privately owned equipment than by a local telephone company. Moreover, it is generally a simple matter to connect such PBXs directly to interexchange carrier facilities, and the newer, digital PBXs provide users with capabilities not currently available from local telephone companies. These two examples indicate the extent and potential risk of facilities bypass in the telecommunications network.

While facilities bypass is a significant long-term problem, a more immediate concern of this Commission is service bypass—that is, the movement of traffic from usage-sensitive switched access service to flat-rated special access service in circumstances in which only the loading of NTS common line costs onto the usage-sensitive rate makes the more cost-based special access service less expensive. Although as in the case of facilities bypass the amount of service bypass activity is difficult to quantify, the present amount of service bypass far exceeds the amount of facilities bypass. We believe this to be the case because customers can obtain special access services from LECs at flat monthly rates, thereby avoiding any requirement that the customer make large capital investments in its own bypass facilities. Indeed, the magnitude of the service bypass threat is confirmed by the Huber Report which estimates that service bypass is approximately four times as large as facilities bypass. Taken together the amount of facility and service bypass estimated in the Huber Report represents approxi-

---

residential and small business customers do not have usage levels high enough to make bypass an affordable alternative means of satisfying their long distance needs, these customers would have no choice but to stay on the switched network and pay sharply increased long distance rates. Bypass can also increase intrastate rates, because similar incentives exist for customers to bypass the intrastate toll network. Once alternative means of transmission exist, customers will use them for all their long distance calling, including intrastate toll calls.

mately 17 percent of all interLATA traffic—a substantial amount of bypass activity by any measure. Because it is unlikely that customers currently are using their means of bypass at full capacity, and because the marginal cost of using the alternative means once purchased is minimal, we expect that the level of bypass estimated in the Huber Report will increase. Therefore we believe it necessary to take this additional step to increase subscriber line charges in order to further limit the amount of bypass activity undertaken in the future.

We also adopt the Joint Board's recommendation to implement a more comprehensive monitoring plan in order to track the impact of this package of recommendations. We believe that a comprehensive monitoring plan will provide a strong record on the effects of these actions on the telecommunications industry. We will keep an open docket in this proceeding to permit comments from all interested parties regarding the nature and scope of the monitoring plan. The reports to Congress and state regulators will assure that all those interested in the progress of this plan will receive current information relevant to their review. We direct the Joint Board to issue in the near future an order delineating the framework of, and schedule for, this monitoring program. . . .

MTS AND WATS MARKET STRUCTURE, RECOMMENDED DECISION

3 F.C.C. Rcd. 4543 (1988)

This order addresses several requests for reconsideration of our . . . 1987 *Report and Order* in this proceeding. In that Order, we adopted, with minor modifications, a comprehensive set of recommendations concerning the implementation of subscriber line charges, the federal lifeline assistance program, high cost assistance, and common line pooling that had been presented by the Docket 80–286 Joint Board in a *Recommended Decision and Order* released on March 31, 1987.

The petitioners seek reconsideration of various aspects of the determinations regarding the level and schedule of subscriber line charge increases, the allocation of the first such increase to reduce the originating carrier common line (CCL) charge, and the rules governing the structure of the non-traffic sensitive (NTS) pool. In addition, NECA requests certain limited revisions to several sections of Part 69 of our Rules to facilitate the administration of these requirements.

Our review of the petitions for reconsideration and the responsive pleadings leads us to conclude that the fundamental decisions reached in the *Order* on the level and timing of subscriber line charge increases, the allocation of the decreases in the CCL charge, and the structure of the NTS pool should be affirmed. We do, however, adopt several limited modifications of our Part 69 Rules in response to technical concerns raised by petitioners.

In our 1983 *Access Charge Order*, this Commission adopted a system of tariffed access charges for the recovery of the cost of local exchange carrier (LEC) plant and expenses used in the origination and termination of interstate calls. This comprehensive access charge plan was designed to further the four fundamental goals of this proceeding: preserving universal service, promoting economic efficiency, eliminating pricing discrimination, and deterring bypass. The recovery of a significant proportion of local loop costs allocated to the interstate jurisdiction directly from telephone subscribers through monthly flat-rate subscriber line charges was a key element of that integrated scheme. Most of these charges, however, were not implemented when the initial access charges became effective. We decided to defer subscriber line charges for residential and single-line business customers in order to examine their effect on those subscribers.

We asked the Docket 80–286 Joint Board to assist us in that examination. That Joint Board issued its initial recommendations on the subscriber line charge, lifeline and high cost assistance issues raised in these proceedings in November 1984. In that decision, the Joint Board recommended that subscriber line charges be implemented subject to an interim cap of $2.00 for residential and single-line business subscribers, and remain at that level until the completion of a further Joint Board proceeding to study the effects of these charges, including their impact on universal service, bypass, and economic efficiency. These Joint Board recommendations were, with minor modifications, adopted by this Commission in December 1984.

Pursuant to the Joint Board's recommendation, in July 1986 we released a *Further Notice of Proposed Rulemaking* to undertake a broad study of the effects of the implementation of the Joint Board's recommendations in terms of the goals of this proceeding. The *Further Notice* also sought the Joint Board's further recommendations on subscriber line charges, high cost assistance, the lifeline programs, and possible modifications to the current provisions for mandatory nationwide pooling of common line costs and revenues.

Based upon its careful study of the record, the Joint Board presented its conclusions and recommendations on these issues in the *Recommended Decision*. The Joint Board concluded that the record before it demonstrated that its 1984 recommended plan had advanced the four goals of this proceeding, introducing increased economic efficiencies, minimizing bypass incentives, and mitigating service pricing discrimination while preserving universal service. From these conclusions, the Joint Board developed further recommendations for progress on these longstanding, interrelated NTS recovery issues. As part of this comprehensive plan, the Joint Board determined that modest subscriber line charge increases would further the four goals of this proceeding, and would also permit needed restructuring of the existing common line tariff and pooling system. In addition, the Joint Board found that efficiencies gained from the increased subscriber line charges and decreased CCL charge would permit more extensive federal lifeline assistant programs. Specifically, the Joint Board recommended that the cap on subscriber line charges for residential and single-line business customers be increased to $2.60 on June 1, 1987, $3.20 on September 1, 1988, and $3.50 on April 1, 1989, and that the cap on subscriber line charges for embedded Centrex lines be increased to $4.00 on June 1, 1987, $5.00 on September 1, 1988, and $6.00 on April 1, 1989. The Joint Board stated that these changes constitute a permanent solution to the NTS recovery issues before it.

The Joint Board's *Recommended Decision* endorsed the existing lifeline assistance program, which exempts qualifying subscribers from subscriber line charges when matching state benefits are provided pursuant to a certificated state plan, and proposed that the federal benefits be increased to correspond with the prescribed subscriber line charge increases.[13] In addition, the Joint Board recommended that the subscriber line charge waiver program be supplemented by a new program targeted to provide assistance to reduce the initial service installation and connection charges that appear to be a major barrier to subscribership for low income groups. This second program, which has become known as "Link Up America," would offset one half of these charges for commencing telephone service, up to $30, for qualifying households. The Link Up America program also encourages LECs to offer deferred payment schedules for these charges by paying an LEC's interest costs, on an amount up to $200, when the LEC establishes a deferred payment schedule and does not charge interest to qualified subscribers. The Joint Board further recommended that the interstate costs associated with the expanded subscriber line charge waiver and Link Up America programs be recovered through charges assessed on interexchange carriers (IXCs).[15]

The Joint Board also reviewed the existing high cost assistance measures, which permit LECs in study areas with above-average loop costs to allocate additional costs to the interstate jurisdiction, and recommended retargeting the high cost assistance to provide greater assistance to small and medium size LECs and less assistance to larger LECs. Finally, the Joint Board recommended significant modifications in the existing common line tariff and pooling system. Under the proposed approach, LECs would be permitted to withdraw from the NECA tariff and pool, and file common line tariffs based on their own costs. LECs leaving the pool would, however, be obligated to make payments to the common line pool to keep the pooled CCL rates essentially unaffected.[16] In this way, the Joint Board concluded, large companies wishing to establish more-cost based CCL rates, for bypass or other reasons, could do so without adversely affecting the CCL rate charged by the smaller carriers that remain in the pool.[17]

---

13. Under this recommendation, federal assistance would be available to match state reductions to local charges on any amount up to the full subscriber line charge of $3.50, so that a customer could receive a total of $7.00 in benefits.

15. Initially, the cost of these lifeline assistance programs would be recovered through the CCL charge. Upon implementation of the proposed revisions to the present pooling mechanism in 1989, the Joint Board recommended that NECA administer a lifeline assistance revenue "pool" and that the costs be recovered through flat-rate, per-line charges assessed on IXCs based on the number of 1+ lines "presubscribed" to each such carrier.

16. LECs that withdraw from the NECA pool are required to contribute long term support (LTS) to LECs that remain in the NECA pool, thus enabling pooling companies, which generally will be smaller high cost companies, to tariff a CCL charge equal to the charge that would result if all LECs remained in the pool. The Joint Board also recommended that four years of transitional support payments (TRS) be provided to qualifying LECs that withdraw from the pool. In order to qualify for TRS, LECs must be net recipients from the pool in 1988 and must withdraw from the NECA tariff and pool in accordance with a schedule that provides the largest companies one opportunity and smaller companies two opportunities to leave the pool and qualify to receive TRS. TRS will be paid by those nonpooling companies that were net contributors to the pool in 1988.

17. The Joint Board's recommendations and the Commission's *Order* intended that once a

In order to assure that the various proposals achieve the desired results, the Joint Board proposed that we establish an expanded monitoring program. The monitoring program would include ongoing quarterly reports and a 90-day review based on these reports in advance of the final subscriber line charge increases.

This Commission adopted the Joint Board's conclusions and integrated recommendations regarding subscriber line charges, expansion of federal lifeline assistance, the retargeting of the high cost assistance fund, and modifications to the pooling system in our May 19, 1987, *Order*. Our *Order* did, however, make minor modifications in the proposed implementation schedule. The *Order* required implementation of the first $.60 subscriber line charge increase on July 1, 1987, rather than June 1, 1987, and of the second $.60 increase on December 1, 1988, instead of September 1988 in order to permit more thorough monitoring of the impact of the initial $.60 increase. We also adopted the expanded monitoring program proposed by the Joint Board in its *Recommended Decision*. This ongoing monitoring process is already underway.

BELL REGIONALS CITE EXTENSIVE BYPASS, HUNDREDS OF MILLIONS LOST

FCC Week, *May 9, 1988*

In spite of what critics say, bypass is no illusion, the Bell regional holding companies (RHC) contend. Ameritech says it loses about $840 million a year to bypass of its network by more than 600 companies and government agencies. And US West counts its losses at more than $373.7 million per year in 650 cases of bypass.

The figures are contained, along with those of the other regionals, in the first semiannual report on bypass to a joint board of FCC and state public utility commissioners.

This initial report is intended to establish an historical record of bypass to determine if FCC decisions such as introduction of the monthly subscriber line charge and the federal lifeline assistance programs influence the occurrence of bypass over time. To prepare a complete record, citations of bypass were not confined to the post-divestiture period. Ameritech noted some instances reaching as far back as the 1950s.

The report covers both varieties of bypass: "facilities based," in which customers build microwave, satellite or other systems to reach directly to another location or to points where they can connect with long distance carriers, and

---

company (or group of affiliated companies) elects to leave the NECA common line pool and file its own CCL tariff, it may not choose to participate in the NECA common line pool at a later date. The new rules implementing the pooling modifications accordingly do not include any mechanism for a company that has left the NECA common line pool to reenter that pool.

Reprinted from *FCC Week*, P.O. Box 1455, Alexandria, Virginia.

"service bypass," in which the customer leases a private line from the phone company and runs it directly to another of his locations or to an interexchange carrier (IXC).

Hundreds of Examples

The report details hundreds of cases in which Bell operating companies' (BOC) switched network customers have turned to other sources for voice and data communications, but inevitably they will be open to dispute. The companies had to make many assumptions in their calculations.

"Because most bypassers do not have an incentive to reveal themselves," US West said, it relied on indirect methods to find out who had avoided its network, including reports of microwave radio license applications maintained by Spectrum Planning, of Richardson, Texas; right-of-way filings; sales teams' knowledge; and magazines and other periodicals. Methods of calculating the cost of both facilities and service bypass relied on complicated computations containing estimates and assumptions, and varied from RHC to RHC.

Nynex said it loses "at least" $418 million a year because of bypass. The RHC has to contend not only with microwave bypass, but also with Teleport Communications of New York City, an alternative local carrier offering private fiber-optic connections.

Bell Atlantic quoted the highest bypass losses, saying, "As of the end of 1987, service bypass and facilities bypass . . . accounted for an annual impact of $888 million on switched access revenues." The company noted that between 1982 and mid-1986, "private microwave based facilities bypass increased tenfold." Bell Atlantic also has an alternate carrier in its backyard, Institutional Communications Co., providing extensive local fiber-optic links.

BellSouth said it loses about $283.1 million each year to all forms of bypass, and Pacific Bell cited $312.4 million in losses to competitors at the end of 1987. Nevada Bell put its bypass losses at $17.6 million. (Pacific Bell and Nevada Bell did not submit combined figures.) Southwestern Bell reported annual losses of $443.7 million.

In most cases, service bypass far surpassed facilities bypass. At the extreme, BellSouth said it lost $10.2 million to competitors who built their own transmission systems, but $272.9 million to service bypass. Ameritech ran counter to the trend, however, putting its facilities bypass at $446.6 million and its services bypass at $393.1 million. Southwestern, too, posted higher facilities bypass, at $240.4 million, and $203.3 million in service bypass.

Different Types of Bypassers

Types of bypassers ran the gamut. Ameritech's losses, for instance, include government agencies, pipelines, railroads, manufacturers, retail outlets, financial institutions, hospitals, electric utilities, brokerages, insurance companies, and even a pharmacy in Oak Brook, Ill.

The most frequent reason given for the defections was lower costs, but in most cases the RHC did not know why the customer left the network. US West customers who elected for facilities bypass often cited greater control over their network as a reason for going out on their own.

Bell Atlantic indicated that occasionally the customer left because a given service was not available from the local BOC, but did not indicate the nature of the service desired. . . .

Questions

1. Prior to divestiture, which services were subsidized? By whom? Could this explain why these subsidies were acceptable for so long? Could these subsidies have been avoided? Do subsidies exist today?

2. Why are local rates more cost-based since divestiture? What factors work against full cost-based pricing? Why are telcos lobbying for measured local service and against flat-rate service?

3. What was the ENFIA plan? How has equal access hampered the OCCs' competitiveness? How might consumers still benefit where access is not equal access? How do people who do not make long-distance calls benefit from lower long-distance rates?

4. Recall the discussion of WATS and MTS service in Chapter 4. How has the subscriber line charge affected arbitrage opportunities for resellers of long-distance service?

5. How has fiber-optic development been affected by long-distance competition? Is the duplicative capacity of the carriers an inefficiency spawned by competition or a factor critical to full competition?

6. Competitive entry into the international market has been slowed by the difficulties OCCs have had obtaining operating agreements with foreign nations. Could this explain why international long-distance rates have decreased more slowly than domestic long-distance rates? What other factors could apply?

7. How can large users bypass the switched network? 1) Can anyone build a microwave tower or install a satellite dish? Is a license needed? 2) Can a private line owner resell its excess capacity to smaller users? Are resellers regulated? 3) Do the private lines leased by the common carriers themselves bypass the switched network?

8. Private lines constitute the most pervasive form of bypass. To use the public network, private line owners pay a reduced carrier charge pursuant to "special access" tariffs. If so, why is bypass a problem?

9. Why does an increase in the subscriber line charge lead to a decrease in the carrier common line charge? Why does reducing the CCL help limit the bypass threat?

10. Why were regulators concerned about long-distance rate deaveraging? How does the NECA pool help allay these concerns? Why does the FCC encourage companies to leave the pool? What safeguards exist to preclude future rate deaveraging?

11. As local rates rise, what programs have been implemented to promote universal service? Who provides the subsidies?

CABLE AS BYPASS TECHNOLOGY

The bypass debate revolves around the ways large business users can avoid the points of presence (POP) in local-exchange switching facilities. These POPs constitute the points at which the telco collects its CCL charge. Long-distance carriers have explored using cable system networks to carry voice traffic, as detailed in the *Commline* decisions.

While Cox Cable abandoned this effort, other alternative access providers (including cable companies), sometimes referred to as metropolitan area networks (MANs), offer larger users facilities to access interexchange carriers without passing through the POP. MANs construct access networks under high-volume business corridors onto which larger users can direct their long-distance traffic. The MANs then connect calls to the customer's selected interexchange carrier. State PUCs must approve these alternative local-access networks.

MANs are part of a group called Competitive Access Providers (CAPs). To promote expanded interconnection—and thereby bring the force of competition to the access business—the FCC has considered changes in the LEC access tariffs, such as the proposal following *Commline*.

COX CABLE COMMUNICATIONS, INC. (COMMLINE): MEMORANDUM OPINION, DECLARATORY RULING AND ORDER

102 F.C.C.2d 110 (1985)

*   *   *

Cox is an operator of cable television systems serving over 1.2 million subscribers in 23 states. Commline, Inc. was formed by Cox to develop and operate "institutional"[3] high speed digital transmission services (including video teleconferencing, electronic mail, and high speed facsimile) in the markets in which Cox's cable television systems are franchised and committed to providing such services. Cox DTS was formed to be the licensee and operator of Digital Termination System (DTS) facilities.[4] Cox Cable of Omaha, Inc. (Cox-Omaha), a subsidiary of Cox, operates a cable television system in Omaha, Nebraska. Pursuant to a non-exclusive franchise granted by the city, two cables have been

---

3. As used in the pleadings, "institutional" services refer to services offered to businesses and institutions, as opposed to those services offered to residential customers.

4. Digital Termination System (DTS) facilities are microwave radio facilities providing local distribution of communications in the Digital Electronic Message Service (DEMS).

installed by Cox-Omaha: cable A, called the "residential" cable, is used to transmit television broadcasts and pay television programming and to provide Cox's INDAX (tm) service;[5] cable B, called the institutional cable, is used by Commline to provide high-speed digital transmission services to governmental and educational institutions and private businesses. According to its petition, Cox plans to interconnect the institutional cable network with DTS facilities for which Cox DTS has filed a construction permit application, in order to expand the coverage and increase the flexibility of the two technologies. Commline expects to provide service to interstate satellite and microwave carriers, such as MCI Telecommunications Corp. (MCI), for whom Commline already originates and terminates interstate traffic.

In December of 1982 when Commline was preparing to provide its transmission services in Omaha, the NPSC instituted an investigation of Cox, Commline and MCI to determine: (1) whether Commline and Cox's INDAX service were subject to NPSC authority and, therefore, whether Cox was required to obtain a certificate of public convenience under Nebraska statutes and (2) the impact of Commline/MCI services on Northwestern Bell Telephone Co. and other telecommunications carriers. On April 19, 1983, after conducting several days of hearings, the NPSC issued an order concluding that Commline "is a carrier furnishing communication services for hire in Nebraska intrastate commerce and, as such, is a common carrier subject to regulation by this Commission. . . . " Thus, the NPSC ordered Commline to "cease and desist from offering communications service for hire in Nebraska" until it had received a certificate of public convenience and necessity from the NPSC.

Shortly thereafter, Cox filed a request for a preliminary injunction against the enforcement of the NPSC cease and desist order in the United States District Court for the District of Nebraska. The court found that it was not possible at that time to know whether the NPSC would grant a certificate to Commline or, if it did grant a certificate, what type of regulation would be imposed. Thus, it decided to abstain from ruling on the constitutional questions raised by the petitioners while Cox sought a certificate from the NPSC, but retained jurisdiction over the case. The court granted a preliminary injunction pending the outcome of the NPSC proceeding.

A. The Cox Petition

In its petition, Cox generally asks that this Commission enter declaratory rulings that it has jurisdiction over and has preempted state and local regulation of all facilities located wholly within one state and used to originate or terminate interstate communications, including such facilities that also distribute intrastate communications. Cox states that the NPSC investigation has had an adverse effect upon Commline's marketing and on the development of its business and that this Commission must preempt state regulation in order to encourage the

---

5. INDAX (tm) is Cox's residential subscriber service, which is offered on cable A and permits a variety of transactional services such as banking and information retrieval. The request for declaratory ruling is directed only to the services offered by Commline on the B cable. . . .

rapid development of new and innovative cable services. State common carrier regulation, like that imposed by the NPSC, presents "a clear and present danger" to the development of cable television technology and new communications services, according to Cox.

In support of the petition, Cox states that its institutional cable will be used to originate and terminate interstate traffic and as such is subject to this Commission's jurisdiction. Although its institutional cable also will be used for intrastate communications, Cox argues that the configuration of Commline's plant is such that a single coaxial cable channel assigned to a Commline customer will carry both the local and interstate traffic on a nonsegregable, combined basis.[10]

Thus, relying on North Carolina Utilities Comm'n v. FCC, 537 F2d 787 [36 RR 2d 1397] (4th Cir.), cert. denied, 429 US 1027 (1976) (NCUC I), and People of the State of California v. FCC, 567 F2d 84 (DC Cir. 1977), it argues that state and local regulation of the intrastate traffic should be preempted because such regulation would be infeasible and impractical and would interfere with interstate services and federal policies. Although some of its customers may not use the Commission facilities for any interstate services (i.e., all their communications would originate and terminate in Omaha) Cox argues that since these wholly intrastate customers will use the same cable and facilities as customers who have some interstate needs, it would be impractical to separate the interstate and intrastate use. Finally, Cox argues that this Commission already has preempted state regulation of DTS facilities and that state regulation that impedes interconnection with DTS likewise has been preempted.

Cox also argues that since it does not hold itself out to serve the public indiscriminately but rather chooses with whom to deal and on what terms, it is not a common carrier.[11] If it is not a common carrier, Sections 2(b) and 221(b) of the Communications Act, 47 USC §§2(b) and 221(b), which reserve to the states jurisdiction over intrastate and "exchange" common carrier services, do not apply and thus are no bar to federal preemption, according to Cox. Additionally, Cox argues that no "telephone exchange" services or facilities are involved in the Commline services or in the interconnection of Commline services with DTS facilities. Finally, Cox states that it intends to offer "enhanced services" and, therefore, under this Commission's Computer II decision state regulation of those services has been preempted.

*   *   *

As is noted above, Cox has asked this Commission to issue an order stating that as it currently operates, Commline is not a "common carrier" within the meaning of Section 3(h) of the Communications Act, 47 USC §153(h). Whether Commline is operating as a common carrier within the meaning of Section 3(h)

---

10. It argues that the only feasible way to segregate the intrastate traffic from the interstate traffic would be to build separate and distinct cables for interstate and intrastate use.

11. In support of this argument Cox cites National Ass'n of Regulatory Util. Comm'rs v. FCC, 525 F2d 630 (DC Cir. 1976) (NARUC I) and National Ass'n of Regulatory Util. Comm'rs v. FCC, 533 F2d 601 (DC Cir. 1976) (NARUC II).

does not affect this Commission's jurisdiction over Commline's interstate facilities and services. But because Section 2(b), 47 USC §152(b), limits this Commission's jurisdiction over intrastate communications of any common carrier, it may affect the preemption analysis. Thus, we shall first decide whether Commline is acting as a common carrier in its provision of service in Omaha for purposes of the Communications Act.

The test most often cited for whether an entity providing communications service is a common carrier was enunciated in NARUC I. . . . In that case the court found that to be a common carrier an entity must either be under a legal compulsion to "hold himself out indiscriminately to the clientele one is suited to serve" or, if not under legal compulsion, in fact to do so.

The Nebraska PSC found that Commline is a common carrier and that "the record clearly shows that Commline would offer to serve any customer along its cable who had need of its service." We do not believe that finding satisfies the test articulated in NARUC I, since it does not include an "indiscriminate holding out" or an indiscriminate offering of the services. In any event, we are not bound by the Nebraska finding for the purposes of determining common carrier status under the Communications Act. We must make our own analysis of Commline's status.

Commline claims that it deals on an individual basis with each potential customer, that it does not have set prices or terms and conditions and that, therefore, it is not a common carrier.[35] No party brought forth evidence that Commline actually operates in a manner different than it claims. The evidence of the commenters on the other side amounts to little more than claims that Commline would like to sell its service to more customers and that if two customers did obtain the exact same service features, they would be charged the same price. An indiscriminate offering requires more than a desire to serve more customers, and the consequent actions taken in order to obtain more customers (e.g., a willingness to discuss the services offered with any interested party). An indiscriminate offering includes an offering to provide service without negotiation of provision of the services on an individualized basis. It appears that Commline does conduct business through individualized negotiations and does not hold itself out to serve the public indiscriminately.

When comparing Commline's services to the Specialized Mobile Radio Service (SMRS) found to be non-common carrier in NARUC I, it appears that Commline's services have most of the attributes of non-common carriage that SMRS has. In NARUC I, the court found SMRS not [to] be common carriage because the service "would involve the establishment of medium to long term relationships"

---

35. In its reply comments, Westinghouse described the specialized nature of these types of services as follows: "cable systems can be configured for a given customer so as to provide the precise bandwidth necessary to meet the particular mix of video, data, and/or audio transmission needs unique to a given user. . . . By selecting among different frequency arrangements and addressability techniques and by incorporating a variety of terminal devices and modems at customer sites, cable services are tailored to meet unique requirements. Cable services necessarily are founded on the given set of requirements that are unique to a given user, rather than a uniform channel or circuit assignment. . . ."

with a fairly stable customer base and because the SMRS operators would make "individualized decisions about the desirability and compatibility of serving new customers." It appears that the Commline services also will tend to involve long term relationships and, since the service is somewhat specialized, . . . it lends itself to individualized determinations as to the ability and desirability of serving new customers.

The second part of the NARUC I test is whether there is any legal compulsion for Commline to hold itself out indiscriminately to the public. See generally Transponder Sales, 90 FCC 2d 1238, 1255–57 (1982), aff'd sub nom. Wold Communications, Inc. v. FCC, 735 F2d 1465 (DC Cir. 1984). Certainly, this Commission has never found Commline to be compelled to hold itself out indiscriminately. The other aspect of this question is whether there is any reason to require Commline to hold itself out indiscriminately, i.e., is there any compelling reason to regulate Commline as a common carrier? We find that there is none.

Commline has little or no market power. Although there are some barriers to entry into the market, they do not appear to be sufficiently high to vest Commline with market power. There are alternative methods of providing similar service. DEMS is one alternative; over a dozen carriers have applied for DEMS in Omaha and several construction permits have been granted. In addition, although Cox was able to lay its cable pursuant to a franchise granted by Omaha, that franchise is not exclusive.

In addition, the Commline service is similar to private line service and we assume that it will be used primarily by companies and institutions with some ability to protect their rights in dealing with Commline. Further, the Commline service does not have the characteristics of, and could compete to only a limited extent with, traditional telephone exchange service and switched access service.[37] Accordingly, we find there is no compelling reason to regulate Commline as a common carrier.[38]

* * *

The second major ruling requested by Cox is that state regulation of facilities like Commline's that are used to originate and terminate interstate communica-

---

37. Although the "cable headend" performs a primitive switching function, the switch is unlike a switch in the telephone hierarchy in that a cable subscriber cannot "call" every other subscriber connected to the switch: subscribers can only communicate with predesignated locations. In that way, the communications service is more like a point-to-point or point-to-multipoint private line service than a switched service or "telephone exchange service," which is defined in Section 3 of the Communications Act, 47 USC §153, as "interconnecting service of the character ordinarily furnished by a single exchange. . . ."

38. We note that the State of California recently completed an investigation into the question of whether intraLATA toll competition should be allowed. While generally refusing to authorize intraLATA competition, it made an exception for high-speed data transmission services over private line networks. It based its decision in part upon finding that private line revenues are less than 2 percent of Pacific Telephone's total local service revenues, private line competition does not threaten the universal network, and competition may solve the problem of customer dissatisfaction with private line service being provided at that time.

tions are preempted because of the effect such regulation would have on interstate communications and federal law and policy. There is no dispute that the service being provided by Commline is a communication service by wire and that at least one of its customers is using the facilities for the origination and/or termination of interstate communications.[39] Section 2(a) of the Communications Act, 47 USC §152(a), provides that the Act's provisions apply to "all interstate and foreign communication by wire or radio." It is also clear that the Commission has end-to-end jurisdiction over facilities used in interstate communication and the interstate services provided over those facilities regardless of the facilities' physical location. See, e.g., People of the State of California v. FCC, supra. See also AT&T, 71 FCC 2d 1 (1979); AT&T (Arco), Mimeo No. 636 (Nov. 8, 1983), reconsideration, Mimeo No. 3267 (April 3, 1984). In addition, it is clear the Commission has jurisdiction over the facilities used in interstate communications even if they are "primarily" used for intrastate service. See, e.g., North Carolina Utilities Comm'n v. FCC, 552 F2d 1036, 1045–47 (4th Cir.), cert. denied, 434 US 874 (1977) (NCUC II); Puerto Rico Telephone Co. v. FCC, 553 F2d 694, 700 (1st Cir. 1977).

As a general matter federal law preempts state law when the state law "stands as an obstacle to the accomplishment and execution of the full purposes and objectives of Congress." Hines v. Davidowitz, 312 US 52, 67 (1941). Other courts have stated the test in slightly different language, but the concept remains one of federal supremacy over conflicting state laws or regulations. See, e.g., Florida Lime and Avocado Growers, Inc. v. Paul, 373 US 132 (1962) (federal law will preempt state law when compliance with both federal and state law regulations is impossible); Fidelity Federal Savings & Loan Co. v. de la Cuesta, 458 US 141 (1982) (nullifies state law to the extent that it actually conflicts with federal law). Moreover, in the communications field, the courts have acknowledged that our authority encompass[es] the power to preempt state regulation that substantially affects federal regulation of interstate communications or federal policy related thereto or when the dual use of the facilities renders separation for regulatory purposes impractical.

*   *   *

With respect to the Commline services, we conclude that this Commission should preempt the Nebraska action requiring Commline to apply for a certificate of public convenience because the state action impermissibly infringes on federal policies. Because some of the Commline customers use the facilities for intrastate communications, the Nebraska order, which only addresses intrastate service, did not exceed Nebraska state jurisdiction. We find, however, that the Nebraska action has had and is likely to continue to have a substantial adverse effect upon interstate communications. Cox has presented evidence, and the evidence has not been convincingly rebutted, that the NPSC investigation of Cox has had an adverse effect upon Commline's marketing and on the development of its services

---

39. As noted above, MCI has been a customer of Commline for some time. Telephone Bypass News (April 1985) reports that Commline now is providing local distribution facilities for GTE/Sprint as well as for MCI.

and business, including interstate access services, and that some customers have delayed taking service because of the NPSC actions. In addition, the Nebraska statute relating to certificates of public convenience and necessity places a substantial burden on entities such as Commline. In the event the application were denied, inefficient use of facilities would result which could lead to a severe increase in interstate costs because interstate charges would have to support the costs of the entire facility.

In addition, Cox testified before the Nebraska District Court that if the Nebraska order were not enjoined, Cox would shut down Commline's operations permanently. Thus, we find that the Nebraska certification requirement has impaired, and likely will continue to impair, Commline's ability to provide interstate services.

We find that Nebraska's certification requirement conflicts with and obstructs several of our national communications policies. Both GTE/Sprint and MCI utilize Cox's cable facility to terminate their interstate telecommunications networks in Omaha. The state entry regulation inherently affects, and may even foreclose, use of these facilities by long distance service providers, and thereby frustrates the federal regulatory policies designed to facilitate competitive long distance services that we have promoted in our Competitive Carrier Rule Making. For almost two decades this Commission has been encouraging competition in the provision of interstate common carrier services. These efforts have been designed to stimulate innovation, lower rates, increase diversity and encourage the efficient use of facilities. Moreover, we have encouraged the interstate carriers to use alternative facilities and technologies in their systems. Indeed, Section 7(a) of the Act, 47 USC §157(a), requires us to encourage new developments and new technologies in communications. It provides that:

> It shall be the policy of the United States to encourage the provision of new technologies to the public. Any person . . . who opposes a new technology or service . . . shall have the burden to demonstrate that such proposal is inconsistent with the public interest.

Commline and Cox are attempting to develop a means of providing interstate communications by originating and terminating interstate common carrier traffic for entities as MCI.[55] The Nebraska state entry regulation presents a clear possibility of barring these services and precluding the new alternatives that this Commission has sought to foster. There appears to be no practical or economical means of preventing Commline's customers from using these facilities for both intrastate and interstate communications. . . . Even if there is a feasible way of preventing Commline customers from using the facilities for intrastate communications, this would result in inefficient use of facilities and, because there are few users, increase the cost of the facilities to Cox's interstate customers. Such

---

55. Some have argued that preemption in this case might result in bypass of telephone company facilities and services. This Commission has not, however, sought to prevent all bypass. We have focused upon cost-based access charges as a means of ensuring only that bypass not justified by service or cost considerations be limited.

an increase in costs could—and Cox stated in its testimony before the District Court would—destroy the viability of the service. Thus, to ensure that interstate services may be provided consistent with our federal policies, the state certification requirement must be preempted.

Moreover, Cox intends to utilize its intrastate institutional cable systems in conjunction with DTS facilities to provide its customers with interstate telecommunications facilities. We have previously authorized and encouraged the use of DTS for interstate communications.[56] In the Fifth Report and Order in the Competitive Carrier Rule Making, 98 FCC 2d 1191, 1205–09 (1984), we determined that a policy of regulatory forbearance would help promote the entry and expansion of DEMS and DTS systems by relieving carriers of the costs and delay of required tariff filings, would help promote competition, and would benefit consumers. Id. at 1207. Indeed, we have already indicated our intention to preempt inconsistent state regulation of DTS facilities because such regulation would impede the development of interstate systems. State entry regulation of institutional cable systems used with DTS facilities could impede efficient development of these various interstate communications systems.

Additionally, since the inception of cable television this Commission has recognized and encouraged the use of cable facilities for services other than traditional cable services. For example, as early as 1972 in our Cable Television Report and Order, 36 FCC 2d 143 (1972), we recognized that cable systems were capable of providing "facsimile reproduction of newspapers, magazines, documents, etc.; electronic mail delivery; merchandising; business concern links to branch offices, primary customers or suppliers; access to computers," and many other services. Id. at 144 n. 10. Throughout the Commission's history of regulation of cable, it has consistently articulated a desire not to interfere with these new services and, in fact, to promote them.

* * *

Preemption of entry barriers will further another important federal policy. Spectrum for private microwave systems is now highly congested in some areas. See First Report and Order in Private Radio Docket No. 83–426, FCC 85–53 (released April 1, 1985). Private cable systems may provide an important alternative to these congested microwave frequencies. Through encouraging the development of private cable systems we can better ensure "a rapid, efficient, nationwide . . . wire and radio communications service. . . . " 47 USC §151.

In sum, we find that if the Commission does not preempt the Nebraska certification requirement, it is likely that the Commline interstate services will be severely impeded, if they are able to develop at all. This would be inconsistent with the federal policies designed to foster the development of new services, a

---

56. In 1981, the Commission allocated radio spectrum for nationwide common carrier digital transmission networks (DEMS systems) providing high-speed, two-way transmissions. The intercity links of these networks employ satellite, microwave, fiber optics, or cable facilities, and the intracity facilities include digital termination systems (DTS) and internodal links.

competitive interstate communications marketplace, and the construction of efficient interstate telecommunications systems.[60]

From the comments received in this proceeding, it appears that other cable companies in other states also are having problems similar to Commline's caused by state certification and other regulatory requirements. It also appears that state certification or other regulatory requirements that have the effect of barring entry into the intrastate provision of institutional services offered by cable television companies generally may have an impact upon and may impede the provision of interstate services by these companies. Any state regulation of institutional services offered by cable companies that acts as a de facto or de jure barrier to entry into the interstate communications market or to the provision of interstate communications must be preempted. At the same time, we recognize there may be instances in which cable companies wish to provide only intrastate service or in which a cable company's ability to provide intrastate service would have little impact upon its ability to provide interstate service. In those cases the federal interest in a state certification requirement would be less. In this order, we do not address those situations in which state regulation would have no effect upon the provision of interstate service. State regulation that does not act as a barrier to the provision of interstate communications may stand.[62]

*   *   *

DISSENTING STATEMENT OF COMMISSIONER JAMES H. QUELLO

I am not prepared to argue, at this point, that the majority has overstepped its authority in preempting entry regulation although that well might be the case. My concern rests with the policy established in this proceeding which seems to say to the states that we will preempt only a little now but stand ready to go further if the states exercise their prerogatives to regulate these new carriers.

---

60. We are mindful of the argument raised by the telephone companies that it is not fair to allow cable companies to provide services similar to services provided by the telephone companies if the cable companies are not subject to the same regulatory constraints as the telephone companies. With respect to our actions here, however, that argument holds little weight because the telephone company already is certificated, to the extent necessary, to provide services over its facilities that are most analogous to the cable facilities.

62. Based on the comments in this proceeding we are unable to determine the effect state rate or other economic regulation would have upon interstate communications or federal law or policies. Cox argues that it is not possible to segregate interstate and intrastate use of its facilities for rate making purposes. The comments of the telephone companies dispute this and state that the telephone companies currently conduct usage studies for separations purposes on those facilities most closely resembling Commline's facilities. Thus, there is clearly a factual dispute as to the feasibility of separating traffic for rate making purposes and we do not rule on whether, in particular circumstances, this Commission would preempt state rate or other economic regulation of Commline-type services. However, economic regulation could become a barrier to entry, and thereby be eligible for preemption if, for example, cable companies were subjected to it and telephone companies were exempted for provision of the same type of service.

It isn't clear to me what significant national policy is to be furthered by forcing the states to accept bypass technology while this Commission remains unable to implement significant strategies to make bypass unattractive. Until we can remove the subsidy that flows to local ratepayers benefits will continue to accrue to those who can avoid paying the subsidy. By its action, the majority has introduced a technology with significant potential to do what the Commission's attenuated subscriber line charge was designed to prevent.

Not to worry, say the proponents of preemption, the cable industry merely wants to provide "broadband" data services, an insignificant contributor to exchange revenues. If this Commission doesn't understand by now that the money is in message telephone service, its institutional memory has been ravaged by some dread malady. And, like Willie Sutton, the new entrants in the local exchange market will simply and unerringly go where the money is.

The states have the incentives to take whatever steps are necessary to prevent serious damage to the local exchange, and I believe that they should retain the means. Therefore, I dissent.

*   *   *

[**Note:** This decision was vacated as moot because the service went out of business (1 F.C.C. Rcd. 561 [1986]).]

Questions

1. Why did Cox petition the FCC? Was FCC approval required? What specific type of regulation is involved in this case? What message was the Commission sending to the states? Note that although this decision was vacated as moot in 1986, cable companies have since deployed access systems for long-distance providers.

2. Commissioner Quello strongly disagrees with the FCC on the bypass issue. Do you share his concerns? What is the Commission's response? How can a policy to discourage bypass be balanced with an interest in promoting new service offerings in cases such as this?

3. Cox relied on *North Carolina Util. Comm'n v. FCC* on the preemption issue. Would Cox have prevailed if *Louisiana PSC v. FCC* had been decided at that time? Would Cox's argument that it could not support the service with interstate revenues alone be strong enough to result in federal preemption?

4. Why did the FCC undertake a common carrier definitional analysis? What were its findings?

5. Why was there a general federal policy to promote cable use over microwave use? To what degree are the technologies substitutable?

6. The FCC noted its strong policy of promoting "nontraditional" cable services that cross over into telco offerings. Conversely, Congress is investigating whether to introduce competition into the cable field by allowing entry by the telcos. What arguments support telco entry? What arguments

oppose telco entry? See Winer, "Telephone Companies Have First Amendment Rights Too: The Constitutional Case for Entry Into Cable," 8 *Cardozo Arts & Entertainment Law Journal* 257 (1990). In the United Kingdom, the government in 1991 decided to allow cable companies to provide local phone service in competition with Mercury and British Telecom and to allow British Telecom to enter the video services business eventually.

EXPANDED INTERCONNECTION WITH LOCAL TELEPHONE COMPANY FACILITIES, NOTICE OF PROPOSED RULEMAKING AND NOTICE OF INQUIRY

CC Docket No. 91–141, 6 F.C.C. Rcd. 3259 (1991)

For many years, local exchange carriers (LECs) faced little or no competition in providing the local access facilities and services used in the provision of interstate telecommunications.[2] Recent changes, however, have facilitated the development of competition in the provision of these facilities and services. Most importantly, fiber optic technology has advanced rapidly, significantly increasing capacity and sharply reducing per-circuit costs. Intensified interstate long-distance competition, when combined with the American Telephone and Telegraph Company's (AT&T's) divestiture of the Bell Operating Companies (BOCs) and the implementation of federal equal access and access charge systems, have greatly increased interexchange carrier (IXC) and end user incentives to seek lower cost options for interstate access. As American business becomes more information-dependent, customer demand for communications services with enhanced reliability has also grown. While the LECs still provide the vast majority of interstate access services, fiber-based carriers, sometimes described as Competitive Access Providers (CAPs), now offer access services to large business customers in the central business districts of many major cities.[3]

Expanded access competition has the potential to produce substantial benefits through expanded customer choice, improved efficiency, and the more rapid deployment of new technology. At the same time, such competition will impact current LEC rates and structures, bringing major changes for the LEC industry and communications users.

The action proposed in this notice is a measured step toward broader competition in the provision of interstate access services and facilities. The improved arrangements for interconnection with LEC facilities which we are proposing

---

2. In perhaps the simplest example, interstate access consists of the delivery by a caller's local telephone company of an originating interstate telephone call to the facilities of an interstate long-distance carrier, and the completion of the call by a second local telephone company from the long-distance carrier to the called party.

3. End users also use microwave and other radio-based facilities in lieu of LEC access services in some cases, and other technologies also have the potential of providing alternatives to LEC access services in certain circumstances.

will substantially expand the universe of customers who can be served by the new competitive entrants, and increase the scope of LEC offerings subject to competition. At the same time, we have restricted our proposal to the provision of special access service, which is used largely by business customers. While this will at least initially limit the potential benefits of expanded competition, this particular step does not require complex adjustments in switched access rates that may indirectly affect residential customers.

The current interstate access tariffs effectively limit the ability of interested parties to substitute their own or a third parties' facilities for portions of LEC special access facilities. The current special access tariffs generally impose a flat charge for transmission between the end user's premises and the local telephone company's end office serving that customer, a distance sensitive charge for transmission between LEC central offices (if both end points on the circuit are not served by the same central office), and a flat charge for transmission between the second LEC central office and the customer designated end point, such as an IXC point of presence (POP).[4] The premises-to-end-office and the end-office-to-POP segments are usually called channel terminations and are subject to the same charge. The interoffice element is usually called channel mileage. The tariffs also contain separate charges for certain central office special features.

This special access rate structure effectively precludes a CAP or other interested party from interconnecting with a LEC to provide either the premises-to-end-office or the end-office-to-POP segment of a special access line. This results from the fact that the CAP or other interconnecting party would be required to pay both LEC channel termination charges regardless of whether it substituted its own facilities for virtually all of one of the LEC transmission segments. Therefore, the CAP or other interconnecting party apparently could not offer the premises-to-end-office or the end-office-to-POP segments alone at an economically competitive price.

For example, under the current tariff structure, a large customer cannot, as a practical matter, deliver its interstate traffic to an IXC POP using LEC access facilities from its location to the LEC central office and CAP transmission facilities from there, or a point just outside the central office, to the IXC premises. Assuming that the customer location and the POP are served by the same central office, a customer using CAP facilities in this manner would pay two channel termination charges to reach the CAP facilities in addition to the CAP charges. By paying the two channel termination charges directly to the LEC, however, the customer could also reach the POP directly without incurring any CAP charges. Accordingly, the customer must choose between using LEC facilities for the entire special access connection or bypassing the LEC entirely through third-party facilities that connect the customer location directly with the IXC.

As a result, CAPs are seeking new interstate interconnection arrangements that would allow them to interconnect at, or near, the LEC central office under rates, terms, and conditions different from those in the present access tariffs. The CAPs seek the right to interconnect with the LECs either by locating their own

---

4. For the sake of simplicity in discussing the special access rate structure, we will assume that the customer is connecting to an IXC POP.

equipment in the LEC central office, or by interconnecting with the LEC at a point adjacent to the central office under rates, terms, and conditions that they argue would more accurately reflect the facilities they use. In particular, Metropolitan Fiber Systems (MFS) filed a Petition for Rulemaking on November 14, 1989, requesting that we develop rules providing CAPs with access to the BOC access networks on reasonable and nondiscriminatory terms through the unbundling of each component of the exchange access network on a cost-supported basis.[5] The Commission sought comment on the MFS Petition and more than thirty parties filed comments or replies, which were considered in deciding to initiate this proceeding.[6]

IXCs and large users have generally supported CAP requests for expanded interstate interconnection rights. While certain LECs have entered into, or are currently negotiating, intrastate arrangements for expanded interconnection. LECs generally have argued that expanded interconnection opportunities for third parties require that regulators permit substantially greater LEC pricing flexibility.[7] Some states have established expanded interconnection policies for intrastate services, while regulators from other states have expressed concern about such initiatives. NARUC and a number of states have also raised questions about the potential effect of federal interconnection actions on state interests.

The Commission has long pursued regulatory policies removing barriers to full competition in telecommunications when possible. In the interstate telecommunications market, the prod of competition has led to greater customer choice, the more efficient provision of products and services desired by customers, and a more rapid deployment of advanced telecommunications technologies. For example, competition in the provision of interstate long-distance service has led to sharply reduced rates, a larger variety of service options, and more rapid deployment of new technologies such as fiber optics and digital switching. Similar advantages have flowed to residential and business consumers with the advent of competition in the provision of Customer Premises Equipment (CPE). In both instances, Commission decisions to mandate new forms of interconnection with telephone company monopoly facilities were crucial to the development of competition.

Based on our past experience with competition and on our understanding of the provision of interstate special access-type services, we tentatively conclude that current LEC interstate special access interconnection arrangements create a significant barrier to the competitive provision of interstate special access transmission links. The customer seeking competitive alternatives must either find a LEC competitor with facilities that interconnect all the necessary points without any use of LEC facilities, or build such a network itself. Expanded interconnection

---

5. MFS has proposed a bidding process to determine whether the LEC or the CAP would provide interconnection facilities.

6. A list of the parties commenting on the MFS Petition is contained in Appendix A. In 1987, Teleport also filed a Petition for Declaratory Ruling which raised similar issues.

7. The LECs which have negotiated expanded interconnection agreements with CAPs include New York Telephone Company, New England Telephone and Telegraph Company, Illinois Bell Telephone Company, and Pacific Telesis.

arrangements would significantly increase the opportunities for special access competition by permitting a customer to choose competitively provided special access links between a LEC central office and a POP, for example, and LEC special access transmission facilities elsewhere.

We believe removing the barriers present in current LEC special access tariffs to allow greater competition will result in substantial benefits. Expanded interconnection will subject LEC operations more directly to the discipline of greater competition, and thus strongly complement the proefficiency incentives of LEC price cap regulation. Increased interstate special access competition should lower the price of services subject to competition, and, in the long term, increase the overall efficiency of LEC operations. It should also provide a competitive spur for the LECs to deploy new technologies and improve service quality.

*   *   *

SEPARATE STATEMENT OF
COMMISSIONER ERVIN S. DUGGAN

I support the NPRM/NOI that we are initiating on expanded interconnection. Competition at the local exchange level is an idea whose time is coming, hastened by technology and consumer demand. This initial proposal, limited to requiring interconnection for competitive special access services, is measured and judicious.

History suggests, however, that modest proposals often turn out to have far-reaching and sometimes unintended consequences. We would do well, then, to reflect upon some issues that may arise from our decision to order expanded interconnection, if that comes to pass.

The oldtimers among us—among whom I cannot count myself—must have a sense of *deja vu*, for the parallels here to the beginnings of long-distance competition are striking.

We hear warnings of "cream-skimming," for example: objections that allowing local exchange competition will tempt competitors to siphon off high-volume customers, leaving lower-volume customers, who produce less revenue, to bear the costs of network operations. Hearing such charges, it's encouraging to remember that in the long-distance market this specter of cream skimming turned out to be overdrawn. But even as we hope that history will repeat itself, we should remember that keeping local and long-distance rates affordable required considerable exertions on the part of the regulators. The demand growth that helped keep rates low, for example, was stimulated in part by the adoption of subscriber line charges. If we hope to see events unfold in the same encouraging way as we move toward competition in the local access market, we must not expect an automatic reenactment of previous history: regulators will have to work hard to preserve reasonably-priced, universally affordable telephone service.

Perhaps we will be able to learn something from the history of emerging competition in other markets—telephone equipment, long-distance and enhanced services, for example. In the past, the advent of competition required us to adopt new rules governing interconnection, to amend our jurisdictional separations rules and to adopt access charge rules. I hope that commenters will tell us how we might build upon, borrow from or change the approaches we have followed in other areas.

On some issues that will confront us, we can't look so easily for guidance from experience. It seems inevitable that if local telephone company special access facilities are supplanted by new entities, telephone companies will feel compelled to change the current special access rate structure, which is now generally averaged. Local telephone companies may respond to competition by filing tariffs to lower their rates on more competitive routes while raising them on less competitive routes. In any event, our current regulatory practice—to allow "competitive" rates for new entrants, while requiring averaged rates for existing carriers' services—will probably prove unsustainable in the long run.

If we allow expanded interconnection along the lines we have proposed, we must also face some fundamental questions about rate structure and rate levels for special access service, and about the need for and scope of local telephone company pricing flexibility. We must also recognize that local competition—and local telephone company responses to competition—may give customers greater incentives to migrate switched traffic to special access facilities—either the local telephone companies' facilities or those of competitors.

The rate structures we propose here will benefit customers who interconnect within one-eighth of a mile of the central office. I hope commenters will address whether this benefit comports with the public interest. In the past, the Commission—hoping to encourage reasonably-priced service to all customers within a carrier's service area—generally was reluctant to endorse special access tariffs which conferred benefits solely on the basis of proximity to the central office. If we depart from this policy, we should do so with our eyes open to the possible impact upon the rates of other special access customers.

Finally, I hope that the comments we receive will discuss the implications of our proposal to require interconnection for special access on competition for switched access traffic—even though I'm fully aware that we do not now propose to require expanded interconnection for switched access. The implications of introducing competition into the market for switched access are probably greater than they are for the special access market. And while the specific implications for each may differ, we face the same formidable task in both: to balance the proven benefits of competition against the potential harm to local carriers and, most important, their customers.

10

DEREGULATED MARKETS

COMPETITION IN TERMINAL EQUIPMENT
(CUSTOMER PREMISES EQUIPMENT)

The first shot for competition arose so innocuously that hardly anyone noticed. The plastic Hush-A-Phone, a device that fit over the mouthpiece of a telephone receiver for user privacy, began the march to deregulating telephone equipment. Yet in challenging the AT&T tariff that prevented usage of Hush-A-Phone, this small company established a precedent that would be used to allow full competition in the customer premises equipment (CPE) market.

CUSTOMER INTERCONNECTION,
FIRST REPORT

61 F.C.C.2d 766 (1976)

The prohibition in the AT&T tariffs against interconnection of customer-supplied terminal equipment[3] generally remained absolute until 1956 when the United States Court of Appeals for the District of Columbia Circuit ruled that the tariff restriction, as applied to the Hush-a-Phone device, was an "unwarranted interference with the telephone subscriber's right reasonably to use his telephone in ways which are privately beneficial without being publicly detrimental" (*Hush-a-Phone v. U.S.*, 238 F.2d 266, 269).[4] The Commission on remand then ordered AT&T to cancel the tariff prohibition against the Hush-a-Phone device "or any other device which does not injure defendants' employees, facilities, the public in its use of defendants' services or impair the operation of the telephone system." *Hush-a-Phone*, Decision and Order on Remand, 22 FCC

---

3. Such forbidden attachments included plastic covers on phone books (as recently as 1975 such a case was taken by the telephone companies to the Supreme Court of North Carolina which overturned the prior State P.U.C. ruling that such a tariff restriction was valid), shoulder rests attached to the receiver, and dial locks to prevent people from calling out from a telephone.

4. The Court reversed the Commission's prior ruling upholding the validity of the tariff against the Hush-a-Phone (20 FCC 391, 425–427 (1955)).

112 (1957).[5] Subsequently, in reliance on the Hush-a-Phone principle, the Commission held that the AT&T broad tariff prohibition was unlawful as applied to Carterfone[6] and other interconnecting devices. *Carterfone,* 13 FCC 2d 420 (1968), *reconsideration denied,* 14 FCC 2d 571 (1969). We found that "the tariff was unlawful, and had been in the past, because it prohibited the use of Carterfone and other interconnecting devices without regard to actual harm caused to the system" (14 FCC 2d 572). In addition to considering the question of technical harm, we recognized that the economic effects were a pertinent public interest consideration but found no showing in the *Carterfone* record to demonstrate economic harm (14 FCC 2d at 572–573).

Following *Carterfone* AT&T filed tariff revisions permitting interconnection of customer-provided terminal equipment subject to requirements for telephone company-provided connecting arrangements (CAs) and network control signalling units (NCSUs). *AT&T Foreign Attachment Tariff Revisions,* 15 FCC 2d 605 (1968), *reconsideration* 18 FCC 2d 871 (1969). The Commission allowed the tariff revisions to go into effect but commenced a Federal-State Joint Board proceeding (Docket No. 19528) to determine whether the CA and NCSU restrictions could be liberalized without technical harm to the telephone network (*Interstate and Foreign MTS and WATS,* 35 FCC 2d 533 (1972)). The question of potential economic harm was deferred pending consideration of our findings in this docket. The *First Report and Order in Docket No. 19528* (56 FCC 2d 593 (1975), *reconsideration* 58 FCC 2d 716) established a registration program to allow users to connect certain terminal equipment to the telephone network without the need for carrier-supplied CAs, provided that the equipment or the connecting protective circuitry has been certified by the Commission pursuant to Part 68 of the Rules which is designed to protect the telephone network from technical harm. The Commission's *Second Report and Order in Docket No. 19528* further amended Part 68 of the Rules to include private branch exchanges (PBXs), key telephone systems, and main station telephones in the registration program (58 FCC 2d 736 (1976)).

*　　*　　*

[**Note:** The United States Court of Appeals for the Fourth Circuit affirmed the Commission's "registration program" in *North Carolina Utilities Commission v. FCC,* 537 F.2d 787 (4th Cir.), *cert. denied,* 429 U.S. 1027 (1976).]

COMPETITION FOR EQUIPMENT
AND ENHANCED SERVICES

The three *Computer Inquiry* decisions mark another FCC effort to deal with evolving telecommunications technology. Competition among telecom-

---

5. The Hush-a-Phone was a plastic cup clipped to the mouthpiece of the telephone to assure privacy and also to promote intelligibility in noisy environments.

6. The Carterfone was an inductive-acoustically coupled device which allowed a mobile telephone user to access the public telephone network through the mobile system's base station, where the Carterfone was installed.

munications enterprises caused some overlap between computing and tele-communications. AT&T had resolved one overlap in its business by a consent decree with the Justice Department in 1956, under which the company agreed not to engage in any business other than communications common carrier services subject to regulation. However, in the 1960s AT&T had excess computer capacity that it could have sold as a hybrid common carrier/data processing service. Such sales could have increased AT&T's revenues, theoretically allowing lower consumer telephone rates.

IBM was in a similar position from the supplier's side. The company developed various computing services, the potential of which it could not fully exploit without becoming involved in common carrier activities.

The FCC began hearings on these issues in 1966, culminating in its *Computer Inquiry I* decision in 1971. *Computer Inquiry I* temporarily resolved the issue in legalistic terms, allowing the Commission to consider "hybrid services" by weighing the characteristics of each service to determine whether it was predominantly a "communications" service or a "data processing" service. By requiring a balancing test, the FCC did little to let companies know in advance with any certainty which technologies might be regulated. Therefore, the cost of regulation could not be factored into a firm's decision to invest in a new technology, because it could not be known in advance whether regulation would be applied or to what extent. The fear was that entrepreneurs would be less willing to invest in risky and costly technologies as a result. Investment decisions in high-risk technologies are difficult enough without the added uncertainty of possible additional costs imposed by a later decision to regulate.

After ruling that an AT&T "smart" data processing terminal was a com-munications service within its regulatory jurisdiction, the FCC received substantial industry opposition, leading to a second round of hearings culminating in a second ruling, *Computer Inquiry II*, in 1980. The Commission ruled that services either were "basic" and regulated as common carrier services, or "enhanced" and excluded from regulation. It also ruled that customer premises equipment should be unregulated. This led to the detar-iffing of equipment and the growth of phone manufacturers providing a wide variety of phones of varying cost and quality.

SECOND COMPUTER INQUIRY

77 F.C.C.2d 384 (1980)

*   *   *

Commonly referred to as the "Second Computer Inquiry," this proceeding focuses on regulatory issues emanating from the greater utilization of computer processing technology and its varied market applications. The thrust of this proceeding is threefold: a) to determine whether enhanced services which are provided over common carrier telecommunication facilities should be subject to regulation and, if so, to what extent; b) to examine the competitive and technological evolution of customer premises equipment, with a view toward determining whether the continuation of traditional regulation of terminal equipment is in the public interest; and c) to determine, consistent with the statutory mandate set forth in the Communications Act of 1934, as amended, 47 U.S.C. §151, the role of communication common carriers in the provision of enhanced services and customer-premises equipment (CPE).

*　*　*

A. First Computer Inquiry

More than a decade ago an inquiry was commenced to address the regulatory and policy problems raised by the interdependence of computer technology, its market applications, and communications common carrier services. In that proceeding, commonly referred to as the "First Computer Inquiry," information was sought regarding actual and potential computer uses of communications facilities and services. Views and recommendations were sought as to whether there was any need for new or improved common carrier service offerings, or for revised rates, regulations, and practices of carriers to meet the emerging communications requirements for the provision of data processing or other computer services involving the use of communication facilities.

A number of regulatory issues were raised in the course of the proceeding. A major issue was whether communications common carriers should be permitted to market data processing services, and if so, what safeguards should be imposed to insure that the carriers would not engage in anti-competitive or discriminatory practices. Concern was also expressed as to the appropriateness of a carrier utilizing part of its communications switching plant to offer a data processing service. The potential existed for common carriers to favor their own data processing activities through cross-subsidization, improper pricing of common carrier services, and related anti-competitive practices which could result in burdening or impairing the carrier's provision of other regulated services. There was also concern over the extent to which data processing organizations should be permitted to engage in transmission as part of a data processing package free from regulation.

Two fundamental regulatory issues were addressed: (a) whether data processing services should be subject to regulation under Title II of the Communications Act, and b) whether, under what circumstances, and subject to what conditions or safeguards, common carriers should be permitted to engage in data processing. In addressing the first issue, we looked to the basic purpose of our regulatory authority as well as specific statutory guidelines and determined that data processing services should not be regulated, even though transmission over common carrier communications facilities was involved in order to link user terminals to central computers. Thus, certain communications-related services involving electronic transmission over common carrier communication facilities were not subject to regulation under the Act.

Regulatory forbearance with respect to data processing services made it necessary to distinguish regulated communications services from unregulated data processing services. Accordingly, in the *First Computer Inquiry* a set of definitions was adopted to assist in making such determinations. See 47 CFR §64.702. The thrust of this definitional approach was to distinguish between unregulated data processing and permissible carrier utilization of computers by establishing a dichotomy between data processing and message or circuit switching. We recognized that entities would offer "hybrid" services combining both communications and data processing functions. We stated that where message-switching is offered as an incidental feature of an integrated service offering that is primarily data processing, there would be total regulatory forbearance with respect to the entire service. However, where the package offering is oriented to satisfy the communications or message-switching requirements of the subscriber, and the data processing function is incidental to the message-switching performance, we concluded that the entire integrated service would be treated as a communications service. We also stated that in making such determinations we would look to whether the service, by virtue of its message-switching capability, has the attributes of the point-to-point services offered by conventional communications common carriers and is basically a substitute therefor.

*   *   *

B. Second Computer Inquiry

The *First Computer Inquiry* was a vehicle for identification and better understanding of problems spawned by the confluence of computer and communications technologies taking place at that time. The scope of the Inquiry was very broad and determinations were made based on the state of the art as it then existed. However, significant advances in computer hardware and software have been made since that time. In particular, dramatic advances in large-scale integrated circuitry and microprocessor technology have permitted fabrication of mini-computers, micro-computers, and other special purpose devices, which are capable of duplicating many of the data-manipulative capabilities which were previously available only at centralized locations housing large scale general-purpose computers. With this new technology, users now find it cost-beneficial to remove some of the computing power from a centralized computer location. The phenomenon of distributed processing allows computers and terminals to perform both data processing and communications control applications within the network and at the customer's premises.

*   *   *

Having concluded that there should be no regulatory distinction between enhanced services, we are left with two categories of services—basic and enhanced. The common carrier offering of basic transmission services are regulated under Title II of the Act. This proceeding does not address the nature and degree of regulation exercised over providers of basic services. Insofar as enhanced services are concerned, there are two options—subject all enhanced services to regulation, or refrain from regulating them *in toto*. We believe that, consistent with our overall statutory mandate, enhanced services should not be regulated under the Act.

We find the public interest benefits inherent in distinguishing basic and enhanced services and regulating only the former far outweigh any regulatory scheme that attempts to regulate some enhanced services and not others. Significant public interest benefits accrue to the Commission, carriers and other service providers, and consumers under this regulatory structure. Moreover, we are convinced that such a regulatory scheme offers the greatest potential for efficient utilization and full exploitation of the interstate telecommunications network. The basis for such conviction becomes apparent when the advantages of this structure are compared to the existing regulatory environment or that proposed in the *Tentative Decision*.

From the perspective of the regulator, a major benefit in not classifying services within the enhanced category is that the scope of Commission regulation is focused on those services which are clearly within the contemplation of the Communications Act and which serve as the foundation for all enhanced services. Moreover, the extent of our regulatory authority is not automatically expanded with advances in technology and the types of enhanced services that can be offered. Semantic distinctions are avoided as to whether a given service is data processing, information processing, process control, communications processing, or some other category. As such, the potential for the development of an inconsistent regulatory scheme to accommodate these services is eliminated; all enhanced services are accorded the same regulatory treatment. To the extent uncertainty creates a regulatory barrier to entry, that barrier is also removed. With the nonregulation of all enhanced services, FCC regulations will not directly or indirectly inhibit the offering of these services, nor will our administrative processes be interjected between technology and its marketplace applications. This structure enables us to direct our attention to the regulation of basic services and to assuring nondiscriminatory access to common carrier telecommunications facilities by all providers of enhanced services.

Service vendors also benefit under this structure. Providers of enhanced services are afforded tremendous flexibility because there is no restriction on the types of services they may provide, except those imposed by the demands of their customers. The boundary between basic and enhanced services raised no such barrier since we believe we have identified a common necessary element in our definition of basic services. The trend in technology is toward new and innovative enhancements that build upon basic services. For computer vendors and entrepreneurs the momentum is away from basic communications services, rather than toward it. As a result, the types of enhanced services they may provide is limited only by their entrepreneurial ingenuity and competitive market constraints. Services need not be artificially structured or limited so as to avoid transgressing a regulatory boundary.

The benefit to consumers is that services which depend on the electronic movement of information can be custom-tailored to individual subscriber needs. Moreover, information systems can be programmed so that users dictate the nature and extent of computer processing applications to be performed on any given amount of information. As greater flexibility is offered consumers to tailor their services, a broader spectrum of the marketplace can be expected to take advantage of information processing services. To the extent regulatory barriers to entry are removed and restrictions on services are lifted there is a corresponding potential for greater utilization of the telecommunications network through greater access to new and innovative service by a larger segment of the populace. Finally, this structure creates the proper economic incentives for vendors to segregate their services such that consumers need pay only for those services necessary for their own information processing requirements.

*   *   *

[Customer Premises Equipment]

Having concluded that we should not classify CPE, our attention is focused on the role of the communication common carrier in offering CPE. Specifically we address whether the objectives of the Communications Act would be better served if carriers were required to sell or lease CPE separate and apart from their regulated transmission services, and whether Title II regulation of carrier provided equipment is warranted. Upon review of the record in this proceeding, we believe that our statutory mandate can best be fulfilled if all CPE is detariffed and separated from a carrier's basic transmission services.

In weighing the merits of this conclusion, we have considered the nature of the terminal equipment market and the effects of advances in technology on equipment design and use, the benefits of competition, and our statutory responsibility to insure the reasonableness of rates charged for interstate services. Beginning with our *Carterfone* decision this Commission has embarked on a conscious policy of promoting competition in the terminal equipment market. As a result of this policy the terminal equipment market is subject to an increasing amount of competition as new and innovative types of CPE are constantly introduced into the marketplace by equipment vendors. We have repeatedly found that competition in the equipment market has stimulated innovation on the part of both independent suppliers and telephone companies, thereby affording the public a wider range of terminal choices at lower costs. See, for example, *First Report in Docket No. 20003*, 61 FCC 2d at 867; *Phase II Final Decision and Order in Docket No. 19129*, 64 FCC 2d 1, 602. Moreover, this policy has afforded consumers more options in obtaining equipment that best suits their communication or information processing needs. Benefits of this competitive policy have been found in such areas as improved maintenance and reliability, improved installation features including ease of making changes, competitive sources of supply, the option of leasing or owning equipment, and competitive pricing and payment options.

*   *   *

The competitive potential of terminal equipment markets is reflected in the fact that there are hundreds of manufacturers and suppliers of modems, terminals, storage devices, front end processors, large and small central processing units, multiplexers, concentrators, and virtually innumerable related devices. While some segments of the CPE market may be more competitive than others, we have been given no evidence that, given certain modifications in the markets, any segment is inherently less competitive than another. In fact, the lack of any significant competition in some segments has been attributable not to any inherent monopoly characteristics, but to those artificial constraints imposed by carrier tariff restrictions which we have struck down as unlawful. There are multiple vendors for almost any type of equipment desired, and consumers are free to select equipment that best suits their needs.

Many different types of CPE are offered in the marketplace and it is virtually impossible for a single supplier to satisfy all the various equipment needs of a user. The number of suppliers in the marketplace and the variety of products they offer is evidence of the severability of CPE from a carrier's transmission service. Moreover, to a large extent, the technological revolution in terminal equipment has occurred independent of common carrier transmission services. Nonregulated equipment vendors have been instrumental in applying computer technology to CPE, and have been the primary leaders in innovation in this area. The degree to which innovation occurs independent of the telecommunications network also reflects the fact that CPE is clearly severable from the underlying utility service to which it is attached. There is nothing inherent in any carrier-provided CPE, including the basic telephone, that necessitates its provision as an integrated part of a carrier's regulated transmission service.

* * *

This separation of the provision of carrier-provided CPE from the carrier provision of regulated communications services complements the regulatory scheme we are adopting for basic and enhanced services. Trends in technology enable CPE to function as an enhancement to basic common carrier services and many enhanced service applications involve interaction with sophisticated terminal equipment. The uses to which these devices may be put are under the user's, not the carrier's control. The structure we are adopting for network services separates the costs of service enhancements from the underlying transmission service. Deregulation of carrier-provided CPE would separate the costs associated with the provision, marketing, servicing and maintenance of CPE from the rates charged for interstate common carrier services. Thus, the deregulation of CPE fosters a regulatory scheme which separates the provision of regulated common carrier services from competitive activities that are independent of, but related to, the underlying utility service. In addition, the separation of CPE from common carrier offerings and its resulting deregulation will provide carriers the flexibility to compete in the marketplace on the same basis as any other equipment vendor. . . .

COMPUTER INQUIRY III

The distinction drawn in *Computer Inquiry II* between basic and enhanced services held firm, but questions remained. First, was structural separation necessary in order to assure competitive opportunity for enhanced services providers (ESPs) other than dominant carriers? For example, an ESP might offer least-cost routing for long distance based on a study of pricing. Or it might offer more detailed billing, coded to clients, than an ordinary phone bill contains. Information services, discussed at the end of the chapter, are another form of enhanced services.

Once faced with such challenges, telcos might want to compete against ESPs. But under a requirement that they provide enhanced services through a structurally separate subsidiary, the telcos face higher costs and adminis-trative burdens in providing such services than ESPs. These burdens were viewed by the telcos as onerous.

In Phase I of *Computer Inquiry III*, the FCC addressed this situation, indicating that telcos could offer enhanced services on a non–separated-subsidiary basis if safeguards were in place (*Computer Inquiry III, Phase I*, 104 F.C.C.2d 958 [1986]). The FCC established five safeguards: network information disclosure, including identification of basic service elements (BSE) that are the network's building blocks; accounting rules under Part 64 of the Commission's rules to prevent cross-subsidies; open network architec-ture (ONA) so the configuration of the telco's system can be known to unaffiliated companies; comparably efficient interconnection (CEI) so out-siders can attach to essential facilities as easily as the telco; and customer proprietary network information (CPNI), data about customers that assists outsiders in developing services on a par with the telcos. For instance, it would be important to know how many times a phone rings busy if you were devising a voice mail product—that would be CPNI.

In *California v. FCC*, 905 F.2d 1217 (9th Cir. 1990), the Ninth Circuit Court of Appeals (which generally does not review FCC orders; the D.C. Circuit does) found the relaxation of requirements in Phase I unlawful. It concluded that the FCC had failed to explain satisfactorily how circumstances had changed to justify substituting nonstructural for structural separation re-quirements for BOCs. It noted that in its 1983 *BOC Separation Order* 95 F.C.C.2d 1117 (1983), decided just fourteen months before *Computer Inquiry III*, the Commission had rejected the BOCs' argument that divestiture had eliminated the need for structural separation. In that order the FCC concluded that the benefits of structural separation—preventing discriminatory access to the switched network for nonrelated ESPs and preventing cross-subsi-dies—outweighed the benefits accruing from nonstructural separation.

Note that in separate orders in 1986, the FCC had permitted AT&T and the BOCs to offer customer premises equipment on a nonseparated basis. As that market has turned out, however, the BOCs have generally found it unprofitable even to offer CPE. And under the divestiture decree, they cannot manufacture it.

In *Computer Inquiry III, Phase II*, 66 R.R.2d 1594 (1987), the FCC took a harder look at defining enhanced services. For example, when a computer's output is fed by telephone lines to another computer but the language of the computer has to be modified to allow the transmission, is the step of translating a basic or enhanced service? The FCC decided it was an enhanced service.

This further inquiry followed on the decision to treat voice message storage services as enhanced. In voice message storage, phone companies integrate answering machines into their service, so messages can be retrieved by touchtone phones. This service has begun to be offered by local telcos under names such as "Message Center."

In response to the 1990 court of appeals decision, the FCC reaffirmed its intention to impose ONA requirements on the BOCs. Regardless of how the structural/nonstructural safeguards issue is resolved, the FCC concluded that ESPs would benefit by having access to the information offered by an ONA disclosure. The Commission also reaffirmed its intention to apply a nonstructural safeguard scheme to AT&T's provision of enhanced services, which the Ninth Circuit left untouched (*Computer III Remand Proceedings*, 68 R.R.2d 873 [1990]).

COMPUTER INQUIRY III
PHASE I (FURTHER RECONSIDERATION)

3 F.C.C. Rcd. 1135 (1988)

* * *

II. Background

We initiated this proceeding in the summer of 1985 to undertake a broad reexamination of the regulatory framework for enhanced services adopted in *Computer II* and related proceedings. In the *Phase I Order*, we concluded that, relative to nonstructural safeguards, structural separation requirements for enhanced services impose significant costs on the public in decreased efficiency and innovation that outweigh their benefit in limiting the ability of AT&T and the BOCs to engage in anticompetitive behavior. We retained, however, the two service categories first established in *Computer II*: basic services, which are subject to common carrier regulation under Title II of the Communications Act of 1934, and enhanced services, which are not subject to such regulation.

In the *Phase I Order*, we replaced structural separation for the enhanced service operations of AT&T and the BOCs with a set of nonstructural safeguards designed to prevent improper cost shifting and discrimination by these carriers in their provision of enhanced services. We permitted AT&T and the BOCs to offer specific enhanced services on an unseparated basis pursuant to the CEI requirements described in the *Phase I Order*. As a precondition to full structural relief for their entire enhanced services operations, we required AT&T and the BOCs to (a) implement approved ONA Plans to be filed February 1, 1988; (b) file cost allocation plans in compliance with the *Joint Cost Order* requirements; (c) adhere to modified versions of the existing network information disclosure requirements; and (d) follow customer proprietary network information (CPNI) procedures.

In the *Phase I Recon Order*, we addressed nine petitions for reconsideration of the *Phase I Order*. Upon reconsideration, we revised the CEI/ONA requirements applicable to AT&T so that AT&T is not required to implement the type of unbundling required in the *Phase I Order* for ONA, but may instead rely on service-specific CEI plans for its enhanced service offering. We also stated that the BOCs and AT&T must file ONA plans by February 1, 1988.

We clarified in the *Phase I Recon Order* that carriers need only address the requirements of enhanced service providers in designing unbundled BSEs for ONA and unbundled basic services for service-specific CEI plans. However, we stated that such BSEs and CEI offerings, when tariffed at the federal level, must be available to any customer for any use. We did not, however, preempt the states from imposing use restrictions on state-tariffed BSEs and CEI services, nor did we preempt pricing of intrastate services. We maintained the requirement of the *Phase I Order* that the technical characteristics of a carrier's CEI offering must be equal to those of the basic services it uses for its own enhanced services. We noted that this equal access standard remains "full technical equality," but that "equality as perceived by end users" is a key factor in fulfilling the standard.

In the *Phase I Recon Order*, we emphasized that ONA implementation is a long-term process. We stated that while we did not expect carriers to complete ONA implementation throughout their entire service area within one year, we declined to modify our requirement that an initial set of key BSEs be implemented within one year of approval of a carrier's ONA plan. We further declined to alter the criteria we established in the *Phase I Order* for determining the initial set of key BSEs, since the criteria well served our pro-efficiency, antidiscrimination goals for ONA. We required that each carrier's ONA plan contain a schedule for the phased introduction of further ONA capabilities after implementation of the initial set of key BSEs, including a schedule for the deployment of the initial set of BSEs throughout a carrier's geographic service area.

We also decided that preemption in *Computer II* of state common carrier regulation of enhanced services should not be changed, and affirmed our actions in the *Phase I Order* that preempted the states from imposing (a) separate subsidiary requirements on the enhanced service operations of AT&T and the BOCs, and (b) state nonstructural safeguards that are inconsistent with our *Computer III* safeguards.

*   *   *

We reaffirm our decision in the *Phase I Recon Order* to impose CEI/ONA requirements on AT&T that differ from those for the BOCs. Under those requirements, AT&T must file a modified ONA plan on February 1, 1988, and also must file service-specific CEI plans for its enhanced service offerings. We clarify that while both AT&T and the BOCs must file ONA plans, we do not require either AT&T or the BOCs to adopt a particular business organization for their enhanced service operations. We simply require, as we did in the *BOC CPE Relief Order*, that any carrier that does not intend to implement full structural relief must demonstrate that the form of structural separation it proposes to retain either satisfies our nonstructural safeguards or provides a fully adequate replacement for them. . . .

COMPUTER INQUIRY III
PHASE II (RECONSIDERATION)

3 F.C.C. Rcd. 1150 (1988)

In the *Phase I Order* in this docket, we established a new regulatory framework to govern the participation of the American Telephone and Telegraph Company (AT&T) and the Bell Operating Companies (BOCs) in the enhanced services marketplace. This framework, based on nonstructural safeguards, replaced the structural separation requirements established in the *Computer II* proceeding. In the *Phase II Order*, we determined how those principles would be applied in the following five subject areas. First, we determined that protocol processing should continue to be treated as an enhanced service and that AT&T and BOC protocol conversion offerings must satisfy specific Comparably Efficient Interconnection (CEI) requirements for the basic services their competitors need to provide enhanced services that include protocol processing. Second, we required AT&T and the BOCs to comply with nonstructural safeguards including: a requirement to provide quarterly reports on the quality and timeliness of their installation and maintenance activities; network information disclosure rules, under which AT&T and the BOCs must inform enhanced service providers of new or modified network services; and rules governing the release and use of customer proprietary network information (CPNI). Third, we retained our general requirement that network channel terminal equipment (NCTE) be treated as unregulated customer premises equipment (CPE), while allowing the BOCs to provide remote loopback testing under tariff. We also retained our existing "multiplexer exception which permits carriers to provide network multiplexers on customer premises as part of a regulated service. Fourth, we concluded that we should not apply *Computer III* requirements to the independent telephone companies. Fifth, we found that the *Computer III* policies should apply to international communications.

Nine parties have filed petitions seeking reconsideration of various aspects of our decision in the first three of these five subject areas. As summarized below, we deny those petitions in substantial part. . . .

Protocol Processing

In the *Phase II Order*, we determined that protocol processing should continue to be treated as an enhanced service and that, when protocol processing is offered by AT&T or a BOC, the carrier must satisfy specific CEI requirements in order to provide efficient, nondiscriminatory, unbundled access to its basic service facilities necessary for competitors to provide enhanced services that include protocol processing. . . .

In this Order we decline to reclassify protocol conversion as a basic service. . . .

Questions

1. Is it true that a basic/enhanced dichotomy removes many uncertainties? What uncertainties remain? Does a basic/enhanced dichotomy benefit non-telco service providers as much as it benefits telco providers?

2. Are enhanced services the same as information services? The whole of *Computer Inquiry III* must be considered in the light of the AT&T divestiture decree. Until 1991 the former Bell Operating Companies had been prohibited from entering the field of information services, with certain limited exceptions. Therefore, if a service could not have been offered under the divestiture decree, it would not matter whether the FCC had classified it as basic or enhanced. Does this mean that the divestiture decree proceeding had the

last word and always will? Is it sound communications policy to have the FCC approve deregulated entry into enhanced services while the courts will be allowed to decide about entry into information services?

3. What safeguards does *Computer Inquiry III* require to protect other enhanced service providers against potential anticompetitive behavior by the BOCs and AT&T? What are the drawbacks of nonstructural safeguards?

4. Recall that the Ninth Circuit invalidated the nonstructural requirements pending a satisfactory justification by the FCC. What kind of record evidence will be sufficient to prove that the risks associated with a nonstructural approach are outweighed by the potential benefits? Is it really only a matter of time?

5. How are consumer interests weighed into the equation by the district court and the FCC? Are the issues here easily understood in terms of consumer stakes?

6. Under the *Computer Inquiry III* scheme, the FCC could preempt state regulation of enhanced services provided by AT&T and the BOCs. The Ninth Circuit, however, has invalidated federal preemption of enhanced services. How can dual federal and state regulation be reconciled? See discussion in question 3 in Chapter 3 *supra*.

7. AT&T has lost ground to foreign manufacturers of service provider equipment (i.e., large systems used by telephone companies). For example, Northern Telecom, a Canadian company, has nearly a 40 percent share of the U.S. market. Much of this loss can be attributed to the fact that most nations ban or restrict foreign suppliers in their markets. U.S. policymakers are particularly concerned about the significant increase in the U.S. trade deficit caused by this situation. (In 1981 the United States had an $817 million trade surplus for telephone equipment. By 1987 the surplus had degenerated to a $2.5 billion deficit.) What should policymakers do to try to remedy the problem? See National Telecommunications and Information Administration, "Maintaining America's Strength in Markets for Telecommunications and Information Services," in *NTIA Telecom 2000*, 115 (1988).

8. How could the 1990 FCC decision continuing the ONA requirement be viewed as a pretext for continuing to pursue the goal of *Computer Inquiry III, Phase I?*

INFORMATION SERVICES

INFORMATION SERVICES

Fredrick Matos
NTIA TELECOM 2000 (1988)

Information services available via the public telephone networks can be generally categorized into seven different types, some of which can be further subcategorized into 222 business and consumer applications. The distinctions among the definitions are not always precise, for there is some overlap among categories, e.g., some database retrieval and messaging systems are available via consumer videotex firms.

The dependence upon public-switched telephone networks of these services, and the costs which they place on such networks, also differ. Credit card verification services, for instance, typically handle many communications, but each message is of very short duration. In contrast, remote access data processing may involve fewer messages, but each message may be of some hours' duration.

Consumer Videotex. These consumer and residential services are relatively easy-to-use, low-cost services allowing residential users to store and retrieve information or perform transactions electronically. They frequently provide access to the other information services described below. Examples of videotext vendors are CompuServe and GEnie. Businesses may also make use of such services.

Access/Retrieval Services. These services provide on-line information on compilations, Government documents, bibliographic information, financial data, and more. Typical users are libraries, researchers, banks, and stock brokers. The information vendors include database/retrieval services such as LEXIS, DIALOG, and pubic announcement services.

Messaging Services. These services permit users to address, dispatch, temporarily store, and retrieve information. Storage may be incidental to delivery and may not be the principal function of the service. Examples include electronic mail, voice storage and retrieval, and opinion polling.

Transactions. These services authorize or perform settlements for transactions such as credit card purchases, bank withdrawals, and shop-by-phone.

Personal/Environmental Management. These services monitor, measure, diagnose, and control the users' information, equipment, entertainment, or environment. Home telemetering alarm service is one example.

Computing Services. These services enable the customer to use the computing and storage power of the remote computer via timesharing. For example, businesses having large inventories often use such services.

Code and Protocol Conversion. These services are low-level network support systems required by many other information services. Examples are the code and protocol services provided by value-added networks such as Telenet and TYM-NET. These services enable incompatible computers and terminals to "communicate" and operate interdependently.

Online databases and interactive services have experienced significant growth in the 1980s in both the business and mass market sectors. The Cuadra/Elsevier *Directory of Online Databases,* for example, indicates that 3,369 databases are available via 528 online services in 1987 compared to 400 data bases and 59 online services in 1979–80. The growth is largely attributed to decreasing costs for computer hardware and increased computer literacy and awareness. The rapid growth in the number of online searches of databases over the past decade is illustrative: from less than 2 million searches in 1974 to 18 million in 1985.

A distinction has evolved in the United States between what, for purposes of this review, are called information vendors and information providers. Information vendors are firms such as DIALOG, The Source, and Compuserve, that for the most part, are retailers of information that is developed by other firms, normally referred to as information providers. Information providers or sources are firms that develop the information, update it, and store it, making it available through vendors. The situation can be viewed as a typical wholesale and retail arrangement. Examples of information providers whose information is available through one or more vendors are the Official Airline Guide, Associated Press, Dun's Marketing Services (Dun and Bradstreet), and McGraw-Hill News.

A few firms are both information vendors and information providers, but these are the exception rather than the rule. Typical examples are Dow Jones News/Retrieval, which provides its own financial information plus information from other sources such as *The Washington Post* and Standard and Poor's Online; and Mead Data Central, which offers its own legal information service, LEXIS, and provides other information such as news from *The Washington Post*, Associated Press, and TASS.

In the context of the information services business, the term "gateway" has a unique definition: a gateway is a service permitting users to access various information sources offered by other vendors by initially accessing only a single vendor. The first vendor, for all practical purposes, provides a transparency to the user. The information vendor CompuServe, for example, provides access to five other information vendors that make many information sources and databases available. Most recently, the term has been used to describe certain of the services that may now be provided by the Bell companies under the AT&T consent decree.

Videotex is the information service that many experts consider most likely to be used by the mass market consumer. It is a type of electronic information service that was developed in the 1970s and which began to grow as an industry in the early 1980s. As a two-way medium, videotex permits users to conduct transactions, send and receive non-entertainment electronic messages, and gain access to a wide range of information services.

The total number of U.S. subscribers to mass market videotex was approximately 720,000 in 1986, and slightly over one million in 1987, with 1987 revenues of $114.8 million.

Although notable, the revenues of these services and their customer bases should be viewed in the context of a U.S. telecommunications industry that in 1987 should have service revenues exceeding $127 billion, and will serve about 83 million American households. Electronic online information services, in short, currently serve only a statistically insignificant percentage of U.S. families. Indeed, total U.S. information subscribers of one million number less than half the current subscribers to France Telecom's Teletel service, despite the fact that there are about five times as many U.S. telephone access lines as in France.

The size of the U.S. business information market is currently about $5 billion with a forecast of $15 billion for 1992. Business usage of information services is primarily for financial, legal, journalistic, library, credit reporting, airline and travel information, and electronic mail purposes. In many cases, businesses make use of an information service provider indirectly through a third party, such as a travel agent or stock broker. The public telephone network and the available businesses providing access to information services in the United States also make it very convenient for consumers to simply call such a third party agent to obtain the information, rather than access the information themselves. Furthermore, there is also widespread use of the toll-free "800" service to obtain various information, whether from airlines, car rental companies, hotels and motels, catalogue shopping, etc.

There are several information vendors in the United States that provide access to a number of information databases, the largest of which are Dow Jones News/Retrieval; Mead Data Central; NewsNet; ORBIT; Data-Times; and DIALOG. Such vendors would typically be used by public libraries and information resource departments of private companies, government agencies, and law firms.

More specialized information vendors are the airline information and reservation services such as SABRE/American Airlines and Apollo/United Airlines.

The vendor-provider relationship can take several forms. The information vendor may have an exclusive contract with an information provider so that the provider does not make its database available to anyone except that vendor. The non-exclusive relationship, in contrast, permits the database provider to make information available through a number of vendors.

The future may see the development of the end-user terminal go in several ways: it may become simpler, evolving towards the simple French Minitel terminal without processing capabilities and with self-contained modems; or it may grow in sophistication such as the terminals that will be required for the IBM/Sears Prodigy information services—with substantial computer memory, software, and color graphics preferred to access the information. A more likely result is a blend of terminals in the mass market ranging from simple, low-cost types to higher level personal computers.

The disadvantage of the low-cost or "dumb" terminals is their lack of processing capability. This prevents the user from "downloading" the information into his terminal and processing it at his convenience. The low-end user must stay connected online to the information source thus running up online usage charges, whereas the user with a personal computer can retrieve ("download") the information quickly, store it, and process it later.

Note

Cable television is a form of information service. Were the public network's capacity to grow to accommodate the transmission of video, cable TV would be a natural extension of the telcos' foray into information service.

The 1991 removal of the MFJ restriction on information services breathed life into the telco's effort to expand in this direction. However, the Communications Act, 47 U.S.C. § 533(b), prohibits telcos from operating cable systems in their service areas. The Act also forbids operating a cable system without a franchise.

In 1991, the FCC tentatively approved "videodial tone" for telcos (Telephone Company–Cable Television Cross-Ownership Rules, 69 R.R. 2d 1613 [1991]). While telcos may not select the programming to be carried, they may transmit single channel offerings, in competition with existing cable operators. Telcos may operate a limited video network without first obtaining local permission or a local franchise. This is opposed by the cable industry, which sees telcos as unfranchised competitors. It also is opposed by local regulators, who want to determine who may operate video and, not unimportantly, want to collect a franchise fee of up to five percent of gross revenues, as provided for in the Communications Act, 47 U.S.C. § 542.

For a discussion of the First Amendment aspects of telco entry into video, see Brenner, "Telephone Company Entry into Video Services: A First Amendment Analysis," 67 *Notre Dame Law Review* 97 (1991).

11

INTERNATIONAL
TELECOMMUNICATIONS

NOTE ON INTERNATIONAL COMMUNICATIONS

In 1962 the United States launched the world's first fully active communications satellites—AT&T's Telstar, which transmitted telephone communications, data, and live television signals, and the National Aeronautics and Space Administration (NASA) Relay Communications Satellite ("Relay I"). In 1965 INTELSAT deployed the first communications satellite in geostationary orbit, INTELSAT I or "Early Bird." Early Bird could relay 240 voice circuits or one television channel. The latest generation of INTELSAT satellites, INTELSAT VI, can transmit 120,000 telephone circuits as well as three television channels.

Satellite Communications Systems

Commercial satellite communications systems may be grouped into three categories: international systems, regional systems, and domestic systems. INTELSAT and INMARSAT are international satellite communications cooperatives. INTELSAT, the International Telecommunications Satellite Organization, has 114 members and provides almost two-thirds of international telephone service and nearly all overseas television broadcasting. INTELSAT also offers domestic services to nations lacking domestic satellite systems. Until recently INTELSAT precluded private satellite systems from transmitting international communications. INMARSAT, the International Maritime Satellite Organization, has fifty-five members and offers ship-to-shore and ship-to-ship communications.

The regional satellite systems include the European Telecommunications Satellite Organization, EUTELSAT, which serves twenty countries; the Arab Satellite Organization, ARABSAT, which serves twenty-two nations; Palapa, an Indonesian system that serves Southeast Asia; and the regional systems of the former Soviet Union, MOLNIYA 1, 2, and 3, EKRAN, RADGYA, and STATSIONAR.

Domestic satellites, or domsats, are the third group of commercial communications satellite systems. More than a dozen nations either operate or are developing domestic satellites. While domsats essentially provide service within one country, the FCC has authorized certain U.S. domsat operators to offer transborder services not provided by INTELSAT (*Transborder Satellite Video Services*, 88 F.C.C.2d 258 [1981]).

Technology

The basic structure of a satellite network consists of an uplink, a downlink, and a satellite. The uplink is an earth station transmitter that relays the signal up to a satellite transponder; the transponder amplifies and beams the signal to the downlink, or earth station receiving dish; from the downlink, terrestrial distribution of the signal may begin via cable or microwave.

One of the technological disadvantages of the early satellites, such as AT&T's Telstar, was that signal transmissions between the earth stations and the satellite were possible only when the satellite was orbiting "in view" of an earth station. As a result, transmitting and receiving antennae were mounted on moving platforms to track the satellites. Continual transmissions required launching additional satellites so one would come into view when another orbited out of sight. This problem was solved by deploying the satellites into geostationary, or geosynchronous, orbit. A geostationary satellite orbits the earth at a speed equal to that of the earth's twenty-four-hour rotation. The satellite appears stationary from any given point on the earth's surface, which allows earth station antennae to remain continually fixed on the satellite.

Technological innovation also allows more efficient use of the radio spectrum. Frequency bands allocated for commercial communications satellites are divided into downlink/uplink pairs, e.g., 4/6 GHz (C Band), 12/14 GHz (Ku Band), and 20/30 GHz (K Band). In addition, technological advances have eased competition between satellite systems and nations by reducing signal interference. This allows satellite orbital slots now to be spaced two degrees apart instead of five degrees apart.

INTELSAT

Through the Communications Satellite Act of 1962, 47 U.S.C. §§701–744, the United States provided primary impetus to establish an international satellite system, INTELSAT. The act called for the incorporation of a private organization empowered to act as U.S. representative to INTELSAT in establishing and managing the international systems. In 1964 the Communications Satellite Corporation (COMSAT) was formed to fulfill this purpose, working with the appointed signatories of each member nation, usually government-owned or quasi–government-owed postal, telephone, and telegraph organizations (PTTs).

Until 1985 COMSAT served as a "carrier's carrier" and as the statutory monopoly provider of international satellite service in the United States. A three-tiered market structure existed: 1) wholesaler, 2) retailer, and 3) end user. COMSAT acted as the wholesaler and the sole means of access to INTELSAT. COMSAT was restricted to leasing capacity to common carriers, who acted as the retailers. The common carriers, in turn, offered their services to the end users. Carriers and end users, however, complained about the high costs and limited service offerings associated with this monopolistic structure. The FCC has since adopted competitive policies to break down the rigid three-tiered system in order to reduce barriers to entry, decrease prices, and increase service options and technological innovation. Many of these policies, however, have received considerable resistance from most other nations.

Not only has COMSAT faced competition, but a communications provider or end user can employ an alternative international communications network to bypass INTELSAT. In 1985 the FCC authorized the establishment of private satellite systems that provide international services separate from INTELSAT (*International Satellite Systems*, 58 R.R.2d 1313 [1985]). The decision allows these separate systems to compete with INTELSAT by offering the sale or long-term lease of transponders to carriers, noncarriers, resellers, and end users. A substantial amount of INTELSAT's business is protected, however, by the restriction against the offering of any switched message services at any level through the separate systems.

In addition, noncarriers and end users can bypass U.S. common carriers by purchasing INTELSAT transmission capacity directly from COMSAT under the same terms and at the same tariffed rates as the common carriers. And COMSAT can offer retail services directly to end users (*Authorized User II*, 90 F.C.C.2d 1394 [1982]). However, the FCC refused to allow carriers to bypass COMSAT and directly access INTELSAT services (*Direct Access Denial*, 97 F.C.C.2d 2906 [1984]). The D.C. Circuit upheld both of these decisions in *Western Union International v. FCC*, 804 F.2d 1280 (D.C. Cir. 1986).

As you read the *International Satellite Systems* decision that follows, think about the extent and types of new service options and prices that might be spurred by the new competitive policies.

ESTABLISHMENT OF SATELLITE SYSTEMS PROVIDING INTERNATIONAL COMMUNICATIONS, REPORT AND ORDER

101 F.C.C.2d 1046 (1985)

On January 4, 1985, we initiated an inquiry and rulemaking about the construction and operation of satellite systems providing international communication services. The purpose of this proceeding was to solicit data and analyses about issues that have arisen in connection with the filing of a series of applications for authority to establish international communications satellite systems separate from INTELSAT and to obtain comments on the recent Executive branch decision that such systems are "required in the national interest" subject to certain limitations. . . .

On November 28, 1984, President Reagan signed a Presidential determination (PD No. 85–2) that alternative satellite systems were "required in the national interest" within the meaning of Sections 102(d) and 201(a) of the Communications Satellite Act. . . .

On February 8, 1985, the Department of State and the Department of Commerce jointly submitted a paper to the Commission stating the policy grounds for the President's determination and reviewing related issues. The paper, entitled, "A White Paper on New International Satellite Systems," (hereinafter referred to as the "White Paper") was completed by the Senior Interagency Group on International Communication and Information Policy.

The White Paper reviews current U.S. telecommunications policies and international obligations to determine whether and under what conditions authorizing satellite systems and services in addition to the INTELSAT system would be: (1) consistent with prevailing U.S. law, practice, and international treaty obligations; (2) compatible with sound foreign policy and telecommunications policy goals; and (3) in the U.S. national interest. The White Paper generally concludes that:

> It is technically feasible, economically desirable, and in the national interest to allow new entry by U.S. firms into the international satellite field. Customers should be afforded both the new service options and the benefits of competition among customized service providers that new entry promises. This can be accomplished, moreover, while maintaining the technical integrity of the INTELSAT global system and avoiding significant economic harm to that system. U.S. foreign policy, and international communications and information policy, require a continued strong national commitment to INTELSAT as 'a single global commercial telecommunications satellite system as part of an improved global telecommunications network.' But our national commitment to INTELSAT and other important goals can be accommodated, provided that new international satellite systems and services are authorized and regulated along the lines discussed in this report.

*   *   *

The White Paper discusses U.S. foreign policy regarding international communications satellite systems, reviews the background of INTELSAT and discusses the U.S. role as the primary force behind the development of that organization. It states that providing communication service to developing countries was a significant goal of the establishment of a global system and that, from the outset, INTELSAT has charged uniform rates for identical services provided on a global basis. The White Paper recognizes that some countries are concerned that the introduction of separate systems in the North Atlantic would lead to an increase in worldwide rates, but concludes that placing conditions restricting the operation of separate systems would avoid significant economic harm to INTELSAT. Thus, if the separate systems only are authorized under regulatory terms and conditions that restrict them to the "customized service" market, the White Paper concludes that an adverse impact on INTELSAT is unlikely. Since the new satellite systems would not be able to provide public-switched services, INTELSAT would retain its "commercial core" of revenues and would not be harmed.

The White Paper further concludes that there would be little possibility of adverse economic harm to developing nations which are concerned that the entrance of satellite systems would divert substantial amounts of traffic from profitable routes and result in increases in communication costs. It reaches this conclusion because: (1) the entrants would be unable to compete with a majority of INTELSAT's service offerings; (2) even with significant cross-elasticities between the conventional and customized markets, both markets are growing rapidly and revenue siphoning would not occur; and (3) INTELSAT is in a good position to compete for the customized services market.

*   *   *

The United States is not the first INTELSAT member to consider the use of non-INTELSAT space segment to meet its international public telecommunications needs. Systems separate from INTELSAT have already been established by other nations, and new ones are planned. A growing number of nations, developing as well as developed, are using, or are considering use of, separate systems to complement INTELSAT in providing their international telecommunications needs. INTELSAT has favorably coordinated several systems under Article XIV(d) finding no significant economic harm. It has yet to reach an unfavorable recommendation for any proposed system. From this record, it is clear that the INTELSAT charter is flexible in recognizing the diverse needs of nations and the challenges and opportunities offered by evolving telecommunications technology. Thus, while the proposals now being considered by the United States may appear from the perspective of other countries to be distinguishable from other non-INTELSAT endeavors that they have undertaken or are planning, the question before INTELSAT in the coordination process is not whether the proposed systems are regional in character or are broader in scope. As with other systems which have been coordinated, the question before INTELSAT is avoidance of significant economic harm and assurance of technical compatibility.

Second, as reflected by the President's policy determination, the Executive branch White Paper and our decision today, the United States is taking extraordinary measures to avoid economic harm to INTELSAT by placing service restrictions on the new systems. Our imposition of these restrictions is voluntary. There is no obligation, either express or implied, in the INTELSAT Agreement or elsewhere to impose such restrictions. To our knowledge, this action is unprecedented.

*   *   *

The Communications Satellite Act of 1962, 47 USC §§701–744 (1984), embodies the United States policy goals on the establishment of international satellite systems. The Act calls for the establishment of a commercial communications satellite system which would meet public needs and national objectives, serve the communication needs of the United States and other countries, and contribute to world peace and understanding by the development of a system through cooperation with other countries. 47 USC §701(a). To effectuate these objectives, the Act states that the system to be established should: (1) provide communication services to the economically less developed countries as well as the highly developed countries; (2) promote the use of the most efficient and advanced technology available; and (3) reflect the efficiencies of the system in its rates and services. 47 USC §701(b).

*   *   *

Although the Satellite Act provides for the establishment of a global commercial satellite system, it clearly does not require or contemplate a monopoly satellite system. The Act specifically provides for the creation of additional satellite systems if "required to meet unique governmental needs or if otherwise required in the national interest." 47 USC §701(d). The President has made the threshold determination that additional satellite systems are "required in the national interest" pursuant to authority under Sections 102(d) and 201(a) of the Act.

*   *   *

The domestic satellite industry exemplifies all the benefits of a competitive market. The Commission initially adopted an "open skies" policy to facilitate the entry of qualified parties in this market. Low entry barriers have resulted in a dynamically growing domestic satellite industry. This industry currently includes six satellite carriers, each with several satellites in operation, and numerous resellers and service providers. The Commission has also eliminated the Section 214 authorization and tariff filing requirements for domestic satellite carriers through its Competitive Carrier Rulemaking. The pressures of the marketplace and the existence of unregulated resale have encouraged efficient innovative service offerings and cost based prices in this industry, as many of the commenters note.

The Commission's Transponder Sales decision allows a customer or end-user several options with respect to obtaining transponder capacity. Users may lease capacity from a carrier, buy capacity in bulk for resale, lease or purchase entire transponders or parts thereof on a long term basis, obtain a percentage ownership interest, or choose to buy capacity from a reseller. By studying these options and selecting the best one for the specified business, the customer can achieve greater operational flexibility, fix costs for transmission, and configure the capacity or transponder to meet the business's particular needs. In addition to the benefits of transponder ownership, a customer has a choice of customer premises, shared use or common use general purpose earth stations and a variety of transmit-receive equipment. Finally, there have been significant advances in the design and operation of the spacecraft and ground equipment which have increased these satellites' use and efficiency and allow for the use of smaller, less expensive earth stations.

We have taken a number of measures to introduce competition in the provision of international services. Our relaxation of entry barriers for new international carriers has resulted in an increasing number of new carriers providing a variety of new services. These new carriers include Western Union, entering the international record market under the terms of the Record Carrier Competition Act of 1981, 47 USC §222, and MCI, GTE Sprint and SBS competing with AT&T for international telephone service. In the TAT-4 decision, we eliminated the voice-record dichotomy in international communications and encouraged the full utilization of digital networks in the international market. We have modified our policy with regard to the ownership and operation of U.S. international earth stations that operate with the INTELSAT global communications satellite system to permit any international carrier or group of carriers to apply for authority to construct and operate such earth stations, whether IBS, television or multi-purpose type. This policy has already resulted in the authorization of 23 new earth stations at several different urban locations to provide video and data services comparable to those proposed by the separate system applicants. Competition in the provision of earth station services is expected to have the indirect benefit of encouraging more equipment manufacturers to enter the market. In our Authorized User decision, we allowed Comsat to lease space segment directly to users and enhanced-service providers and to provide earth-station and end-to-end service through a common carrier subsidiary. Finally, we granted Cable Landing Licenses to two private companies, Tel-Optik Ltd. and Submarine Lightwave Cable Company, for authority to construct and operate fiber-optic submarine cables in the North Atlantic. We concluded that the introduction of private cable systems would provide users of North Atlantic transmission capacity with new alternatives to satisfy their needs and would further stimulate technology and service development to the benefit of international communications users. We concluded further that, with the advent of these cables, the benefits of owning and leasing transmission capacity available to domestic satellite communications users would now be available to the international communications user.

In these decisions, we found that competition in the international area would give users increased choice of services and carriers, provide more accurate cost information for users to make an informed choice, give users more flexibility in tailoring a communication system to meet their specific needs, result in technically superior service to consumers, enhance the efficient use of facilities and create downward pressure on costs and rates for the designated services. We also stated that the introduction of competition in the aforementioned areas of the international market would present no major economic hurdles and would not greatly affect our foreign partners in INTELSAT.

* * *

To implement the Executive branch service restrictions, we will condition the license for any separate system that we authorize to limit its operation to the provision of services through the sale or long-term lease of transponders or space segment capacity for communications not interconnected with public-switched message networks (except for emergency restoration service). No communications provided over a separate satellite system's space segment may interconnect with the public facilities of common carriers to provide switched message services such as MTS, telex, TWX, telegraph, teletext facsimile and high speed switched data services. The "no-interconnection" and "sale and long-term lease" restrictions apply not only to separate system operators, but also to all levels of resellers and users of the facilities. In view of the "sale and long-term lease" requirement, separate system licensees may not operate as common carriers. Finally, we have determined the following: (1) there is no need to establish a minimum unit of space segment capacity which a separate system must provide; (2) the minimum lease period for the "long-term lease" of capacity is to be one year; (3) space segment capacity may be obtained and resold by common carriers and enhanced service providers to provide communications services not interconnected with any public-switched message network; and (4) there is no basis to establish a "sunset" date for the Executive branch service restrictions absent a finding from the Executive branch that these restrictions are no longer necessary to fulfill U.S. international obligations.

In addition, consistent with the Presidential determination that separate systems are required in the national interest, we will not issue a license permitting any separate system applicant to begin operating its proposed system until the United States has completed coordination of that system with INTELSAT pursuant to Article XIV(d) of the INTELSAT Agreement and we have been informed by the Department of State that the United States has fulfilled its obligations under Article XIV(d).

Questions

1. Can Congress, the FCC, and the courts adopt and enforce a new competitive order in the international telecommunications market as they do in the domestic telecommunications market? What are the obstacles? What are the limits?

2. Did the United States waver in its commitment to INTELSAT by approving separate systems in the *International Satellite Systems* decision? How might other nations respond to such U.S. actions?

3. There is growing concern among less-developed nations that all orbital slots and frequencies will be allocated to developed countries before these other nations establish satellite capacity. The slots are granted on a first come, first served basis. The International Telecommunications Union (ITU) has convened a number of World Administrative Radio Conferences on the Use of the Geostationary-Satellite Orbit (Space WARC) to examine these issues. Less-developed nations would like some form of guaranteed access, whether or not they currently need the orbital slot. Developed countries, on the other hand, argue that technological advances will continue to expand the number of slots to accommodate all parties, and that, in any case, first come, first served is the fairest mechanism. How should these concerns be resolved?

4. The United States has adopted policies to promote the "free flow of information" necessary to fuel our increasingly service-oriented economy. Most other nations, however, have laws that restrict the flow of data across their borders. Their concerns are rooted in protecting the privacy of individuals (the United States agrees), protecting national sovereignty, and preserving cultural autonomy. These obstacles to the free flow of information, coupled with the relatively common barriers to foreign markets faced by U.S. firms, harm U.S. competitiveness because many of our exports are information-based. Do these foreign policies limit the effectiveness of U.S. attempts to spur competition and innovation in global communications? How

should the United States resolve these conflicts? Is it technologically feasible to guarantee the protection of international information flows?

5. NASA is developing an Advanced Communications Technology Satellite (ACTS) to process and switch signals—like a telephone company central switching office in space—and then selectively distribute them to any of several dozen earth stations using a spot beam. Could this become a form of bottleneck facility in space? Could it provide competition to the traditional bottleneck facilities? What are the regulatory implications?

6. In 1982 the FCC authorized domestic satellite licensees to sell individual transponders on satellites, along the lines of a space condominium. Such domsats are considered "coordinators" of the transponders rather than tariffed common carriers. What is conveyed in a transponder sale? Who has ultimate responsibility for the signal transmission? Satellite operators are subject to Title III regulation because radio waves are involved, but transponder owners and dealers are not. What does the coordinators' non–common carrier status amount to in regulatory terms? Recall the Tuxxedo Network case discussed in Chapter 2. How might a transponder sale to Tuxxedo have affected the outcome? Would Alabama's actions have been as swift or effective with the satellite operators no longer in a carrier mode?

12

THE FUTURE OF REGULATION

DEREGULATION:
LOOKING BACKWARD AND LOOKING FORWARD

Alfred E. Kahn

We have a surfeit of deregulatory anniversaries to celebrate or deplore: it is now more than thirty years since the Federal Communications Commission (FCC) authorized substantial competition in long-distance communications, more than eleven since we deregulated the airlines, and almost ten years since we did substantially the same to the railroad and trucking industries. Can we, by examining this long and varied experience with deregulation, draw any conclusions about the likelihood and desirability of its continuation in the decade ahead?

In this attempt to place deregulation in historical perspective, I feel compelled to emphasize, in contradiction of the widespread popular impression that President Reagan deserves most of the credit—or blame—how much of it occurred between 1978 and 1980.

While deregulation has dramatically transformed the transportation industries, its effect on the traditional public utilities, while substantial, can easily be exaggerated. Two years ago, in a symposium on "The Surprises of Deregulation," Robert Crandall shrewdly observed that the greater surprise in the case of telecommunications was how little had actually occurred. Customer premises equipment aside, the overwhelming majority of transactions continue to be thoroughly regulated. And AT&T, which had agreed to divest its putatively naturally monopolistic services and confine itself to competitive operations, continues nonetheless to be heavily regulated.

* * *

Of especial significance, the major issues of regulatory policy these days in the public utility arena are not whether or how to return to the closed world of franchised, thoroughly regulated monopolies, but how to accommodate traditional regulation to the increasing intrusion of competition. Among the leading examples of that intrusion are:

Copyright 1990 by the *Yale Journal on Regulation*, Box 401A, Yale Station, New Haven, CT 06520. Reprinted from Volume 7 by permission. All rights reserved.

- the total deregulation of telephone equipment, which is now highly competitive; and
- the burgeoning of private communications networks, to such a point that more business phones are now linked in the first instance to their own switches than to those of the local telephone company.

Despite these developments, most transactions at the core of the traditional public utilities, such as the local provision of telephone, electric and gas service, continue to be tightly regulated, and there seems little prospect or desirability of that situation changing fundamentally in the next decade. In these circumstances, my predictions and prescriptions about the future course of deregulation in the structurally competitive industries, on the one side, and the structurally monopolistic markets, on the other, will necessarily differ from one another.

There will, however, be a common theme and a consistent set of conclusions:

> The case for deregulation has been that direct regulation typically suppressed competition, or at least severely distorted it, and that competition, freed of such direct restraints, is a far preferable system of economic control. I read the recent experience as having essentially vindicated that proposition, making substantial reversal of the deregulatory trend unlikely.
>
> Where competition is not feasible throughout an industry or market, as in the traditional public utilities, entry of unregulated competition can introduce distortions so severe as to make the mixed system the worst of both possible worlds. The preferable remedy is not to suppress the competition, but to make the residual regulation as consistent as possible with it. That seems to be the direction in which regulators are moving.
>
> The abolition of direct economic regulation is by no means synonymous with *laissez faire*. On the contrary, it may call for government interventions no less vigorous than direct regulation itself, but fundamentally different in character and intent. The progressive realization of this fact in recent years makes for a bifurcated prognosis for the 1990s: the historic trend of direct economic deregulation is unlikely to be reversed, but government will play an increasingly active role in attempting to preserve competition and remedy its imperfections. And that is what it should do.

*   *   *

One way of trying to judge whether the recent deregulatory trends are likely to continue or be reversed is to consider the root causes of these remarkable historical changes and appraise the likelihood of their persistence.

Perhaps the most fundamental of these has been the rediscovery all over the world of the virtues of the free market. It was obviously no accident that many of the comprehensive governmentally-administered cartelizations overturned during the late 1970s and early 1980s were established during the Great Depression, when confidence in the market economy was at its nadir. While the present enthusiasm for market capitalism will doubtless be subject to ebbs and flows in the years ahead, it is difficult to envision an early return to centralized governmental command and control systems, of which our regimes of economic regulation were an exemplar in microcosm.

There is no sign of let up, either, in the technological explosion that made inevitable the collapse of almost all the historic regulatory barriers against competitive interpenetrations in telecommunications, and bids fair to do the same among financial institutions. It was the development of microwave that presented large users with the irresistible opportunity to escape the regulatorily-dictated overcharging of interexchange services. Similarly, the geometrically declining cost and increased versatility of switching has made possible the proliferation of privately-owned networks and privately-provided sophisticated telecommunications services; and fiber optics will probably doom the present artificial separation of cable television and information services from telephony.

*   *   *

The deregulations of the last fifteen years were powerfully motivated also by changes in the configuration of the private interests most directly affected. The Staggers Act was passed in large measure because of the growing disenchantment of the railroads with their historic regulatory bargain with government that protected them from competition but also systematically impeded them from competing effectively, forced them to maintain thousands of miles of track on which they were losing money, and limited their ability to raise their charges to customers with relatively inelastic demands. Similarly, airline deregulation owed a great deal to the unhappiness of United Airlines with the CAB's systematic denial to it of the ability to enter new markets or desert old ones. The insistence of large customers that they be released from the burdens of cross-subsidization to which they had been subjected by the FCC and state commissions was an important part of the reason for the breakup of AT&T's monopoly.

*   *   *

It is the converse of the foregoing proposition that is the more relevant for the future. There are now vested interests in deregulation itself—politically or economically powerful entities that, having now achieved freedom from regulation, will not readily surrender it. That is part of what I intended when I said that my colleagues and I at the CAB were going to get the airline eggs so scrambled that no one was ever going to be able to unscramble them.

*   *   *

Where the deregulatory process has been only partial, the companies that remain thoroughly regulated devote most of their energies to demanding "symmetry," by which they mean not a restoration of restraints on their newer competitors, but corresponding freedom for themselves. The principle applies symmetrically to deregulation and regulation: once instituted, they tend to be progressive and cumulative.

These forces explain why the process can be essentially inadvertent, as it was in the case of telecommunications. No planner laid out in advance the path of decisions from Hush-a-Phone and Above 890 through Carterphone, MCI, Specialized Common Carriers, Execunet, AT&T's stonewalling response, the Modified Final Judgment concluding the ensuing antitrust litigation, and the FCC's MTS/WATS Market Structure and three Computer Inquiries. Yet each step led logically to the next, and they were all in the same direction.

*   *   *

In the electric and gas utilities, partial deregulation has introduced a host of asymmetries and distortions, which have been and are still being resolved primarily by further liberalizations. The basic problem is that the rates charged by the utility companies, which inevitably play a central role in deciding which competitive transactions take place and which do not, contain a very large component of capital carrying charges on investments valued at embedded (i.e., at depreciated original) cost, not marginal cost. Under partial deregulation, therefore, many competitive purchase and production decisions are made on the basis of comparisons between those economically meaningless, traditionally regulated rates, on the one side, and competitive costs or prices on the other. Businesses will decide whether to generate their own electric power or construct their own communications systems by comparing the current, true economic cost to them of doing so with the regulated rates they would otherwise have to pay.

* * *

The legal obligation of utility companies to serve on demand, which requires them to incur the costs of installing the capacity necessary to fulfill that obligation, creates a similar distortion.

* * *

The still emerging resolution of these distortions has had several components.

Legislatures and regulatory commissions have been giving the utility companies increased freedom to reduce prices as low as their incremental costs to meet competition. Occasionally, this freedom has extended to the point of total deregulation of some services or transactions, such as Centrex, telephone equipment on the customer's premises, and some electric bulk power sales.

Also, both regulators and the passage of time have presided over a partial writing off, settling out, accelerated recovery, and disallowance of the heavy sunk costs—the multi-billion dollar take-or-pay obligations of the gas pipelines, the long-term contractual purchase obligations of the local gas distribution companies, the inflated costs of recently constructed or abandoned electric generating plants, and inadequately depreciated telephone company plant—that have constituted the major source of discrepancy between the companies' average revenue requirements for regulatory purposes and their own incremental costs.

* * *

There has been no abatement in the zeal of regulatory commissions to protect residential and small commercial customers, almost all of whom remain captive to the local utility companies, from being forced to assume the sunk costs that the competitive markets can no longer be forced to bear. To some extent, they have continued to do so by discouraging "cream-skimming" competition—for example, by competitive providers of long-distance telephone service intrastate, or by proprietors of "smart buildings," providing telecommunications services for their tenants. Increasingly, however, regulators have been developing methods consistent with, rather than obstructive of, the new competition—a tendency most fully developed in the field of telecommunications.

The simplest of these new methods has been a rate freeze for basic telephone service, accompanied by stipulations that service quality not deteriorate. The freeze may consist in a simple directive or undertaking to maintain existing rates for a number of years. Alternatively, it may provide for automatic adjustment to reflect inflation or changes in taxes or interstate separations. The indexations typically incorporate an automatic downward adjustment predicated on a targeted improvement in productivity, thereby ensuring a continuation of the long-term decline of these rates in real terms.

Such freezes or "social compacts" have some obvious virtues, both political and economic. They provide direct, straightforward protection for consumers of the services that are the subject of most intense regulatory concern. More important in the present context, they sever the link between those rates and the revenues from the more competitive services, and in this way, in principle, prevent cross-subsidization of the latter offerings by the former. By so doing, once again in principle, they make it possible to give the utility companies greater freedom to compete for the business on which they are challenged. Finally, by focusing regulation on prices rather than rates of return, and fixing the course of those prices over a period of time, these freezes or indexations mitigate the cost-plus character of traditional regulation, and therefore enhance the incentives of the companies to improve their efficiency.

These beneficent tendencies are sometimes reinforced by an explicit or implicit acceptance of a wider than usual range within which achieved rates of return are permitted to vary. Sometimes there is an accompanying provision for companies and ratepayers to share surplus profits, up to limits (before sharing) that would have seemed unacceptably high by historical standards. The consequently wider range of possible earnings, for longer periods of time, presumably provides carriers with enhanced incentives not only to minimize costs, but also to undertake risky investments and innovations that would be discouraged if the returns from successful ventures were limited to levels traditionally regarded as reasonable.[28]

Finally, the FCC now subjects AT&T's basic and non-basic interstate services to separate rate caps—ceilings on average prices (rather than on each individual one) indexed to inflation minus a productivity target. It has decided to do the same with the services of the local companies under its jurisdiction, and some states as well are now actively considering rate caps for intrastate services.

*   *   *

The future course of regulation and deregulation will be determined not only by the changing configurations of private interests, prevailing political and economic philosophies and macroeconomic conditions, but also by how we collectively appraise the record so far

*   *   *

---

28. These direct restraints on prices—whether in the form of freezes, indexation provisions, "social compacts," or rate caps—do not represent an abandonment of traditional rate of return regulation. They typically contemplate periodic reexamination of the results and readjustment of the formulas when and as rates of return range outside of acceptable limits. In the last analysis, therefore, they are all forms of rate of return regulation.

I believe most economists would agree on the following two broad propositions:

First, wherever even quite imperfect competition is feasible, it is superior to command-and-control regulation. This proposition has a corollary: where such regulation continues to be necessary, as in major sectors of the traditional public utilities, it should, to the greatest extent possible, be designed in such a way as to be compatible with competition rather than obstructive of it; and

Second, if competition is to work well, it requires a great variety of governmental interventions to remedy imperfections and market failures—interventions that, however validly they may be characterized as regulatory, differ fundamentally from the kind of direct economic regulation previously administered by such agencies as the CAB and ICC, and still practiced by most of the state public utility commissions.

To these propositions I would attach a third, somewhat less obvious one. A central part of the case for deregulation is the severe deficiencies of regulation—deficiencies of information, wisdom, and incentives, along with a strong inherent tendency to suppress competition. If, however—as I will argue presently—the response to the imperfections we have observed in the performance of the deregulated industries is that a large share of the fault lies in the failure of government to perform its essential competition-supplementing functions, such as antitrust enforcement, then the case for deregulation may rest upon assumptions about the ability of the government to fulfill those supplementary responsibilities just as unrealistic as the assumptions behind the case for direct economic regulation. This last consideration could, in some situations, take us full circle, back to an acceptance of full-scale regulation as the less imperfect of the two alternatives. In most instances, I believe, it does not.

The deregulated industries are unquestionably more competitive today than they were previously. This is not to deny the significance of the increased concentration at the national level in less-than-truckload (LTL) carriage or, marginally, in airlines, or to claim that the competition is sufficiently effective in all markets to have fully taken over the role previously played by governmentally-enforced price ceilings. It is to say that market concentration route-by-route has definitely declined, on average, in markets of all sizes and dimensions, and that the several indicia of competitive behavior support the same conclusion. The same is true of telecommunications, particularly in customer and central office equipment, long-distance telephony, and the provision of high-speed, high-volume transmission of data. Because of the competition unleashed by deregulation, average prices of air travel, trucking, and long-distance telephoning are down substantially, producing not only consumer savings but net welfare improvements in the billions of dollars each year.

The effect of deregulation on the relationship between the structure of prices and costs has been more complicated. In general, regulators tend to equalize rates to different customers despite differences in the costs of serving them; correspondingly, competition since deregulation has apparently—despite some increases in price discrimination, to which I will return—forced prices for the several categories of service into closer conformity with their respective costs. Prominent examples of this economically beneficial change have been the increased sensitivity of air fares to the effects on cost of length of trip and traffic density, and of transportation rates generally to the differences between peak and off-peak and front- and back-haul. In telephony, the prices of long-distance calling and basic residential service have likewise come into closer conformity with their respective costs.[41]

*   *   *

Purchasers are being offered a greatly expanded range of price/service options, most strikingly in financial services, telecommunications and transportation.

*   *   *

There remain three glaring apparent exceptions to the beneficent consequences of deregulation—the deterioration in the quality of air travel, a sharp increase in certain kinds of price discrimination, and—reflecting a loss of the safety or stability that the previous pervasive restrictions on competition were supposed to preserve—the savings and loan fiasco.

*   *   *

Competition can in some circumstances make unrealistic demands on consumers as well—assuming a greater ability on their part to make complex choices, on pain of suffering penalties to which they had not previously been subjected, than they either have or are willing to take the trouble to acquire. A poignant illustration of the resulting dilemma has been provided in recent years by providers of alternative telephone operator services, which have entered into arrangements with non-telephone-company owners of public telephones, hotels, and other such institutions serving transient customers, under which, in exchange for commissions to the owners, they receive the right to provide operator services and charge what they please. The problems arise because the transient caller is an often unwitting captive to such arrangements between the other two parties. The competitive solution would be to permit this kind of free entry, while requiring comprehensive disclosure of the system of charges and, probably also, that callers be offered the opportunity to be transferred without charge to the long distance carrier of their own choice. Conceivably, however, the burden on consumers of digesting such information and choosing may outweigh the benefits of competition; one is reminded of Oscar Wilde's analogous observation: "The trouble with Socialism is that it uses up too many evenings."

*   *   *

---

41. Between December 1983 and December 1989, the local telephone charges component of the Consumer Price Index increased 19.3 percent in real terms, while the average price of long-distance calling declined 44.5 percent interstate and 24.1 percent intrastate. FEDERAL-STATE JOINT BOARD, U.S. BUREAU OF LABOR STATISTICS, MONITORING REPORT CC DOCKET NO. 87–339, at 246 (1990). This has been more the indirect than the direct consequence of intensified competition: the FCC initially required local exchange companies to charge long-distance companies rates far above marginal costs for access to interstate callers. When institutional customers and interexchange carriers began to bypass the local phone companies in order to evade these inflated charges, the FCC gradually reduced them and substituted a direct charge on ultimate subscribers.

I can take solace from the equivocal nature of these observations in the fact that I have been consistent in my equivocation. The beginning of wisdom in the devising of regulatory and deregulatory policies must be, as I put it in celebrating the "passing of the public utility concept,"

> a skepticism of the universal efficiency of both the unregulated market, on the one side, and of government enterprise on the other, sufficient to make it impossible for me simply to abandon the regulatory tool. Competition and regulation are both highly imperfect institutions. So is antitrust. It should not be surprising, therefore, that there is no single choice between them equally valid for all times and places. . . .[59]

The experience of the last decade or so justifies a somewhat less fatuous conclusion. I believe it has confirmed our historic presumption in favor of competitive markets: against the deregulatory fiasco of the S&Ls must be weighed the regulatory fiascos of nuclear power plant construction and the shortages and extreme distortions of natural gas markets during this same decade. Our recent experience demonstrates also that free markets may demand governmental interventions just as pervasive and quite possibly more imaginative than direct regulation; but its lesson is that those interventions should to the greatest extent possible preserve, supplement, and enhance competition, rather than suppress it. Finally, to the extent direct economic regulation continues to be required, it is preferable that it be of a kind compatible with competition, rather than obstructive of it.

In short, the lesson I take from recent history is that the evolution of regulatory policy will never come to an end. The path it takes—and we should make every effort to see that it takes—however, is the path not of a full circle or pendulum, which would take us back to where we started, but of a spiral, which has a direction. This is in a sense only an expression of a preference for seeking

---

59. It is important for me to make clear what it is that I have been consistently equivocal about. It has to do with selecting the set of institutional arrangements best suited to achieving economically optimal results, not with the propriety of economic efficiency as the primary goal of regulatory (or deregulatory) policy.

In contrast, the debate between advocates of regulation and deregulation is in very large measure about the latter, not the former issue. Opponents of deregulation will often protest— sometimes truculently, I can attest—that efficiency is not and should not be the sole or even the primary end of economic regulation. While I endorse the proposition that fairness and a more equitable distribution of income should be central goals of public policy, I also insist that proponents of such goals have every obligation to be just as rigorous in thinking about how they may best be served as the advocates of pure economic efficiency. And "best," in a world of scarcity, must mean "at minimum social cost." Restrictions on entry and price competition and distortions of the relationship between prices and marginal cost are usually irrational ways of achieving those ends, and to the extent regulation has served them in these ways, it has typically done so at excessive social cost. From this standpoint, one of the major accomplishments of deregulation has been to force us to seek more rational ways of achieving those goals. Neither privately nor governmentally-administered syndicalism or cartelization is a sensible way either to remedy the failures of unregulated market capitalism or to achieve a more humane distribution of income.

consistently to move in the direction of the first-best functioning of a market economy, rather than the second- or third-best world of centralized command and control.

Questions

1. According to Kahn, was deregulation primarily caused by the lobbying efforts of regulated industries or by independent factors such as technology? To what extent is the deregulation process independent of the affected industries?

2. What is "symmetry" in the regulatory process? Can regulators leave an industry to competitive forces until symmetry of the players has been accomplished?

3. Kahn faults government failure to "perform its essential competition-supplementing functions, such as antitrust enforcement," for many of the imperfections in the performance of deregulated industries. Is relaxed enforcement of antitrust laws inevitable in a deregulated environment? Is not rate-of-return regulation a form of antitrust regulation? If not, how does it differ from antitrust enforcement?

APPENDIX A:
TELECOMMUNICATIONS
GLOSSARY

Access Charge: Refers to two types of charges. The first is known as the *carrier common line (CCL) charge* or *carrier's carrier charge*. It is assessed by local-exchange carriers against toll carriers for interconnecting them with the local-exchange network. The second, the *subscriber line charge (SLC)*, is paid by exchange customers for access to the local-exchange network to make interexchange calls.

Bell System: A term synonymous with the predivestiture American Telephone and Telegraph Company, which principally consisted of twenty-three local-exchange operating companies, Western Electric Company, Bell Laboratories, and Long Lines. Long Lines became the core of postdivestiture AT&T.

BOCs: Bell Operating Companies. The twenty-two operating companies divested from the Bell system under the MFJ. They provide intraexchange transport of calls and local access to interexchange service.

Bypass: The circumvention of a charge for a particular service by use of a lower-cost alternative. Potential for bypass exists when a service is priced substantially above cost or when a different technology is available at a lower cost. Toll and exchange bypass occurs by means of satellite, microwave, private line, and/or cable television facilities.

CEI: Comparably Efficient Interconnection. A postdivestiture service requirement imposed on the BOCs to assure that unaffiliated companies can attach to the network as efficiently as the BOCs.

Class 5 Office: An industry designation of a local-dial switching office providing connections between customers within a town or local calling area and/or access to the toll network.

Class 4 Office: An industry designation of a toll switching office that provides routing decisions and connections to distant offices on the long-distance network; Class 4 offices interconnect with local-network facilities through the Class 5 offices.

Coaxial Cable: A cable consisting of an outer tube with an insulated wire center. Coaxial cable has a very large capacity for transmitting information and can carry about four dozen TV channels or thousands of voice conversations. Coaxial cable has been in use since about 1940; fiber-optic lines are being substituted for coaxial cable.

COMSAT: Communications Satellite Corp. A private organization created pursuant to the Communications Act of 1964 to serve as the U.S. signatory to INTELSAT.

CPE: Customer Premises Equipment. Any customer-supplied terminal equipment that is interconnected with the network at the customer's location. It includes everything from a fax machine to an answering machine to a telephone.

Domsat: Domestic Satellite System. A satellite system that generally provides service to a single nation. Fourteen countries operate domsats, including the United States.

Downlink: The transmission of radio signals from a satellite to an earth station.

Earth Station: A ground station that uses a parabolic antenna ("dish") to transmit or receive radio signals to or from a satellite.

ESP: Enhanced Service Provider. A company that provides a service beyond basic transmission service.

Fiber-Optic: A lightware technology that transports information more efficiently than copper or coaxial wire. One advantage is its capacity to carry data long distances without signal diminution.

Geostationary/Geosynchronous Orbit: A satellite orbit in which satellites are deployed 22,300 miles above the equator. In this position, the orbit is synchronized with the speed of the earth's rotation so that the satellite appears stationary from any point on the earth's surface. This allows earth station antennae to remain fixed on the satellite at all times.

High-Cost Pooling Arrangements: Companies serving rural areas experience higher costs of local-distribution facilities because of low customer density per mile of line. The high-cost pooling concept allows a subsidy to high-cost companies so that their rates are affordable to rural customers.

Independent Telephone Company: A telephone utility not affiliated with one of the Bell Operating Companies.

Information Services: A category of activities from which BOCs are prohibited under the MFJ. Generally a form of enhanced service that involves the content, rather than transmission, of communication.

ISDN: Integrated Services Digital Network. An end-to-end digital transmission network capable of transmitting voice, data, and video.

IXC: Interexchange Carrier. A telecommunication carrier authorized to provide service between LATAs, e.g., AT&T, US Sprint, MCI.

Jurisdictional Separations: A process by which costs of service are allocated between the intrastate and interstate jurisdictions.

LAN: Local Area Network. A private network providing high capacity transmission facilities, often in connection with computer-based services.

LEC: Local Exchange Carrier. A phone company providing intraLATA service and access to interLATA service.

"Lifeline" Service: A need-based program designed to promote universal telephone availability by subsidizing basic service to qualifying households. Similarly, the "Link Up America" program subsidizes installation costs for qualifying households.

Local Access & Transport Area (LATA): The designation of areas served by the Bell Operating Companies following divestiture from AT&T. The definition of LATAs is based on SMSAs (Standard Metropolitan Statistical Areas), which are specified by the U.S. Census Bureau.

Measured Service: An alternative to flat-rate service. Charges are based on number of calls, duration, length of haul, and/or time of day.

Microwave: A system of radio transmission that is limited to a line of sight between stations. It has a large capacity like coaxial cable systems and has been in use since the 1940s.

Modified Final Judgment (MFJ): The term applied to the divestiture agreement between the Department of Justice and AT&T settling the 1974 antitrust suit against AT&T. Among other things, it created seven regional holding companies comprising twenty-two Bell Operating Companies. The Bell Operating Companies provide intraLATA service. AT&T is restricted to interLATA service.

NTS: Non–Traffic Sensitive. This term describes a local distribution plant used to connect the customer with the telephone central office. The plant consists of the cable, inside wire, and customer premises equipment. The characteristic of this plant is that costs do not vary with usage.

OCC: "Other common carriers" providing long-distance telephone service (such as US Sprint and MCI). The use of this term has become less common.

OCMS: Optional Calling Measurement Service. Telephone service allowing residential customers outside, say, the San Francisco and Los Angeles metropolitan areas to call over specified routes within a forty-mile radius at reduced rates.

POP: Point of Presence. The point of connection of an interexchange carrier to a local-exchange carrier within a LATA. The carrier's carrier charge (or common line charge) is assessed at this point.

POTS: Plain Old Telephone Service. The term applied to regular telephone service without any enhanced feature.

Private Line: A leased telephone line permitting unlimited service between two points at a special rate and not connected to the regular telephone network. Private lines are available for voice and data transmission and for use as fire and burglar alarm circuits. Access for private lines to the local-exchange network is provided under *special access* tariffs.

Resale Carrier: A provider of long-distance service that primarily resells toll service provided by a telephone utility or toll carriers. Usually, a reseller owns a PBX switch but owns no circuits to distant points. Resellers charge customers rates below regular toll rates by "reselling" bulk services such as WATS and private line. The FCC has deregulated all interstate resale carriers.

ROC/RHC: Regional operating companies or regional holding companies. These seven companies, each serving more than one state, became the non–long-distance portion of the divested AT&T in 1984.

Separations and Settlement: The process by which two or more operating telephone companies divide revenues for jointly provided telephone service.

SMSA: A term applied by the U.S. Office of Management and Budget to counties, or aggregations of counties, that have one or more central core cities and that meet specified criteria of population, population density, commuting patterns, and social and economic integration.

Specialized Common Carrier: A somewhat dated term to describe a company offering telecommunications service between two or more points to large-volume users, generally using microwave or other advanced technology.

Subscriber Line Usage (SLU): Relative use of subscriber plant for various purposes (e.g., interstate toll, intrastate toll, local).

Subscriber Plant Factor (SPF): A basis of allocation of costs of subscriber plant between intrastate and interstate operations.

TS: Traffic Sensitive. Applied to costs of telephone plant on which the requirements vary with the volume of traffic carried. This plant consists of switches, trunk lines, and associated hardware.

Transponder: The component of a satellite that 1) receives an uplink signal; 2) shifts the frequency and amplifies the signal; and 3) retransmits it to the receiving earth station.

Trunk: A connection between two switching offices that is jointly used by a large number of customers.

Universal Service: A concept that telephone service should be available to everyone that wishes to have it. Universal service has not been specifically defined, but discussion of the subject usually relates to the fact that over 90 percent of the residences in the United States now have telephone service.

Uplink: The transmission of radio signals from an earth station to a satellite.

Value of Service: A monetary measure of the usefulness or necessity of utility service to a customer group.

VAN: Value-Added Network. Networks designed to provide an enhanced service to customers.

WATS: Wide Area Telephone Service. A bulk rate for message toll telephone service offered both on an Outward WATS and Inward WATS basis. Outward WATS allows a customer toll calling to a specified area at WATS rates instead of toll rates. Inward WATS permits any caller from a specified geographical area to call a specific customer, who pays the charges at WATS rates.

ZUM: Zone Usage Measurement. A method of pricing local calls and interexchange calls between rate centers. Messages are timed in one-minute increments. Evening and night discounts of 35 percent and 60 percent apply. The method is used by intraLATA carriers.

APPENDIX B:
COMMUNICATIONS ACT OF 1934

Title 47—Telegraphs, Telephones, and Radiotelegraphs

§ 151. Purposes of Chapter; Federal Communications Commission Created

For the purpose of regulating interstate and foreign commerce in communication by wire and radio so as to make available, so far as possible, to all the people of the United States a rapid, efficient, Nation-wide, and world-wide wire and radio communication service with adequate facilities at reasonable charges, for the purpose of the national defense, for the purpose of promoting safety of life and property through the use of wire and radio communications, and for the purpose of securing a more effective execution of this policy by centralizing authority heretofore granted by law to several agencies and by granting additional authority with respect to interstate and foreign commerce in wire and radio communication, there is created a commission to be known as the "Federal Communications Commission", which shall be constituted as hereinafter provided, and which shall execute and enforce the provisions of this chapter.

§ 152. Application of Chapter

(a) The provisions of this chapter shall apply to all interstate and foreign communication by wire or radio and all interstate and foreign transmission of energy by radio, which originates and/or is received within the United States, and to all persons engaged within the United States in such communication or such transmission of energy by radio, and to the licensing and regulating of all radio stations as hereinafter provided; but it shall not apply to persons engaged in wire or radio communication or transmission in the Canal Zone, or to wire or radio communication or transmission wholly within the Canal Zone. The provisions of this chapter shall apply with respect to cable service, to all persons engaged within the United States in providing such service, and to the facilities of cable operators which relate to such service, as provided in subchapter V-A.

(b) Except as provided in section 224 of this title and subject to the provisions of section 301 of this title and subchapter V-A of this chapter, nothing in this chapter shall be construed to apply or to give the Commission jurisdiction with respect to (1) charges, classifications, practices, services, facilities, or regulations for or in connection with intrastate communication service by wire or radio of any carrier, or (2) any carrier engaged in interstate or foreign communication solely through physical connection with the facilities of another carrier not directly or indirectly controlling or controlled by, or under direct or indirect common control with such carrier, or (3) any carrier engaged in interstate or foreign communication solely through connection by radio, or by wire and radio, with facilities, located in an adjoining State or in Canada or Mexico (where they adjoin the State in which the carrier is doing business), of another carrier not directly or indirectly controlling or controlled by, or under direct or indirect common control with such carrier, or (4) any carrier to which clause (2) or clause (3) of this subsection would be applicable except for furnishing interstate mobile radio communication service or radio communication service to mobile stations on land vehicles in Canada or Mexico; except that sections 201 to 205 of this title shall, except as otherwise provided therein, apply to carriers described in clauses (2), (3), and (4) of this subsection.

§ 153. Definitions

For the purposes of this chapter, unless the context otherwise requires—

(a) "Wire communication" or "communication by wire" means the transmission of writing, signs, signals, pictures, and sounds of all kinds by aid of wire, cable, or other like connection between the points of origin and reception of such transmission, including all instrumentalities, facilities, apparatus, and services (among other things, the receipt, forwarding, and delivery of communications) incidental to such transmission.

(b) "Radio communication" or "communication by radio" means the transmission by radio of writing, signs, signals, pictures, and sounds of all kinds, including all instrumentalities, facilities, apparatus, and services (among other things, the receipt, forwarding, and delivery of communications) incidental to such transmission.

(c) "Licensee" means the holder of a radio station license granted or continued in force under authority of this chapter.

(d) "Transmission of energy by radio" or "radio transmission of energy" includes both such transmission and all instrumentalities, facilities, and services incidental to such transmission.

(e) "Interstate communication" or "interstate transmission" means communication or transmission (1) from any State, Territory, or possession of the United States (other than the Canal Zone), or the District of Columbia, to any other State, Territory, or possession of the United States (other than the Canal Zone), or the District of Columbia, (2) from or to the United States to or from the Canal Zone, insofar as such communication or transmission takes place within the United States, or (3) between points within the United States but through a foreign country; but shall not, with respect to the provisions of subchapter II of this chapter (other than section 223 of this title), include wire or radio communication between points in the same State, Territory, or possession of the United States, or the District of Columbia, through any place outside thereof, if such communication is regulated by a State commission.

(f) "Foreign communication" or "foreign transmission" means communication or transmission from or to any place in the United States to or from a foreign country, or between a station in the United States and a mobile station located outside the United States.

(g) "United States" means the several States and Territories, the District of Columbia, and the possessions of the United States, but does not include the Canal Zone.

(h) "Common carrier" or "carrier" means any person engaged as a common carrier for hire, in interstate or foreign communication by wire or radio or interstate or foreign radio transmission of energy, except where reference is made to common carriers not subject to this chapter; but a person engaged in radio broadcasting shall not, insofar as such person is so engaged, be deemed a common carrier.

*   *   *

§ 154. Federal Communications Commission

(a) Number of commissioners; appointment

The Federal Communications Commission (in this chapter referred to as the "Commission") shall be composed of five commissioners appointed by the President, by and with the advice and consent of the Senate, one of whom the President shall designate as chairman.

(b) Qualifications

(1) Each member of the Commission shall be a citizen of the United States.

(2)(A) No member of the Commission or person employed by the Commission shall—

(i) be financially interested in any company or other entity engaged in the manufacture or sale of telecommunications equipment which is subject to regulation by the Commission;

(ii) be financially interested in any company or other entity engaged in the business of communication by wire or radio or in the use of the electromagnetic spectrum;

(iii) be financially interested in any company or other entity which controls any company or other entity specified in clause (i) or clause (ii), or which derives a significant portion of its total income from ownership of stocks, bonds, or other securities of any such company or other entity; or

(iv) be employed by, hold any official relation to, or own any stocks,bonds, or other securities of, any person significantly regulated by the Commission under this chapter;

except that the prohibitions established in this subparagraph shall apply only to financial interests in any company or other entity which has a significant interest in communications, manufacturing, or sales activities which are subject to regulation by the Commission.

(B)(i) The Commission shall have authority to waive, from time to time, the application of the prohibitions established in subparagraph (A) to persons employed by the Commission if the Commission determines that the financial interests of a person which are involved in a particular case are minimal, except that such waiver authority shall be subject to the provisions of section 208 of title 18. The waiver authority established in this subparagraph shall not apply with respect to members of the Commission.

(ii) In any case in which the Commission exercises the waiver authority established in this subparagraph, the Commission shall publish notice of such action in the Federal Register and shall furnish notice of such action to the appropriate committees of each House of the Congress. Each such notice shall include information regarding the identity of the person receiving the waiver, the position held by such person, and the nature of the financial interests which are the subject of the waiver.

(3) The Commission, in determining whether a company or other entity has a significant interest in communications, manufacturing, or sales activities which are subject to regulation by the Commission, shall consider (without excluding other relevant factors)—

(A) the revenues, investments, profits, and managerial efforts directed to the related communications, manufacturing, or sales activities of the company or other entity involved, as compared to the other aspects of the business of such company or other entity;

(B) the extent to which the Commission regulates and oversees the activities of such company or other entity;

(C) the degree to which the economic interests of such company or other entity may be affected by any action of the Commission; and

(D) the perceptions held by the public regarding the business activities of such company or other entity.

(4) Members of the Commission shall not engage in any other business, vocation, profession, or employment while serving as such members.

(5) The maximum number of commissioners who may be members of the same political party shall be a number equal to the least number of commissioners which constitutes a majority of the full membership of the Commission.

(c) Terms of office; vacancies

Commissioners shall be appointed for terms of five years and until their successors are appointed and have been confirmed and taken the oath of office, except that they shall not continue to serve beyond the expiration of the next session of Congress subsequent to the expiration of said fixed term of office; except that any person chosen to fill a vacancy shall be appointed only for the unexpired term of the commissioner whom he succeeds. No vacancy in the Commission shall impair the right of the remaining commissioners to exercise all the powers of the Commission.

§157. New Technologies and Services

(a) It shall be the policy of the United States to encourage the provision of new technologies and services to the public. Any person or party (other than the Commission) who opposes a new technology or service proposed to be permitted under this chapter shall have the burden to demonstrate that such proposal is inconsistent with the public interest.

(b) The Commission shall determine whether any new technology or service proposed in a petition or application is in the public interest within one year after such petition or application is filed or twelve months after December 8, 1983, if later. If the Commission initiates its own proceeding for a new technology or service, such proceeding shall be completed within 12 months after it is initiated or twelve months after December 8, 1983, if later.

SUBCHAPTER II—COMMON CARRIERS

§ 201. Service and Charges

(a) It shall be the duty of every common carrier engaged in interstate or foreign communication by wire or radio to furnish such communication service upon reasonable request therefor; and, in accordance with the orders of the Commission, in cases where the Commission, after opportunity for hearing, finds such action necessary or desirable in the public interest, to establish physical connections with other carriers, to establish through routes and charges applicable thereto and the divisions of such charges, and to establish and provide facilities and regulations for operating such through routes.

(b) All charges, practices, classifications, and regulations for and in connection with such communication service, shall be just and reasonable, and any such charge, practice, classification, or regulation that is unjust or unreasonable is declared to be unlawful: *Provided,* That communications by wire or radio subject to this chapter may be classified into day, night, repeated, unrepeated, letter, commercial, press, Government, and such other classes as the Commission may decide to be just and reasonable, and different charges may be made for the different classes of communications: *Provided further,* That nothing in this chapter or in any other provision of law shall be construed to prevent a common carrier subject to this chapter from entering into or operating under any contract with any common carrier not subject to this chapter, for the exchange of their services, if the Commission is of the opinion that such contract is not contrary to the public interest: *Provided further,* That nothing in this chapter or in any other provision of law shall prevent a common carrier subject to this chapter from furnishing reports of positions of ships at sea to newspapers of general circulation, either at a nominal charge or without charge, provided the name of such common carrier is displayed along with such ship position reports. The Commission may prescribe such rules and regulations as may be necessary in the public interest to carry out the provisions of this chapter.

§ 202. Discriminations and Preferences.

(a) Charges, services, etc.

It shall be unlawful for any common carrier to make any unjust or unreasonable discrimination in charges, practices, classifications, regulations, facilities, or services for or in connection with like communication service, directly or indirectly, by any means or device, or to make or give any undue or unreasonable preference or advantage to any particular person, class of persons, or locality, or to subject any particular person, class of persons, or locality to any undue or unreasonable prejudice or disadvantage.

(b) Charges or services included

Charges or services, whenever referred to in this chapter, include charges for, or services in connection with, the use of common carrier lines of communication, whether derived from wire or radio facilities, in chain broadcasting or incidental to radio communication of any kind.

(c) Penalty

Any carrier who knowingly violates the provisions of this section shall forfeit to the United States the sum of $6,000 for each such offense and $300 for each and every day of the continuance of such offense.

§ 203. Schedules of Charges

(a) Filing; public display

Every common carrier, except connecting carriers, shall, within such reasonable time as the Commission shall designate, file with the Commission and print and keep open for public inspection schedules showing all charges for itself and its connecting carriers for interstate and foreign wire or radio communication between the different points on its own system, and between points on its own system and points on the system of its connecting carriers or points on the system of any other carrier subject to this chapter when a through route has been established, whether such charges are joint or separate, and showing the classifications, practices, and regulations affecting such charges. Such schedules shall contain such other information, and be printed in such form, and be posted and kept open for public inspection in such places, as the Commission may by regulation require, and each such schedule shall give notice of its effective date; and such common carrier shall furnish such schedules to each of its connecting carriers, and such connecting carriers shall keep such schedules open for inspection in such public places as the Commission may require.

(b) Changes in schedule; discretion of Commission to modify requirements

(1) No change shall be made in the charges, classifications, regulations, or practices which have been so filed and published except after one hundred and twenty days notice to the Commission and to the public, which shall be published in such form and contain such information as the Commission may by regulations prescribe.

(2) The Commission may, in its discretion and for good cause shown, modify any requirement made by or under the authority of this section either in particular instances or by general order applicable to special circumstances or conditions except that the Commission may not require the notice period specified in paragraph (1) to be more than one hundred and twenty days.

(c) Overcharges and rebates

No carrier, unless otherwise provided by or under authority of this chapter, shall engage or participate in such communication unless schedules have been filed and published in accordance with the provisions of this chapter and with the regulations made thereunder; and no carrier shall (1) charge, demand, collect, or receive a greater or less or different compensation for such communication, or for any service in connection therewith, between the points named in any such schedule than the charges specified in the schedule then in effect, or (2) refund or remit by any means or device any portion of the charges so specified, or (3) extend to any person any privileges or facilities in such communication, or employ or enforce any classifications, regulations, or practices affecting such charges, except as specified in such schedule.

(d) Rejection or refusal

The Commission may reject and refuse to file any schedule entered for filing which does not provide and give lawful notice of its effective date. Any schedule so rejected by the Commission shall be void and its use shall be unlawful.

(e) Penalty for violations

In case of failure or refusal on the part of any carrier to comply with the provisions of this section or of any regulation or order made by the Commission thereunder, such carrier shall forfeit to the United States the sum of $6,000 for each such offense, and $300 for each and every day of the continuance of such offense.

§ 204. Hearings on New Charges; Suspension Pending Hearing; Refunds; Duration of Hearing; Appeal of Order Concluding Hearing

(a)(1) Whenever there is filed with the Commission any new or revised charge, classification, regulation, or practice, the Commission may either upon complaint or upon its own initiative without complaint, upon reasonable notice, enter upon a hearing concerning the lawfulness thereof; and pending such hearing and the decision thereon the Commission, upon delivering to the carrier or carriers affected thereby a statement in writing of its reasons for such suspension, may suspend the operation of such charge, classification, regulation, or practice, in whole or in part, but not for a longer period than five months beyond the time when it would otherwise go into effect; and after full hearing the Commission may make such order with reference thereto as would be proper in a proceeding initiated after such charge, classification, regulation, or practice had become effective. If the proceeding has not been concluded and an order made within the period of the suspension, the proposed new or revised charge, classification, regulation, or practice shall go into effect at the end of such period; but in case of a proposed charge for a new service or an increased charge, the Commission may by order require the interested carrier or carriers to keep accurate account of all amounts received by reason of such charge for a new service or increased charge, specifying by whom and in whose behalf such amounts are paid, and upon completion of the hearing and decision may by further order require the interested carrier or carriers to refund, with interest, to the persons in whose behalf such amounts were paid, such portion of such charge for a new service or increased charges as by its decision shall be found not justified. At any hearing involving a charge increased, or sought to be increased, the burden of proof to show that the increased charge, or proposed charge, is just and reasonable shall be upon the carrier, and the Commission shall give to the hearing and decision of such questions preference over all other questions pending before it and decide the same as speedily as possible.

(2)(A) Except as provided in subparagraph (B), the Commission shall, with respect to any hearing under this section, issue an order concluding such hearing within 12 months after the date that the charge, classification, regulation, or practice subject to the hearing becomes effective, or within 15 months after such date if the hearing raises questions of fact of such extraordinary complexity that the questions cannot be resolved within 12 months.

(B) The Commission shall, with respect to any such hearing initiated prior to November 3, 1988, issue an order concluding the hearing not later than 12 months after November 3, 1988.

(C) Any order concluding a hearing under this section shall be a final order and may be appealed under section 402(a) of this title.

(b) Notwithstanding the provisions of subsection (a) of this section, the Commission may allow part of a charge, classification, regulation, or practice to go into effect, based upon a written showing by the carrier or carriers affected, and an opportunity for written comment thereon by affected persons, that such partial authorization is just, fair, and reasonable. Additionally, or in combination with a partial authorization, the Commission, upon a similar showing, may allow all or part of a charge, classification, regulation, or practice to go into effect on a temporary basis pending further order of the Commission. Authorizations of temporary new or increased charges may include an accounting order of the type provided for in subsection (a) of this section.

§ 205. Commission Authorized to Prescribe Just and Reasonable Charges; Penalties for Violations

(a) Whenever, after full opportunity for hearing, upon a complaint or under an order for investigation and hearing made by the Commission on its own initiative, the Commission shall be of opinion that any charge, classification, regulation, or practice of any carrier or carriers is or will be in violation of any of the provisions of this chapter, the Commission is authorized and empowered to determine and prescribe what will be the just and reasonable charge or the maximum or minimum, or maximum and minimum, charge or charges to be thereafter observed, and what classification, regulation, or practice is or will be just, fair, and reasonable, to be thereafter followed, and to make an order that the carrier or carriers shall cease and desist from such violation to the extent that the Commission finds that the same does or will exist, and shall not thereafter publish, demand, or collect any charge other than the charge so prescribed, or in excess of the maximum or less than the minimum so prescribed, as the case may be, and shall adopt the classification and shall conform to and observe the regulation or practice so prescribed.

(b) Any carrier, any officer, representative, or agent of a carrier, or any receiver, trustee, lessee, or agent of either of them who knowingly fails or neglects to obey any order made under the provisions of this section shall forfeit to the United States the sum of $12,000 for each offense. Every distinct violation shall be a separate offense, and in case of continuing violation each day shall be deemed a separate offense.

§ 206. Carriers' Liability for Damages

In case any common carrier shall do, or cause or permit to be done, any act, matter, or thing in this chapter prohibited or declared to be unlawful, or shall omit to do any act, matter, or thing in this chapter required to be done, such common carrier shall be liable to the person or persons injured thereby for the full amount of damages sustained in consequence of any such violation of the provisions of this chapter, together with a reasonable counsel or attorney's fee, to be fixed by the court in every case of recovery, which attorney's fee shall be taxed and collected as part of the costs in the case.

§ 207. Recovery of Damages

Any person claiming to be damaged by any common carrier subject to the provisions of this chapter may either make complaint to the Commission as hereinafter provided for, or may bring suit for the recovery of the damages for which such common carrier may be liable under the provisions of this chapter, in any district court of the United States of competent jurisdiction; but such person shall not have the right to pursue both such remedies.

§ 208. Complaints to Commission; Investigations; Duration of Investigation; Appeal of Order Concluding Investigation

(a) Any person, any body politic, or municipal organization, or State commission, complaining of anything done or omitted to be done by any common carrier subject to this chapter, in contravention of the provisions thereof, may apply to said Commission by petition which shall briefly state the facts, whereupon a statement of the complaint thus made shall be forwarded by the Commission to such common carrier, who shall be called upon to satisfy the complaint or to answer the same in writing within a reasonable time to be specified by the Commission. If such common carrier within the time specified shall make reparation for the injury alleged to have been caused, the common carrier shall be relieved of liability to the complainant only for the particular violation of law thus complained of. If such carrier or carriers shall not satisfy the complaint within the time specified or there shall appear to be any reasonable ground for investigating said complaint, it shall be the duty of the Commission to investigate the matters complained of in such manner and by such means as it shall deem proper. No complaint shall at any time be dismissed because of the absence of direct damage to the complaint.

(b)(1) Except as provided in paragraph (2), the Commission shall, with respect to any investigation under this section of the lawfulness of a charge, classification, regulation, or practice, issue an order concluding such investigation within 12 months after the date on which the complaint was filed, or within 15 months after such date if the investigation raises questions of fact of such extraordinary complexity that the questions cannot be resolved within 12 months.

(2) The Commission shall, with respect to any such investigation initiated prior to November 3, 1988, issue an order concluding the investigation not later than 12 months after November 3, 1988.

(3) Any order concluding an investigation under paragraph (1) or (2) shall be a final order and may be appealed under section 402(a) of this title.

§ 209. Orders for Payment of Money

If, after hearing on a complaint, the Commission shall determine that any party complainant is entitled to an award of damages under the provisions of this chapter, the Commission shall make an order directing the carrier to pay to the complainant the sum to which he is entitled on or before a day named.

§ 210. Franks and Passes: Free Service to Governmental Agencies in Connection with National Defense

(a) Nothing in this chapter or in any other provision of law shall be construed to prohibit common carriers from issuing or giving franks to, or exchanging franks with each other for the use of, their officers, agents, employees, and their families, or, subject to such rules as the Commission may prescribe, from issuing, giving, or exchanging franks and passes to or with other common carriers not subject to the provisions of this chapter, for the use of their officers, agents, employees, and their families. The term "employees", as used in this section, shall include furloughed, pensioned, and superannuated employees.

(b) Nothing in this chapter or in any other provision of law shall be construed to prohibit common carriers from rendering to any agency of the Government free service in connection with the preparation for the national defense; *Provided,* That such free service may be rendered only in accordance with such rules and regulations as the Commission may prescribe therefor.

§ 211. Contracts of Carriers; Filing with Commission

(a) Every carrier subject to this chapter shall file with the Commission copies of all contracts, agreements, or arrangements with other carriers, or with common carriers not subject to the provisions of this chapter, in relation to any traffic affected by the provisions of this chapter to which it may be a party.

(b) The Commission shall have authority to require the filing of any other contracts of any carrier, and shall also have authority to exempt any carrier from submitting copies of such minor contracts as the Commission may determine.

§ 212. Interlocking Directorates; Officials Dealing in Securities

After sixty days from June 19, 1934, it shall be unlawful for any person to hold the position of officer or director of more than one carrier subject to this chapter, unless such holding shall have been authorized by order of the Commission, upon due showing in form and manner prescribed by the Commission, that neither public nor private interests will be adversely affected thereby: *Provided,* That the Commission may authorize persons to hold the position of officer or director in more than one such carrier, without regard to the requirements of this section, where it has found that one of the two or more carriers directly or indirectly owns more than 50 per centum of the stock of the other or others, or that 50 per centum or more of the stock of all such carriers is directly or indirectly owned by the same person. After this section takes effect it shall be unlawful for any officer or director of any carrier subject to this chapter to receive for his own benefit directly or indirectly, any money or thing of value in respect of negotiation, hypothecation, or sale of any securities issued or to be issued by such carrier, or to share in any of the proceeds thereof, or to participate in the making or paying of any dividends of such carriers from any funds properly included in capital account.

§ 213. Valuation of Property of Carrier

(a) Hearing

The Commission may from time to time, as may be necessary for the proper administration of this chapter, and after opportunity for hearing, make a valuation of all or of any part of the property owned or used by any carrier subject to this chapter, as of such date as the Commission may fix.

(b) Inventory

The Commission may at any time require any such carrier to file with the Commission an inventory of all or of any part of the property owned or used by said carrier, which inventory shall show the units of said property classified in such detail, and in such manner, as the Commission shall direct, and shall show the estimated cost of reproduction new of said units, and their reproduction cost new less depreciation, as of such date as the Commission may direct; and such carrier shall file such inventory within such reasonable time as the Commission by order shall require.

(c) Original cost

The Commission may at any time require any such carrier to file with the Commission a statement showing the original cost at the time of dedication to the public use of all or of any part of the property owned or used by said carrier. For the showing of such original cost said property shall be classified, and the original cost shall be defined, in such manner as the Commission may prescribe; and if any part of such cost cannot be determined from accounting or other records, the portion of the property for which such cost cannot be determined shall be reported to the Commission; and, if the Commission shall so direct, the original cost thereof shall be estimated in such manner as the Commission may prescribe. If the carrier owning the property at the time such original cost is reported shall have paid more or less than the original cost to acquire the same, the amount of such cost of acquisition, and any facts which the Commission may require in connection therewith, shall be reported with such original cost. The report made by a carrier under this subsection shall show the source or sources from which the original cost reported was obtained, and such other information as to the manner in which the report was prepared, as the Commission shall require.

(d) Easement, license or franchise

Nothing shall be included in the original cost reported for the property of any carrier under subsection (c) of this section on account of any easement, license, or franchise granted by the United States or by any State or political subdivision thereof, beyond the reasonable necessary expense lawfully incurred in obtaining such easement, license, or franchise from the public authority aforesaid, which expense shall be reported separately from all other costs in such detail as the Commission may require; and nothing shall be included in any valuation of the property of any carrier made by the Commission on account of any such easement, license, or franchise, beyond such reasonable necessary expense lawfully incurred as aforesaid.

(e) Improvements; changes in condition

The Commission shall keep itself informed of all new construction, extensions, improvements, retirements, or other changes in the condition, quantity, use, and classification of the property of common carriers, and of the cost of all additions and betterments thereto and of all changes in the investment therein, and may keep itself informed of current changes in costs and values of carrier properties.

(f) Additional information; access to records and data

For the purpose of enabling the Commission to make a valuation of any of the property of any such carrier, or to find the original cost of such property, or to find any other facts concerning the same which are required for use by the Commission, it shall be the duty of each such carrier to furnish to the Commission, within such reasonable time as the Commission may order, any information with respect thereto which the Commission may by order require, including copies of maps, contracts, reports of engineers, and other data, records, and papers, and to grant to all agents of the Commission free access to its property and its accounts, records, and memoranda whenever and wherever requested by any such duly authorized agent, and to cooperate with and aid the Commission in the work of making any such valuation or finding in such manner and to such extent as the Commission may require and direct, and all rules and regulations made by the Commission for the purpose of administering this section shall have the full force and effect of law. Unless otherwise ordered by the Commission, with the reasons therefor, the records and data of the Commission shall be open to the inspection and examination of the public. The Commission, in making any such valuation, shall be free to adopt any method of valuation which shall be lawful.

(g) Interstate Commerce Commission

Notwithstanding any provision of this chapter the Interstate Commerce Commission, if requested to do so by the Commission, shall complete, at the earliest practicable date, such valuations of properties of carriers subject to this chapter as are now in progress, and shall thereafter transfer to the Commission the records relating thereto.

(h) State commissions

Nothing in this section shall impair or diminish the powers of any State commission.

§ 214. Extension of Lines or Discontinuance of Service: Certificate of Public Convenience and Necessity

(a) Exceptions; temporary or emergency service or discontinuance of service; changes in plant, operation or equipment

No carrier shall undertake the construction of a new line or of an extension of any line, or shall acquire or operate any line, or extension thereof, or shall engage in transmission over or by means of such additional or extended line, unless and until there shall first have been obtained from the Commission a certificate that the present or future public convenience and necessity require or will require the construction, or operation, or construction and operation, of such additional or extended line: *Provided,* That no such certificate shall be required under this section for the construction, acquisition, or operation of (1) a line within a single State unless such line constitutes part of an interstate line, (2) local, branch, or terminal lines not exceeding ten miles in length, or (3) any line acquired under section 221 or 222 of this title: *Provided further,* That the Commission may, upon appropriate request being made, authorize temporary or emergency service, or the supplementing of existing facilities, without regard to the provisions of this section. No carrier shall discontinue, reduce, or impair service to a community, or part of a community, unless and until there shall first have been obtained from the Commission a certificate that neither the present nor future public convenience and necessity will be adversely affected thereby; except that the Commission may, upon appropriate request being made, authorize temporary or emergency discontinuance, reduction, or impairment of service, or partial discontinuance, reduction, or impairment of service, without regard to the provisions of this section. As used in this section the term "line" means any channel of communication established by the use of appropriate equipment, other than a channel of communication established by the interconnection of two or more existing channels: *Provided, however,* That nothing in this section shall be construed to require a certificate or other authorization from the Commission for any installation, replacement, or other changes in plant, operation, or equipment, other than new construction, which will not impair the adequacy or quality of service provided.

(b) Notification of Secretary of Defense, Secretary of State and State Governor

Upon receipt of an application for any such certificate, the Commission shall cause notice thereof to be given to, and shall cause a copy of such application to be filed with, the Secretary of Defense, the Secretary of State (with respect to such applications involving service to foreign points), and the Governor of each State in which such line is proposed to be constructed, extended, acquired, or operated, or in which such discontinuance, reduction, or impairment of service is proposed, with the right to those notified to be heard; and the Commission may require such published notice as it shall determine.

(c) Approval or disapproval; injunction

The Commission shall have power to issue such certificate as applied for, or to refuse to issue it, or to issue it for a portion or portions of a line, or extension thereof, or discontinuance, reduction, or impairment of service, described in the application, or for the partial exercise only of such right or privilege, and may attach to the issuance of the certificate such terms and conditions as in its judgment the public convenience and necessity may require. After issuance of such certificate, and not before, the carrier may, without securing approval other than such certificate, comply with the terms and conditions contained in or attached to the issuance of such certificate and proceed with the construction, extension, acquisition, operation, or discontinuance, reduction, or impairment of service covered thereby. Any construction, extension, acquisition, operation, discontinuance, reduction, or impairment of service contrary to the provisions of this section may be enjoined by any court of competent jurisdiction at the suit of the United States, the Commission, the State commission, any State affected, or any party in interest.

(d) Order of Commission; hearing; penalty

The Commission may, after full opportunity for hearing, in a proceeding upon complaint or upon its own initiative without complaint, authorize or require by order any carrier, party to such proceeding, to provide itself with adequate facilities for the expeditious and efficient performance of its service as a common carrier and to extend its line or to establish a public office; but no such authorization or order shall be made unless the Commission finds, as to such provision of facilities, as to such establishment of public offices, or as to such extension, that it is reasonably required in the interest of public convenience and necessity, or as to such extension or facilities that the expense involved therein will not impair the ability of the carrier to perform its duty to the public. Any carrier which refuses or neglects to comply with any order of the Commission made in pursuance of this paragraph shall forfeit to the United States $1,200 for each day during which such refusal or neglect continues.

§ 215. Examination of Transactions Relating to Furnishing of Services, Equipment, etc.; Reports to Congress

(a) Access to records and documents

The Commission shall examine into transactions entered into by any common carrier which relate to the furnishing of equipment, supplies, research, services, finances, credit, or personnel to such carrier and/or which may affect the charges made or to be made and/or the services rendered or to be rendered by such carrier, in wire or radio communication subject to this chapter, and shall report to the Congress whether any such transactions have affected or are likely to affect adversely the ability of the carrier to render adequate service to the public, or may result in any undue or unreasonable increase in charges or in the maintenance of undue or unreasonable charges for such service; and in order to fully examine into such transactions the Commission shall have access to and the right of inspection and examination of all accounts, records, and memoranda, including all documents, papers, and correspondence now or hereafter existing, of persons furnishing such equipment, supplies, research, services, finances, credit, or personnel. The Commission shall include in its report its recommendations for necessary legislation in connection with such transactions, and shall report specifically whether in its opinion legislation should be enacted (1) authorizing the Commission to declare any such transactions void or to permit such transactions to be carried out subject to such modification of their terms and conditions as the Commission shall deem desirable in the public interest; and/or (2) subjecting such transactions to the approval of the Commission where the person furnishing or seeking to furnish the equipment, supplies, research, services, finances, credit, or personnel is a person directly or indirectly controlling or controlled by, or under direct or indirect common control with such carrier; and/or (3) authorizing the Commission to require that all or any transactions of carriers involving the furnishing of equipment, supplies, research, services, finances, credit, or personnel to such carrier be upon competitive bids on such terms and conditions and subject to such regulations as it shall prescribe as necessary in the public interest.

(b) Wire telephone and telegraph services

The Commission shall investigate the methods by which and the extent to which wire telephone companies are furnishing wire telegraph service and wire telegraph companies are furnishing wire telephone service, and shall report its findings to Congress, together with its recommendations as to whether additional legislation on this subject is desirable.

(c) Exclusive dealing contracts

The Commission shall examine all contracts of common carriers subject to this chapter which prevent the other party thereto from dealing with another common carrier subject to this chapter, and shall report its findings to Congress, together with its recommendations as to whether additional legislation on this subject is desirable.

§ 216. Receivers and Trustees; Application of Chapter

The provisions of this chapter shall apply to all receivers and operating trustees of carriers subject to this chapter to the same extent that it applies to carriers.

§ 217. Agents' Acts and Omissions; Liability of Carrier

In construing and enforcing the provisions of this chapter, the act, omission, or failure of any officer, agent, or other person acting for or employed by any common carrier or user, acting within the scope of his employment, shall in every case be also deemed to be the act, omission, or failure of such carrier or user as well as that of the person.

§ 218. Management of Business; Inquiries by Commission

The Commission may inquire into the management of the business of all carriers subject to this chapter, and shall keep itself informed as to the manner and method in which the same is conducted and as to technical developments and improvements in wire and radio communication and radio transmission of energy to the end that the benefits of new inventions and developments may be made available to the people of the United States. The Commission may obtain from such carriers and from persons directly or indirectly controlling or controlled by, or under direct or indirect common control with, such carriers full and complete information necessary to enable the Commission to perform the duties and carry out the objects for which it was created.

§ 219. Reports by Carriers: Contents and Requirements Generally

(a) The Commission is authorized to require annual reports from all carriers subject to this chapter, and from persons directly or indirectly controlling or controlled by, or under direct or indirect common control with any such carrier, to prescribe the manner in which such reports shall be made, and to require from such persons specific answers to all questions upon which the Commission may need information. Except as otherwise required by the Commission, such annual reports shall show in detail the amount of capital stock issued, the amount and privileges of each class of stock, the amounts paid therefor, and the manner of payment for the same; the dividends paid and the surplus fund, if any; the number of stockholders (and the names of the thirty largest holders of each class of stock and the amount held by each); the funded and floating debts and the interest paid thereon; the cost and value of the carrier's property, franchises, and equipment; the number of employees and the salaries paid each class; the names of all officers and directors, and the amount of salary, bonus, and all other compensation paid to each; the amounts expended for improvements each year, how expended, and the character of such improvements; the earnings and receipts from each branch of business and from all sources; the operating and other expenses; the balances of profit and loss; and a complete exhibit of the financial operations of the carrier each year, including an annual balance sheet. Such reports shall also contain such information in relation to charges or regulations concerning charges, or agreements, arrangements, or contracts affecting the same, as the Commission may require.

(b) Such reports shall be for such twelve months' period as the Commission shall designate and shall be filed with the Commission at its office in Washington within three months after the close of the year for which the report is made, unless additional time is granted in any case by the Commission; and if any person subject to the provisions of this section shall fail to make and file said annual reports within the time above specified, or within the time extended by the Commission, for making and filing the same, or shall fail to make specific answer to any question authorized by the provisions of this section within thirty days from the time it is lawfully required so to do, such person shall forfeit to the United States the sum of $1,200 for each and every day it shall continue to be in default with respect thereto. The Commission may by general or special orders require any such carriers to file monthly reports of earnings and expenses and to file periodical and/or special reports concerning any matters with respect to which the Commission is authorized or required by law to act. If any such carrier shall fail to make and file any such periodical or special report within the time fixed by the Commission, it shall be subject to the forfeitures above provided.

§ 220. Accounts, Records, and Memoranda

(a) Forms

The Commission may, in its discretion, prescribe the forms of any and all accounts, records, and memoranda to be kept by carriers subject to this chapter, including the accounts, records, and memoranda of the movement of traffic, as well as of the receipts and expenditures of moneys.

(b) Depreciation charges

The Commission shall, as soon as practicable, prescribe for such carriers the classes of property for which depreciation charges may be properly included under operating expenses, and the percentages of depreciation which shall be charged with respect to each of such classes of property, classifying the carriers as it may deem proper for this purpose. The Commission may, when it deems necessary, modify the classes and percentages so prescribed. Such carriers shall not, after the Commission has prescribed the classes of property for which depreciation charges may be included, charge to operating expenses any depreciation charges on classes of property other than those prescribed by the Commission, or after the Commission has prescribed percentages of depreciation, charge with respect to any class of property a percentage of depreciation other than that prescribed therefor by the Commission. No such carrier shall in any case include in any form under its operating or other expenses any depreciation or other charge or expenditure included elsewhere as a depreciation charge or otherwise under its operating or other expenses.

(c) Access to information: burden of proof

The Commission shall at all times have access to and the right of inspection and examination of all accounts, records, and memoranda, including all documents, papers, and correspondence now or hereafter existing, and kept or required to be kept by such carriers, and the provisions of this section respecting the preservation and destruction of books, papers, and documents shall apply thereto. The burden of proof to justify every accounting entry questioned by the Commission shall be on the person making, authorizing, or requiring such entry and the Commission may suspend a charge or credit pending submission of proof by such person. Any provision of law prohibiting the disclosure of the contents of messages or communications shall not be deemed to prohibit the disclosure of any matter in accordance with the provisions of this section.

(d) Penalty for failure to comply

In case of failure or refusal on the part of any such carrier to keep such accounts, records, and memoranda on the books and in the manner prescribed by the Commission, or to submit such accounts, records, memoranda, documents, paper, and correspondence as are kept to the inspection of the Commission or any of its authorized agents, such carrier shall forfeit to the United Sates the sum of $6,000 for each day of the continuance of each such offense.

(e) False entry; destruction; penalty

Any person who shall willfully make any false entry in the accounts of any book of accounts or in any record or memoranda kept by any such carrier, or who shall willfully destroy, mutilate, alter, or by any other means or device falsify any such account, record, or memoranda, or who shall willfully neglect or fail to make full, true, and correct entries in such accounts, records, or memoranda of all facts and transactions appertaining to the business of the carrier, shall be deemed guilty of a misdemeanor, and shall be subject, upon conviction, to a fine of not less than $1,000 or more than $5,000 or imprisonment for a term of not less than one year nor more than three years, or both such fine and imprisonment: *Provided,* That the Commission may in its discretion issue orders specifying such operating, accounting, or financial papers, records, books, blanks, or documents which may, after a reasonable time, be destroyed, and prescribing the length of time such books, papers, or documents shall be preserved.

(f) Confidentiality of information

No member, officer, or employee of the Commission shall divulge any fact or information which may come to his knowledge during the course of examination of books or other accounts, as hereinbefore provided, except insofar as he may be directed by the Commission or by a court.

(g) Use of other forms; alterations in prescribed forms

After the Commission has prescribed the forms and manner of keeping of accounts, records, and memoranda to be kept by any person as herein provided, it shall be unlawful for such person to keep any other accounts, records, or memoranda than those so prescribed or such as may be approved by the Commission or to keep the accounts in any other manner than that prescribed or approved by the Commission. Notice of alterations by the Commission in the required manner or form of keeping accounts shall be given to such persons by the Commission at least six months before the same are to take effect.

(h) Exemption; regulation by State commission

The Commission may classify carriers subject to this chapter and prescribe different requirements under this section for different classes of carriers, and may, if it deems such action consistent with the public interest, except the carriers of any particular class or classes in any State from any of the requirements under this section in cases where such carriers are subject to State commission regulation with respect to matters to which this section relates.

(i) Consultation with State commissions

The Commission, before prescribing any requirements as to accounts, records, or memoranda, shall notify each State commission having jurisdiction with respect to any carrier involved, and shall give reasonable opportunity to each such commission to present its views, and shall receive and consider such views and recommendations.

(j) Report to Congress on need for further legislation

The Commission shall investigate and report to Congress as to the need for legislation to define further or harmonize the powers of the Commission and of State commissions with respect to matters to which this section relates.

§221. Consolidations and Mergers of Telephone Companies

(a) Notification of State Governor and State commission; public hearing; certification

Upon application of one or more telephone companies for authority to consolidate their properties or a part thereof into a single company, or for authority for one or more such companies to acquire the whole or any part of the property of another telephone company or other telephone companies or the control thereof by the purchase of securities or by lease or in any other like manner, when such consolidated company would be subject to this chapter, the Commission shall give reasonable notice in writing to the governor of each of the States in which the physical property affected, or any part thereof, is situated, and to the State commission having jurisdiction over telephone companies, and to such other persons as it may deem advisable, and shall afford such parties a reasonable opportunity to submit comments on the proposal. A public hearing shall be held in all cases where a request therefore is made by a telephone company, an association of telephone companies, a State commission, or local governmental authority. If the Commission finds that the proposed consolidation, acquisition, or control will be of advantage to the persons to whom service is to be rendered and in the public interest, it shall certify to that effect; and thereupon any Act or Acts of Congress making the proposed transaction unlawful shall not apply. Nothing in this subsection shall be construed as in anywise limiting or restricting the powers of the several States to control and regulate telephone companies.

(b) State jurisdiction over services

Subject to the provisions of sections 225 and 301 of this title, nothing in this chapter shall be construed to apply, or to give the Commission jurisdiction, with respect to charges, classifications, practices, services, facilities, or regulations for or in connection with wire, mobile, or point-to-point radio telephone exchange service, or any combination thereof, even though a portion of such exchange service constitutes interstate or foreign communication, in any case where such matters are subject to regulation by a State commission or by local governmental authority.

(c) Determination of property used in interstate toll service

For the purpose of administering this chapter as to carriers engaged in wire telephone communication, the Commission may classify the property of any such carrier used for wire telephone communication, and determine what property of said carrier shall be considered as used in interstate or foreign telephone toll service. Such classification shall be made after hearing, upon notice to the carrier, the State commission (or the Governor, if the State has no State commission) of any State in which the property of said carrier is located, and such other persons as the Commission may prescribe.

(d) Valuation of property

In making a valuation of the property of any wire telephone carrier the Commission, after making the classification authorized in this section, may in its discretion value only that part of the property of such carrier determined to be used in interstate or foreign telephone toll service.

§ 222. Competition Among Record Carriers

(a) Definitions

For purposes of this section:

(1) The term "primary existing international record carrier" means any record carrier which (A) derives a majority of its revenues during any calendar year from the provision of international record communications services between points of entry into or exit from the United States and points outside the United States; (B) is eligible, on December 29, 1981, to obtain record traffic from a record carrier in the United States for delivery outside the United States; and (C) is engaged in the direct provision of record communications services between the United States and four or more continents.

(2) The term "record carrier" means a common carrier engaged in the offering for hire of any record communications service, including service on interstate network facilities between two points located in the same State. Such term does

not include any common carrier which derives a majority of its revenues during any calendar year from the provision of services other than record communications service.

(3) The term "record communications service" means those services traditionally offered by telegraph companies, such as telegraph, telegram, telegram exchange, and similar services involving an interconnected network of teletypewriters.

(b) Exercise of authorities by Commission

(1) The Commission shall, to the maximum extent feasible, promote the development of fully competitive domestic and international markets in the provision of record communications service, so that the public may obtain record communications service and facilities (including terminal equipment) the variety and price of which are governed by competition. In order to meet the purposes of this section, the Commission shall forbear from exercising its authority under the chapter as the development of competition among record carriers reduces the degree of regulation necessary to protect the public.

(2) In furtherance of the purposes of this section, record carriers shall not impose upon users of any regulated record communications services the costs of any other services or facilities (including terminal equipment), whether regulated or unregulated.

(c) Implementation by Commission; procedures applicable

(1)(A)(i) In implementing its responsibilities under section 201(a) of this title, the Commission shall require each record carrier to make available to any other record carrier, upon reasonable request, full interconnection with any facility operated by such record carrier, and used primarily to provide record communications service. Such facility shall be made available, through written agreement, upon terms and conditions which are just, fair, and reasonable, and which are otherwise consistent with the purposes of this section.

(ii)(I) Subject to the provisions of subclause (II), if a request for interconnection under clause (i) is for the purpose of providing international record communications service, then the agreement entered into under clause (i) shall require that the allocation of record communications service between points outside the United States and points of entry in the United States shall be based upon a pro rata share of record communications service between points of exit out of the United States and points outside the United States provided by the carrier making such request for interconnection.

(II) The requirement established in subclause (I) shall not apply in any case in which the customer requesting any record communications service between a point outside the United States and a point of entry in the United States has the option to specify the international record carrier which will provide such record communications service.

(B) The Commission shall require that—

(i) if any record carrier engages both in the offering for hire of domestic record communications services and in the offering for hire of international record communications services, then such record carrier shall be treated as a separate domestic record carrier and a separate international record carrier for purposes of administering interconnection requirements;

(ii) in any case in which such separate domestic record carrier furnishes interconnection to such separate international record carrier, any interconnection which such separate domestic record carrier furnishes to other international record carriers shall be (I) equal in type and quality; and (II) made available at the same rates and upon the same terms and conditions; and

(iii) in any case in which such separate international record carrier furnishes interconnection to such separate domestic record carrier, any interconnection which such separate international record carrier furnishes to other domestic record carriers shall be (I) equal in type and quality; and (II) made available at the same rates and upon the same terms and conditions.

The requirements of clauses (i), (ii), and (iii) shall not apply to a record carrier if such record carrier does not have a significant share of the market for record communications services.

(2) If any request made by a record carrier under paragraph (1)(A)(i) will require an agreement under which any record communications service or facility operated by one of the parties to such agreement will be used by any other party to such agreement, then such agreement shall establish a nondiscriminatory formula for the equitable allocation of revenues derived from such use between the parties to such agreement, except that each party to such agreement shall have the right to establish the total price charged by such party to the public for any such service which is originated by such party, consistent with the provisions of section 203 of this title. To the extent possible, and consistent with the provisions of paragraph (3)(B)(ii), the Commission shall require that such equitable allocation of revenues be based upon the costs of the record communications service or facility employed as a result of such agreement.

(3)(A) The Commission, as soon as practicable (but not later than fifteen days) after December 29, 1981, shall convene a meeting among all record carriers which the Commission determines would be parties to any agreement required by paragraph (1)(A)(i). Such meeting shall be held for the purpose of negotiating any such agreement. Representatives of the Commission shall attend such meeting for purposes of monitoring and presiding over such negotiations.

(B)(i) In the case of any such required agreement, if—

(I) the record carrier subject to the interconnection requirement; and

(II) a majority of the primary existing international record carriers involved in the meeting convened by the Commission under subparagraph (A); fail to enter into an agreement before the end of the forty-five day period following the beginning of such meeting, then the Commission shall issue an interim or final order which establishes a just, fair, reasonable, and nondiscriminatory agreement which is consistent with the purposes of this section. Any such agreement established by the Commission shall be binding upon such parties.

(ii) Such interim or final order shall be issued not later than ninety days after the date on which the Commission convenes the meeting under subparagraph (A). In the case of any such required agreement, if—

(I) the record carrier subject to the interconnection requirement; and

(II) a majority of the primary existing international record carriers involved in the meeting convened by the Commission under subparagraph (A);

reach an agreement which complies with the requirements of this section, and such agreement is entered into before the issuance of such order by the Commission under this subparagraph, then such agreement of the parties shall take effect and the Commission shall not be required to issue any such order.

(C) Any record carrier which is not subject to the agreement entered into, or established by the Commission, under this paragraph may elect to be subject to the terms of such agreement upon furnishing written notice to the Commission and to all existing parties to such agreement. After a carrier makes such an election, the terms and arrangements established by the agreement shall apply to such carrier to the extent practicable, as determined by the Commission.

(4) The Commission shall have authority to vacate or modify any agreement entered into by any record carriers under this section if the Commission determines that (A) such agreement is not consistent with the purposes of this section; or (B) such agreement unjustly or unreasonably discriminates against any record carrier.

(5) If the Western Union Telegraph Company submits an application to the Commission for authority to provide international record communications service, the Commission shall not have any authority to take any final action with respect to such application until the end of the one hundred and twenty-day period following the date a written agreement is entered into between such Company and other record carriers under paragraph (3), or following the effective date of any interim or final order issued by the Commission under paragraph (3)(B) with respect to such carriers. The limitation upon Commission authority established in this paragraph shall expire at the end of the two hundred and ten-day period following December 29, 1981.

(d) Domestic and international market service

Subject to the provisions of subsection (c)(5) of this section, each record carrier may provide record communications service in the United States domestic market and in the international market. Any record carrier seeking to provide domestic record communications service may provide such service without submitting an application to the Commission under section 214 of this title unless the Commission requires such a submission. The Commission shall act expeditiously upon any application submitted pursuant to section 214 of this title.

(e) Termination of certain statutory oversight authorities of Commission

(1) At the end of the 36-month period following December 29, 1981, the provisions of subsection (c) of this section, other than paragraph (1)(B) of such subsection, shall cease to have any force or effect.

(2) The provisions of paragraph (1) shall not be construed to affect the obligation of any carrier to interconnect with any other carrier pursuant to this chapter.

§ 223. Obscene or Harassing Telephone Calls in the District of Columbia or in Interstate or Foreign Communications

(a) Prohibited general purposes

Whoever—

(1) in the District of Columbia or in interstate or foreign communication by means of telephone—

(A) makes any comment, request, suggestion or proposal which is obscene, lewd, lascivious, filthy, or indecent;

(B) makes a telephone call, whether or not conversation ensues, without disclosing his identity and with intent to annoy, abuse, threaten, or harass any person at the called number;

(C) makes or causes the telephone or another repeatedly or continuously to ring, with intent to harass any person at the called number; or

(D) makes repeated telephone calls, during which conversation ensues, solely to harass any person at the called number; or

(2) knowingly permits any telephone facility under his control to be used for any purpose prohibited by this section.

shall be fined not more than $50,000 or imprisoned not more than six months, or both.

(b) Prohibited commercial purposes; defense to prosecution

(1) Whoever knowingly—

(A) within the United States, by means of telephone, makes (directly or by recording device) any obscene communication for commercial purposes to any person, regardless of whether the maker of such communication placed the call; or

(B) permits any telephone facility under such person's control to be used for an activity prohibited by subparagraph (A),

shall be fined in accordance with Title 18, or imprisoned not more than two years, or both.

(2) Whoever knowingly—

(A) within the United States, by means of telephone, makes (directly or by recording device) any indecent communication for commercial purposes which is available to any person under 18 years of age or to any other person without that person's consent, regardless of whether the maker of such communication placed the call; or

(B) permits any telephone facility under such person's control to be used for an activity prohibited by subparagraph (A), shall be fined not more than $50,000 or imprisoned not more than six months, or both.

(3) It is a defense to prosecution under paragraph (2) of this subsection that the defendant restrict access to the prohibited communication to persons 18 years of age or older in accordance with subsection (c) of this section and with such procedures as the Commission may prescribe by regulation

(4) In addition to the penalties under paragraph (1), whoever within the United States intentionally violates paragraph (1) or (2) shall be subject to a fine of not more than $50,000 for each violation. For purposes of this paragraph, each day of violation shall constitute a separate violation.

(5)(A) In addition to the penalties under paragraphs (1), (2), and (5), whoever, within the United States, violates paragraph (1) or (2) shall be subject to a civil fine of not more than $50,000 for each violation. For purposes of this paragraph, each day of violation shall constitute a separate violation.

(B) A fine under this paragraph may be assessed either—

(i) by a court, pursuant to civil action by the Commission or any attorney employed by the Commission who is designated by the Commission for such purposes, or

(ii) by the Commission after appropriate administrative proceedings.

(6) The Attorney General may bring a suit in the appropriate district court of the United States to enjoin any act or practice which violates paragraph (1) or (2). An injunction may be granted in accordance with the Federal Rules of Civil Procedure.

(c) Restriction on access to subscribers by common carriers; judicial remedies respecting restrictions

(1) A common carrier within the District of Columbia or within any State, or in interstate or foreign commerce, shall not, to the extent technically feasible, provide access to a communication specified in subsection (b) of this section from the telephone of any subscriber who has not previously requested in writing the carrier to provide access to such communication if the carrier collects from subscribers an identifiable charge for such communication that the carrier remits, in whole or in part, to the provider of such communication.

(2) Except as provided in paragraph (3), no cause of action may be brought in any court or administrative agency against any common carrier, or any of its affiliates, including their officers, directors, employees, agents, or authorized representatives on account of—

(A) any action which the carrier demonstrates was taken in good faith to restrict access pursuant to paragraph (1) of this subsection; or

(B) any access permitted—

(i) in good faith reliance upon the lack of any representation by a provider of communications that communications provided by that provider are communications specified in subsection (b) of this section, or

(ii) because a specific representation by the provider did not allow the carrier, acting in good faith, a sufficient period to restrict access to communications described in subsection (b) of this section.

(3) Notwithstanding paragraph (2) of this subsection, a provider of communications services to which subscribers are denied access pursuant to paragraph (1) of this subsection may bring an action for a declaratory judgment or similar action in a court. Any such action shall be limited to the question of whether the communications which the provider seeks to provide fall within the category of communications to which the carrier will provide access only to subscribers who have previously requested such access.

§ 224. Pole Attachments

(a) Definitions

As used in this section:

(1) The term "utility" means any person whose rates or charges are regulated by the Federal Government or a State and who owns or controls poles, ducts,

conduits, or rights-of-way used, in whole or in part, for wire communication. Such term does not include any railroad, any person who is cooperatively organized, or any person owned by the Federal Government or any State.

(2) The term "Federal Government" means the Government of the United States or any agency or instrumentality thereof.

(3) The term "State" means any State, territory, or possession of the United States, the District of Columbia, or any political subdivision, agency, or instrumentality thereof.

(4) The term "pole attachment" means any attachment by a cable television system to a pole, duct, conduit, or right-of-way owned or controlled by a utility.

(b) Authority of Commission to regulate rates, terms, and conditions; enforcement powers; promulgation of regulations

(1) Subject to the provisions of subsection (c) of this section, the Commission shall regulate the rates, terms, and conditions for pole attachments to provide that such rates, terms, and conditions are just and reasonable, and shall adopt procedures necessary and appropriate to hear and resolve complaints concerning such rates, terms, and conditions. For purposes of enforcing any determinations resulting from complaint procedures established pursuant to this subsection, the Commission shall take such action as it deems appropriate and necessary, including issuing cease and desist orders, as authorized by section 312(b) of this title.

(2) Within 180 days from February 21, 1978, the Commission shall prescribe by rule regulations to carry out the provisions of this section.

(c) State regulatory authority over rates, terms, and conditions; preemption; certification; circumstances constituting State regulation

(1) Nothing in this section shall be construed to apply to, or to give the Commission jurisdiction with respect to rates, terms, and conditions for pole attachments in any case where such matters are regulated by a State.

(2) Each State which regulates the rates, terms, and conditions for pole attachments shall certify to the Commission that—

(A) it regulates such rates, terms, and conditions; and

(B) in so regulating such rates, terms, and conditions, the State has the authority to consider and does consider the interests of the subscribers of cable television services, as well as the interests of the consumers of the utility services.

(3) For purposes of this subsection, a State shall not be considered to regulate the rates, terms, and conditions for pole attachments—

(A) unless the State has issued and made effective rules and regulations implementing the State's regulatory authority over pole attachments; and

(B) with respect to any individual matter, unless the State takes final action on a complaint regarding such matter—

(i) within 180 days after the complaint is filed with the State, or

(ii) within the applicable period prescribed for such final action in such rules and regulations of the State, if the prescribed period does not extend beyond 360 days after the filing of such complaint.

(d) Determination of just and reasonable rates; "usable space" defined

(1) For purposes of subsection (b) of this section, a rate is just and reasonable if it assures a utility the recovery of not less than the additional costs of providing pole attachments, nor more than an amount determined by multiplying the percentage of the total usable space, or the percentage of the total duct or conduit capacity, which is occupied by the pole attachment by the sum of the operating expenses and actual capital costs of the utility attributable to the entire pole, duct, conduit, or right-of-way.

(2) As used in this subsection, the term "usable space" means the space above the minimum grade level which can be used for the attachment of wires, cables, and associated equipment.

§ 225. Telecommunications Services for Hearing-Impaired and Speech-Impaired Individuals

(a) Definitions

As used in this section—

(1) Common carrier or carrier

The term "common carrier" or "carrier" includes any common carrier engaged in interstate communication by wire or radio as defined in section 153(h) of this title and any common carrier engaged in intrastate communication by wire or radio, notwithstanding sections 152(b) and 221(b) of this title.

(2) TDD

The term "TDD" means a Telecommunications Device for the Deaf, which is a machine that employs graphic communication in the transmission of coded signals through a wire or radio communication system.

(3) Telecommunications relay services

The term "telecommunications relay services" means telephone transmission services that provide the ability for an individual who has a hearing impairment or speech impairment to engage in communication by wire or radio with a hearing individual in a manner that is functionally equivalent to the ability of an individual who does not have a hearing impairment or speech impairment to communicate using voice communication services by wire or radio. Such term includes services that enable two-way communication between an individual who uses a TDD or other nonvoice terminal device and an individual who does not use such a device.

(b) Availability of telecommunications relay services

(1) In general

In order to carry out the purposes established under section 151 of this title, to make available to all individuals in the United States a rapid, efficient nationwide communication service, and to increase the utility of the telephone system of the Nation, the Commission shall ensure that interstate and intrastate telecommunications relay services are available, to the extent possible and in the most efficient manner, to hearing-impaired and speech-impaired individuals in the United States.

(2) Use of general authority and remedies

For the purposes of administering and enforcing the provisions of this section and the regulations prescribed thereunder, the Commission shall have the same authority, power, and functions with respect to common carriers engaged in intrastate communication as the Commission has in administering and enforcing the provisions of this title with respect to any common carrier engaged in interstate communication. Any violation of this section by any common carrier engaged in intrastate communication shall be subject to the same remedies, penalties, and procedures as are applicable to a violation of this chapter by a common carrier engaged in interstate communication.

(c) Provision of services

Each common carrier providing telephone voice transmission services shall, not later than 3 years after July 26, 1990, provide in compliance with the regulations prescribed under this section, throughout the area in which it offers service, telecommunications relay services, individually, through designees, through a competitively selected vendor, or in concert with other carriers. A common carrier shall be considered to be in compliance with such regulations—

(1) with respect to intrastate telecommunications relay services in any State that does not have a certified program under subsection (f) of this section and with respect to interstate telecommunications relay services, if such common carrier (or other entity through which the carrier is providing such relay services) is in compliance with the Commission's regulations under subsection (d) of this section; or

(2) with respect to intrastate telecommunications relay services in any State that has a certified program under subsection (f) of this section for such State, if such common carrier (or other entity through which the carrier is providing such relay services) is in compliance with the program certified under subsection (f) of this section for such State.

(d) Regulations

(1) In general

The Commission shall, not later than 1 year after July 26, 1990, prescribe regulations to implement this section, including regulations that—

(A) establish functional requirements, guidelines, and operations procedures for telecommunications relay services;

(B) establish minimum standards that shall be met in carrying out subsection (c) of this section;

(C) require that telecommunications relay services operate every day for 24 hours per day;

(D) require that users of telecommunications relay services pay rates no greater than the rates paid for functionally equivalent voice communication services with respect to such factors as the duration of the call, the time of day, and the distance from point of origination to point of termination;

(E) prohibit relay operators from failing to fulfill the obligations of common carriers by refusing calls or limiting the length of calls that use telecommunications relay services;

(F) prohibit relay operators from disclosing the content of any relayed conversation and from keeping records of the content of any such conversation beyond the duration of the call; and

(G) prohibit relay operators from intentionally altering a relayed conversation.

(2) Technology

The Commission shall ensure that regulations prescribed to implement this section encourage, consistent with section 157(a) of this title, the use of existing technology and do not discourage or impair the development of improved technology.

*   *   *

§226. Telephone Operator Services

(a) Definitions

As used in this section—

(1) The term 'access code' means a sequence of numbers that, when dialed, connect the caller to the provider of operator services associated with that sequence.

(2) The term "aggregator' means any person that, in the ordinary course of its operations, makes telephones available to the public or to transient users of its premises, for interstate telephone calls using a provider of operator services.

(3) The term 'call splashing' means the transfer of a telephone call from one provider of operator services to another such provider in such a manner that the subsequent provider is unable or unwilling to determine the location of the origination of the call and, because of such inability or unwillingness, is prevented from billing the call on the basis of such location.

(4) The term 'consumer' means a person initiating any interstate telephone call using operator services.

(5) The term 'equal access' has the meaning given that term in Appendix B of the Modification of Final Judgment entered August 24, 1982, in United States v. Western Electric, Civil Action No. 82–0192 (United States District Court, District of Columbia), as amended by the Court in its orders issued prior to the enactment of this section.

(6) The term 'equal access code' means an access code that allows the public to obtain an equal access connection to the carrier associated with that code.

(7) The term 'operator services' means any interstate telecommunications service initiated from an aggregator location that includes, as a component, any automatic or live assistance to a consumer to arrange for billing or completion, or both, of an interstate telephone call through a method other than—

(A) automatic completion with billing to the telephone from which the call originated; or

(B) completion through an access code used by the consumer, with billing to an account previously established with the carrier by the consumer.

(8) The term 'presubscribed provider of operator services' means the interstate provider of operator services to which the consumer is connected

when the consumer places a call using a provider of operator services without dialing an access code.

(9) The term 'provider of operator services' means any common carrier that provides operator services or any other person determined by the Commission to be providing operator services.

(b) Requirements for Providers of Operator Services

(1) In general

Beginning not later than 30 days after the date of enactment of this section, each provider of operator services shall, at a minimum—

(A) identify itself, audibly and distinctly, to the consumer at the beginning of each telephone call and before the consumer incurs any charge for the call;

(B) permit the consumer to terminate the telephone call at no charge before the call is connected;

(C) disclose immediately to the consumer, upon request and at no charge to the consumer—

(i) a quote of its rates or charges for the call;

(ii) the methods by which such rates or charges will be collected; and

(iii) the methods by which complaints concerning such rates, charges, or collection practices will be resolved;

(D) ensure, by contract or tariff, that each aggregator for which such provider is the presubscribed provider of operator services is in compliance with the requirements of subsection (c) and, if applicable, subsection (e)(1);

(E) withhold payment (on a location-by-location basis) of any compensation, including commissions, to aggregators if such provider reasonably believes that the aggregator (i) is blocking access by means of "950" or "800" numbers to interstate common carriers in violation of subsection (c)(1)(B) or (ii) is blocking access to equal access codes in violation of rules the Commission may prescribe under subsection (e)(1);

(F) not bill for unanswered telephone calls in areas where equal access is available;

(G) not knowingly bill for unanswered telephone calls where equal access is not available;

(H) not engage in call splashing, unless the consumer requests to be transferred to another provider of operator services, the consumer is informed prior to incurring any charges that the rates for the call may not reflect the rates from the actual originating location of the call, and the consumer then consents to be transferred;

(I) except as provided in subparagraph (H), not bill for a call that does not reflect the location of the origination of the call; and

(J) not bill an interexchange telephone call to a billing card number which—

(i) is issued by another provider of operator services, and

(ii) permits the identification of the other provider, unless the call is billed at a rate not greater than the other provider's rate for the call, the consumer requests a special service that is not available under tariff from the other provider, or the consumer expressly consents to a rate greater than the other provider's rate.

(2) Additional requirements for first 3 years

In addition to meeting the requirements of paragraph (1), during the 3-year period beginning on the date that is 30 days after the date of enactment of this section, each presubscribed provider of operator services shall identify itself audibly and distinctly to the consumer, not only as required in paragraph (1)(A), but also for a second time before connecting the call and before the consumer incurs any charge.

(c) Requirements for Aggregators

(1) In general

Each aggregator, beginning not later than 30 days after the date of enactment of this section, shall—

(A) post on or near the telephone instrument, in plain view of consumers—

(i) the name, address, and toll-free telephone number of the provider of operator services;

(ii) a written disclosure that the rates for all operator-assisted calls are available on request, and that consumers have a right to obtain access to the interstate common carrier of their choice and may contact their preferred interstate common carriers for information on accessing that carrier's service using that telephone; and

(iii) the name and address of the enforcement division of the Common Carrier Bureau of the Commission, to which the consumer may direct complaints regarding operator services;

(B) ensure that each of its telephones presubscribed to a provider of operator services allows the consumer to use "800" and "950" access code numbers to obtain access to the provider of operator services desired by the consumer; and

(C) ensure that no charge by the aggregator to the consumer for using an "800" or "950" access code number, or any other access code number, is greater than the amount the aggregator charges for calls placed using the presubscribed provider of operator services.

(2) Effect of state law or regulation

The requirements of paragraph (1)(A) shall not apply to an aggregator in any case in which State law or State regulation requires the aggregator to take actions that are substantially the same as those required in paragraph (1)(A).

*   *   *

ABOUT THE BOOK & AUTHOR

This casebook-plus-commentary offers a basic introduction to the regulation of the telephone and other common carriers. Drawing on historical and contemporary court decisions as well as on FCC and legislative reports, Professor Brenner documents and evaluates the changes that have taken place during the deregulation of the telecommunications industry. He deals not just with the obviously important telephone industry but also with cable, broadcast, and video distribution companies.

The voluminous materials relating to telecommunications regulation are critically important to understanding the legal and policy landscape of telecommunications today, but this is the first time these materials have been sifted, excerpted, given context, and ordered in a readily accessible way.

Law and Regulation of Common Carriers in the Communications Industry presumes no specialized background in technology, law, or economics and therefore provides an ideal introduction to this increasingly important field for professionals as well as for scholars and students interested in any aspect of communications and communications policy.

Daniel L. Brenner is vice president, law and regulatory policy, of the National Cable Television Association. From 1986 to 1992 he was director of the Communications Law Program at the School of Law at the University of California–Los Angeles.

CASE INDEX

Note: Principal cases appear in boldface.

INDEX